ALSO BY GLENN BECK

The Great Reset: Joe Biden and the Rise of Twenty-First Century Fascism

Arguing with Socialists

Addicted to Outrage

Liars

The Immortal Nicholas

It Is About Islam

Agenda 21: Into the Shadows

Dreamers and Deceivers

Conform: Exposing the Truth About Common Core and Public Education

Miracles and Massacres

The Eye of Moloch

Control: Exposing the Truth About Guns

Agenda 21

Cowards: What Politicians, Radicals, and the Media Refuse to Say

Being George Washington

The Original Argument: The Federalists' Case for the Constitution, Adapted for the 21st Century

The 7: Seven Wonders that Will Change Your Life

Broke: The Plan to Restore Our Trust, Truth and Treasure

The Overton Window

Arguing with Idiots: How to Stop Small Minds and Big Government

Glenn Beck's Common Sense: The Case Against an Out-of-Control Government, Inspired by Thomas Paine

The Christmas Sweater

An Inconvenient Book: Real Solutions to the World's Biggest Problems

The Real America: Early Writings from the Heart and Heartland

DARK FUTURE

UNCOVERING
THE GREAT
RESET'S
TERRIFYING
NEXT PHASE

GLENN BECK

WITH **JUSTIN HASKINS**

CONTRIBUTOR
DONALD KENDAL

Forefront
BOOKS

MERCURY
INK

Dark Future: Uncovering the Great Reset's Terrifying Next Phase

Copyright © 2023 by Mercury Radio Arts, Inc.
Mercury Ink is a trademark of Mercury Radio Arts, Inc.

Published by Forefront Books and Mercury Ink.

Distributed by Simon & Schuster.

Library of Congress Control Number: 2023907498

Print ISBN: 978-1-63763-211-6

Cover Design by Alexander Somoskey.
Interior Design by Bill Kersey, KerseyGraphics.

In honor of those who came before us and dedicated

to all those who will come afterward. We have done our best,

knowing that He will make up for our shortcomings.

The God of Abraham, Isaac, and Jacob is

real. His righteous judgment will come, and His

forgiving arms are available to all of us.

CONTENTS

ACKNOWLEDGMENTS

MAKING A LIST OF PEOPLE TO ACKNOWLEDGE IS ALWAYS hard. There are so many in my life who play an important role. It's simply not conceivable that I could name them all. But know that it is not possible to do what I do without a team of people assisting, guiding, and building at my side on all things. To every one of you, I am grateful. I get the spotlight, but please know that I recognize that it is those of you who are often not seen that give purpose and meaning to that light.

I also need to acknowledge all of you who have listened, watched, and read my work over the many years. Thank you. You give me strength and hope. It is an honor to serve you and call you *friends*.

1

THE GREAT RESET WAS JUST THE BEGINNING

JANUARY 17, 1961

President Dwight D. Eisenhower gathered a stack of papers and walked swiftly toward his desk in the Oval Office.

"Just two minutes before you go live, Mr. President," noted a staffer standing confidently behind an awkwardly large, box-shaped television camera.

Two minutes. After decades of service to his country, Eisenhower—popularly referred to as "Ike," a nickname that dated back to his days as a young child in Abilene, Kansas—was now mere moments away from his final act of service and just three days from formally leaving the White House for the last time.

Eisenhower had been planning to retire to his large farmhouse in Gettysburg, Pennsylvania, for several years. Since 1954, the house—which sat adjacent to the Gettysburg battlefield—had been a place of calm for the Eisenhower family, as well as an important setting for meeting world leaders.[1] Soon it would be his permanent home.

Ike's successor, John F. Kennedy, was young and captivating. Whether he would be prepared for the troubles ahead, Eisenhower didn't know. After all, Kennedy was just forty-three years old at the time he took office. When Kennedy had been elected president, Eisenhower, who was born on October 14, 1890, had been serving his nation longer than Kennedy had been alive.[2]

Eisenhower sat at his wooden desk and placed his papers beside a large box from which emerged two microphones. He shuffled the documents and briefly scanned the opening lines of his farewell speech.

Ike adjusted his glasses and then quietly read, taking note of the various last-minute, handwritten adjustments he had made to the text.[3]

Good evening, he thought silently. *Remember to say, "Good evening."*

Replace "people" with "nation."

Thank Americans for the "opportunity"—no, the *"privilege"—of addressing them.*

Ike's concentration was suddenly broken by a shout behind the camera. "Thirty seconds, Mr. President!"

In those final moments prior to delivering his culminating address, Eisenhower's storied career flashed before him, from his enrollment at the U.S. Military Academy at West Point in 1911 to the immense challenges of commanding the D-Day invasion of Nazi-occupied France during World War II. Of course, Eisenhower wasn't perfect. No one knew that better than Ike himself. But if there are any certainties in the world, it's that Dwight Eisenhower loved his country and would always say and do whatever was necessary to protect it, no matter how difficult the challenge might be.

"Ten seconds!" shouted the cameraman.

Ten seconds, Eisenhower thought. *Were the American people ready to hear what desperately needed to be said?*

A television producer held up his hand, signifying five seconds, then steadily folding one finger after another into his palm until none remained. It was time. Eisenhower's final moment in the spotlight had come.

"Good evening, my fellow Americans," Eisenhower said.[4] "Three days from now, after half a century in the service of our country, I shall lay down the responsibilities of office as, in traditional and solemn ceremony, the authority of the presidency is vested in my successor. This evening, I come to you with a message of leave-taking and farewell, and to share a few final thoughts with you, my countrymen."

Eisenhower then masterfully and succinctly worked through his final speech. First, he wished Kennedy good fortune and thanked the members of Congress, whom he said had "cooperated well" during Ike's presidency to "serve the national good rather than mere partisanship."

Eisenhower then outlined the "noble" goals that lay at the heart of what it means to be American.

"Throughout America's adventure in free government," Ike said, "our basic purposes have been to keep the peace; to foster progress in human achievement, and to enhance liberty, dignity, and integrity among people and among nations. To strive for less would be unworthy of a free and religious people."

Then, in a clear reference to the rise of communism around the world, Eisenhower warned that the "progress" the American people have made in their endeavors "is persistently threatened by the conflict now engulfing the world."

"It commands our whole attention, absorbs our very beings," Eisenhower added. "We face a hostile ideology—global in scope, atheistic in character, ruthless in purpose, and insidious in method. Unhappily the danger it poses promises to be of indefinite duration. To meet it successfully, there is called for, not so much the emotional and transitory sacrifices of crisis, but rather those which enable us to carry forward steadily, surely, and without complaint the burdens of a prolonged and complex struggle—with liberty the stake."

To this point in Eisenhower's speech, the concerns he outlined were important but expected. Eisenhower understood, however, that what would come next would surprise, even shock, many of his fellow citizens. Few presidents in the decades that followed would have had the courage to deliver Ike's urgent message of reform, and almost none of them would have had the humility to do so during a farewell address. But if President Eisenhower was anything, it was patriotic and courageous.

Sensing the immense gravity of the moment, Eisenhower paused, stared with great seriousness into the camera, into the homes of millions of Americans, and said:

> A vital element in keeping the peace is our military establishment. Our arms must be mighty, ready for instant action, so that no potential aggressor may be tempted to risk his own destruction.
>
> Our military organization today bears little relation to that known by any of my predecessors in peacetime, or indeed by the fighting men of World War II or Korea.
>
> Until the latest of our world conflicts, the United States had no armaments industry. American makers of plowshares could, with time and as required, make swords as well. But now we can no longer risk emergency improvisation of national defense; we have been compelled to create a permanent armaments industry of vast proportions. Added to this, three and a half million

men and women are directly engaged in the defense establishment. We annually spend on military security more than the net income of all United States corporations.

This conjunction of an immense military establishment and a large arms industry is new in the American experience. The total influence—economic, political, even spiritual—is felt in every city, every state house, every office of the federal government. We recognize the imperative need for this development. Yet we must not fail to comprehend its grave implications. Our toil, resources, and livelihood are all involved; so is the very structure of our society.

In the councils of government, we must guard against the acquisition of unwarranted influence, whether sought or unsought, by the military-industrial complex. The potential for the disastrous rise of misplaced power exists and will persist.[5]

Before Eisenhower's farewell address began, I am willing to bet almost no one would have guessed that his speech would end up becoming one of the most influential and memorable in American history. The number of presidential speeches that have truly stood the test of time like Eisenhower's is exceptionally small, to say the least, and even fewer have been used by such a wide variety of ideological factions. Even to this day, both tinfoil-hat-wearing conspiracy theorists on the right and socialist politicians such as Bernie Sanders on the left regularly allude to the dangers of a "military-industrial complex," often without providing any meaningful context.[6] In fact, I would argue that despite its widespread use, most of those who have spoken about Ike's military-industrial complex speech, at least for as long as I can remember, have largely misunderstood its meaning. Many have missed the mark entirely.

Contrary to popular belief, Eisenhower's speech was *not* about the dangers of industry coercing Americans or their elected representatives into participating in future wars. Nor was it meant to express a concern that the military-industrial complex is engaged in star-chamber-like conspiracies to create foreign conflicts. In fact, at its heart, Eisenhower's warning wasn't about war at all; it was meant to call attention to the growing threat of *cronyism* and the threat to liberty that inevitably comes from it. This is why Eisenhower emphasized that the "total influence—economic, political, even spiritual—is felt in every city, every state house, every office of the federal government." Of course, the decision to go to war is *not* made in cities, state houses, nor in most offices of the federal government. Cronyism, however, *does* impact all those institutions in our society.

The point Eisenhower was making is that in 1961, after decades of war and the rise of the Soviet Union, the public-private partnerships that had developed between military-related industries and governments—local, state, and federal—had become so strong that corruption and cronyism were driving policy decisions, not the will of the people. You do not need to take my word for it, either. Eisenhower himself confirmed this interpretation of his speech in an often-overlooked correspondence sent in 1967 to an academic at Michigan State University.

In response to a letter from Professor Theodore R. Kennedy asking whether the meaning of Ike's warning was linked to Eisenhower's experience investigating "war profits" while serving on the War Policies Commission in 1932, Eisenhower responded, "Concerning your question about any connection between that experience and the caution I expressed in my final Presidential address, I assure you I find none whatsoever."[7]

"I became convinced in those early studies that industry wanted anything but war," Eisenhower continued, "in other words the hope of profits by industry was in no way a cause of war."

And if that is not clear enough for you, Eisenhower further added in his letter to Kennedy, "My 1961 caution in this matter was not inspired by any belief that any sector in the United States now wanted war." Rather, Ike said he "wanted to point out that so many sectors of our nation—defense forces, industry and political officials—were all influenced toward greater and greater armament production in time of peace."

Even more importantly, most commentators and historians who discuss Eisenhower's farewell address typically leave out the next section, which is much more relevant today for the American people, and, indeed, for all of humanity. According to Eisenhower:

> Akin to, and largely responsible for the sweeping changes in our industrial-military posture, has been the technological revolution during recent decades.
>
> In this revolution, research has become central; it also becomes more formalized, complex, and costly. A steadily increasing share is conducted for, by, or at the direction of, the federal government.
>
> Today, the solitary inventor, tinkering in his shop, has been overshadowed by task forces of scientists in laboratories and testing fields. In the same fashion, the free university, historically the fountainhead of free ideas and scientific discovery, has experienced a revolution in the conduct of research. Partly because of the huge costs involved, a government contract becomes virtually a substitute for intellectual curiosity. For every old blackboard there are now hundreds of new electronic computers.[8]

Even if Eisenhower were to stop his speech here, it would be a remarkable indictment and warning about the relationship between science, technology, and powerful government forces. As Eisenhower understood well, when government works with institutions, it often corrupts them, altering their purpose—intentionally or unintentionally—so that they conform to the desires and plans of one or more politicians or government agencies. The freedom necessary to seek out the truth and to use those findings to improve society, one of the core goals underlying most scientific and techno-logical achievements, cannot exist when institutions are beholden to an army of government bureaucrats.

But Eisenhower did not end his comments there. Soon after lamenting that a "government contract" can become "virtually a substitute for intellectual curiosity," he warned, "The prospect of domination of the nation's scholars by Federal employment, project allocations, and the power of money is ever present and is gravely to be regarded. Yet, in holding scientific research and discovery in respect, as we should, we must also be alert to the equal and oppo-site danger that public policy could itself become the captive of a scientific-technological elite."[9]

For Eisenhower, the threat of elites taking public policy "captive" wasn't simply a passing concern. It was an exceptional danger to the preservation of the American way of life.

"As we peer into society's future," Eisenhower said later in his farewell address, "we—you and I, and our government—must avoid the impulse to live only for today, plundering, for our own ease and convenience, the precious resources of tomorrow. We cannot mortgage the material assets of our grandchildren without risking the loss also of their political and spiritual heritage. We want democracy to survive for all generations to come, not to become the insolvent phantom of tomorrow."[10]

In 1961, it would have been impossible for Eisenhower to see all that would soon change in the Western world, such as the immense globalization of the late twentieth and early twenty-first centuries; the development of the personal computer, Internet, and artificial intelligence; smartphone technology; the rise of central-bank digital currencies; the importance of social media and e-commerce; twenty-four-hour cable news networks; and the rewriting of the meaning of humanity itself. But what had become evident for Eisenhower after decades of experience serving in the highest ranks of the military and government, working closely with allies from around the world, was that a ruling class, empowered by a technological and scientific revolution, had started to develop in the United States, and that if its power were left unchecked, it could make freedom the "insolvent phantom of tomorrow."[11]

We are now living in a country that is teetering on the edge of Eisenhower's worst nightmares. What we say, think, and do is so heavily impacted by an alliance composed of major multinational corporations, government agencies, financial institutions, and scientific-technological elites that for many, freedom has become, at best, a clever illusion.

The United States has become a corrupted, confused, and, at times, borderline authoritarian society. In America today, a president running an annual budget deficit of well over $1 trillion can—without getting laughed out of the room—brag about how well he has "prioritized fiscal responsibility."[12] People have lost good-paying jobs for refusing to inject themselves with a vaccine. Once universally held, science-based understandings of humanity and the universe have been designated backward forms of "bigotry." Well-documented, factual investigative reports from mainstream media outlets have been labeled "misinformation" and banned from being shared or discussed on social media platforms.[13]

The U.S. economy has become a funhouse-mirror distortion of capitalism, where companies regularly engage in activist causes that alienate large segments of their customers and employees. For example, in recent years, Coca-Cola has instructed its staff to be "less white," so that they can be "less oppressive," "less arrogant," and "less ignorant."[14] Nothing screams, "Buy Coke!" more than, "Stop being so white!" am I right?

CEOs from hundreds of companies, including Amazon, American Express, Facebook, and Major League Baseball, have actively campaigned against election-integrity laws—because they contain crazy, horribly racist things such as asking people for a form of identification when they vote and mandating that the state start counting its absentee ballots prior to Election Day to ensure election results are reported earlier.[15] And how can I forget reckless provisions such as those establishing a voter fraud hotline, so citizens who witness voter intimidation and fraud can immediately report it.[16] Oh, the horror!

Strangely, despite having made massive amounts of money by lending to job-creating fossil-fuel companies, every single one of the six largest banks in the United States—including JPMorgan Chase & Co., Bank of America, Wells Fargo, and Citibank—have promised to completely phase out fossil fuels from their entire business portfolios over the next few decades, because they care *oh so much* about stopping climate change.[17]

Most disgusting of all, Disney has launched a campaign to overturn legislation in Florida that prohibits teachers from discussing sexuality with children in the third grade or younger.[18,19] (Yes, the same Disney that has made the bulk of its fortune building family-friendly theme parks and developing films featuring talking cartoon lions and toys that come to life when no one is watching.)

What is happening to our country and our supposedly "free-market" economy? The answer can be summarized in just three words: the Great Reset.

A "GREAT RESET" OF CAPITALISM

If you're reading this book, there's a decent chance you have already read my latest book on a closely related topic, *The Great Reset: Joe Biden and the Rise of Twenty-First Century Fascism*, which was published in January 2022.[20] To say *The Great Reset* book was a "success" is an immense understatement. Within forty-eight hours of its release, *The Great Reset* sold out at nearly every book retailer in the United States, making it the number-one bestselling book in the country and one of the most successful book launches of my career.

I wish I could say that the book's popularity is due to my super-exceptional writing talents or because of my even more super-exceptional charm and good looks. But the truth is, the reason people came out in droves to buy *The Great Reset* is because tens of millions of everyday Americans have known for several years now that something just isn't right. Their country has been radically transformed, but many of them couldn't quite figure out how this sweeping alteration of society had occurred so quickly or who was behind it. Understanding the Great Reset offers a clear picture of the driving forces behind our changing world. After more than a year of research, speaking with countless experts, and digging into a wealth of important primary sources, I was able to piece together how the Great Reset works and why it answers so many of the questions we have all been wondering about.

Once you slip on the Great Reset decoder ring provided by the research in my last book, the seemingly nonsensical, bizarre, authoritarian actions regularly taken by government officials, banks, corporations, and financial firms will make *a lot* more sense.

However, this book isn't merely about the Great Reset. It is about the future. It is about your future and your family's future, and how that future could be greatly improved or severely harmed in a world in which there is a period of great technological trans-formation built on top of a Great Reset framework—a concept often referred to by its supporters as the *Great Narrative*. And I will reveal the truth of this important topic by providing you with numerous quotes and primary sources from leaders in the fields of technological development and futurism, as well as from many of the most influential figures backing the Great Reset.

Just as importantly, in this book, I will explain why millions of Americans, Canadians, and Europeans will in the coming decades be tempted to enter into the seemingly warm embrace of the traditionalist movement promoted by China, Russia, and other nations that are actively fighting against the Great Narrative for all the wrong reasons. Thanks, in part, to the authoritarian, disturbing nature of the Great Reset and its total rejection of all traditional ideals, national fascism is now sweeping many parts of the globe. Hundreds of millions of people struggle to find someone, *anyone*, who will stand up against the anti-religion, anti-traditionalism brand of international fascism promoted by Great Reset elites. We must do everything we can to stop this movement, as it is absolutely no friend of freedom and will almost certainly end in unimaginable tragedy.

I will further show that a new world war has already started to emerge between those who support the Great Reset and those who are seeking to protect national fascistic governments—and no, I am not merely referring to the conflict between Ukraine and Russia, although that war is undoubtedly part of this story. The battle being waged is much more complex and far-reaching, and it is intimately connected with the Great Narrative.

Before we can dive into those important topics, though, it is vital that you have a strong understanding of exactly what the Great Reset is, how it works, and who is pushing for its expansion—all of which are topics covered throughout the remainder of this chapter. If you do not understand the Great Reset, it is impossible to grasp what is ahead, what is at stake, and why an emerging technological revolution and the new Great Narrative that elites are trying to build around it are two of the greatest issues facing humanity today. (Yes, all of humanity, not just America. And no, I am *not* exaggerating.)

In the coming years, advancements in artificial intelligence, quantum computing, blockchain technologies, bioengineering, automation, the metaverse, and countless other areas will challenge the human race in unprecedented ways. How these technologies are used will alter all our lives, whether we want them to or not. The question is *not* whether life is going to change; that unstoppable freight train has already left the station. The real question—the most important one of this century—is, Will the emerging technological revolution improve life and make mankind freer, or will it enslave, impoverish, or perhaps even destroy it? At its foundation, it really is a simple decision. Will we choose good or evil? Freedom or control? Light or darkness?

The issues surrounding those questions should be discussed, considered, and decided with input from every part of society through democratic institutions, but because of the Great Reset movement, that isn't happening now and might not occur in the future, either—unless, that is, we stop the Reset from fully going into effect. Of course, that cannot happen unless everyone understands what the Great Reset is in the first place. That's where our journey in this book begins, although it's quite far from our final destination.

If you regularly listen to my radio show or watch me on BlazeTV, some of the concepts presented throughout the rest of this chapter about the Great Reset will be familiar to you. But there's also a lot of information included on the following pages that I haven't had the time to present in a comprehensive way on radio or television. So if you blow by this chapter because you think you have heard all of this before, you are going to miss out on some extremely important details and new developments that have occurred since I wrote *The Great Reset* book. I urge you to avoid making that mistake.

If you aren't as familiar with the Great Reset, then this chapter will provide you with more than enough facts, figures, and evidence to help you understand the seriousness and significance of the other topics I will discuss in later chapters, although I would still encourage you to read my *Great Reset* book as well. There is nowhere near enough space in this chapter to reveal everything that is included in my previous book. Also, thanks to President Biden's boneheaded policies, I could really use the extra gas money.

WHAT IS THE GREAT RESET?

In June 2020, at the height of the COVID-19 pandemic, a group of highly influential, exceptionally wealthy, extremely powerful leaders from governments, corporations, international institutions, banks, activist organizations, and investment firms gathered to launch a campaign to "push the reset button" on the global economy.

The initial launch event featured a laundry list of prominent figures, including Antonio Guterres, the United Nations secretary-general; Bradford Smith, president of Microsoft; Bernard Looney, CEO of BP; Ajay Banga, CEO of Mastercard; Gina Gopinath, chief economist at the International Monetary Fund (IMF); and Kristalina Georgieva, the IMF's managing director, among many others.[21] In subsequent events and interviews, countless other business, activist, and government leaders expressed their support for the Reset too, including Al Gore; John Kerry, who now serves as President Biden's special climate envoy, a cabinet-level position; and Larry Fink, CEO of BlackRock, the wealthiest investment firm on the planet and the single largest owner of stock in American corporations.[22,23,24]

The hosts of the Great Reset launch event were Prince Charles and the World Economic Forum (WEF), the same organization that holds a lavish gathering of thousands of government bureaucrats, Hollywood celebrities, and activists in the Swiss resort town of Davos every year. Davos is one of those rare events where jet-setting government workers and millionaires get to simultaneously live out their fantasy of "saving the world" while enjoying $100 shrimp cocktails at George Soros dinner parties and extravagant wine tastings hosted by Anthony Scaramucci.[25] But they deserve it, don't they? Being a ruling-class elite is hard work.

Perhaps the most influential figure promoting the Great Reset is the Davos man himself, Klaus Schwab, founder and head of the World Economic Forum. In an article published in conjunction with the June 2020 event, titled "Now is the Time for a 'Great Reset,'" Schwab outlined what he and many others in the Reset movement believe are essential reforms for changing the global economy in the twenty-first century and beyond.[26]

"COVID-19 lockdowns may be gradually easing, but anxiety about the world's social and economic prospects is only intensifying," Schwab wrote. "There is good reason to worry: a sharp economic downturn has already begun, and we could be facing the worst depression since the 1930s. But, while this outcome is likely, it is not unavoidable."[27]

How does Schwab think we should face this "likely" economic collapse?

"To achieve a better outcome," Schwab wrote, "the world must act jointly and swiftly to revamp all aspects of our societies and economies, from education to social contracts and working conditions. Every country, from the United States to China, must participate, and every industry, from oil and gas to tech, must be transformed. In short, we need a 'Great Reset' of capitalism."[28]

According to Schwab, his plan for a Great Reset of "all aspects of our societies and economies" is "not some impossible dream." In fact, Schwab says one "silver lining of the [COVID-19] pandemic is that it has shown how quickly we can make radical changes to our lifestyles. Almost instantly, the crisis forced businesses and individuals to abandon practices long claimed to be essential, from frequent air travel to working in an office."

Let's pause for a moment and think about what our old pal Klaus is saying here. For him and the others who back the Great Reset, hundreds of millions of people being confined to their homes, millions of jobs lost, tens of millions more forced to work from home, and restrictions placed on air travel and all the good that comes with it (such as visiting family members) are a "silver lining"? Really? A "silver lining"? Even by extremely high supervillain standards, Schwab has managed to push the envelope with that one. But to be fair, as truly awful of a statement as Schwab's "silver lining" comment is, I suppose it is *slightly* better than what Klaus's Great Reset event cohost Prince Charles—now King Charles—said about the pandemic. While promoting the Great Reset, he called COVID-19 "a golden opportunity" to enact reforms, made possible because the pandemic's "unprecedented shockwaves" made people "more receptive to big visions of change."[29]

The "big visions of change" King Charles is referring to here is a shift to an economic model called "stakeholder capitalism." (Don't be fooled by the name. This isn't "capitalism.") Under a stakeholder economic model, businesses are not rewarded primarily based on economic metrics such as profit, loss, customer satisfaction, or the quality of a company's products and services. Instead, businesses are rated based on their commitment to social and environmental causes chosen by the elites themselves, often to their own benefit.

This stakeholder system is contrasted by "shareholder capitalism"—a term used derisively by people such as King Charles and the wannabe emperor Schwab to describe an economic system in which businesses, especially corporations, focus primarily on the desires of their customers, owners, and employees. (Sounds terrible, doesn't it?)

In an agonizingly boring book published in 2021 about his stakeholder capitalism model, Schwab explained that although traditional capitalist ideas have led to tremendous amounts of economic growth, capitalism is "selfish" and unsustainable. Only by adopting *his* grand, genius, innovative, insightful plan to save the universe can we fix society's woes.[30]

"We can't continue with an economic system driven by selfish values, such as short-term profit maximization, the avoidance of tax and regulation, or the externalizing of environmental harm," Schwab wrote. "Instead, we need a society, economy, and international community that is designed to care for all people and the entire planet."[31]

Take note of Schwab's use of the word *designed* here. For Schwab and dozens of other leaders linked to the Great Reset and Great Narrative, *designing* future societies is a core concept. In their minds, only when academic, industrial, financial, and government elites work together to "design" the world can social, environmental, and economic problems be fully dealt with. This is going to be a reoccurring theme throughout this book, and as you'll find out in later chapters, "designing" society is meant in a creepier, more authoritarian way than most people realize.

The switch to an economic system focused on the *stakeholders*— which is really just another way of saying *collective*—is not meant to focus solely on one component of the economy. Remember what Schwab wrote back in June 2020 about the Great Reset: "every industry, from oil and gas to tech, must be transformed."[32] Additionally, the Reset will impact "all aspects of our societies . . . from education to social contracts and working conditions."[33]

Schwab and King Charles aren't alone in their focus on changing all of society, either. For example, Sharan Burrow, general secretary of the International Trade Union Confederation, noted in a conversation about the pandemic and the Great Reset, "I can see how we could use this opportunity to design a better world, but we need both national and multilateral institutions to make it work. Solidarity and sharing and deciding on how you protect people—both within nations and globally—is absolutely critical at the moment."[34]

Similarly, at a Great Reset event hosted by the World Economic Forum in late June 2020, John Kerry lamented, "Forces and pressures that were pushing us into crisis over the social contract are now exacerbated. The world is coming apart, dangerously, in terms of global institutions and leadership."[35]

"What we never did was adequately address the social contract," Kerry added, just before saying, "The World Economic Forum—the CEO capacity of the Forum—is really going to have to play a front and center role in refining the Great Reset to deal with climate change and inequity—all of which is being laid bare as a consequence of COVID-19."[36]

HOW DOES THE GREAT RESET WORK?

It is clear that the purpose of the Great Reset is to transform countries around the world, but how, exactly, do those elites who support the Reset plan on accomplishing such an ambitious goal? There is no formal, published, all-encompassing Great Reset instruction manual, confession of faith, or constitution. There are, however, hundreds—perhaps even thousands—of speeches, presentations, articles, and books discussing various aspects of the Great Reset and how a post-Reset world would look. *TIME* magazine even devoted an entire issue to promoting Klaus Schwab and the Great Reset in October 2020. (Way back in 2020, it was still cool for elites to admit they want to "reset" every country on earth. Today, they usually—but not always—try to be a little more deceitful when they make their case for global domination.)[37]

To really understand exactly what Reseters are proposing, you need to tediously gather all the scattered parts of their plan, rearrange the pieces, and then meticulously connect one piece to the next. It is sort of like building a gigantic fascism-themed puzzle. That's exactly what I and my team of researchers have done for the better part of the past three years. It has been an exceptionally difficult project at times, and I think that's by design. Those who support the Great Reset do not make it easy for the little "stakeholders" they supposedly care so much about to know what they are up to, because if everyday Americans, Canadians, and Europeans were to figure it out, the jig would be up and the massive game of authoritarian Jenga would end with an ugly crash. (Wow. References to both making puzzles and playing Jenga in one paragraph. I guess all those family game nights are really starting to affect my writing.)

The Great Reset has two main components. The first is a call for gargantuan new government social, economic, and welfare spending programs—everything from proposals related to spending trillions on the Green New Deal and European Green Deal to basic income programs and government-run health care.[38] In my *The Great Reset* book, I spend substantially more time discussing this part of the plan, so I encourage you to read more about it there.[39] For now, though, it's enough to say that if you have any familiarity at all with the many political fights ongoing in the United States, Canada, or Europe today, it won't be hard for you to imagine what Great Reset elites have in mind when they talk about increasing government welfare programs.

However, the second big component of the Great Reset is much more complex and insidious, and as such, it requires a longer discussion. Unlike the first piece of the Reset, the second can be put into place without long, drawn-out political battles, making it much easier to achieve. That does not mean it would be less important, though. It would provide elites with transformative authority over—well, just about everything. It is called environmental, social, and governance (ESG) metrics, and it functions as the heart of Schwab's stakeholder-capitalism model.

ESG metrics are a kind of social credit scoring system, similar to the ones now being used by the Chinese Communist Party to control its vast population and economy. ESG measures a company based on its devotion to environmental and social justice causes, rather than solely by examining business and economic considerations, and then assigns businesses with numerical or letter scores. This is not to say that revenue, product development, and other more traditional concerns no longer matter; businesses are still expected to attempt to earn a profit. But ESG systems add a complicated set of additional criteria, so that investors, government officials, and financial institutions know who the "good" businesses are and can identify (and eventually destroy) the "bad" ones.

There are many different ESG ratings agencies, including numerous ones that are affiliated with some of the most powerful institutions on Wall Street. For example, prominent ESG ratings reports are offered by Moody's Investors Service, Morningstar, MSCI, and S&P Global.[40]

One of the most influential new set of metrics was recently published in a report titled *Measuring Stakeholder Capitalism: Toward Common Metrics and Consistent Reporting of Sustainable Value Creation*. The World Economic Forum and the International Business Council published the report in September 2020, just three months after the WEF launched the Great Reset.[41]

The World Economic Forum's ESG standards, which were developed with help from many prominent business leaders—notably Brian Moynihan, CEO of Bank of America and a vocal advocate of ESG—include twenty-one "core metrics" and thirty-four "expanded metrics." The metrics are grouped into four "pillars": Principles of Governance, Planet, People, and Prosperity.[42]

Not every ESG scoring category is bad or designed to coerce businesses into promoting causes that provide more power to elites. For example, some ESG systems penalize companies that benefit from child labor in their supply chain. And if that's all ESG were, few would have any problems with it. But environmental, social, and governance metrics reach much further.

For instance, the WEF's ESG system gives a social credit score penalty to companies with a relatively low "Percentage of active workforce covered under collective bargaining agreements." So if companies do not hire enough union labor, their ESG scores take a hit.

Companies are also evaluated based on their "Percentage of employees per employee category, by age group, gender and other indicators of diversity (e.g. ethnicity)." Further, businesses are rated based on "The total global tax borne by the company, including corporate income taxes, property taxes, non-creditable VAT and other sales taxes, employer-paid payroll taxes, and other taxes that constitute costs to the company, by category of taxes." They are also evaluated in light of their commitment to battling climate change and reducing their use of water—even when their business models rely heavily on fossil fuels, such as an energy company, or water use, such as a farmer.[43]

In other words, the businesses that pay the most in taxes, have the "right" ratio of Hispanic to Black employees (whatever that means), agree with and adopt Al Gore's and Joe Biden's views on climate change, and have lots of union workers will be given an ESG boost compared to those that don't perform quite as well in those and other categories—regardless of how successful, popular, and important that "bad" business might be.

Other metrics include land and plastic use, the "Percentage of revenue from products and services designed to deliver specific social benefits or to address specific sustainability challenges," and a company's "Total Social Investment," which seeks to measure, in part, the degree to which a company is financially supporting social justice causes.[44]

Although these and many other ESG metrics tend to favor left-wing causes at present, it is important to note that in the United States the metrics can change at any time. Today, they are in line with many left-wing ideals, but that doesn't mean they will be tomorrow. In America, ESG metrics are developed and applied by non-government institutions that are largely unaccountable to voters. So while you might agree with some of what ESG has to offer, keep in mind that this could rapidly change in the future, and there would be little, if anything, you could do about it.

So the question is not really, "Do you agree with today's ESG standards?" The better question is, "Do you want a system in place by which nameless, faceless, unaccountable, unelected bureaucrats can impose arbitrary rules on corporations and dictate how they do business based on nothing but cultural and political whims?" And if you answer yes, would you still want that if all the players suddenly switched political allegiances and started promoting causes you despise?

This does not mean government is staying out of the ESG business, however. For example, as you'll learn later in this chapter, government and government-backed central banks are the primary drivers of the ESG movement, and they are working closely alongside some of the biggest players of the Great Reset in the private sector to help ensure ESG is adopted worldwide. This "public-private partnership"—a fancy way for Great Reset elites to say *cronyism*—is *exactly* the sort of threat to freedom Eisenhower warned about way back in 1961.

The reason ESG systems are so worrisome is that they are being used to change virtually every part of society. Large corporations now dominate much of the U.S., Canadian, and European market-places, so if you can alter how these businesses operate, change who they will or will not do business with, and, among other things, manipulate how they advertise to the public, you can transform people's jobs, educational experiences, and even the culture they live in. And because these corporations are not directly owned by the government, they can infringe on individual rights normally protected by government constitutions and other national laws.

For instance, the U.S. federal government was not permitted to ban citizens from sharing and discussing a news story in 2020 that revealed a recovered laptop owned by Hunter Biden may offer proof that both he and Joe Biden—who, remember, was campaigning to become the most powerful person in the world at the time the story broke—had been engaged in deeply disturbing business arrangements with companies tied to the Chinese and Russian governments. But social media companies such as Twitter could (and did) kill the story. It didn't matter that there was (and is) plenty of evidence suggesting the Hunter Biden laptop story is 100 percent true, or that many of the very same people and media outlets who dismissed it as "Russian misinformation" at first have since completely changed their assessment—after the election ended, of course.[45]

There is no First Amendment right to free speech, free press, or free association that currently applies to Facebook, Google, and Twitter. That makes them, as well as all corporations, very valuable allies for ruling-class elites in government, banking, and international organizations who have been wanting to expand their influence and power for more than a century in the United States but haven't made the same kind of progress here—and by "progress," I mean the expansion of elites' influence—as they have in the peaceful bastion of enlightenment that is Europe. (Oh, and pay no attention to all the world wars, cold wars, civil wars, and financial chaos that has occurred in Europe over the past hundred years. I heard we're just a year or two away from paradise over there.)

THE ROOT OF THE PROBLEM

ESG social credit systems are already incredibly popular with large corporations in America, Canada, and much of Europe. According to a report by KPMG, one of the largest accounting firms in the world, *thousands* of companies located in more than fifty countries have ESG systems in place, including 82 percent of large corporations in the United States. Even more remarkably, 96 percent of the G250—"the 250 largest companies by revenue as defined in the *Fortune* 500 ranking"—produce ESG reports.[46]

In all of these reports, corporations—many of which have hired dozens of employees to work exclusively on ESG—brag endlessly about how woke they are, how their bleeding hearts ache for the plight of Mother Earth, and how the members of their leadership team begin each day in their corporate yoga studios flogging themselves to atone for their business's climate sins and for their failure to produce more commercials that empower drag queens to be their "most authentic selves." OK, so that last part is a *bit* of an exaggeration, but not by a whole lot.

Of course, corporations don't really care about any of these issues. Drag queens have been around for a *long* time. Believe me, I know. The executive producer of my radio show, Stu, used to be one. In fact, I'm pretty sure his stage name was Madam Beef Stu. Yet corporations such as Old Navy didn't start hiring drag queens to hawk Christmas-themed full-bodied pajamas until recently.[47] Further, executives in corporate boardrooms have privately advocated for gay rights for more than a decade, but it wasn't until the past couple of years that many of them developed large-scale advertising campaigns to shout their support for gay pride from the mountaintops. And I am sure the executives at Amazon have loathed all sorts of books about controversial topics that have been sold on Amazon.com since the company was first created, but only now have they started to ban books they disagree with. Al Gore has been bloviating about the "existential threat" of climate change for more than two decades, but only now are corporations taking it seriously. *Why?*

I am sure if you were to ask the heads of most *Fortune* 500 companies in America to identify the root cause of their recent leftward shift, they would blather on about how they have been touched in recent years by the pain and suffering of "marginalized communities" and how scientists have convinced them about the dangers of climate change. But that isn't what's really going on, and I can prove it with just one very inconvenient word: China. The Communist Party of China has one of the most monstrous, blood-soaked records in human history, but that has not stopped virtually every major corporation in America—most of whom are champions of the Great Reset—from doing business, in one way or another, either *in* or *with* China.

If corporations, banks, and Wall Street firms care so much about the marginalized and oppressed, why would they do business with the same political party that has murdered tens of millions of people;[48] locked away millions of ethnic and religious minorities in "re-education" camps;[49] severely restricted access to cultural ideas that are in opposition to the views of the leaders of the Communist Party, including issues such as homosexuality;[50] limited families from having more than one child, then two children, and now three children;[51] and dramatically increased China's coal-fired power plants, even though elites in Europe and North America say coal is going to kill the planet?[52] Oh, and then there's that whole mysterious origins-of-the-global-coronavirus-pandemic thing. But I probably shouldn't get started on that one. I wouldn't want this book to be banned the first day it comes out.

If you did not read my book covering the Great Reset in detail, or if you have chosen to block the experience out so that you can sleep a little better at night, the big questions on your mind are probably: If many large institutions don't truly care about all the causes they *say* they support, why would so many corporations and businesses go along with a plan to reset capitalism? What is the real motivation behind this decision? Wouldn't they prefer to have more control over their own businesses, build better relationships with their customers, pay lower taxes, and focus on products and services, rather than engage in endless social justice advocacy?

Like many of you, I admit that I struggled with these questions when I first started to research the Great Reset. Corporations have their problems, sure, and many of the big ones have been promoting cronyism and sending armies of lobbyists to Washington, D.C., for decades to help ensure that regulations and laws are written in a way that disproportionately benefits them. But why would they, of all people, be so interested in a Great Reset of capitalism? Last I checked, capitalism has been *very* good to them.

If I have learned anything over the past couple of decades of researching, watching, and analyzing the actions of wealthy, powerful institutions and governments, it's that they aren't irrational. There are *always* reasons behind the decisions that they make. The reasons might be stupid—and when it comes to the federal government, they often are—but there is always a justification for the behavior taken by large institutions and individuals vested with authority. And more often than not, when it comes to large corporations, that reason is cold, hard cash—or, more accurately, digital Fed coins (more on that in chapter 4).

The most important reason corporate America is going woke is because, contrary to the popular slogan adopted by some on the right, if you go woke, you actually *don't* go broke. You get filthy rich. At least, that is what many of the businesses caught up in the Great Reset believe. But everyone involved is under the impression that this is only true for those companies that agree to become good little soldiers in the battle to save the planet, or whatever else might be the cause of the day for the powerful elites crafting national and international narratives. And you know what? They aren't wrong.

Ungodly sums of money have streamed into ESG causes over the past decade, and the momentum in recent years has been building even more rapidly in favor of ESG than many analysts expected just a few years ago. Popular business website *Fast Company* reported—in an article published in their section titled "New Capitalism," by the way—that 2021 "was a record year for ESG, with an estimated $120 billion poured into sustainable investments, more than double the $51 billion of 2020."[53]

Fast Company further noted that by the end of 2021, "an estimated one-third of all assets contain sustainable investments," and "the amount invested in ESG increased tenfold from 2018 to 2020, and 25-fold from 1995 to 2020."[54] As shocking as these numbers appear at first glance, they are just a drop in the bucket. *Fast Company's* report is limited to ESG investment funds, which, while important, do not tell the whole story, or even 1 percent of it, in fact.

In addition to massive ESG-dedicated investment funds, there are trillions upon trillions of dollars in capital that have been committed to promoting ESG and other forms of "sustainable investment" and capital allocation. Take Principles for Responsible Investment (PRI), for example. PRI, a leading force behind ESG, began at a meeting coordinated by the United Nations in 2005. Initially, it included a group of just twenty influential investors from twelve countries.[55] But just one year later, when PRI officially launched, it had one hundred signatories, eighty more than PRI's first meeting. Today, more than three thousand wealthy individuals and institutions belong to PRI. Together, these investors, pension funds, and asset managers control more than $100 trillion.[56] That's about five times the size of the entire gross domestic product of the United States, and it's a figure that's greater than the combined total GDP for the *entire world*, including America.[57] With that kind of cash in mind, is it really so surprising that corporations are eager to be on fascist Santa's "nice" list?

Keeping a close eye on powerful groups like PRI, not the amount of cash being dumped into sustainable investment funds, is the best way to track the influence of ESG on business. If investment inflows and outflows were the primary measure, then the ESG movement should be dying right now, not thriving. In 2022, ESG funds experienced one of their worst years in a decade, yet the push for ESG in Western economies has never been stronger.[58]

THE STOCK MARKET MAFIA

Although investment trends are a vital part of the ESG equation, corporations are not adopting ESG social credit scoring systems solely because they suspect or hope that they will receive a flood of investment from the members of PRI and other, similar groups. They are being told that they *must* do this by the most powerful figures on Wall Street, as well as by countless banks and other financial institutions.

Many players in the Great Reset movement have suggested that everyone involved is adopting ESG out of the goodness of their hearts, but in reality, a super-wealthy band of goons are the ones imposing this system on U.S. businesses, breaking the financial kneecaps of anyone who gets in the way.

Some of the biggest thugs involved in this system are asset managers such as BlackRock, State Street Global Advisors, and Vanguard. BlackRock, State Street, and Vanguard are three of the wealthiest private organizations on the planet,[59] and they regularly use the wealth they control and the stock they buy with it to force companies to promote ESG causes. Note that I said *the wealth they control*. BlackRock and other asset managers have boatloads of their own cash, but most of the wealth they manage is actually owned by others, including many large institutions, which give their money to "experts" like BlackRock in the hopes of getting a better return.

According to BlackRock's website, "We provide a broad range of investment solutions to official institutions worldwide including central banks, sovereign wealth funds, multilateral entities, public pension schemes, and government ministries and agencies."[60] BlackRock also offers services to foundations and endowments, wealthy families, and many others.

One of the primary ways companies like BlackRock throw their weight around is by purchasing stock and then using their shares to ensure corporate leadership is willing to do their bidding. In most cases, threats alone are persuasive enough to get corporate bigwigs onboard with whatever BlackRock and other large asset managers want, including ESG.

As an analyst for S&P Global, another giant on Wall Street, noted in a January 2022 report, "BlackRock has long been a prominent player in the environmental, social and governance arena. In January 2020, for example, the New York–based money manager signed up to Climate Action 100+, an investor-led initiative that's pushing companies to move toward net zero emissions by 2050 or sooner."[61]

S&P further supported its claim about BlackRock's devotion to ESG by noting that in "March 2021, BlackRock also committed to the goal of net zero greenhouse gas emissions by 2050 or earlier. And in May that year, the asset manager caused a stir when it voted to replace three directors at Exxon Mobil Corp. because it believed the oil company wasn't moving quickly enough to incorporate clean energy sources."[62]

The saga involving Exxon is now infamous among Wall Street elites and illustrates well how the ESG stock market mafia operates. In 2021, a relatively small and mostly unknown activist hedge fund called Engine No. 1 led a campaign to force Exxon Mobil—one of the largest oil and gas companies—to reduce its carbon footprint, which, of course, is intimately tied to the very same oil and gas it sells.[63] This would be like going to McDonald's and demanding that it stop selling so many cheeseburgers. Of course, if many left-wing politicians have it their way, including Vice President Kamala Harris, cheeseburgers probably will be the next target on activists' hit list.[64]

According to a *New York Times* report about the campaign, "The tiny firm [Engine No. 1] wouldn't have had a chance were it not for an unusual twist: the support of some of Exxon's biggest institutional investors. BlackRock, Vanguard and State Street voted against Exxon's leadership and gave Engine No. 1 powerful support."[65] When all was said and done, three of Exxon's directors were replaced because of their unwillingness to take a hard line on fossil fuels. (And who could blame them? Exxon is a fossil-fuel company, remember?)

The *Times* further reported that in the wake of the ousting, "Engine No. 1 instantly became a Wall Street name. The firm is among a new breed of shareholder activists, ones driven by the idea that social good also benefits the bottom line, just as policy and public sentiment on the environment are evolving. Chris James, the founder of Engine No. 1, argued that Exxon's management wasn't making needed changes fast enough."[66]

"The firm convinced the mighty BlackRock," the *Times* added. "'We believe more needs to be done in Exxon's long-term strategy'" on reducing climate risk, which threatens shareholder value, it [BlackRock] said in a statement explaining why it had sided with Engine No. 1."[67]

It is rare for BlackRock and other big asset managers to play second fiddle to lesser-known groups like Engine No. 1. Usually, if BlackRock wants to impose its will on a corporation or even an entire industry, it has no problem leading the charge.

Although the force put on display in the fight over Exxon's leadership surprised some journalists, it didn't shock me one bit. BlackRock's CEO, Larry Fink, is on the Board of Trustees of the World Economic Forum and is a close ally of Klaus Schwab.[68] Fink has also repeatedly and openly defended Schwab's "stakeholder capitalism" Great Reset model. In fact, Fink's 2022 "Letter to CEOs" was devoted entirely to providing a full-throated response to critics of the Great Reset like me.

"Stakeholder capitalism is not about politics," Fink wrote. "It is not a social or ideological agenda. It is not 'woke.' *It is capitalism*, driven by mutually beneficial relationships between you and the employees, customers, suppliers, and communities your company relies on to *prosper*. This is the power of capitalism."[69]

Fink's insistence that "stakeholder capitalism" isn't about a "social or ideological agenda" would be laughable if the whole "pushing the reset button" on society thing weren't so terrifying. On its face, it is a ridiculous claim that is easily disproven. There is no debate over whether ESG is designed to promote a "social" agenda. It obviously is.

If stakeholder capitalism and the ESG system that is such a big part of it aren't about politics, ideology, or a "social agenda," why does the ESG system developed by the World Economic Forum—which, again, is where Fink serves as a board member—include measures evaluating the racial composition of a company's workforce or how well it supports labor unions?[70]

Why does WEF's ESG scoring system include the "Percentage of revenue from products and services designed to deliver specific *social* benefits or to address specific sustainability challenges"?[71] Similarly, why does it measure a business's "Total *Social* Investment," which seeks to measure, in part, the degree to which a company is financially supporting *social* justice causes?[72][73] In fact, the World Economic Forum's ninety-six-page report laying out its ESG framework includes the word *social* 132 times. Heck, *social* is one of just three words in ESG—environmental, *social*, and governance. But don't worry about all that, America. BlackRock promises none of this "stakeholder capitalism" stuff has anything to do with a "social or ideological agenda," and if ever there were a trustworthy organization, it's BlackRock, right? How stupid does Larry Fink think we are?

Of course, like all authoritarians, Fink couldn't conceal his desire to control others for long. In this case, he couldn't even manage to write a single letter without spicing it up with a few threats directed at CEOs who might be getting cold feet about Larry's plan to transform all of society.

In the very same epistle to CEOs in which he promised stakeholder capitalism isn't "woke," Fink wrote, "Capital markets have allowed companies and countries to flourish. But access to capital is not a right. It is a privilege. And the duty to attract that capital in a responsible and sustainable way lies with you."[74]

Elsewhere in the letter, Fink warned, "Companies not adjusting to this new reality and responding to their workers do so at their own peril." He also wrote, "Every company and every industry will be transformed by the transition to a net zero world. *The question is, will you lead, or will you be led?*"[75] Does any of this sound like BlackRock is merely trying to persuade corporations, or is it more likely Fink is threatening companies still refusing to go along with the ESG agenda?

BlackRock isn't the only one cracking corporate skulls either. Vanguard, another massive Wall Street firm, has been on a crusade for several years to force companies to transform the gender and racial ratios of their workforces and leadership teams. For instance, in December 2020, Reuters reported Vanguard promised it "will continue pressing companies to make their boards and workforce more diverse, but stopped short of setting specific targets as rivals have done."[76]

"Pennsylvania-based Vanguard will encourage boards to take other steps toward diversity such as looking for candidates among human-resources executives and other untapped talent groups, or increasing their sizes," Reuters reported.[77] Reuters also noted that Vanguard's global head of investment stewardship, John Galloway, warned that "Vanguard may vote against directors at companies not making any progress."[78]

Vanguard's ESG team has been analyzing and tracking corporate diversity for years. "By Vanguard's count among Russell 3000 company boards, some 200 lack gender diversity and about 500 appear to lack racial diversity," Reuters reported.[79]

Not to be outdone by its rivals, State Street Global Advisors, yet another Wall Street behemoth, has been even more aggressive when it comes to board diversity linked to its ESG and stakeholder capitalism initiatives. In 2018, the publication *Institutional Investor* reported State Street expanded its board diversity policy, saying it "will vote against the entire slate of board members on the nominating committee of any company not meeting its gender diversity criteria."[80] As a result of its demands, "State Street says that more than 300 companies have added a female board director in response to its demands, and that another 28 have pledged to do so."[81]

Oh, but none of this has anything to do with "a social or ideological agenda," right, Larry?

All of this is made worse by the fact that asset managers like BlackRock have become increasingly richer over the past decade. BlackRock, the biggest of all money managers, controlled $10 trillion in assets in early 2022, about $8.7 trillion more than it did in 2008.[82] And BlackRock is just one of dozens of asset managers who have been weaponizing ESG. The total assets controlled by the ten largest investment groups on Wall Street—BlackRock, Vanguard, UBS Group, Fidelity, State Street, Morgan Stanley, JPMorgan Chase & Co., Allianz, Capital Group, and Goldman Sachs—were worth more than $34 trillion in 2021.[83]

These asset managers and financial institutions have been swallowing up available stock at a breakneck speed, giving them increasingly more influence in corporate boardrooms. As I pointed out in my book *The Great Reset*:

> According to research by Lucian Bebchuk, a professor at Harvard Law School, and Scott Hirst, an associate professor at the Boston University School of Law, the average ownership stake of the "Big Three" investment firms was 5.2 percent in 1998. In 2017, it was 20.5 percent. Even more importantly, the Big Three "collectively cast an average of about 25 percent of the votes at S&P 500 companies." That means when the Big Three firms demand that corporate America jumps, most CEOs can only respond with, "How high?"
>
> This consolidation of voting power is likely to get worse in the coming years too. Bebchuk and Hirst believe "that the Big Three could well cast as much as 40 percent of the votes in S&P 500 companies within two decades." If that were to occur, *three* Wall Street firms, working in conjunction with a relatively small group of other shareholders, could effectively control nearly all of corporate America.[84]

CORPORATE BONDS GO "WOKE"

The control of vast amounts of stock isn't the only way for elites to ensure that ESG scores are adopted. There are important systemic changes that have been made in recent years that help to guarantee the rise of ESG as well, most notably that ESG scores have been widely adopted by corporate ratings agencies, especially when issuing bond ratings.

As the U.S. Securities and Exchange Commission (SEC) explains, "A bond is a debt obligation, like an IOU. Investors who buy corporate bonds are lending money to the company issuing the bond. In return, the company makes a legal commitment to pay interest on the principal and, in most cases, to return the principal when the bond comes due, or matures."[85]

How is the interest rate on bonds determined? The SEC explains, "Like all investments, bonds carry risks. One key risk to a bondholder is that the company may fail to make timely payments of interest or principal. If that happens, the company will default on its bonds. This 'default risk' makes the creditworthiness of the company—that is, its ability to pay its debt obligations on time—an important concern to bondholders."[86]

So the more "risk" a bond is associated with, the more interest corporations and governments must pay to attract investors. But how can that risk be accurately determined? A gigantic sector of the financial industry has developed over many decades to address that very question, by providing high-quality risk assessments, commonly called "bond ratings."

Bond ratings make a lot of sense. After all, if you are going to buy an IOU from a company, you should have some sense of how likely it is the debt will be repaid. But in recent years, rating agencies have stopped relying solely on traditional metrics when crafting bond ratings, inserting ESG metrics into many of their bond assessments, a trend that experts predict is likely to pick up speed in the years to come.

In a 2021 report produced by FitchRatings titled *ESG in Credit*, Fitch—one of the "big three" ratings agencies, along with S&P and Moody's Investors Service—notes that although ESG "was once a niche investment strategy and a distinct fund class," it is "now

practiced in many (if not all) major financial markets and by investment firms worldwide, including in emerging markets."[87]

According to FitchRatings, "ESG Relevance Scores (ESG.RS)
are assigned by Fitch's 1,500 credit analysts as part of their regular
risk analysis. These analysts are the primary point of contact for
industry participants on all aspects of risk, including ESG. This
strong link to Fitch's core business ensures ESG remains a fully
embedded and relevant aspect of our work."[88]

You might be tempted to think that concerns over climate
change have the greatest impact on a company's credit rating,
because energy-related issues tend to have the biggest financial
impact on a company's bottom line. But Fitch claims its "initial
research across its global ratings portfolio clearly shows that
Governance overall is the most dynamic ESG factor from a credit
perspective," although it acknowledges that "Social factors also
play a key role in non-financial corporates and structured finance
ratings."[89] The "Governance" section of ESG incorporates factors
that include (but are not limited to) the company's impact on
society, ethical standards and practices, and even the diversity of
the company's boardroom.

ESG scores have become so embedded in corporate finance
that almost no corporation has managed to avoid their influence.
Fitch reports that since its "launch of our ESG Relevance Scores
in January 2019, our coverage has expanded to cover all analytical
groups and we now maintain over 140,000 individual environmental, social and governance scores for more than 10,000 entities
and transactions worldwide."[90]

That means ESG scores are already having a real impact on
corporate finances. If you are a corporation looking to issue a bond
to raise capital, a bad ESG score could literally cost you hundreds
of thousands or even millions of dollars over the long term. And all
signs point to ESG becoming an even greater part of the corporate

bond market over the next decade, further incentivizing corporations to enact sweeping ESG reforms.

FOLLOW THE MONEY

It is clear from the evidence presented so far that ESG social credit scores are being used to transform society by altering corporate behavior. This is impacting nearly every aspect of your life in ways you often don't realize. The products you buy, the price of gasoline at the pump, the things you're allowed to say and do online—all these things and more are being influenced directly or indirectly by ESG scores, because corporations have been infected with environmental, social, and governance metrics, and there's almost no part of our society that isn't already touched by what corporations do.

Corporations are being coerced and incentivized into adopting ESG by financial institutions, investment firms like BlackRock, and banks. But all this begs the question: Why are asset managers, banks, credit rating agencies, and others in the financial services industry so committed to ESG? Why are they working night and day to impose ESG on the wider economy? What's in it for *them*?

This is where modern monetary theory (MMT) and the vast money-printing operations of the Federal Reserve bank come to the fore. A slightly moderated version of MMT, once a fringe economic theory, has become the standard operating system for governing monetary policy in the United States. Under MMT, debts and deficits don't matter.[91] Central banks and governments can print as much money as they need to bring an economy to full employment and accomplish goals deemed essential by elites, such as fighting climate change or societal "inequities"—but only if a country controls its own currency, as we do in the United States.

You don't need to be an expert on monetary policy to see that the Federal Reserve has adopted a quasi-MMT strategy. From

January 2020 to December 2022, the Fed added *at least* $15 trillion to the U.S. money supply.[92] I say *at least*, because there's actually no way to know precisely how much money the Fed has pumped into the global financial system. They keep some of it a secret from the less-enlightened, more-deplorable members of society, like you and me. But even if we assumed $15 trillion was the total added, it would mean about 80 percent of all U.S. dollars in existence in 2022 had been created *in just two years.* If that's not modern monetary theory, I don't know what is.

Supporters of MMT say that, instead of focusing on debt, central banks and governments should be worried only about inflation. When inflation rises, which, you know, seems likely when you are endlessly printing money, MMTers say the central bank and national government should alleviate those inflationary pressures by targeting the parts of the economy the "experts" believe are driving the inflation. The government and central bank can then issue a slew of government rules, price controls, subsidies, spending programs, or whatever else the bureaucrats decide will help to address the problem. In other words, to control inflation, MMTers say government should have more direct authority over the economy.

In my previous two books, *Arguing with Socialists* and *The Great Reset,* I spent a substantial amount of time explaining the details of MMT and why it would lead to runaway inflation, contrary to the bat-crap-crazy claims made by its supporters. No need to beat that decrepit old horse with the bum leg again here. Besides, every single American experienced firsthand the impacts of modern monetary theory in 2021 and 2022, when inflation reached levels not seen in decades.

In a December 2022 report titled "2022 Has Been a Year of Brutal Inflation," *The Economist* (which has a long track record of *supporting* liberal policies) noted, "What made 2022 so unusual was the breadth of price pressures. The global rate of inflation will finish the year at roughly 9%. For many developing countries high inflation is a recurrent challenge. But the last time that inflation was so elevated in rich countries was the early 1980s. In America consumer prices are on track to have risen by about 7% in 2022, the highest in four decades."[93]

As bad as these numbers were, they actually appeared to be much better than what the inflation rate would have been had the U.S. government calculated inflation in 2022 using the same formulas they relied on in the 1980s and 1990s. In fact, according to an analysis published on John Williams's popular economics website ShadowStats.com, the inflation rate in 2022 topped out at over 15 percent, using the 1980s CPI model.[94] And general inflation only tells part of the story. Housing prices, one of the most important indicators of inflation driven by monetary policy, rose by a whopping $152,800 from the first quarter of 2020 to the fourth quarter of 2022, a 39 percent increase.[95] So, yeah, nearly endless money-printing causes inflation. Who knew? (Literally *everyone* with a shred of common sense, that's who.)

What does all of this have to do with the Great Reset and the commitment made by much of Wall Street and the U.S. financial system to impose the Reset using ESG metrics? Well, let's do a quick thought exercise. We know for a fact that there was at least five times the amount of money in circulation in 2022 than there was at the start of 2020, but did your bank account swell by 400 percent? Maybe you have $10,000 laying around the house that you forgot about, or perhaps the tens of thousands of dollars you've been getting from the Fed simply slipped in between your couch cushions. Wait, *you* haven't been getting jumbo-sized Fed checks in the mail every month? Well, then, where did all that money go?

In recent times of economic crisis, when the Federal Reserve adds dollars to the money supply, it doesn't send everyone a check in the mail for tens of thousands of dollars. Instead, the Fed purchases U.S. treasuries and other assets available in financial markets. The Fed also spurs lending in an attempt to increase economic growth by lowering interest rates. The theory is that if it's cheaper to get a loan, more people and businesses will go into greater amounts of debt, helping to slow or even reverse an economic downturn.

All these actions disproportionately benefit financial institutions, investors, governments, and banks. Lower interest rates allow big institutions and governments to gain access to greater amounts of capital, giving them more money to spend and invest, and banks end up with a lot more dollars to lend out, which is one of the primary ways banks make money. After all, regardless of who initially gains access to newly printed dollars, most of the money eventually ends up in someone's bank account.

Many of these institutions are using their newfound wealth to buy up assets, such as real estate, bonds, businesses, and stock, giving them increasingly more economic power. For example, do you remember what I said about asset managers like BlackRock earlier in this chapter? BlackRock, the country's largest owner of stock, controlled $10 trillion in assets at the start of 2022.[96] Where did all that money come from, and how has BlackRock been able to purchase so much stock in recent years? In 2008, BlackRock's managed assets totaled just $1.31 trillion.[97] That means BlackRock increased its assets seven-fold in a little more than a decade—a decade that included two large recessions.

It is no coincidence that BlackRock's growth coincided with the Fed policies that have kept interest rates historically low and expanded the money supply well beyond anything Americans have ever seen before. BlackRock, like many other asset managers, has become exceptionally wealthier in recent years because a sizeable chunk of the money created by the Fed has ended up in the hands of a relatively small group of businesses, financial institutions, and

Wall Street firms. Regular folks typically only gain access to newly created money when government uses dollars added by the Fed to launch a shiny new social welfare or infrastructure program, or when money given to financial institutions trickles down to the rest of the economy. But because these policies also cause inflation and price increases in important parts of the economy, such as the housing industry, the benefits of money printing for most Americans are far outpaced by the harm it causes.

Of course, every major institution involved in this gigantic modern monetary theory Ponzi scheme wants to keep the good times rolling, and they know that the only way that can happen is if government and the Federal Reserve stay happy. But that can't happen in an environment with frequent anti–Wall Street rallies or unified political opposition from Democrats and Republicans. So—and this part of my analysis, I admit, does involve some speculation—the elites profiting from this colossal scam made a crafty and politically astute decision: Instead of trying to wage ideological and political wars with the Right and the Left, they chose to go all-in on left-wing causes (at least for now) in an attempt to alleviate some of the pressure they were starting to experience in the wake of the Occupy Wall Street movement that began in 2011. Why fight a political opponent if you can just buy him or her off?

This, of course, doesn't mean most Occupy activists and democratic socialists have sold out to the Great Reset—although we know some, such as millionaire Black Lives Matter cofounder Patrisse Khan-Cullors, absolutely have.[98] But the Left's establishment wing, including President Biden, Kamala Harris, Greenpeace, BlackRock, John Kerry, Al Gore, and countless other Davos elites, is another story entirely. There is simply no doubt that these groups and individuals have profited immensely from modern monetary theory and have sold their souls to the Great Reset to ensure their endeavors remain profitable. And why not? If they can accomplish their goals using the financial system and the Western world's biggest corporations—all while getting rich in the process—why not sign up for the Great Reset?

A NEW GREAT NARRATIVE

Banks, the Federal Reserve, governments, corporations, big tech companies, Wall Street, international organizations such as the United Nations and World Economic Forum, and financial institutions are all working together to "reset capitalism" and rewrite the social contract in the West. The Great Reset is the biggest public-private partnership we have ever seen, and it is exactly the kind of threat to liberty Dwight Eisenhower warned Americans about more than sixty years ago.

But as terrifying as the Great Reset is—and it *is* Stephen King, killer-clowns-murdering-kids-in-a-sewer level of scary—its ESG scores, huge new government programs, widespread social media censorship, COVID-style government lockdowns, and deconstruction of the social contract are a foundation for something even bigger and more troubling than the Great Reset. They are the framework for a new call to action called *the Great Narrative*, a plan that has the potential to transform life on earth forever and usher in a terrifying new dark future for you and your family.

The Great Narrative, like the Great Reset, is a campaign developed by the World Economic Forum that's meant to promote a new model for society.[99] But unlike the Great Reset, the Great Narrative doesn't describe a set of policies or a specific blueprint for changing economies today. Rather, it's a call to rethink the way humans live and how their societies function in light of an emerging *Fourth Industrial Revolution*—a term WEF head Klaus Schwab and many others use to describe the vast changes occurring in our society due to scientific and technological advancements, many of which haven't yet occurred but are expected to soon.

The Great Reset is, in so many ways, the framework upon which a new Great Narrative for the world will be built, because the Reset gives institutions the tools needed to ensure future technological and scientific developments are made with the values of the Great Reset embedded within them. For instance, artificial intelligence systems designed using ESG would likely look very different from a truly neutral form of artificial intelligence. The same would be true of almost any technological advancement, from quantum computing systems used by governments to craft public policy to the development of new digital currencies.

What will the world look like in five, ten, twenty, fifty, or even one hundred years if the Great Reset system is adopted as a key part of the Fourth Industrial Revolution (a.k.a. Industry 4.0 or 4IR)? How will humanity be impacted by the tremendous amount of economic and societal disruption that's sure to come our way over the next couple of decades? What will most people do to earn a living when automation becomes the primary means of production? What are the most important ethical questions we need to be thinking about as technology and science begin to bleed into the realm of bioengineering? Will humans own property or have any privacy in the future? What will it even mean to be "human" in a world in which the lines between man and machine are blurred? These and many other questions related to the looming Fourth Industrial Revolution are all a part of the discussions surrounding the Great Narrative, as well as the extreme reaction against the Great Reset and Great Narrative from authoritarian leaders in countries like Russia.

These important topics, as well as questions surrounding how Americans can maintain their freedom when faced with these remarkable challenges, are the focus of the rest of this book, which has been one of the most important and difficult projects of my career. And be forewarned, throughout this book, I use a lot of direct and often lengthy quotes from the leaders of the Great Reset movement. I don't want you to simply "take my word for it," because in many cases, these global elites expressly state their plans and intentions about redesigning our future.

There is no denying that the Great Reset is one of the truly colossal challenges of this generation. If we allow elites controlling the West's most important institutions—especially those related to government, finance, and technology—to work together to impose their ideas on every country on earth, liberty will die. At the very least, it will be so horrifically wounded that whatever freedoms remain become virtually worthless. But the truth is, as uncomfortable and worrisome as it might be to hear, the Great Reset was never meant to be the final stage of elites' vision for the future. Quite the contrary, in fact. The Great Reset was just the beginning.

— 2 —

THE "GREAT NARRATIVE" IN THE FOURTH INDUSTRIAL REVOLUTION

NARRATIVES AND STORYTELLING ARE POWERFUL. THEY CAN inspire, inform, or transport listeners to another part of the world, or even another universe. For many, stories are infinitely more persuasive than charts and figures, and they are substantially more intimate. A great storyteller doesn't merely teach you something, whether it's about life, history, or even God; he or she makes you feel it in your bones, so that even the deepest part of your soul believes something is true. Narratives and storytelling are as much a part of the human experience as breathing. And although many often fail to recognize their importance, human beings cannot and do not live without narratives.

Of course, the narratives and stories we develop and tell each other are not always based in the truth. People formulate fictional stories for all sorts of reasons—for entertainment, to teach morality, and, of course, to deceive others (and sometimes even ourselves). And together, these untrue stories can become larger narratives that move entire civilizations to act, for better or worse, in remarkable ways.

Although this makes storytelling and societal narratives potentially problematic, people are not machines. They don't take in raw data and coldly spit out reactions based only on the information they have been given. Humans typically understand facts *in context*, based on larger narratives and their emotional connections to those narratives.

You might be surprised to hear that on this topic, I mostly (but not totally) agree with our old World Economic Forum buddy, Klaus Schwab. In a book titled *The Great Narrative*, Schwab and his coauthor, Thierry Malleret, wrote:

> The rich scholarly literature about narratives makes it clear that we think, act and communicate in terms of narratives, and each interpretation, understanding or model of how the world operates begins with a story. Narratives provide the context in which the facts we observe can be interpreted, understood and acted upon. In that sense, they equate to much more than the stories we tell, write or illustrate figuratively; they end up being the truths, or the ideas we accept as truths, that underpin the perceptions that shape our "realities" and in the process form our cultures and societies. Through narratives, we explain how we see things, how these things work, how we make decisions and justify them, how we understand our place in the world and how we try to persuade others to embrace our beliefs and values. To sum up: narratives shape our perceptions, which in turn form

our realities and end up influencing our choices and actions. They are how we find meaning in life.[100]

Schwab's emphasis on the importance of narrative is refreshing. Rarely do you see someone in a position as influential as his carefully think through such a foundational issue, never mind take the time to talk about it. However, I also fear that it makes his ideas for reshaping society all the more dangerous. Schwab has no interest in settling for pushing the "reset button" on the global economy. In fact, his proposal for a Great Reset is meant to serve as the foundation for a much greater transformation in the future, one that will largely be driven by new advancements in technology and the further development of international institutions and global multilateral agreements between world powers. Together, these ideas form a new Great Narrative for the planet, one that reimagines humanity and its cultures, governing institutions, and priorities.

Schwab doesn't believe his own personal understanding of what a Great Narrative could look like is all that matters. He's committed to bringing together other "stakeholders" and elites to help develop and implement a new narrative for the world. But in the end, that narrative must, in Schwab's own words, "help guide the creation of a more resilient, inclusive and sustainable vision for our collective future."[101]

On the surface, this sort of flowery language might sound unremarkable and even tedious. How many times have we heard the United Nations and other internationalists and organizations suggest that their vision for society will improve our "collective future" and be "inclusive" and "sustainable," and that if only we were to listen to them, the world would be a much better place?

However, Schwab's ideas, as well as those of many who have allied themselves with him, go so much further than meaningless slogans. Schwab is a deeply serious individual who has devoted much of his life to advancing the Great Reset by building relationships with thousands of leaders from corporations, banks, Wall Street, central banks, governments, and nonprofit organizations. The names of his foundational concepts have evolved over the years and come in many forms, such as "stakeholder capitalism" and "Davos manifesto," but the underlying ideas and their associated policy proposals have largely remained the same. And when he and others have discussed the Great Narrative in detail, as you will see later in this chapter, they often propose specific ways their values could be put into action. So when Schwab speaks, we should listen and take him deathly seriously.

THE FOURTH INDUSTRIAL REVOLUTION

Throughout his writings, Schwab and many of those he has partnered with express a sense of urgency when calling for a new Great Narrative, a new story for mankind. This is because, like myself, Schwab is an amateur futurist. He often thinks and writes about the emergence of new technologies and what impacts they might have on countries large and small.[102] This, as you'll see throughout the rest of this book, is an essential part of understanding what Schwab has in mind when thinking about a new Great Narrative.

Schwab believes, and rightfully so, that technological, social, environmental, and economic developments are rapidly changing the way people live, and significantly more changes are coming soon. In his mind, many of these alterations, including the "convergence of the physical, digital and biological worlds," are, to varying extents, unstoppable and will cause immense changes and upheaval. As Schwab wrote in his book, "Disruption is coming. It will be both good and bad, and major."[103]

As noted in chapter 1, this period of innovation and disruption is often referred to by global elites in the West as the Fourth Industrial

Revolution, a term CNBC reports was coined by Schwab himself at a Davos meeting in 2016.[104] Schwab says the Fourth Industrial Revolution—along with the "digitization of countless economic activities"—was "the defining issue of the pre-pandemic era."[105] And now that the COVID-19 pandemic is not raging to the extent it once was, the Fourth Industrial Revolution will once again become a primary concern for thinkers, activists, and government officials.

As the World Economic Forum notes, there have been three Industrial Revolutions prior to the current one. The development of the steam engine led to the birth of the First Industrial Revolution in the United Kingdom in about 1760.[106]

The Second Industrial Revolution began in the nineteenth century, with the development of technologies that allowed for the mass production and/or distribution of oil, electricity, and steel.[107]

The Third Industrial Revolution ushered in the Digital Era, the revolution we are most familiar with today. This marked the birth of personal computers, the Internet, smartphones, the proliferation of software, and other, similar developments.[108]

The World Economic Forum claims the Fourth Industrial Revolution "represents a fundamental change in the way we live, work and relate to one another. It is a new chapter in human development, enabled by extraordinary technology advances commensurate with those of the first, second and third industrial revolutions."[109]

According to a CNBC report summarizing the views of Zvika Krieger, the head of technology policy and partnerships at WEF, although every Industrial Revolution has involved remarkable changes to economies and societies, the Fourth Industrial Revolution differs from the most recent one because "the gap between the digital, physical and biological worlds is shrinking, and technology is changing faster than ever."[110] These changes and the speed with which they are occurring offer "huge promise and potential peril."[111]

In the minds of many Davos attendees, it is up to elites and powerful institutions—acting with input from and in the best interests of those they lord over—to ensure the transition to the next era of humanity is "inclusive" and respectful of ideas Schwab values, such as advancing globalism and protecting the environment from climate change. This can only occur, according to Schwab, if we avoid totalitarian government interventions (as he would understand them) and if nations agree to "move on" from free-market economics and what he believes to be a misguided emphasis on individuals.[112]

As Schwab once wrote, "Free-market fundamentalism has eroded worker rights and economic security, triggered a deregulatory race to the bottom and ruinous tax competition, and enabled the emergence of massive new global monopolies. Today's consumers do not want more and better goods and services for a reasonable price. Rather, they increasingly expect companies to contribute to social welfare and the common good. There is both a fundamental need and an increasingly widespread demand for a new kind of 'capitalism.'"[113]

To fix these problems, Schwab says "we must rethink what we mean by 'capital' in its many iterations, whether financial, environmental, social, or human."[114] In other words, we need a Great Reset of the global economy.

It's important to understand that the Great Narrative isn't merely another name for the Great Reset. The Great Reset is only one small part of the much bigger, much scarier Great Narrative. The Great Reset, as destructive as it is, is just a stepping stone on the way to something even worse. The Great Narrative is a call to rethink every part of life, to prepare for the emergence of a new world. In Schwab's mind, this rethinking ought to include environmental, social, and governance (ESG) metrics and other components of the Great Reset, but the Great Narrative includes broader issues related to how we think about morality, trade, geopolitics, technology, and other topics.

In other words, the Great Narrative seeks to come up with an answer to the question: What should the human experience look like in the decades to come? And for Schwab, that begs another question: How can we use the Great Reset's stakeholder capitalist approach to ensure this vision for the future is fulfilled? Additionally, how can the ruling class embed ESG ideals into most, if not every, part of life?

Schwab doesn't pretend to know the answers to every aspect of these questions, and he has repeatedly suggested that others—mostly people who already agree with much of his approach, of course—must be involved in this important conversation. But over and over again, Schwab insists that whatever comes next must produce a more "resilient, inclusive and sustainable" international society.

DESIGNING THE FUTURE

At its heart, the Great Narrative is a call for elites and well-connected nonprofit organizations to develop a plan for the future of humanity, one that considers the numerous disruptions going on today and, more importantly, the disruptions of the future. This will, in the eyes of many who support the Great Narrative, involve discussing issues that are "a bit out of the mainstream," such as, for example, "gene editing," applied artificial intelligence, and "synthetic biology."[115] I don't know about you, but anytime the world's most powerful people gather together to develop a new "narrative" for humanity and to discuss how to embed their values into the future of things such as synthetic biology and gene editing, I think it's probably a good idea to start paying attention.

To say that the conversations that have occurred over the past few years surrounding the Great Narrative and the Fourth

Industrial Revolution are creepy and incredibly terrifying is really underselling them. But that's a good thing—a *really* good thing, in fact. If those affiliated with the Great Narrative weren't so openly and bluntly acknowledging their intentions, the vast majority of Americans would never find out about them. Most people don't spend their Saturday afternoons jet-setting to Switzerland to attend (for the seventeenth time this year) a ski/brunch/take-over-the-world conference. In the old days—you know, like the 1990s—power-hungry elites used to quietly draw up their proposals in cigar-smoke-filled backrooms and closed-door meetings. They're still doing that, of course, but now they are also brash (and foolish) enough to proudly boast about their proposals at elaborate, multi-million-dollar conferences too.

The first time I heard the Great Narrative openly discussed was in a speech delivered at just such an event. From November 10–13, 2021, the World Economic Forum and the Government of the United Arab Emirates hosted an historic Great Narrative conference in Dubai.[116] Although it was relatively small by WEF standards, the discussions were absolutely astonishing and serve as a helpful guide to better understanding what the Great Narrative is and could become.

According to the event's official description, "The Great Narrative meeting is a linchpin of the Great Narrative initiative, a collaborative effort of the world's leading thinkers to fashion longer-term perspectives and co-create a narrative that can help guide the creation of a more resilient, inclusive and sustainable vision for our collective future. Top thinkers from a variety of geographies and disciplines—including futurists, scientists and philosophers—will contribute fresh ideas for the future."[117]

At the opening event, titled "Narrating the Future," Klaus Schwab hosted a truly shocking discussion with Mohammad Abdullah Al Gergawi, the UAE's minister of cabinet affairs.

In his introduction to the discussion, Schwab said that the purpose of the conference was "to develop the Great Narrative—a story for the future. And I would like to refer to his highness Sheik Mohammad bin Rashid Al Maktoum, the vice chairman and prime minister of the United Arab Emirates and the ruler of Dubai, who told us that, 'In order to shape the future, you have first to imagine the future, you have to design the future, and then you have to execute.'"[118]

Schwab later echoed these points in his presentation, saying that over the course of the conference, "We will look at how we imagine, how we design, how we execute the Great Narratives. How we define the story of our world for the future."[119]

Note the repeated use of the words *imagine, design,* and *execute.* As I explained earlier in this chapter, *designing* and *imagining* are themes used throughout Great Narrative events, discussions, and literature, and the expectation is often stated that ruling-class elites and their allies are the ones responsible for ensuring that a proper Great Narrative is constructed and implemented.

Following Schwab's brief comments, Al Gergawi offered a revealing speech about the Great Narrative and its purpose. "The world has gone through a very difficult time in the past couple of months," Al Gergawi said. "People are looking for a way for a Great Transformation. We need, as a world, a new blueprint. In fact, a new Great Narrative."[120]

Al Gergawi then referenced a couple of the run-of-the-mill WEF justifications for upending the global order with a new "blueprint" for society, arguing, "We need the new Great Narrative because the world has been through one of the largest economic downturns in its history" due to the COVID-19 pandemic and its associated government-imposed lockdowns.[121]

However, Al Gergawi went beyond the standard Great Reset talking points, introducing a striking concept that nearly caused me to fall out of my chair when I first read it. (And that's not easy to do, by the way. Like all elite athletes, I have exceptional balance.)

"We need a new Great Narrative because *our digital world will be as important as the physical world,*" Al Gergawi declared. "Already, there are more connected devices than people in the world. And by 2025, there will be five times more devices than people on this planet."[122]

Our digital world will be as important as the physical world. Do not forget those words. They are an essential component of the future envisioned by advocates of the Great Narrative, and it's important that you keep this idea in mind when we talk later about some of the more detailed ideas Schwab and others have about future technological innovation.

Later in the discussion with Schwab, Al Gergawi went even further. "We have to understand that today we sit in a very interesting time zone when it comes to human history," he said. "We have to look at our current situation as a part of human evolution, and this is part of human history." It is a "second wave of human evolution," one "based on technology."[123]

Al Gergawi claimed that to address the issues arising from this "second wave of human evolution," "We need the new Great Narrative," which "will inspire both hope and action. And governments, first and foremost, are in the business of installing hope."[124]

Really? *Installing hope?* I thought government was in the business of protecting human rights and defending our communities, not "installing" inspiration—whatever that means—into the citizens that government is supposed to be serving.

Under a new Great Narrative, it is not enough for individual governments on their own to strive for a better future by utilizing the principles and strategies of the Great Reset. Every country must participate.

"It is time to imagine what role government should play to enable this new Great Narrative," Al Gergawi said. "As you know, a global challenge requires a global solution."[125]

And don't forget that this "global solution" isn't driven by government alone. As I explained in chapter 1, Schwab insists that "To achieve a better outcome, the world must act jointly and swiftly to revamp all aspects of our societies and economies, from education to social contracts and working conditions," and "every industry, from oil and gas to tech, must be transformed."[126]

Similarly, Al Gergawi said during the Great Narrative conference, "A whole of government approach is simply not enough. We need a whole of society and a whole of humanity approach."[127]

Schwab admits that such a far-reaching "Great Transformation" of the world will require "stronger" governments,[128] but you have nothing to worry about, I'm sure. Schwab, Al Gergawi, and others have repeatedly promised that under their new Great Narrative international society, they and the other overlords in the ruling class will make the interests of all the stakeholders, even little people like you and me, their primary concern. When Schwab is toiling away in his elaborate office in Switzerland, described by the *Independent* newspaper as "a glam corner affair decked out in white leather panels and furnished with gentlemen's club–style armchairs in a chocolate brown,"[129] or lamenting the plight of the poor at "extravagant dinners" hosted in what *Vanity Fair* calls a "palatial home in the Cologny neighborhood of Geneva—the Beverly Hills of Switzerland,"[130] I'm sure *you* are the first and only thing on his mind.

The truth is, the core belief behind the Great Narrative is that elites in business, academia, international institutions, central and private banks, Wall Street firms, and government agencies are much better qualified to "design the future" than the rest of society. They pay lip service to the idea that the little people should have a say in what the future looks like, but in the end, those who attend Davos are the ones charting our course. As Al Gergawi proclaimed to his elitist audience at the 2021 Great Narrative conference, "Professor Klaus Schwab, ladies and gentlemen, collectively, we are the author of this new chapter. We cannot be passive and reactive."[131]

Even more explicitly, Al Gergawi later added, "Going back to the role of government, our job is to design a better future. Always, we believe that. And in the Emirates, we believe that. I don't want to say we are government officials. We are designers."[132]

They are *designers*. That's their job. What about the rest of us? Well, Schwab says that "the people" are one of the great "difficulties" standing in the way of a new Great Narrative taking hold. Schwab said that they have struggled to "shape the future" because "people have become much more self-centered—to a certain extent egotistic. So in such a situation, it's much more difficult to create a compromise because shaping the future, designing the future usually needs a common will of the people."[133]

You see, in the minds of people like Klaus Schwab and others trying to impose a new Great Narrative, those of us who believe in individual rights are the problem. If only we would just shut up and sit down, our betters could rule society more effectively and to our benefit.

THE CHALLENGES AHEAD

It is clear that Klaus Schwab and the other madmen in Davos—and madwomen too; this book is committed to gender-balanced insults of the ruling class—believe that large-scale technological changes are going to create serious problems, issues that they believe justify a new "blueprint" and "design" for the world's economy and social contracts everywhere. But what, exactly, do they say they are worried about, and is there any merit to their fears?

Earlier in this chapter, I referenced two of the broad concerns often cited by supporters of developing a new Great Narrative: technological innovations and rebuilding the global economy in the wake of the COVID-19 pandemic. However, in his 2021 book about the Great Narrative, Klaus Schwab, following conversations he had with dozens of academics and leaders in business, outlined a long list of other, often much more detailed concerns he and other World Economic Forum members share, along with their proposed "narrative" solutions.

For example, Johan Rockstrom, the joint director of the Potsdam Institute for Climate Impact Research, claims that climate change is causing the world to "irreversibly start drifting away to a state that would no longer be able to support the modern world as we know it. Perhaps it will take 100, 200 or 300 years before we sit there with 40% of the land area on Earth being uninhabitable, sit there with a 10-metre sea-level rise, and sit there with extreme weather events, fires, and disease."[134]

Schwab and Al Gergawi agree with Rockstrom's climate change fears. Schwab has said climate change is the "greatest collective action problem we've ever been confronted with,"[135] and Al Gergawi said during the 2021 Great Narrative conference that humanity "cannot afford to waste more time on inaction or denial about the climate change."[136]

Rockstrom's "grand narrative" to fix this alleged climate "emergency" is that humanity "must reconnect to the planet, must become stewards to the planet, and must recognize that the planet has boundaries that are non-negotiable. The big new future for humanity is to be successful, equitable and profitable, all the desirable attributes within the safe operating space of a stable planet."[137]

Schwab says another significant concern is wealth inequality. According to Schwab, "Among the many societal challenges we collectively face, the most damaging and deep-rooted is inequality. As UN Secretary-General António Guterres puts it, 'Inequality defines our time.'"[138]

In Schwab's eyes, the problem of inequality has become increasingly more important in recent years:

> COVID-19 has exacerbated pre-existing conditions of inequality, making them worse in several respects. The first was to magnify the challenge of social inequalities by spotlighting the shocking disparities in the degree of risk to which different social classes are exposed (the upper and middle classes have been much less affected by COVID than members of the working class). The second was to expose the profound disconnect between the essential nature and innate value of a job done and the economic recompense it commands. Put another way: COVID made it plain that we value least economically the individuals that society needs the most in times of crisis (such as nurses, delivery personnel, or cleaners).[139]

If you read my book *The Great Reset*, this will all sound very familiar. Climate change and the economic fallout from the COVID-19 pandemic are two of the most common issues Great Reset supporters cite when talking about the need for blowing up the existing global economy. However, as I explained in great length in *The Great Reset*, the evidence is very strong that these justifications are nothing more than a smokescreen that obscures many elites' true motivations.[140] It's hard to take seriously Great Reseters who say they are concerned about climate change and the effects of the COVID-19 lockdowns when many of them:

1. Have made their fortunes in part by utilizing fossil fuels.
2. Fly in private jets all over the world on a weekly basis, spewing carbon dioxide into the atmosphere.[141]

3. Buy houses or support politicians who live on beaches that are supposedly on the verge of being swallowed up by the ocean because of climate change.[142]

4. Are the ones largely responsible for closing down the economy during the pandemic in the first place.

Concerns about a human-caused climate change catastrophe are especially hypocritical coming from Al Gergawi, a government official who benefits immensely from the fact that his country, the United Arab Emirates, is the seventh-largest oil producer on the planet, with outputs typically surpassing ten million barrels of oil per day.[143]

Climate change and economic inequality aren't the only societal problems that supposedly justify a new Great Narrative. For instance, Schwab says, "The risks associated with cybercrime are the most current and tangible because they have affected or will affect most of us and millions of companies around the world. Cybercrime, cyberattacks and ransomware are on the increase globally, becoming ever more targeted and 'strategic' in nature." Citing a report by *Cybercrime Magazine*, Schwab claims the cost of cyberattacks, ransomware, and other, similar problems could be as high as $10.5 trillion by 2025.[144] Some experts estimate cybercrime already costs around $1 trillion to $6 trillion annually.[145]

Another problem identified by Schwab is that the "foundational premise of equity—i.e. that governments serve the people and apply the rule of law equally," has been "seriously undermined" and could be "ultimately destroyed" because of unfair tax and regulatory rules that favor some big businesses and the wealthy.[146]

"As a result, people become angry, convinced that the system is rigged, and lose faith or hope that things might one day get better for them," Schwab wrote. "A toxic sentiment of unfairness permeates their lives."[147] These "rigged" rules have led to a dangerous "increase in dissatisfaction, often expressed via demonstrations and social unrest."[148]

Schwab says unrest has or will soon cause countries across the globe to "redefine the terms of their social contract," which he describes as the "set of arrangements and expectations that govern the relations between individuals and institutions" and the "glue" that "binds" the members of society.[149]

What will new social contracts look like in a Great Narrative world? Schwab admits that the answer to that question will vary from country to country, but, ultimately, "they could all share some common features and principles, the absolute necessity for which has been made ever-more obvious by the social and economic consequences of the pandemic crisis."[150]

Two features "stand out" for Schwab as essential parts of building a "fairer," more inclusive future: "(1) a broader, if not universal, provision of social assistance, social insurance, healthcare and basic quality services; and (2) a move towards enhanced protection for workers in the form of mandatory benefits, a minimum decent wage and help to adapt to (the disruptive effects of) innovation."[151]

In other words, Schwab believes the best way to stave off a dissatisfied populace is to further expand the West's already massive welfare programs, and to further inject government rules and regulations into the economic bloodstream. And why not, right? It's not like these strategies have been tried thousands of times over the past century in America and Europe, with disastrous results. Oh, shoot. That's right. They have. Huh.

Oh, and all of this, of course, would be coupled with Schwab's plan for a Great Reset of the global economy that would "steer the market toward fairer outcomes" by, in part, improving "coordination" between nations on tax, fiscal, and regulatory policy; altering trade agreements; and imposing an ESG-dominated "stakeholder economy."[152]

Concerns about the economy, environment, and social contracts are not the only things World Economic Forum intellectuals are thinking about. Many are pondering the potential wonders and catastrophes that might occur once humans further develop artificial intelligence (AI).

Take, for example, the role of AI in the lives of our children. The World Economic Forum notes that AI technologies "can be used to educate and empower children and youth," and in the years to come AI "will determine the future of play, childhood, education and societies."[153] However, WEF warns that there are serious risks associated with using AI to help develop our children, because "children and youth can be especially vulnerable to the potential risks posed by AI, including bias, cybersecurity and lack of accessibility."[154]

To guard against these potentially unsafe, racist, sexist AI systems, WEF says, "AI technology must be created so that it is both innovative and responsible. Responsible AI is safe, ethical, transparent, fair, accessible and inclusive."[155]

If you thought concerns over AI's influence on your kids is as scary as it gets, think again. The World Economic Forum also has substantial fears about an AI-inspired nuclear holocaust, and an even scarier plan to avoid it. An article published to the WEF's website, in partnership with the RAND Corporation, warns, "Stunning advances in AI have created machines that can learn and think, provoking a new arms race among the world's major nuclear powers. It's not the killer robots of Hollywood blockbusters that we need to worry about; it's how computers might challenge the basic rules of nuclear deterrence and lead humans into making devastating decisions."[156]

In the article, the RAND Corporation's Doug Irving, summarizing the views of various other RAND experts, rightly notes that, among other things, a shared belief among nuclear powers in mutually assured destruction has prevented a nuclear war for more than a half-century. If one nation knows that its adversary could respond in kind to a nuclear strike with another, potentially deadlier nuclear launch, it's unlikely either side will attack in the first place.

However, Irving notes, "The situation gets more dangerous and uncertain if one side loses its ability to strike back or even just thinks it might lose that ability. It might respond by creating new weapons to regain its edge. Or it might decide it needs to throw its punches early, before it gets hit first."[157]

According to RAND, "That's where the real danger of AI might lie. Computers can already scan thousands of surveillance photos, looking for patterns that a human eye would never see. It doesn't take much imagination to envision a more advanced system taking in drone feeds, satellite data, and even social media posts to develop a complete picture of an adversary's weapons and defenses."

You might be wondering, *What's the harm in having too much information?* According to Irving, "A system that can be everywhere and see everything might convince an adversary that it is vulnerable to a disarming first strike—that it might lose its counterpunch. That adversary would scramble to find new ways to level the field again, by whatever means necessary. That road leads closer to nuclear war."

Edward Geist, a specialist in nuclear security at RAND, says, "Autonomous systems don't need to kill people to undermine stability and make catastrophic war more likely. New AI capabilities might make people think they're going to lose if they hesitate. That could give them itchier trigger fingers. At that point, AI will be making war more likely even though the humans are still quote-unquote in control."[158]

What's RAND's Great Narrative solution to the problem? Surely it is to keep AI as far from the nuclear launch codes as possible, right? Wrong again.

Although the technology is "still far in the future," RAND says, "It's possible that a future AI system could prove so reliable, so coldly rational, that it winds back the hands of the nuclear doomsday clock. To err is human, after all. A machine that makes no mistakes, feels no pressure, and has no personal bias could provide a level of stability that the Atomic Age has never known."[159]

I don't know about you, but nothing makes me feel safer than knowing that the entire fate of the human race could soon be put into the "coldly rational" machine hands of a future AI system. What could go wrong? If we do move in this direction, I suggest naming the AI system SkyNet. That name has a familiar ring to it, doesn't it?

BUILDING A FOUNDATION

As crazy as it might sound, all we have done thus far is lightly scratch the surface of the Great Narrative. In future chapters, we'll go into much greater detail about artificial intelligence and Klaus Schwab's vision for a future stakeholder economy, as well as discuss a number of other important topics that are regularly part of conversations surrounding the Great Reset and Great Narrative. This includes automation and self-driving cars, robotics, the so-called Internet of Things and 5G technology, quantum computing, transhumanism, cryptocurrencies and digital central bank currencies, the metaverse, a new international system of ethics and morality, the promise that "you'll own nothing and be happy," and, the creepiest topic of them all, synthetic biology and gene editing. Yes, you read that correctly; I said *gene editing*.

Before we discuss those and other topics, though, I want to make something crystal clear: I share many of Klaus Schwab and the World Economic Forum's concerns that we've looked at so far, as well as many more we'll talk about in future chapters. I, too, believe that we are on the verge of experiencing unprecedented levels of disruption caused by technological advancements and issues related to globalization. I am also deeply worried about the role that artificial intelligence could soon play in our lives, and not just when it comes to our children and weapons defense systems. I agree that cybersecurity and ransomware attacks pose substantial threats to key infrastructure, and I absolutely believe that we are on the brink of seeing once-unfathomable levels of unrest and demands for a new social contract—including here in the United States.

What troubles me about the Great Narrative and Great Reset movements is not that the issues that have allegedly inspired them are unworthy of our time or consideration. In fact, one of the main reasons I wanted to write this book is to help inspire *all* of us—not just the uber-wealthy, well-connected, and CEOs of *Fortune* 500 companies blessed with an invitation to Davos—to start thinking through and talking about these complex problems. I hate to say it, but in our current social, economic, cultural, and political climate, the American people are completely unprepared for the challenges ahead. We're so busy brawling with each other over who gets to sit in the most comfortable chair at the beach that we've missed the thousand-foot-high tsunami that's about to drown the country. We must change our priorities or the United States, and perhaps even the entire human race, might not survive the next century—and no, Greta Thunberg, I'm not talking about climate change. I'm talking about *real* crises, such as killer robots and the emergence of Nazi-style eugenics. (A bit later in the book, you'll see that's not a joke.)

The biggest divergence between where I and most other Americans stand compared to Klaus Schwab and the enlightened masterminds at Davos is that their so-called solutions to these problems involve expanding the power of government, internationalizing virtually all of the world's most important policy decisions, and using ESG social credit scores, the power of the global financial system, and other aspects of the Great Reset to serve as the foundation for the coming technological advancements of the Fourth

Industrial Revolution. In other words, their answer to the question, what should the human experience look like in the decades to come, is giving more control of our economies and societies to an international ruling class that plans to "design" our future so that American individuals and families have less property, power, and wealth. Does that sound like the future *you* want to live in?

THE RESISTANCE

Libertarian and conservative Americans like me aren't the only ones worried about what will happen to the United States' future if Great Reset principles are merged with revolutionary technological advancements and economic and cultural changes. Concerns over the Great Reset have spread well beyond America's borders, to places such as Canada, France, and the United Kingdom.

In fact, in many ways, the United Kingdom's decision to leave the European Union—which finally occurred on January 31, 2020, after years of political wrangling—was one of the first major shots fired against the emerging Great Reset movement.[160] Brexit, as it is commonly referred to, may have started before the World Economic Forum launched its official Great Reset campaign, but the foundation for the Great Reset had been built long before 2020. The people of the United Kingdom may not have understood most of what the Great Reset entails at the time they voted to leave the EU, but they did know their country was losing its sovereignty to elitist internationalists on continental Europe, and they wanted to chart their own course and have control over their own destiny.

Freedom from Davos and its allies is the heart of the resistance to the Great Reset.

However, not everyone pushing back against Klaus Schwab and the other power-hungry globalists in the World Economic

Forum are friends of liberty. Far from it, in fact. Some of the biggest adversaries of the Great Reset are also fascists, but instead of advocating for an internationalist, twenty-first-century brand of fascism beloved in Davos, these fascists are nationalists, traditionalists, and, in many cases, violent.

Although most Americans don't know it yet, there is a growing ideological divide between governments, financial institutions, and even corporations in the West—especially Canada, Europe, and the United States—and governments and their allies in the East, most notably China, Russia, Turkey, and Iran. This conflict between international fascists in the West and national fascists in the East is, as I'll argue extensively in chapter 9, one of the reasons Russian president Vladimir Putin chose to invade Ukraine in early 2022, and it will very likely play a significant role in global affairs for decades to come.

I believe we have entered a Third World War—perhaps a Fourth World War, depending on how you view the Cold War. That doesn't mean we're going to see Chinese and Russian tanks rolling into France anytime soon. (Although, after watching what has occurred in Ukraine, can anyone really rule out that possibility?) But what I do think we're going to see is the continued expansion of cyber, financial, and economic warfare. I say "continued" because the evidence is clear that these tactics have already been utilized by the major forces in this conflict.

I will say a lot more about the possibility that World War III has already started later on, but for now, all I'll ask from you is to think carefully as we work our way through the next several chapters about how a nationalistic, traditionalist, fascist government such as the Chinese Communist Party, Putin's regime in Russia, or the radical Islamic states in the Middle East would view the Great Narrative and its goals of embedding Great Reset, non-traditional, globalist values into future technologies.

Do not forget that one of the primary goals of the Great Reset and Great Narrative movements is to rework social contracts and economies around the world, not just in the West. As I noted earlier, Klaus Schwab said, *"Every country, from the United States to China, must participate, and every industry, from oil and gas to tech, must be transformed."*[161]

Do you think China and Russia want to participate in Schwab's grand vision of the future? Of course not, and they are doing everything they can to show the West that they won't be part of a new Great Narrative formulated in Davos—even if they do on occasion pretend, rather unconvincingly, to be willing to collaborate with Western nations to appease elites like Schwab.

A FAIR WARNING

Whenever humanity has gone through periods of intense change, opportunity knocks. The big question is, who will answer the door? That's what the remainder of this book is about.

In chapters 3 and 4, I will detail the technological and social changes that are headed our way, and then I'll briefly outline some of the opportunities and dangers associated with those changes.

In chapter 5, I'll talk about how the ongoing consolidation of property ownership poses significant risks for freedom, as well as explain what the World Economic Forum has in mind when its writers talk about "owning nothing."

In chapter 6, I will introduce you to the Great Narrative's "new blueprint" for the Western world, which includes huge amounts of data collection, "smart cities," and the expansion of artificial intelligence. Chapter 6 is when we'll start to dive into the specific ways supporters of the Great Narrative could use the Fourth Industrial Revolution to transform Western civilization and even what it means to be human.

And if you're head hasn't exploded by the end of chapter 6, then you'll read in chapter 7 about the threats that the Fourth Industrial Revolution poses to basic human rights and even all of humankind, including those related to bioengineering, gene editing, and brain implants.

In chapter 8, I'll show you what the Biden administration, large corporations and financial institutions, and globalist organizations are doing today to build the foundation for a new Great Narrative.

As I mentioned earlier, in chapter 9 I'll discuss how national fascistic regimes in Russia and China are using the Great Reset and Great Narrative movements to advance their own tyrannical agendas.

Finally, in chapter 10, I'll show you what we can all do to save the United States—and humanity along with it.

Prior to starting to dig into these topics, though, I want to provide you with a couple of important notes. First, I have intentionally packed this book with a metric ton of quotations that come directly from the Davos crowd, because I want you to see what the elite leaders of the movement have to say for themselves, in their own words. They aren't hiding the ball here. They're putting it all out there for anyone to see and hear. All you have to do is listen and take what they have to say seriously.

Second, and more importantly, I want to provide you with a fair warning: this book isn't for the faint of heart nor the weak-willed. Once you learn about the full extent of the Great Narrative, there's no turning back the clock. You will *never* look at the world the same way again.

Remember the famous scene in that wonderful documentary film *The Matrix*, where Morpheus gives that handsome actor from *Bill and Ted's Excellent Adventure* a choice of taking two pills?

"This is your last chance," Morpheus warns Neo. "After this, there is no turning back. You take the blue pill, the story ends. You wake up in your bed and believe whatever you want to. You take the red pill, you stay in Wonderland, and I show you how deep the rabbit hole goes. Remember, all I'm offering is the truth. Nothing more."[162]

If you don't want to know how deep the rabbit hole goes, you can close the book now and walk away. Of course, that won't stop the world around you from changing, and it won't guard you against the Great Narrative's effects. But perhaps for a while, you will sleep a little better at night.

However, if you take the red pill, then you will be confronted with economic, social, and ethical problems that are unlike anything humanity has dealt with before. You'll then need to decide for yourself whose side you are on. What do you believe and why? And is America, as well as the rest of Western civilization, still worth saving?

How you and tens of millions of others answer those difficult questions will shape the course of human events for generations to come. I know that sounds dramatic, but if you stick with me throughout this book, keep an open mind, and, most importantly, do your own homework, I guarantee you'll agree about the importance of what we are up against.

So which is it going to be—the blue pill or the red pill? Remember, all I'm offering is the truth. Nothing more.

3

THE AGE OF DISRUPTION, PART I: THE AUTOMATION BOMB

"STUBBORN," "OLD-FASHIONED," "RESISTANT TO CHANGE," "technophobes," "extremists," "fools"—these are just some of the many negative assumptions that typically come to mind for modern Americans when they hear the word *Luddites*.

For two centuries, these machine-breaking radicals have served as a cautionary tale to all those who would stand in the way of economic and societal development. We have repeatedly heard that those who make the terrible mistake of opposing technological development will, just like the Luddites, be swept away by the inevitable march of progress. "You don't want *that* to be your legacy too," they often say.

I am guessing that most people reading this book have heard the term *Luddite* before, probably in passing from a more "enlightened" politician, or perhaps just before dozing off in your high school history class. But how much do you *really* know about the Luddites and their true motivations? I am willing to bet the answer is not a whole lot. Before doing the research for this book, I also assumed that everything I'd heard about the Luddites was true, only to discover that our understanding of the Luddites, like so many other figures in history, is miles away from what those involved in the movement actually believed and fought for.

The Luddite movement emerged in the United Kingdom in early 1811, predominantly in manufacturing centers in the north of England and Midlands regions, including in the city of Nottingham.[163] Over a six-year period in the heart of the Industrial Revolution, angry textile workers stormed countless factories located across a swath of land stretching seventy miles. They smashed valuable equipment and sometimes engaged in deadly shootouts with government officials and factory security guards.[164] Some Luddites unlucky enough to be caught by government agents ended up going to the gallows, while others were shipped off to Australia back when it was still a British penal colony.

The name Luddites came from their proclaimed legendary leader, Edward "Ned" Ludd, who was often referred to by his "followers" as "Captain," "General," or "King Ludd."[165] I put "followers" in quotation marks because good ole' King Ludd wasn't a real person. He was a fictional character ingeniously created by the rioters to personify their movement and draw attention away from the Luddites' real organizers.

The violent groups of disaffected workers who took on the name "Luddites" didn't merely destroy factory equipment; when they raged against the machines, they did it in style. For example, they often sent threatening letters or poetic notes to factory owners before or after attacks. Occasionally, rioters even dressed up as women—"General Ludd's wives"—while they smashed factory equipment. Some sang catchy songs as they marched triumphantly through the streets.[166]

My personal favorite tune from these rowdy, cross-dressing, anti-technology fanatics was their smash hit involving the legend of Robin Hood, another likely mythological figure who emerged from the Midlands region of England. "Chant no more your old rhymes about bold Robin Hood," Luddite rioters would sing. "His feats I but little admire. I will sing the achievements of General Ludd, now the hero of Nottinghamshire."[167] (Now, if that isn't deserving of becoming a Top 40 hit, I'm not sure what is.)

A common description of the Luddites suggests that the movement focused on destroying all new factory technologies because they erroneously believed their livelihoods would soon be threatened by these novel machines. But the truth is, Luddites typically targeted *specific kinds of machines* in their attacks, not machinery in general, and their favorite targets were typically tools that had been around for many decades. For example, Luddites were fond of smashing stocking frames, a machine that had been invented by William Lee two centuries before the Luddite movement commenced.[168]

Contrary to popular belief, Luddites were not motivated by a hatred of technology or societal change, but rather by what they perceived to be a completely unjust social and economic situation that had developed in England over several decades. Luddites worked under poor conditions, and they had grown increasingly angrier after factory owners started to rely further on machines that workers believed produced shoddy, poorly made products. More importantly, employers typically hired lower-wage, unskilled workers called *colts* to operate the machines. This enraged the Luddites, many of whom were *required by law* to complete a seven-year-long apprenticeship to work their trade.[169] Making matters even worse, Britain and many of its workers had suffered immensely from the seemingly never-ending wars with Napoleonic France, and food shortages had reduced the quality of life for many Luddite families in the years leading up to their riots.

Luddites also had few political or economic rights. In England at the end of the eighteenth century and beginning of the nineteenth century, only a tiny fraction of the populace could vote. According to the United Kingdom's National Archives, "A survey conducted in 1780 revealed that the electorate in England and Wales consisted of just 214,000 people—less than 3% of the total population of approximately 8 million. In Scotland the electorate was even smaller: in 1831 a mere 4,500 men, out of a population of more than 2.6 million people, were entitled to vote in parliamentary elections."[170] Even after Parliament passed the 1832 Reform Act, which significantly improved the electoral system, only 18 percent of the total number of adult males could vote in elections.[171] (Women in the United Kingdom weren't allowed to cast votes until 1928.)

Political power had also been dramatically skewed in favor of rural regions with ties to influential British families, rather than more-populated urban centers, where factories were typically located. According to the UK National Archives records in the time of the Luddites, "Large industrial cities like Leeds, Birmingham and Manchester did not have a single MP [member of Parliament] between them."[172] It was also common for wealthy factory owners to benefit from close relationships with government officials, who commonly suppressed, sometimes with great brutality, protests against the unfair treatment of workers.[173]

The Luddites were not, as many imagine today, low-income, starving, backwoods haters of progress; they were mostly highly skilled artisans rebelling against a crony, corrupt, public-private partnership between oligarchs and the governments who protected them. The Luddite movement wasn't a fight against technology; it was a rebellion against the elites of their day who had for decades used the incredible technological and societal transformations ushered in by the Industrial Revolution to enhance their own wealth and power, often at the expense of working-class families. You might even say that before anyone had ever heard of Klaus Schwab, Joe Biden, or the World Economic Forum, the Luddites were waging a war against a "great reset" of their own time.

Like the Luddites, today's Westerners are living in an age of remarkable disruption, an era that will usher in more substantial changes to society than the world has ever seen before. But as tempting as it might be to take a page out of the Luddites' playbook, we cannot and should not smash and riot our way out of the trouble we have found ourselves in. Instead, we should take advantage of the technological achievements of the present and future to empower individuals and fight back against the centralization of wealth and authority of the Great Reset and Great Narrative movements. But before we can even begin to understand the best road ahead, we need to first gain a greater understanding of our own disruptive era by learning about the dangers, opportunities, and challenges of emerging technologies.

Throughout the remainder of this chapter and chapter 4, I will outline some of the most revolutionary ideas and technologies that have developed in recent years, as well as many that are expected to come our way over the next decade. If you are someone who is, to put it bluntly, a little technologically challenged, don't worry; my research team and I have worked tirelessly to develop this chapter so that all readers can understand these groundbreaking concepts and then share what they have learned with their friends and family.

Before we get started, though, I want to offer another word of warning: Predicting the future of technology is like predicting the weather. Sometimes you get it exactly right. But other times, you find yourself blindsided by a torrential rainstorm and have to run into the nearest convenience store, only to find they are all out of umbrellas. Then you're forced to buy some embarrassing plastic pink poncho that's clearly fifteen sizes too small and made for middle-school girls with a passion for unicorns. But you know it's either *this* or spending the rest of the night sitting through your child's latest high school musical soaked to the bone, wondering if you're going to catch pneumonia and die. So you end up buying the embarrassing pink unicorn poncho and hope that it holds up throughout the worst storm of your life. (It doesn't, and you end up getting soaked anyway.)

OK, so maybe predicting the future isn't *exactly* like that, but you get the idea. No one, not even the best futurists on the planet, knows for sure which technological changes will take hold and which will end up in the dustbin of history. And for that reason, it is almost guaranteed that more than one of my predictions in this chapter will end up looking incredibly stupid in the not-so-distant future. But one thing is undoubtedly certain: our lives *will* change dramatically over the next decade and longer, whether we like it or not. And if we are not prepared for those changes, Davos elites—or maybe someone even worse—will take advantage of our ignorance to elevate their own position.

If we want the free world to survive the next fifty years, and if we want to avoid becoming the Luddites of the twenty-first century, we must first learn as much as we can about the future and take advantage of technological advancements, all while avoiding the pitfalls of the past and attempts by elites to use innovation to consolidate wealth and power. It's not going to be easy, but who said saving Western civilization would be a walk in the park?

THE AUTOMATION REVOLUTION

I love a good science fiction book or movie. Whether it's *Star Wars*, *Star Trek*, or a planet full of machine-gun-toting, warmongering apes, I can't get enough sci-fi. However, something has always bothered me about how sci-fi writers describe a typical watering hole in the far-flung future that's filled with humanoid robots and ships traveling at the speed of light. If there's a bar scene in space, you almost always see the same kind of working-class stiffs serving drinks that you'd see in your local Applebee's. The bartenders might have eight eyeballs and tentacles for arms, but otherwise there's no noticeable advancement in the food service industry.

Of course, there are exceptions. In the 2016 sci-fi movie *Passengers*, Chris Pratt and Jennifer Lawrence play characters who are trapped alone on a large interstellar ship traveling through space. Well, almost alone. Their primary companion is a robot bartender who is extremely lifelike, nearly indistinguishable from an actual human being.[174]

So in the minds of Hollywood's best and brightest screenwriters, in *some* galaxies far, far away, our coffee and pie will be served to us by blue-collar, working-class octo-aliens seeking to earn a "living wage"—which will probably be $19,000 per hour by then, if Alexandria Ocasio-Cortez has it her way—while in others, people will build exceptionally advanced, highly intelligent robots to mix our alcoholic beverages, tell us dirty jokes, and give us advice about our love lives. In reality, neither scenario is likely to occur. It is far more probable that future space cantinas will be run entirely by nameless, faceless kiosks and robotic machine arms. And we likely won't need to wait hundreds or thousands of years for that change to occur. It's already happening, and the effects of the ongoing transformation of work will soon have an even more far-reaching impact on all of our lives.

Perhaps the biggest immediate economic transformation of the Fourth Industrial Revolution is the automation of work and the replacement of human workers with machines. You don't need to be an expert on technology to see how rapidly many business places are changing today. The next time you find yourself running errands around town, make a concerted effort to take note of all the interactions you see between human customers and business machines, and then consider how many people would have been required to work these jobs in previous decades.

When you go to your local grocery store chain, for example, how many self-check-out aisles are there compared to human-run check-out lanes? At my local grocery store, I counted twelve self-check-out lanes to just three human-run registers. When you factor in that it used to be standard practice for grocery stores to bag your purchases in every aisle, twelve self-check-out lanes run by machines and one human overseer would have required about twenty-four workers just a decade or two ago. That's twenty-four jobs replaced by just one person.

After a long morning of grocery shopping, perhaps you'll stop by your local Panera Bread for a soup and sandwich. Most Panera locations still have people taking orders, but the vast majority now use more self-service kiosks than humans to take orders. Customers can now order whatever they want without ever having to talk to a person. That's another half-dozen jobs lost to machines, and Panera isn't done innovating.

In April 2022, food-service publication *FSD* reported, "Panera Bread is testing a new, artificially intelligent coffee system designed to ensure every cup of joe is hot and fresh. The 2,121-unit fast-casual chain has partnered with Miso Robotics ... to use its CookRight Coffee technology at some locations this year."[175]

According to *FSD*, "CookRight will monitor the coffee station, measuring things such as volume, temperature and time, and using AI to anticipate demand. This lets Panera staff know precisely when to brew a new batch and also eliminates the need for them to manually check on the coffee throughout the day, the companies said." Of course, fewer human-employee responsibilities mean fewer human employees will be needed.

Panera is not the only restaurant chain replacing human workers with machines. Flipdish, a business that helps restaurants with "end-to-end ordering, marketing and management," notes that "demand for restaurant kiosks is rapidly rising."[176] Flipdish, using data compiled by Statista, claims "market revenue for kiosks worldwide was an estimated $28.34 (billion) in 2021, up from $26.63 (billion) in 2020, and this is expected to further rise to $45.32 (billion) in 2028. These projections chime with our data here in Flipdish, where we have seen dramatic growth in the number of stores with kiosks and the number of orders through kiosks, a 10x increase in 2021."[177]

Although many restaurant jobs replaced thus far have been associated with customers ordering food items, some of the biggest changes now in the works will occur in kitchens, out of view from most customers. In 2020, fast-food burger chain White Castle implemented a test program for replacing human fry cooks with a robot called Flippy.[178] Flippy could successfully flip burgers, drop fries in hot oil, and perform other tasks that normally come with the risk of burning human workers.

In late 2021, Miso Robotics, the maker of Flippy, released an upgraded version of its technology, Flippy 2, which was designed in part using data collected from the White Castle test. According to Miso Robotics, "Flippy 2 takes over the work for an entire fry station and performs more than twice as many food preparation tasks compared to the previous version including basket filling, emptying and returning."[179]

Unlike the original Flippy, Flippy 2 uses artificial intelligence to identify different kinds of foods, fry foods for the correct amount of time, and ensure food stays warm for customers—all without help from a human.[180] And you're likely going to be seeing more of Flippy in the years to come. With the ongoing labor shortage exacerbated by government policies enacted during the COVID-19 pandemic, increasingly more restaurants are turning to machines when humans stop filling out job applications.[181] In fact, White Castle announced in February 2023 that it will install Flippy 2 in more than one-fourth of its locations throughout the United States over the following two years.[182]

As remarkable as the technology behind Flippy is, however, it's just the tip of the food-service automation iceberg. At the 2022 National Restaurant Show, tech companies proudly showed off an army of new innovations designed to replace human workers. Reporter Thai Phi Le noted that "walking through the aisles of the National Restaurant Show, it appears the future is here. There is Adam, your friendly robot barista, and the peppy-voiced Blue Robot, who wanders the show floor to offer you PepsiCo products."[183]

Further, according to Le, Autec sales representative Takuro Iwamoto claimed that demand for his company's sushi-building robots is skyrocketing, with waitlists topping out at six months. And Nala Robotics announced it now has "three fully automated eateries, including One Mean Chicken, Surya Tiffins and Thai 76."[184] In each of the three Nala Robotics restaurants, only one human is on staff.

Le reports, "The current version of Nala Robotics can perform all the jobs of a chef except cleaning and plating," although the company claims "the next version will include those features."[185] Nala's mostly automated restaurant robots have "sensor-processing capabilities that help it detect its surroundings," so that it can recognize virtually every item of importance in the restaurant, including something as small as a pepper shaker.[186]

So one employee and a sidekick robot (or is the human the sidekick?) can now operate an entire restaurant on their own. But surely the one human still involved must be a technological genius, right? According to Nala Robotics, the answer is no. Le reports, "Training is fairly minimal, with most of it focused on how to upload recipes into Nala Robotics and maintain the machine. It requires regular cleaning."[187]

Wow, technology so simple even Glenn Beck can use it. (Maybe.)

AUTOMATED BANKING

Restaurants aren't the only industry getting overhauled by automation. Perhaps on your next round of errand-running, you'll need to stop by your local bank to deposit a check. Sure, you could go inside the bank building and speak to a teller, but what year is it, 1987? Why talk to humans when your friendly neighborhood automated teller machine (ATM) can provide you with a slew of banking services that once required a trained banker?

Now that I think about it, why are you going to the ATM at all? What year is it, 2007? Most large banks in the United States offer virtually every banking service imaginable through the Internet or a smartphone application. Today, you can deposit checks, pay bills, send money to friends and family, or even apply for a mortgage or credit card without stepping foot in a brick-and-mortar bank. Artificial intelligence, not a skilled human teller, can analyze online check deposits to verify the check is legitimate, look at account and check numbers, and ensure that consumers are depositing correct amounts.

Banking probably isn't the first industry that comes to mind when most people think of automation and job displacement. However, the changes ahead in the financial services industry due to automation and other technological innovations are likely to be some of the most disruptive, especially in the near term.

CBS News reported in October 2021 that, despite the banking sector's "outsized role in the U.S. economy for decades," over the next few years, "thousands of frontline workers in the industry are likely to find themselves with a shrinking part to play as their jobs succumb to automation."[188]

CBS News reporter Khristopher Brooks further warned, "About 100,000 positions could vanish over the next five years as large U.S. banks invest more in digital banking and other technologies," according to a report by Wells Fargo analysts.[189]

"Roles slated to disappear include branch managers, call center employees and tellers," Brooks added. "Artificial intelligence, cloud computing and robots will play a larger role in daily banking functions like taking payments, approving loans and detecting fraud."[190]

And this is just the start. Blockchain technology and blockchain-based decentralized finance systems, which we're going to discuss extensively in chapter 4, could end up transforming or replacing the modern banking system in its entirety over the next decade or two. By automating transactions and streamlining verification, blockchain—the same technology behind cryptocurrencies such as Bitcoin—could help individuals lend money to others securely and without risk of losing money.[191]

Even more remarkably, large groups of individuals could band together to effectively become blockchain banks. Why lend with a massive traditional bank when you could cut out the middleman entirely for a fraction of the cost and with substantially more convenience? This one innovation alone has the potential to forever transform one of the world's longest-standing, wealthiest industries, a development most analysts would have said was impossible just twenty years ago.

SELF-DRIVING, 5G-POWERED DISRUPTORS

For those of you who have been listening, reading, and watching my work for a while, you know that I have been talking about the inevitability of self-driving cars for more than a decade, as well as how important self-driving motor vehicles will be for the future economy. Self-driving cars have the potential to completely alter the way we spend our time on roadways, improve highway safety, increase economic efficiency, and alter how we think about car ownership. (More on that topic in chapter 5.) The day is rapidly approaching when your errand-running Saturdays will involve an automated vehicle driving you and your children around town, making life a little easier and much more convenient.

Self-driving cars will also change the way workers think about commuting. Soon, automated vehicles will give tens of millions of Americans a mountain of additional time to work, study, or consume entertainment as they travel from home to their jobs. A study published in 2021 by the U.S. Census Bureau found that the average American spends 27.6 minutes commuting to work each day, a little less than an hour roundtrip.[192] That's roughly four to five hours spent in the car each week. Over the course of an individual's career, many workers end up spending more than 8,400 hours commuting, which is nearly a full year of a person's life. Many spend two or even three times that amount.[193]

Although I know some of us truly enjoying driving, myself included, others of us *hate* it and would much rather spend their time taking a course online to improve career prospects, finishing work on the road so that they can make it home a little earlier in the evening, or even watching insightful television specials hosted by handsome hosts on BlazeTV—and no, I'm not talking about Dave Rubin. Once the technology is perfected and affordable, readily available self-driving cars will revolutionize how people spend a large chunk of their day, freeing up tens of millions of commuters in a way that has never been possible.

Self-driving cars would also change the way we think about other kinds of travel experiences. For example, long family road trips to Yellowstone could be enjoyed while both the adults and kids in the car are distracted by the latest Hollywood blockbuster, rather than the not-so-peaceful screaming and punching many of us parents have become grudgingly accustomed to. And automated cars will make traveling through the middle of the night much safer and more convenient too. (The only thing better than distracted children is sleeping children, am I right?)

Additionally, because automated cars will eventually be fully capable of driving without humans behind the wheel, and because self-driving vehicles will also be capable of knowing where other cars are located on the road, vehicles in the future will likely operate at much faster speeds than the current generation of cars and trucks. As a result, longer road trips will suddenly become more manageable, and for many of us, perhaps even preferable to air travel. Our already "small," interconnected world will become even smaller.

Although there are many ways self-driving technology could develop, one of the most exciting and innovative depends on the expansion of 5G technology. When people hear "5G" or "4G," they usually think of little bars on their smartphones or one of what seems like thousands of annoying cell phone commercials. But 5G technology has the potential to impact far more than the speed at which you can scroll through Instagram or download videos of waterskiing squirrels on your phone. When coupled with other technological innovations, self-driving cars being one of the top items on the list, 5G could prove to be one of the most impactful innovations of the century.

The name 5G stands for *fifth generation*, a reference to the fifth major development in cellular network technology.[194] However, don't be fooled into thinking 5G is all about cell phones. 5G is a tool for wireless communication of many kinds, from laptops and iPads to toasters and the "smart" refrigerators of the future. (More on smart homes in chapter 6.)

As Prasenjit Mitra, an electrical engineer at Penn State University, explains in an article for *The Conversation*, "Over and above low and medium frequency radio waves, 5G uses additional higher-frequency waves to encode and carry information,"[195] providing substantially more bandwidth than previous network generations.

Bandwidth is sort of like a highway or plumbing; the size of roadways or piping is directly linked to the number of cars or the amount of water that can flow through a passageway without clogging. Of course, bandwidth isn't concerned with trucks or water flow, but the principle is similar—the greater the bandwidth, the greater "the volume of information that can be sent over a connection in a measured amount of time."[196]

5G's higher-frequency radio waves provide more bandwidth than ever before, allowing it to connect to the Internet at speeds that blow its predecessors out of the water. 5G has ten times more bandwidth than 4G, delivering speeds as fast as 1 gigabit per second.[197] Because 5G utilizes higher-frequency waves, the technology needs more towers than 3G and 4G to work effectively, which means it could be several years or more before 5G's potential is fully realized.

Mitra notes that currently, 5G's "higher frequency comes at a higher cost and thus is deployed only where it's most needed: in crowded urban settings, stadiums, convention centers, airports and concert halls."[198] So if you live on a farm in rural Ohio, you probably don't have 5G and might not for a very long time. Eventually, however, 5G will be virtually everywhere, other than in the most remote regions, giving hundreds of millions of people across America access to high-speed wireless Internet that's comparable to connections made over a Wi-Fi network.

5G technology could end up being an essential and revolutionary part of the future of self-driving vehicles. Because the best kinds of 5G allow information to be transmitted at lightning-fast speeds, self-driving cars operating on a well-functioning 5G network will be able to communicate with one another in real time, constantly exchanging important, detailed information.[199]

At the risk of driving readers away—see what I did there?—I think it's important to explain a little bit about how autonomous cars could work in the future. After all, your life could soon be in the hands of this revolutionary new technology. But if you're the kind of person who isn't interested in the details, you can skip ahead to the next subsection on page 101 about "Factories of the Future" instead.

One report about 5G by McKinsey & Company notes that car manufacturers and designers are developing "vehicle-to-everything (V2X) communication" that utilizes 5G, which the report's authors say "will support latency at ten milliseconds end to end (to and from the application layer) and one millisecond over the air." That means in the near future, even the fastest-moving vehicles could be able to communicate with each other and the Internet-connected infrastructure that surrounds them in near-instantaneous fashion.[200] This would make driverless cars capable of offering high-tech comfort features that no one has today, such as turning a motor vehicle into a high-speed office, complete with a webcam, desk, fully functioning computer, and advanced microphones for conference calls. Workers in the future will be able to do all or nearly all their job responsibilities while cruising down the highway alone.

More importantly, 5G-empowered automated vehicles will eventually make driving much safer. Once vehicle-to-everything communication has been fully developed, every vehicle on the road will know the travel speeds, vehicle weight, safety features, tire quality, and other data about every other car traveling nearby. Equipped with powerful computer processers and 5G data, the self-driving cars of the future will be able to foresee and thus avoid potential accidents, coordinate with other vehicles to improve traffic conditions, and make life-or-death decisions in milliseconds that are much more likely to end in the least tragic outcome compared to situations where humans are driving their vehicles.

Even if 5G technology never develops well enough for the advancements I just discussed, self-driving cars will likely become safer than traditional vehicles, because automated cars can utilize numerous sensors, internal and external cameras, and computer processers that far surpass the abilities of humans.[201, 202] Many self-driving vehicles are now even being equipped with heat-seeking cameras and laser-based radar called LiDAR, which are helping developers improve the safety of automated cars.[203, 204] In fact, some experts believe self-driving vehicles, which have over the past several years been tested by traveling tens of millions of miles,[205] have since at least 2018 been just as safe as cars driven by humans.[206] This is why the U.S. National Highway Traffic Safety Administration (NHTSA) now acknowledges, "Vehicle safety promises to be one of automation's biggest benefits."[207]

On a website dedicated entirely to automated-vehicle safety, NHTSA further claims that the best available evidence shows, "Types of automated technologies, such as advanced driver assistance system technologies already in use on the roads and future automated driving systems at their mature state, have the potential to reduce crashes, prevent injuries, and save lives."[208] NHTSA further notes, "In some circumstances, automated technologies may be able to detect the threat of a crash and act faster than drivers. These technologies could greatly support drivers and reduce human errors and the resulting crashes, injuries, and economic tolls."[209]

As important as all these innovative uses of autonomous vehicles would be, however, the biggest impact self-driving cars are likely to have on our lives is economic. Self-driving vehicles will dramatically improve delivery times, speed up the supply chain, increase economic efficiency throughout countless industries, and make deliveries of all sizes much more reliable. After all, humans must sleep, eat, plan trips, and rest, but self-driving fleets of vehicles will only need minimal and periodic breaks, mostly for maintenance.

According to a study produced by a team of academic researchers and economists working with Securing America's Future Energy (SAFE), by 2030, automated vehicles are projected to provide more than $100 billion in annual consumer and societal benefits.[210] By 2040, less than two decades from now, the SAFE study estimates the benefits will top $600 billion. And by 2050, the annual benefits offered by automated vehicles could reach $800 billion.[211]

Make no mistake about it, though: the advent of automated cars and trucks will come at a great cost. Once the technology is fully adopted, automated vehicles will destroy a vast number of jobs, and the job losses will likely occur rapidly.

There are between 300,000 and 500,000 long-haul truck drivers in the United States, and more than a million more drivers operate other heavy and tractor-trailer trucks.[212] The U.S. Postal Service alone employs 133,000 rural letter carriers operating 80,000 delivery routes.[213] Even more incredibly, there are now about 250,000 drivers who deliver packages for Amazon,[214] and those are just the people tasked with fulfilling my wife's online orders.

All told, *millions* of people now work in the trucking industry. The U.S. Census Bureau reported in 2019 that there are about 3.5 million truck drivers in America, and the Census Bureau further noted, "Driving large tractor-trailers or delivery trucks is one of the largest occupations in the United States."[215] Once self-driving vehicles become a reality, nearly *all* of these workers will not only be looking for new employment; they will also be looking for new employment in a completely different industry. Within just the next couple of decades, jobs that have been essential since the creation of the motor vehicle will become almost entirely extinct.

The use of the word *will* throughout this section is very deliberate; there is no question that when self-driving vehicles are successfully developed and distributed, they *will* become a major disruptive force in the global economy. It's not an issue of *if* self-driving cars and trucks will cause disruption; it's a matter of *when*. But on that question, there does remain much debate.

I will be the first one to admit that I am really bad when it comes to timing when future events will occur. I have a long track record of getting *predictions* right, but an equally long record of being terribly off about *when*. However, I feel confident in saying that because self-driving vehicles are still far from perfect, it would be unreasonable to expect widespread distribution by the end of 2023, 2024, or even 2025. A lot more progress is needed before self-driving cars are ready for prime time, especially when it comes to safety. And many of today's car companies are more interested in electrifying vehicles and solving supply-chain issues than they are developing autonomous cars and trucks.

In June 2022, the Associated Press published an article noting that, according to the National Highway Traffic Safety Administration, "Automakers reported nearly 400 crashes of vehicles with partially automated driver-assist systems, including 273 involving Teslas"[216]— rather large numbers considering how few self-driving vehicles are on the road today.

Instead of expecting most automakers to roll out streams of fully automated vehicles in the next year or two, a safer bet is that automated-driving features will become increasingly more advanced over time, with fully automated vehicles becoming common at some point after 2030. Consulting firm Accenture, which specializes in information technology, estimates that by 2030 about six in ten new vehicles will feature some kind of automation. However, only about 5 percent of the vehicle market will include cars equipped with Level 3 or 4 automation—the levels that require very little action from human drivers (and in some cases, none at all). However, Accenture also predicts that by 2030 it's unlikely there will be any publicly available cars with Level 5 automation, the most advanced level of autonomous driving, featuring cars that can drive on any road at any time without any help from a human being.[217]

With that said, some truly brilliant developers are much more optimistic. In January 2022, Elon Musk—one of the world's foremost experts on self-driving technology, electric vehicles, and trolling rivals on Twitter—claimed that Tesla Motors, a company Musk founded and for which he serves as CEO, will develop fully autonomous vehicles by the end of the year.[218] "I would be shocked if we do not achieve full-self-driving safer than a human this year," Musk said during Tesla's fourth-quarter earnings call. "I would be shocked."[219] Musk later in 2022 predicted 2023 was a more likely target.[220] That means we could be just a couple of years away from consumers being able to purchase self-driving Teslas.

In November 2022, Tesla unveiled its full-self-driving beta for North American Tesla owners. The beta, which costs consumers $15,000 to access, allows "drivers" to sit back while their car tackles every aspect of a commute—from leisurely traversing side roads to navigating heavily congested city streets.[221] Having watched a few videos where users test this new software, I will say it is eerie how well the vehicles are able to react to and handle complex traffic patterns.

It's also important to note that Tesla is not the only car company working to get self-driving cars on the road. In addition to Tesla, there is Waymo, formerly a project of Google; Cruise, which has received financial support from General Motors; Argo.Ai, which is working with Ford and Volkswagen; as well as projects launched by Walmart, Honda, and Microsoft.[222]

Musk has also said that in 2023 Tesla will unveil its Robotaxi, a self-driving car service (imagine Uber or Lyft without the human driver), and he says production could begin as early as 2024.[223]

Musk's predictions have been wrong before, though, and there remain many challenges to the development of self-driving cars, including issues regarding legal liability, cost, and humans' skepticism about the safety of computer-controlled motor vehicles. But that's true of every new technology. A fair look at the progress that has already been made in the arena of automated vehicles shows that barring some totally absurd government regulations that aim to stifle innovation (a very real possibility, of course), in the end, fully automated cars will be available in America and most of Europe during the lives of most of the readers of this book. It's just a matter of time.

THE FACTORIES OF THE FUTURE

When most people think about machines replacing human workers, they typically think first of blue-collar Americans being forced out of manufacturing jobs by a wave of massive industrial machines and gigantic robotic arms—and that's for good reason. There has been a substantial amount of automation in U.S. factories over the past three decades. As the World Economic Forum rightly notes, "Assembly-line tasks such as welding and spray-painting were among the first jobs to migrate from people to robots. But humans were on hand to supervise the machines. As the technology has improved, the range of jobs passed on to robots has expanded to cover more complex procedures, such as fixing windscreens into vehicles. They are also widely used to move heavy and bulky items through factories."[224]

New studies show that although the transition from human-centered manufacturing to increased use of robots and other forms of automation has improved productivity and led to higher profits, it has had a disruptive effect on workers. According to the Massachusetts Institute of Technology (MIT), researchers from MIT and Boston University found, "Industrial robots grew fourfold in the U.S. between 1993 and 2007," to a rate of about one new robot for every one thousand workers.[225] MIT notes that the researchers concluded "the increase in robots (about one per thousand workers) reduced the average employment-to-population ratio in a zone by 0.39 percentage points, and average wages by 0.77%, compared to commuting zones with no exposure to robots."[226] These figures might not sound like a lot, but when you apply them to a large population of workers, it means that "adding one robot to an area reduces employment in that area by about six workers."[227] By 2020, U.S. regions had experienced a net loss of 400,000 jobs due to industrial robots, according to MIT.[228]

The job losses are due to the relationship between the *displacement effect* and *productivity effects*. Although adding robots and automation to industrial processes increases productivity and profits substantially, researchers have found that industrial robots have a stronger displacement effect, offsetting productivity gains for workers. In other words, robots improve economic growth generally, but those gains are not enough to add a sufficient number of new jobs to offset the ones taken by robots.[229]

The transition to industrial robots and other forms of automation has grown in recent years too, especially in the wake of the American government's response to the COVID-19 pandemic. By closing much of the economy, putting draconian mask and social-distancing requirements in place, and encouraging Americans to stay home instead of work via the creation of extremely costly coronavirus relief and stimulus programs, local and state governments effectively incentivized many manufacturing and industrial workers to leave their jobs. Making matters worse, governments and the U.S. Federal Reserve artificially kept demand for products and services high through a laundry list of spending programs, adding trillions of new dollars to the economy.

These and other policies imposed in Europe and North America created the conditions for a rapid move toward automation. In

February 2022, Reuters reported, "More robots joined the U.S. workforce last year than ever before, taking on jobs from plucking bottles and cans off conveyor belts at trash recycling plants to putting small consumer goods into cardboard boxes at e-commerce warehouses."[230]

Reuters further reported, "Companies across North America laid out more than $2 billion for almost 40,000 robots in 2021 to help them contend with record demand and a pandemic-fueled labor shortage. Robots went to work in a growing number of industries, expanding well beyond their historic surge in the automotive sector."[231]

Industrial businesses and factories increased robot orders by 28 percent from 2020 to 2021, shattering the record previously set in 2017.[232] Some of the biggest increases were seen in the consumer goods, food, and metals industries—not industries traditionally known for leading the pack in robotics.[233]

Some manufacturers have even gone so far as to build factories where there are more robots than humans. For example, the Associated Press reported in 2021 that car manufacturer Nissan's "intelligent factory" in Kamino Kawa, Japan, "hardly has any human workers."[234] AP further reported, "The robots do the work, including welding and mounting. They do the paint jobs and inspect their own paint jobs."[235]

Nissan's "intelligent factory" isn't completely without a human presence, however. For now, human workers at the factory "focus on more skilled work such as analyzing data collected by the robots, and on maintaining the equipment."[236] But in future years, many of these jobs could also be automated.

By the middle of the 2030s, manufacturing's automation revolution will be nothing short of breathtaking. PwC—one of the West's "big four" accounting firms and an organization with intimate ties to the World Economic Forum[237]—provides detailed analyses and predictions about automation and its impact on the future of economies around the world. PwC's economists and futurists predict that although "AI, robotics and other forms of smart automation have the potential to bring great economic benefits, contributing up to $15 trillion to global GDP by 2030," these technologies will also result in tremendous economic disruption, especially in the manufacturing sector of the United States.[238]

According to PwC, by around 2025, 37 percent of manufacturing jobs in the United States could be replaced by automation.[239] By the mid-2030s, the jobs replaced by robots and other machines in manufacturing could be as high as 53 percent, with the greatest disruption related to workers with "low" and "medium" education levels, such as a high school diploma.[240]

American manufacturing workers aren't alone. PwC estimates 40–60 percent of the manufacturing jobs could ultimately be lost to automation in Austria, Belgium, the Czech Republic, Germany, Denmark, Spain, Finland, France, Ireland, Israel, Italy, Lithuania, the Netherlands, Poland, Slovakia, Slovenia, Sweden, Turkey, and the United Kingdom.[241] And that's just the beginning. PwC's analysis only includes twenty-nine countries and excludes many of the largest manufacturers in the world, such as China, Indonesia, and India.[242]

You may be thinking, *Well, I'm sorry to hear about all those poor long-haul truck drivers, waiters and waitresses, bankers, delivery drivers, and factory workers, but none of those job losses will affect me and my job. Like tens of millions of other American workers today, my job won't be disrupted because a robot can't possibly perform my daily work responsibilities. Sure, perhaps someday, hyper-intelligent robots will be walking around filling out paperwork, coming up with marketing plans, and performing the jobs of many modern workers, but that's not likely to happen anytime soon, Glenn, so I'm in good shape. Right?*

For those of you who have taken comfort in such a view, I have some very bad news for you: there's a good chance that no matter what industry you are in, your job could over the next decade or longer be at risk because of automation. In fact, some of the jobs requiring the least amount of physical labor are the ones at greatest risk of disappearing quickly.

ARTIFICIAL INTELLIGENCE IN THE AGE OF DISRUPTION

Although it is true robots won't soon be heading off to work in their self-driving cars to take jobs away from unsuspecting American office workers, there is already a massive push from businesses to automate many core functions of their businesses using artificial intelligence. AI is a massive topic that we're going to discuss and describe in more detail in chapter 6, but for now, the primary thing you need to understand about AI is that artificial intelligence involves machines that are capable of *thinking*, to various degrees, like a human being. Or, as IBM puts it, "Artificial intelligence leverages computers and machines to mimic the problem-solving and decision-making capabilities of the human mind."[243]

In an article for *Forbes*, Archil Cheishvili, CEO and cofounder of GenesisAI, a global network of AI services and products, explains, "Artificial intelligence can be broadly categorized into three main types: artificial narrow intelligence (ANI), artificial general intelligence (AGI) and artificial superintelligence (ASI)."[244]

Artificial general intelligence and artificial superintelligence are the advanced forms of AI you usually see in sci-fi movies, where machines are capable of functioning like humans, or perhaps even superior to humans. At this point, AGI and ASI do not exist—and boy am I glad about that, because the world isn't ready for the challenges we're going to face when they do. But "narrow" artificial intelligence *does* exist today. In fact, there's a good chance you use it almost every single day.

As *Forbes* contributor and AI expert Naveen Joshi explains, artificial narrow intelligence "represents all the existing AI, including even the most complicated and capable AI that has ever been created to date."[245]

"Artificial narrow intelligence refers to AI systems that can only perform a specific task autonomously using humanlike capabilities," Joshi wrote. "These machines can do nothing more than what they are programmed to do, and thus have a very limited or narrow range of competencies."[246]

Descriptions of narrow AI sometimes make it sound unimpressive, but narrow AI is one of the most advanced technologies humans have ever produced. These systems are capable of performing tasks at a rate that far surpasses anything a human being could ever achieve, and contrary to what you might think, narrow AI already has a remarkable effect on our daily lives.

Futurist Bernard Marr notes that although many "might imagine that artificial intelligence is only something the big tech giants are focused on, and that AI doesn't impact your everyday life," the truth is "artificial intelligence is encountered by most people from morning until night."[247] For example, whenever you visit a social media site, including Facebook, Twitter, Instagram, or YouTube, artificial intelligence is there, "working behind the scenes to personalize what you see on your feeds (because it's learned what types of posts most resonate with you based on past history)."[248] Social media AI is also "figuring out friend suggestions," and "machine learning is working to prevent cyberbullying."[249]

Artificial intelligence programs are further utilized to help users compose messages and identify grammatical mistakes and spelling errors in emails. And AI is used by Google to learn users' interests and offer website and news recommendations, often along with some good old-fashioned Google ideological bias.[250] The advertisements you see online, the navigation applications you use to help you drive around, the movie recommendations offered to you by Netflix, and the fraud-detection alerts sent to you by your bank or credit card company are all dependent on narrow artificial intelligence.[251]

Further, nearly all the products you buy and shipments you receive will also soon be heavily impacted by narrow forms of artificial intelligence. Many already are. The complexity of the modern, highly globalized economy has made supply chains incredibly difficult to manage. Timing shipments and transportation within narrow windows, something that used to be virtually impossible, is now commonplace because of advanced computers running artificial intelligence programs, rapidly improving supply-chain operations.

McKinsey & Company notes that modern AI solutions "include demand-forecasting models, end-to-end transparency, integrated business planning, dynamic planning optimization, and automation of the physical flow—all of which build on prediction models and correlation analysis to better understand causes and effects in supply chains."[252]

According to McKinsey, "Successfully implementing AI-enabled supply-chain management has enabled early adopters to improve logistics costs by 15 percent, inventory levels by 35 percent, and service levels by 65 percent, compared with slower-moving competitors."[253]

Narrow artificial intelligence is most effective when it has access to large amounts of data, which allows it to detect patterns, recognize efficiencies and inefficiencies, and offer recommendations or make decisions based on more information than humans are physically capable of processing. Modern AI can process millions or even billions of pieces of data, and it can do so in a tiny fraction of the time required for people to manually produce the same result. This impressive processing power improves economic efficiency, making economies wealthier and increasing quality of life for most people. However, it is also beginning to push many workers out of their jobs, a trend that will increase rapidly over the next decade.

In a book titled *Futureproof: 9 Rules for Humans in the Age of Automation*, *New York Times* technology columnist Kevin Roose details countless studies, news reports, and personal interviews and experiences that illustrate the high level of disruption already being caused by businesses' move toward artificial intelligence, as well as the even bigger challenges ahead.[254]

According to Roose, existing data show "white-collar workers may actually be more likely to be automated out of a job than blue-collar workers," and many mid-level workers with good-paying jobs in human resources, accounting, and other data-intensive positions are already being phased out by well-designed narrow artificial intelligence programs.[255]

Roose highlights throughout his book that, as artificial intelligence continues to develop, AI algorithms will far surpass the abilities of even many of the highest-skilled workers. Not even lawyers and doctors will be safe from the coming AI-driven automation revolution.

"In 2018, a Chinese tech company built a deep learning algorithm that diagnosed brain cancer and other diseases faster and more accurately than a team of fifteen top doctors," Roose wrote. "The same year, American researchers developed an algorithm capable of identifying malignant tumors on a CT scan with an error rate twenty times lower than a human radiologist."[256]

Roose further noted, "In a 2018 study, twenty top U.S. corporate lawyers were pitted against an algorithm developed by an AI start-up called LawGeex. Their task was to spot legal issues in five nondisclosure agreements—a staple of basic contract law—as quickly as possible. The algorithm crushed the lawyers with an average 94 percent accuracy rate, compared to the average human accuracy rate of 85 percent."[257]

Some of these figures may seem difficult to comprehend. How exactly would AI displace jobs with such disruptive force? The release of OpenAI's ChatGPT product in November 2022 has provided some insight into this important question.[258]

ChatGPT is a cutting-edge technology developed by OpenAI that can understand and respond to natural language input, a skill normally only possessed by humans. It has been trained on a massive amount of data, allowing it to generate high-quality responses to a wide range of questions and topics. Simply put, ChatGPT is a game-changer.

In the customer service industry, businesses can use ChatGPT as a virtual assistant to handle simple customer inquiries, freeing up human agents to focus on more complex issues. ChatGPT can also be used in education, health care, and finance to provide personalized support to customers and patients.

This technology has the potential to transform numerous business practices. It can automate tasks, improve customer experiences, and provide valuable support for workers and consumers.

ChatGPT is so important because it's one of the first AI technologies released to the public that can effectively and believably mimic humans' writing and research abilities on a wide array of topics. It learns and adapts in a way that other lesser-impressive forms of AI in the past have been unable to do.

Don't believe me? The three previous paragraphs were written almost completely by ChatGPT. I simply asked ChatGPT to describe itself and its potential impacts "in the style of Glenn Beck," and in a matter of seconds, it provided me with text good enough to fool just about everyone, including my editors. As good as ChatGPT is, though, I do admit I had to edit a few words here and there before publication. Apparently, ChatGPT thinks I like to include the word "folks" a lot in my writing.[259]

THE AUTOMATION DISRUPTION BOMB

It is difficult to find much agreement among today's policy "experts" and academics. For example, just ask one of them, "What is a woman?" and you'll see exactly what I mean. But when it comes to the future of robotics, artificial intelligence, and automation, nearly every expert in the field agrees that disruption—I'm talking nuclear-bomb-sized disruption—is right around the corner. And not just in one or two industries in three or four countries, but across entire economies, virtually everywhere on Earth.

The McKinsey Global Institute (MGI) estimates "between 400 million and 800 million individuals could be displaced by automation and need to find new jobs by 2030 around the world, based on our midpoint and earliest (that is, the most rapid) automation adoption scenarios."[260] MGI further predicts, "Of the total displaced, 75 million to 375 million may need to switch occupational categories and learn new skills."[261]

In a separate analysis published in 2021, MGI predicted that because of companies' rapid expansion of automation in the wake of the COVID-19 pandemic, automation could displace 45 million workers in America alone by 2030.[262]

Similarly, PwC estimates nearly one in three jobs worldwide could be at risk of automation by the mid-2030s due to advancements in robotics and AI.[263]

Forrester Research predicts that 12 million jobs will be lost to automation in Europe by 2040.[264]

Our pals at the World Economic Forum have a particularly shocking estimate. According to WEF's analysis, compared to 2020 employment figures, "by 2025, 85 million jobs may be displaced by a shift in the division of labour between humans and machines."[265]

It is vital that you understand I'm not saying these lost jobs will never be replaced. Economists' and futurists' opinions vary wildly on that question, from millions of jobs lost to more than 10 million jobs *gained*. But in the end, the really important issues we need to consider aren't related to whether automation will lead to job losses or gains. It's whether there will be immense disruption in the near future, and how policymakers, businesses, activists, and others will react to that disruption.

Hundreds of millions of people, perhaps even more, are going to be put in an incredibly difficult situation because of the coming Fourth Industrial Revolution. There is absolutely no doubt about that. After all, we can't expect sixty-year-old truck drivers to suddenly learn to code because a self-driving vehicle took their jobs. Nor can we ask an experienced loan officer at a bank, a factory worker, or a fry cook to suddenly become a well-trained mathematician capable of designing AI algorithms. These, and millions of other workers, will inevitably be asked to suffer through the coming automation revolution. And whenever there is suffering, there will be people in positions of power trying to use that suffering to increase their power, wealth, and/or influence. That is exactly what the Great Narrative is all about. It is an attempt by elites to "design the future"[266] in the coming Age of Disruption, and to do it in a way that improves *their* position at the expense of *yours*. That's not how they will describe it, of course, but the evidence is simply overwhelming.

TAKING ADVANTAGE

The Great Reset and Great Narrative movements aim to use the disruption of the Fourth Industrial Revolution as a catapult to enact societal and economic changes—changes that advocates of those movements say will ultimately lead to better outcomes for all "stakeholders," even the little people like you and me. Disruption creates incredible opportunity in the eyes of the WEF and its friends, and in this case, the disruption will give the WEF and other Davos elites a chance to reshape the world forever. But you don't need to take my word for it. The WEF and others have spent countless hours openly discussing and publishing materials on this very topic.

For example, in the same World Economic Forum report about economic disruption that predicted 87 million jobs could soon be displaced by automation, which I discussed earlier in this chapter, WEF founder and executive chairman Klaus Schwab and Saadia Zahidi, a member of the WEF's managing board, offered stunning insights about the connection between automation and building a new global society:

> We find ourselves at a defining moment: the decisions and choices we make today will determine the course of entire generations' lives and livelihoods. We have the tools at our disposal. The bounty of technological innovation which defines our current era can be leveraged to unleash human potential. We have the means to reskill and upskill individuals in unprecedented numbers, to deploy precision safety nets which protect displaced workers from destitution, and to create bespoke maps which orient displaced workers towards the jobs of tomorrow where they will be able to thrive.[267]

However, according to Schwab and Zahidi, these efforts are not keeping up with "the speed of disruption." It is now "urgent," Schwab and Zahidi insist, to impose newer, better, kinder social and economic models.[268]

Further, they say only through "global, regional and national public-private collaboration" can the necessary changes occur"—and only if the transition is implemented "at an unprecedented scale and speed."[269]

It doesn't take a genius to understand that the "global, regional and national public-private collaboration" Schwab and Zahidi mention is a reference to the Great Reset and its associated ESG-based stakeholder capitalism model, which I outlined in chapter 1 of this book. But in case you are still skeptical, Schwab and Zahidi hammer the point home in terms that couldn't possibly be clearer: "It is now urgent to enact a Global Reset towards a socio-economic system that is more fair, sustainable and equitable, one where social mobility is reinvigorated, social cohesion restored, and economic prosperity is compatible with a healthy planet."[270]

Who, you might be wondering, has the power, influence, and prestige to help the world's leaders take advantage of the Fourth Industrial Revolution's disruption? Why, the World Economic Forum, of course!

In the words of Schwab and Zahidi, "The Platform for the New Economy and Society at the World Economic Forum works as a 'docking station' for such collaboration on economic growth, revival and transformation; work, wages and job creation; education, skills and learning; and diversity, equity and inclusion."[271]

And in case you were thinking that perhaps the disruption, the public-private cooperation, and the "Global Reset" discussed by Schwab and Zahidi in their report have few, if any, supporters outside the walls of the WEF, consider that in the very same study, Schwab and Zahidi thank "the many partners whose views created the unique collection of insights in this report." The report includes a long list of these "many partners"—more than one hundred businesses and nonprofit organizations—at the end of the publication. It features some of the most powerful organizations in America, including AARP, Bank of America, Bloomberg, the Bill and Melinda Gates Foundation, Dell Technologies, NBC Universal, IBM, Johnson & Johnson, Google, Hewlett-Packard, PayPal, Salesforce, Nestle, and my favorite World Economic Forum "partner," George Soros's multibillion-dollar activist group, the Open Society Foundations.[272, 273]

The disruption caused by the automation that will unquestionably be part of the emerging Fourth Industrial Revolution is, like the COVID-19 pandemic of 2020 and 2021, yet another "golden opportunity" for the supporters of the Great Reset to enact an additional phase of their planned economic and societal transformation.[274] This isn't speculation. It is an undeniable fact.

When faced with serious questions about the Great Reset, the World Economic Forum and its friends in corporations, financial institutions, governments, and nonprofits often deflect concerns by alleging that anyone worried about a "Global Reset" in the midst of 87 million people having their jobs displaced is engaging in "conspiracy theories" and "misinformation." On other occasions, they admit that they want radical changes to the world order, but that no one should be concerned, because these changes are for the better. Yes, automation is happening, they admit, but you have nothing to worry about, because millions more jobs will suddenly become available. Great-Reset–aligned corporations want to build a better, "human-centered" workplace in the future, wherein man and machine work side by side in loving harmony.

For instance, in one World Economic Forum article about artificial intelligence, a chief technology officer of an AI-data company wrote, "Human-centred technology considers the [human] operator to be an asset rather than an impediment. It recognises the value of the operator's skill, knowledge, flexibility and creativity."[275]

Later in the same article, the writer said, "AI isn't meant to rely on the machine or the human exclusively; rather, leveraging a combination of the two can enhance each other's strengths and promote successful outcomes."

In private, however, they are telling a very different story. Rather than trying to ease workers into a human-friendly Fourth Industrial Revolution, many big corporations are running as fast as they can toward eliminating as many workers as possible. Elites at the WEF aren't trying to protect the public from disruption; they are actively attempting to create it.

Perhaps the best illustration I have heard yet of the World Economic Forum's true feelings about automation comes from Kevin Roose's book *Futureproof*.[276] (Don't forget that Roose works for the *New York Times*, which isn't exactly a big fan of me or my views about the Great Narrative, to say the least.) The following are lengthy excerpts from Roose's book. Normally, I wouldn't reprint so much text from another writer, especially someone who works for the *Times*, but the story Roose tells is just too good to pass up. According to Roose:

> The third, and clearest, sign that something was off came in 2019, when I started hearing snippets of a more honest automation conversation.
>
> This conversation wasn't the rosy, optimistic one playing out on tech conference stages and in glossy business magazine spreads. It was happening privately among elites and engineers, like the start-up founder who told me about his Boomer Remover software. These people had seen the future of AI and automation up close, and they had no illusions about where these technologies were headed. They knew that machines are, or soon will be, capable of replacing humans in a wide range of jobs and activities.[277]

Roose then tells his readers about his "first glimpse" of the "other automation conversation" at an annual event in Davos hosted by the World Economic Forum:

> My bosses at the *Times* had invited me to cover that year's forum, which was focused on "Globalization 4.0"—the essentially meaningless term Davos types had concocted for the emerging economic era defined by this new, transformative wave of AI and automation technology. Every day, I went to panels with titles such as "Shaping a New Market Architecture" and "The Factory of the Future," where powerful executives vowed to build "human-centered AI" that would be great for companies and workers alike.
>
> But at night, after their public events were over, the Davos attendees took off their humanitarian masks and got down to business. At lavish, off-the-record dinners and cocktail parties, I watched them grill tech experts about how AI could help transform their companies into sleek, automated profit machines. They gossiped about which automation products their competitors were using. They struck deals with consultants for "digital transformation" projects, which they hoped would save them millions of dollars by shrinking their reliance on human workers.
>
> I ran into one of those consultants one day. His name is Mohit Joshi, and he's the president of a company called Infosys, an India-based consulting firm that helps big businesses automate their operations. When I asked Joshi how his meetings with executives were going, his eyebrows arched, and he told me that the Davos elite's obsession with automation was even more intense than he—a guy who literally automates jobs for a living—had expected.
>
> Once, he said, his clients had wanted to reduce their workforces incrementally, keeping maybe 95 percent of their human workers while automating around the edges.

"But now," he told me, "they're saying, 'Why can't we do it with one percent of the people we have?'"

In other words, when the cameras and microphones were off, these executives weren't talking about helping workers. They were fantasizing about getting rid of them completely.[278]

Take a moment to let that story sink in, especially Roose's final lines: *When the cameras and microphones were off, these executives weren't talking about helping workers. They were fantasizing about getting rid of them completely.*

Davos elites love to present themselves as saviors. Tyrants always do. But if I have learned anything over the years, it is that you don't really find out who people are, especially famous and powerful people, until the public stops watching. It's easy to have a bleeding heart when your "blood" is little more than red food dye mixed with water.[279] Truly thinking about and acting in the best interests of others is hard. The reason the World Economic Forum makes it look so easy is because many of its members do not actually care for the "stakeholders" they want so desperately to lord over.

Sure, Davos pays lip service to the ideas of "fairness," "inclusivity," and "equity." But in the end, Great Narrative global elites are doing little more than chasing wealth and influence, just as big institutions have done since the birth of human civilization. When it comes to politics and power, it is true that the more things change, the more they stay the same.

A NEW REALITY

I wish I could tell you that the only major challenges we are going to face over the next half-century will be limited to self-driving cars, tens of millions of job displacements, and massive economic changes unlike anything we have ever seen before. I also wish that banks and financial institutions colluding with government to utilize ESG to control and manipulate every part of society were the only way in which the Great Narrative could take hold. But as difficult as the Great Reset and its public-private partnerships are to stop, and as important as preventing the emergence of ESG is, the Great Narrative involves so much more than elites taking advantage of automation-related economic disruptions and employing the use of ESG social credit scores.

Remember that the purpose of the Great Narrative is to formulate a completely new way of thinking about virtually every part of life, all within the context of a new, technology-rich industrial revolution. Robots and AI taking jobs, self-driving cars, and 5G technology are undeniably a big part of that equation, but they are hardly the only factors.

In the next chapter, I will pull the curtain back on some of the other incredibly important disruptive technologies that are now emerging or in the early stages of being developed, including virtual reality, augmented reality, the metaverse, cryptocurrencies and other blockchain technologies, and quantum computers. And in chapters 5, 6, and 7, I will discuss a variety of other technological disruptions, including incredible developments in artificial intelligence, gene editing and other health-care-related innovations, and the World Economic Forum's now-infamous "You'll Own Nothing" pledge.

There are a number of other technologies I wish I could have included in this book, but I've been told by people a lot smarter than me that no one will read a book that's a million words long and costs $1,000 per copy, so I had to make some difficult cuts, and, more importantly, had to keep some of the descriptions and discussions of the topics I did include shorter than I would like.

With that said, I'm confident there's far more than enough information about the coming technological revolution contained throughout the rest of this book to make your head explode, and there's no time to waste. So sit back, take a moment to gather your thoughts, try to relax, and then join me in going deeper down the rabbit role of the Fourth Industrial Revolution in the next chapter.

4

THE AGE OF DISRUPTION, PART 2: VIRTUAL REALITY, DIGITAL MONEY, QUANTUM COMPUTERS, AND THE METAVERSE

O NE OF THE MOST IMPORTANT AND OVERLOOKED WAYS LIFE could soon change is through a greater adoption of virtual and augmented reality systems. There are a lot of different ways to think about virtual reality (VR), but the most basic understanding is that VR "entails presenting our senses with a computer generated virtual environment that we can explore in some fashion."[280] Although VR doesn't always involve users' active participation in a three-dimensional virtual world, it's common for people using VR to have the ability to manipulate virtual space, move objects, or even communicate with others while operating within the VR environment.[281]

To enter a virtual world, users put on a VR headset, which features "a display split between the eyes to show each eye a different feed," thereby creating "a stereoscopic 3D effect with stereo sound."[282] VR headsets also track the position of users in real space, allowing a VR system to orient users properly within a virtual reality environment.[283] For those of you who love sci-fi movies, when you think of VR, imagine the universe presented in Disney's recent hit film *Ready Player One.*

Augmented reality (AR) is a mix between virtual reality and the real world. Like VR, augmented reality involves users wearing something over their eyes, like a headset or glasses. But unlike virtual reality, AR users do not operate in a three-dimensional virtual space. Instead, users look at the real world through a pair of lenses that project virtual items onto whatever they're looking at.[284]

For example, instead of buying and hanging an actual television set on the wall of your living room, you could literally sit on your couch and stare at what appears to others as a blank wall. But through the magic of AR glasses, you could be seeing a massive screen playing your favorite movie in crystal clarity on that same wall. And unlike a real television set, your virtual TV could be made bigger or smaller at will, and without any limitations. Have you always dreamed of having a 100-inch television? Well, AR technology could give you the opportunity to have a 100-inch television in every room of your house! By combining the real world with virtual reality, augmented reality offers the chance to enhance our experiences in ways that were nearly unimaginable just a decade ago.

Whenever I talk about virtual reality or even augmented reality, most people think first of video games and other forms of entertainment. It's true that VR is already being used by millions of people around the world to step into the boots of a swashbuckling pirate or to fight off Darth Vader with a virtual lightsaber using something like Meta's popular Quest line of headsets, but the future of VR and AR is potentially much more exciting *and* disruptive.

The possible use cases for virtual reality are endless. Nearly anything you can do in your daily life could be done in a virtual environment. Instead of physically pushing a shopping cart down the aisle of a grocery store, for example, VR could someday allow users to "walk" through a virtual store, pick out items from virtual shelves, and put these representations of real products and services into a three-dimensional shopping cart. The items could then be shipped to your doorstep within a day, similar to services now offered by Amazon and DoorDash.

Augmented reality could be used to help shoppers see how they would look if they bought that fancy new suit or dress they have been eyeing online, or to see whether the best size for a new pair of shoes is a seven or an eight.

Although AR and VR shopping is still in its infancy, retailers are moving quickly to adopt these strategies, in the hopes that they can slowly scale down or even phase out brick-and-mortar stores, which are significantly more expensive to maintain than virtual environments. For example, Bernard Marr notes in a *Forbes* article, "BMW's augmented reality experiences allow car shoppers to go into showrooms and customize cars with different colors or styles using their tablets or phones. Or they can put on virtual reality goggles and experience what it's like to drive the cars, so they understand their options and can make the perfect choice for their new vehicle."[285]

Marr also notes that cosmetic giant L'Oréal "now offers augmented reality–powered makeup try-on experiences, delivered in collaboration with Facebook."[286] And furniture retailer IKEA developed an augmented reality experience called The Place, "which allows shoppers to use augmented reality with their smartphone camera to place furniture items into their homes so they can visualize exactly how the item will look in their setting."[287]

This is becoming so prevalent that you probably *already* have a shopping app on your phone that incorporates AR. Apple's Apple Store app, which comes preinstalled on every iPhone, can use your phone's camera to show you what a shiny new MacBook Pro would look like sitting on your desk.

AR and VR can be utilized for a lot more than virtual shopping sprees. Virtual reality technology can be used to transport students to historical times and places, giving them a firsthand understanding of the past. Imagine what it would be like if children didn't merely *read* about the Boston Tea Party in textbooks but were instead *transported* using VR technology to Boston Harbor in 1773, where they could watch with their own eyes the Sons of Liberty rebel against the tyranny of the British crown. Or how incredibly educational it would be for young Americans to see and hear Founding Fathers discuss the importance of the Bill of Rights, or to hear members of the Continental Congress debate which provisions should be in the Constitution and which proposals ought to be excluded.

VR also allows users to travel to every continent on the planet, giving people the ability to see the Great Pyramids of Egypt, to climb ice shelves in Antarctica, and to visit Machu Picchu in Peru— all while sitting on their couch.

These technologies are also quickly becoming an important part of various kinds of employee and specialty training, including medical education. Onix Systems reports, "FundamentalVR offers simulator-based training programs for surgeons, with all its simulations being approved by the Royal College of Surgeons of England. The simulations are aimed at helping surgeons in training to rehearse and improve their techniques and skills by providing a safe, controlled virtual environment. It also has a tactile feedback feature," allowing future surgeons to "feel" virtual bodies as they make incisions, and to remove or repair injured organs and broken bones from their virtual patients.[288]

Onix further reports the Chicago-based med-tech company Augmedics has "developed the first augmented reality (AR) navigation system aimed at being used in surgery." It's called xvision.[289] Augmedics' xvision "projects a 3D representation onto the surgeon's retina using a headset to see the patient's anatomy through skin and tissue as if using X-ray vision," helping a surgeon "attend to the patient and see the navigation data simultaneously."[290] According to Onix's review of Augmedics, "xvision's system has demonstrated a 98.9% overall placement accuracy when tested on spinal screws in cadavers."[291] When coupled with the hyper-fast speeds of 5G technology and robotic surgery arms, systems similar to xvision could someday be used so that the best surgeons in the world are able to operate on patients 1,000 miles away or even farther, even in semi-remote locations.

Robot-assisted surgeries are already becoming readily available in major academic medical centers, because robot assistance "allows doctors to perform many types of complex procedures with more precision, flexibility and control than is possible with conventional techniques," especially when minimally invasive surgery, which involves very small incisions, is preferable.[292]

ENTER THE METAVERSE

Although many businesses today are focused on ways to use AR and VR to sell more shoes or perform better surgeries, some are spending loads of cash to build entirely new, interconnected virtual and digital worlds, wherein users can do almost anything, including socializing with friends in virtual living rooms, working a nine-to-five job, or owning virtual property. This grander, more all-encompassing use of AR, VR, and digital spaces is often referred to as the *metaverse*, a term coined by author Neil Stevenson in his 1982 dystopian novel *Snow Crash*.[293]

The most notable and well-financed attempt to create a true metaverse is being led by Mark Zuckerberg's $400 billion company Meta. Zuckerberg made massive waves in 2021 when he announced Facebook had changed its name to Meta and that the company's long-term plan had shifted away from its social media foundation toward developing a vast metaverse.[294] Meta is hiring thousands of employees to build its new virtual universe, which has already cost the company substantially. In 2021 alone, Meta spent $10 billion designing, developing, and operating the metaverse.[295]

If Zuckerberg's metaverse were to become fully operational, it could prove to be revolutionary. It would offer to people in every country on the planet the ability to socialize, do business, and be entertained through a series of interconnected, two- and three-dimensional environments, often mixing reality and the real world seamlessly.

For example, in one Meta promotional video, the company offers a vision of what it could be like to go to music concerts in the future.[296] In the video, a user attends a concert with a friend, except the friend isn't there in person. Using the power of augmented reality, virtual reality, and the metaverse, the friend *appears* to be present at the concert with the human user, who is wearing AR glasses. The friend can experience the concert as if she were there in person by using a virtual reality device. Together, these technologies give both friends the feeling of experiencing a live concert together, even though they might be in physical locations that are hundreds or even thousands of miles away.

If the technology behind the metaverse develops sufficiently and enough people decide that life in virtual and digital worlds is better than reality, then the ramifications of the widespread adoption of VR, AR, and the metaverse would be far-reaching and exceptionally disruptive. Of course, there are countless benefits to these technologies, such as bringing people who live far apart closer together, enhancing our real environments with augmented reality, improving safety and reducing the spread of disease, allowing workers who need to closely collaborate with others the ability to live far from physical office spaces, and making luxuries available to people with limited resources, among many other benefits.

But there are also significant dangers associated with a greater dependence on living within virtual spaces and the mass adoption of VR and AR technologies, many of which are directly connected to the Great Narrative.

Remember that the institutions and powerful figures behind the Great Narrative believe they can "design the future" by altering, manipulating, and developing breakthrough technologies such as AR, VR, and the metaverse to make them more aligned with *their* vision for society. Also keep in mind that many of the institutions working with the World Economic Forum—including Meta, Microsoft, and Google—are both official WEF partners and the primary forces behind the creation and distribution of Fourth Industrial technologies such as AR, VR, and the metaverse.[297] Klaus Schwab's vision of embedding his ESG and other stakeholder ideals into the next generation of technological breakthroughs is exactly what the Great Narrative is all about, and it's happening right now.

This isn't a secret. The biggest corporations driving the Fourth Industrial Revolution are also openly and deeply devoted to the Great Reset and Great Narrative movements. For example, Meta has a mountain of data, publications, websites, and other resources touting its commitment to ESG, including an official company policy supporting the very same UN *sustainable development goals* (SDGs) that serve as the foundation for most ESG models such as the one endorsed by the World Economic Forum.[298, 299, 300]

For example, Meta proudly declares on its website:

Our mission is to give people the power to build community and bring the world closer together. We believe in supporting inclusive communities, in which everyone has a voice and access to opportunities. That's why Meta is supporting the advancement of the United Nations Sustainable Development Goals (SDGs) and working alongside our partners to drive progress towards these goals by 2030. While it's possible to link Meta's work to all SDGs, best practice challenges companies to prioritize specific sectors where they can move the needle the most.[301]

Meta also touts its ESG "social impact" and its commitment to ESG goals that advance "peace, justice and strong institutions," as well as those that battle climate change and reduce CO_2 emissions—all of which are standard talking points of the Great Reset and Great Narrative movements.[302]

The question you need to ask yourself is, *How would a company such as Meta that is committed to using ESG social credit scores—and don't forget that Meta is hardly the only big corporation involved— build technologies such as AR, VR, and the metaverse?* Would they create bastions of freedom, or would they be tightly controlled virtual environments that fit nicely into Schwab's Great Narrative agenda? Given the close ties between these businesses and the World Economic Forum, ESG, and other, similar movements and ideas, the answer is obvious.

There's no need for wild speculation, however, because Meta and many other businesses have plainly stated that they will design the Fourth Industrial Revolution's breakthrough technologies in line with ESG goals. In an article titled "How We're Helping Build the Metaverse with Diversity, Equity and Inclusion in Mind," Maxine Williams—who serves as Meta's chief diversity officer, which is apparently a profession now—acknowledges that Meta hopes its metaverse will become "a great technological equalizer," but that this "can only happen if we get involved during these early stages to help steer the direction of what we want the future to look like."[303]

Williams suggests throughout the article, which focuses mostly on diverse hiring practices and inclusive-looking metaverse avatars, that the metaverse can only "reflect everyone under the sun" if its designers represent a variety of racial, gender, and other viewpoints, because, "Our success in realizing this vision depends on our investments, our commitment and *who* is at the table making decisions."[304]

Williams concludes by stating, "Meta is committed to involving people from all backgrounds from the very beginning to create a future where everyone can prosper on the same playing field."[305]

Of course, there's nothing wrong with ensuring that a virtual environment looks and feels authentically diverse, but Williams's statements clearly go beyond racially diverse avatars. When Williams claims that "who is at the table making decisions"—referring to various kinds of diversity—is essential for building a fair and equitable metaverse, she is herself engaging in discrimination. The idea that one race, gender, or sexual orientation cannot possibly build a virtual environment for other races, genders, and sexual orientations is the epitome of bigotry.

Further, it's telling that Williams emphasizes "the same playing field" and creating a "great technological equalizer" as important goals for Meta in developing its metaverse, rather than values that used to be universally applauded in the Western world, like liberty, freedom, and competition.

You might think I'm reading too much into Meta's commitment to diversity in the metaverse, but take a moment to really think about what they're saying. In a truly equitable, inclusive metaverse where people live, work, own virtual property, and are entertained, will religious groups be allowed to hold worship services? Will freedom of association and political freedom be tolerated in Meta's new world? Will those who express their support for Donald Trump's presidency be allowed to speak or hold virtual campaign rallies? (Don't forget, many of the people designing the metaverse insist Trump is a horrific racist who shouldn't be allowed on social media platforms, including Meta's Facebook.) Will metaverse bookstores feature every book, or only those deemed "inclusive" enough to satisfy Meta? What about the movies watched in the metaverse? And the television shows? Will you someday be able to sit in a virtual metaverse living room and watch BlazeTV or Fox News, or will you be limited to more left-leaning outlets such as MSNBC and CNN?

There are already special-interest groups and nonprofits demanding strict limits on every type of freedom imaginable in the emerging metaverse. In an article for *TIME* titled "An Industry-Backed Group Thinks the Metaverse Can Avoid the Ills of Social Media. Here's How," writer Andrew Chow notes that a think tank called OASIS Consortium is actively working with tech developers to design metaverse applications with "safety" in mind. But the OASIS Consortium isn't merely worried about *physical* safety or various forms of sexual abuse in the metaverse; it's also deeply concerned about preventing another "Jan. 6 insurrection."

"You can think of the Jan. 6 insurrection as a result of not having safety guardrails 15 years ago," OASIS founder Tiffany Xingyu Wang told *TIME*. "This time in the metaverse, either the impact will be much bigger, or the time to get to that catastrophic moment will be much shorter."[306]

Chow writes that "Wang's solution" to the problem of preventing the next January 6 "insurrection" is not "to seek government intervention—but instead work with metaverse builders to self-regulate and think about safety first in a way that most social media platforms did not."[307]

In other words, Wang knows the American government cannot legally silence free speech or association in the metaverse—because of that stupid, pesky Bill of Rights thing—but there is nothing stopping non-government-owned businesses like Meta or its many partners from creating and enforcing restrictions on free speech, just as many social media companies do already.

Although many influential companies have joined the OASIS Consortium, Meta and other tech giants have not—at least, as far as I can tell. But if you're concerned that Meta's emerging metaverse will have too much freedom and not enough ESG censorship, fear not. Meta might not be working with the OASIS Consortium, but it has a much bigger, even more powerful partner to help ensure that the platforms of the future limit freedom: the World Economic Forum.

In a post published by the *MIT Technology Review*, writer Tanya Basu highlights the work of the OASIS Consortium and Meta's plans for regulating the metaverse.[308] According to Basu, after requesting more information from Zuckerberg's company about the metaverse, Meta pointed her to a revealing website post by Andrew Bosworth, Meta's chief technology officer, and Nick Clegg, president of global affairs at Meta.[309]

In the post, titled "Building the Metaverse Responsibly," Bosworth and Clegg noted that in May 2022, the World Economic Forum launched a "Defining and Building the Metaverse" initiative, which "brings together key stakeholders to build an economically viable, interoperable, safe and inclusive metaverse."[310] Clegg, one of the leaders of Meta's metaverse project, joined the WEF initiative on behalf of his company.[311]

Initially, the WEF's new project brought together "more than 60 leading technology and other sector companies, alongside experts, academics and civil society."[312] But at the time of publication of this book, the number of member companies and organizations exceeded one hundred, including some of the biggest names in technology, media, and business—Microsoft, Sony, NBC Universal, Walmart, Accenture, the United Nations, JPMorgan Chase & Co., and Mastercard.[313] INTERPOL, the international community's police organization, and the government of the United Arab Emirates, one of the leaders of the Great Narrative movement, are also members.[314] Interestingly, although Meta is not a part of the OASIS Consortium, the OASIS Consortium is a member of WEF's metaverse initiative, serving alongside Meta.[315]

In one article outlining some of the objectives of the Davos metaverse initiative, titled "How to build an economically viable, inclusive and safe metaverse," one member of the initiative noted, "We must establish ground rules that create an inclusive public commons, recognizing that such live, always-on spaces are vital public spaces that must be supported and regulated as town squares and parks are today."[316]

The same article includes a quote from Meta's Nick Clegg that argues the metaverse must "be developed openly with a spirit of cooperation between the private sector, lawmakers, civil society, academia and, most importantly, the people who will use these technologies."[317]

Although Clegg and others in the WEF like to put a smiley face on their fascism, it's obvious what they are saying here: the metaverse cannot be free. It must be designed for "inclusivity," "equity," and "safety"—all of which are loaded terms regularly used by members of the WEF to limit free speech and other liberties. And while the WEF initiative might *say* that the "people who use these technologies" will be part of their design, none of us regular folk were invited to be part of the WEF's metaverse initiative. Big-tech companies, banks, and other financial institutions, governments, the United Nations, activist groups who want to silence free speech, and billion-dollar corporations were all given their golden tickets to the party, though. Maybe our invitations just got lost in the mail.

The metaverse is not the only important technological development of the Fourth Industrial Revolution, and it is possible that the idea will never really catch on at all, or at least not in the way so many of its advocates and designers imagine it will today. But it does serve as a remarkable cautionary tale for the Fourth Industrial Revolution.

The rules for the metaverse of the future, like those of so many other emerging technologies, are being written in the present by the very same activists, governments, nonprofit organizations, financial institutions, tech companies, and massive corporations that have been calling for a Great Reset of the global economy. They're also the same institutions who are working tirelessly to build an elaborate ESG social credit scoring system throughout the Western world. If the metaverse does end up becoming the place where people spend most of their time (or even just a large chunk of it), then they will be living in a world designed by the supporters of the Great Reset, and it will not, I assure you, be a place where true freedom of religion, thought, expression, or association is tolerated.

BITCOIN, BLOCKCHAIN, AND THE DIGITAL DOLLAR

Of all the disruptive technologies discussed in this book, none have received more press in recent years than blockchain technology, especially as it relates to cryptocurrencies such as Bitcoin. But despite all the hype, most Americans still have no idea what blockchain and cryptocurrencies are, how they work, or how they could soon change the world, so in the remainder of this section, I will outline the basics of blockchain and cryptocurrency, and then I'll discuss why increasingly more governments are so worried about them.

BREAKING DOWN BLOCKCHAIN

At first, blockchain might sound really confusing, and if you get into the weeds of the technology, there's a pretty good chance you're never going to be able to climb your way out. But don't be intimidated; the basics of blockchain are a lot easier to understand than you might think, and if I can grasp it—a man who still hasn't figured out how to program his universal TV remote—you can get it too.

Coinbase, one of the leading platforms for buying, selling, and storing cryptocurrencies, describes blockchain as "a list of transactions that anyone can view and verify."[318] When you read about blockchain, you will often see it referred to as a "ledger," because just as Coinbase noted, blockchain is fundamentally nothing more than a list of transactions available to the public.

Other researchers and writers have thought that it's helpful to describe blockchain as a kind of distributed database. "A database is a giant collection of information stored on servers that can be easily accessed, managed and updated," wrote Luke Conway for *TheStreet*, an online business news publication.[319] And "distributed databases are stored in servers separated by location instead of one central location for security reasons."[320]

Conway says, "You can think of a blockchain as a version of a database, more specifically, a distributed database. The main differences are in the type of data it stores, the way it stores it, who is allowed access and that data on a blockchain cannot be manipulated or deleted."[321]

How do blockchain systems store data? This is what makes blockchain technology so special. With blockchain, data is encrypted and stored in blocks, which are really just groups of information, sort of like little digital filing cabinets. As Conway notes,

These blocks only have room for so many transactions, and when a block fills up, it is chained onto the previous block and added to the long chain of transactions (hence the "blockchain").

This creates a chronological history of transactions, like a ledger, from the first transaction in the first block to the last transaction in the most recent block. The blockchain saves these blocks in a format that allows us to view a perfectly recorded history of … transactions.[322]

Whenever new information is added to a ledger, such as someone buying or selling a Bitcoin, that transaction is recorded in a new block on the blockchain, along with information about the previous block. Blocks are designed with identity markers linking each new block with the previous block, and before a new block can be added, it first must be approved by the users—called "nodes"—of a decentralized blockchain system. This makes it very difficult for a nefarious actor to alter information already recorded in the ledger, because the actor would need control of most of the users (nodes) in the system to verify that the new information fits within the blockchain.

Investopedia describes this aspect of blockchain like so:

What a blockchain does is to allow the data held in that database to be spread out among several network nodes at various locations. This not only creates redundancy but also maintains the fidelity of the data stored therein—if somebody tries to alter a record at one instance of the database, the other nodes would not be altered and thus would prevent a bad actor from doing so. If one user tampers with Bitcoin's record of transactions, all other nodes would cross-reference each other and easily pinpoint the node with the incorrect information. This system helps to establish an exact and transparent order of events. This way, no single node within the network can alter information held within it.[323]

In a helpful article published by *The Verge* that breaks down the blockchain in really simple, easy-to-understand terms, Mitchell Clark writes,

> You can think of a blockchain like an obsessive club filled with members who love to keep track of things. The club has a ton of complicated rules to make sure that every member writes down the exact same set of records about what happens each day (whether it's bird sightings, or beer tastings, or flower sales) and that once data is recorded and accepted, it becomes exponentially more difficult to change as more and more records are added on top of it. Then, usually, outsiders can come by and check out all their records and go, 'Oh, wow, a cardinal flew by at 10AM in front of Mike's house. Cool.'[324]

Clark further explains, "Public blockchains provide a place to put information that anyone can add to, that no one can change, and that isn't controlled by any single person or entity.... Instead of one company or person keeping track of everything, that responsibility is spread out to everyone on the network."[325]

To make blockchain even more secure, in order for a new block of information to be added to the chain, nodes—which, remember, are the computer users—in the blockchain system don't merely validate transactions by reviewing data alone. Instead, a special validation technique that requires computer processing power is also used, making it even harder for a bad actor to alter the blockchain record. The two most popular validation techniques are called *proof of work* and *proof of stake*.

Under a *proof of work* model, transactions can only be verified after a mathematical problem is solved that has been provided by an algorithm to the nodes in the system. As *Forbes* contributor Kate Ashford explained in a 2022 article about the basics of cryptocurrency, under *proof of work*, "Each participating computer, often referred to as a 'miner,' solves a mathematical puzzle that helps verify a group of transactions—referred to as a block—then adds them to the blockchain ledger. The first computer to do so successfully is rewarded with a small amount of cryptocurrency for its efforts."[326]

Ashford further added, "The race to solve blockchain puzzles can require intense computer power and electricity. That means the miners might barely break even with the crypto they receive for validating transactions after considering the costs of power and computing resources."[327]

Proof of stake validation requires a lot less power than *proof of work*. Under *proof of stake*, "the number of transactions each person can verify is limited by the amount of cryptocurrency they're willing to 'stake,' or temporarily lock up in a communal safe for the chance to participate in the process," Ashford notes.[328]

With *proof of stake*, "Each person who stakes crypto is eligible to verify transactions," and thus receive rewards, "but the odds you'll be chosen typically increase with the amount you front."[329]

Still confused about the basics of blockchain? An example might be helpful. Imagine that you and four of your friends go on a road trip and agree beforehand to share the costs equally. To ensure that everyone splits the costs fairly, you create a spreadsheet, perhaps in Microsoft Excel, and each line in the spreadsheet contains information about every transaction made on the trip. For example, perhaps you buy dinner for the group on the first night of the trip. You might write out the cost of the dinner, exactly what was bought, the time of the meal, the date, and other details.

To ensure that the spreadsheet isn't lost or that your degenerate friends don't alter the spreadsheet to make it look like they put more money into the trip than they actually did, you create four copies of the spreadsheet every time you add a new transaction and then distribute the new spreadsheets to the other members of the group, so everyone has exactly the same records.

On the second day of the trip, one of your friends buys lunch, and then that evening, another friend buys gas. To make sure the spreadsheets are accurate and haven't been tampered with, before each of these transactions is entered into the spreadsheet and new copies of the spreadsheets are made, a majority of the friends must agree that the records contained in the newest version of the spreadsheet perfectly match with previous versions, and thus that the records on file have not been tampered with. If someone tries to provide the group with an updated spreadsheet that contains a transaction record for the first night that the rest of the group doesn't agree with, then the new spreadsheet is rejected. Because the group must agree on the record before new transactions can be added, it makes it far more likely the information shared is accurate.

This is essentially how blockchains work—well, kind of. It's actually a lot more complicated than that, but for most people, they won't need to know anything more than what I described.

BLOCKCHAIN BENEFITS

Now you have a basic understanding of blockchain, but it might be difficult for you to understand why so many people are so excited about it. After all, we're talking about spreadsheets here, right? The reason blockchain is a big deal is largely because it's very secure and reliable, and that means the role played by many intermediary institutions in modern transactions can be cut out of the process, saving time and money.

For example, much of the value that financial institutions offer to their customers is related to verification and security. How does a retailer know you have the money available in your bank account to pay for a good or service? Because a financial institution holds your funds, keeps track of them, and can communicate with retailers via payment processers, assuring them that you're good for the money, even if you don't have any dollar bills in your pocket. These institutions can also transfer those funds to other accounts at the same or other institutions, allowing customers to quickly and securely pay vendors.

Blockchain makes this financial middleman unnecessary, because a blockchain system can verify that you have the funds available in a digital wallet to complete a transaction, and it can do so relatively quickly and securely. It's also largely automated, so human error typically does not enter into the equation at all.

Further, blockchain is globally available, so it's much easier for people to use blockchain internationally than to go through institutions operating across numerous countries, all with their own rules, regulations, and taxes. It's also decentralized and publicly available, so decision-making and control is never in the hands of one or two organizations or individuals.

These benefits make blockchain, when set up properly, much more efficient, affordable, and secure compared to bloated financial institutions, potentially saving economies and consumers huge amounts of money.

BITCOIN, ETHEREUM, AND OTHER CRYPTOCURRENCIES

At this point, you could be wondering what any of this has to do with Bitcoin, Ethereum, and other cryptocurrencies. Well, cryptocurrencies such as Bitcoin and Ethereum, as well as thousands of others, run on blockchain technology. That's what makes them so secure and reliable. Two people exchanging goods or services using

Bitcoin can do so from anywhere in the world securely, quickly, and without a traditional financial institution. And many cryptocurrencies designed to be mediums of exchange, such as Bitcoin, are designed in such a way that there is a limited amount of the currency available or a limited amount added to the currency's supply over a specified period. Bitcoin's lifetime supply is capped at 21 million coins, so there will never be more than 21 million Bitcoin, no matter what users or banks want.[330]

The supply restrictions that are part of some cryptocurrency designs help make them more valuable than even the most valuable government-backed currencies on the planet, including the U.S. dollar. In November 2021, Bitcoin's value reached nearly $70,000 per coin.[331] In May 2021, Litecoin, another blockchain-based cryptocurrency, topped $400 per coin.[332]

Central banks that control their own fiat currencies such as the U.S. Federal Reserve—and by *fiat*, I mean currencies not backed by a hard asset such as gold or silver—have the ability to "print" as many new dollars as they want, whenever they want. If this creation of new currency is done responsibly, inflation, which is the devaluation of currency, will occur slowly over time and can, according to many economists, have beneficial effects on an economy. Too much money-printing, however, can cause high amounts of inflation, literally destroying people's wealth overnight. (See my discussion of modern monetary theory in chapter 1 for more on this topic. Or just stop living under a rock and look at the price of gasoline, food, or just about anything else today compared to the period prior to the COVID-19 pandemic, during which governments and central banks in Europe and North America pursued insane levels of spending and money printing.)

People unfamiliar with cryptocurrencies often think that every currency on the market is essentially the same as Bitcoin, which was designed to be a store of value and medium of exchange. But many cryptocurrencies are tied to blockchain ecosystems that serve a completely different function.

In a helpful article written for the popular financial website *The Motley Fool* about various kinds of cryptocurrencies, Nicholas Rossolillo noted that there are two main kinds of cryptocurrencies: coins and tokens. "A digital coin is created on its own blockchain and acts in much the same way as traditional money," Rossolillo wrote. "It can be used to store value and as a means of exchange between two parties doing business with each other."[333]

"Tokens, on the other hand, have far more uses than just digital money," Rossolillo added. "Tokens are created on top of an existing blockchain and can be used as part of a software application (such as to grant access to an app, to verify identity, or to track products moving through a supply chain)."[334] Although most people who have heard of cryptocurrencies don't know it, many of the most valuable currencies are tokens used in blockchain systems, not coins like Bitcoin.

For example, the second-largest cryptocurrency, based on market cap, is a token called Ethereum. As Rossolillo noted, "Ethereum is a platform that uses blockchain technology to enable the creation of smart contracts and other decentralized applications (meaning the software doesn't have to be distributed on app exchanges such as Apple's App Store or Alphabet's Google Play Store, where they might have to give a 30% cut of any revenue to the tech giants). Ethereum is both a cryptocurrency (the actual coins are measured in units called Ether) and a software development sandbox."[335] In many respects, the Ethereum Network is actually closer to being an operating system, such as Microsoft's Windows or Apple's iOS, or even computer hardware, than it is a true currency like Bitcoin.

Another one of the most popular cryptocurrencies is ada, the native token used on the Cardano *proof of stake* blockchain platform. (In case you were wondering, the ada token was "named after

Ada Lovelace: a nineteenth-century mathematician who is recognized as the first computer programmer, and is the daughter of the poet Lord Byron."[336])

According to the Cardano Foundation:

> Ada is a digital currency. Any user, located anywhere in the world, can use ada as a secure exchange of value—without requiring a third party to mediate the exchange. Every transaction is permanently, securely, and transparently recorded on the Cardano blockchain.
>
> Every ada holder also holds a stake in the Cardano network. Ada stored in a wallet can be delegated to a stake pool to earn rewards—to participate in the successful running of the network—or pledged to a stake pool to increase the pool's likelihood of receiving rewards. In time, ada will also be usable for a variety of applications and services on the Cardano platform.[337]

> Cardano aims to be "a flexible, sustainable, and scalable blockchain platform for running smart contracts—which will allow the development of a wide range of decentralized finance apps, new crypto tokens, games, and more."[338] In many ways, Cardano's leadership wants it to be a platform that's similar to Ethereum, except more effective and efficient.

One of the most promising uses of both Ethereum and Cardano involves the development of smart contracts, a kind of digital contract stored on a blockchain system that automatically operates when certain conditions are met. As IBM notes, "They typically are used to automate the execution of an agreement so that all participants can be immediately certain of the outcome, without any intermediary's involvement or time loss. They can also automate a workflow, triggering the next action when conditions are met."[339] Smart contracts built on blockchain have the potential to completely transform global finance, among other parts of the world's economy, because they could make many of the functions of the traditional financial system mostly or totally obsolete.

The greater use of blockchain and smart contracts in the financial system is often referred to as "DeFi," which stands for "decentralized finance." Academics Benedikt Eikmanns and Isabell Welpe, along with Philipp Sandner, a professor and founder of the Frankfurt School Blockchain Center, outlined in a 2021 article for *Forbes* some of the many opportunities associated with DeFi, including its potential for improving or even displacing traditional bank lending:

> The primary business model of commercial banks is to accept deposits and to give loans to its clients. Borrowing and lending are an elementary cornerstone of an efficient financial system as holders of funds get an incentive to provide liquidity to the markets and in exchange earn a return on their otherwise unproductive assets.[340]
>
> DeFi protocols enable for the first time to borrow or lend money on a large scale between unknown participants and without any intermediaries. Those applications bring lenders and borrowers together and set interest rates automatically in accordance with supply and demand. Moreover, those protocols are truly inclusive, as anybody can interact with them at any time, from any location, and with any amount.
>
> In fact, the recent hype around DeFi applications is largely driven by the advancement of borrowing and lending protocols, such as Compound. In contrast to traditional finance, loans in DeFi are commonly secured by over-collateralization. However, companies such as Aave are currently working on enabling uncollateralized loans similarly to traditional finance.

If DeFi takes off, and it certainly looks like it will, it could someday be possible for you to, in effect, become your own bank, offering the money you have to borrowers via smart contracts on a blockchain application. Borrowers would then pay you back with interest. How could you be sure that you'll be paid back? The blockchain application would keep track of payments made, payments missed, and determine if and when the collateral offered by the borrower when the loan first went into effect should be released to the lender because the borrower failed to make a sufficient number of payments. Perhaps even more likely, blockchain DeFi applications will make it possible for groups of people to gather together, pool their resources, and act as their own financial institution—all without needing any employees, and with minimal, if any, risk. Blockchain apps will do all the work for them.[341]

Bitcoin, Ethereum, Cardano, Compound, and Aave are just the beginning too. There are countless other impressive blockchain applications being built today that have the potential to completely revolutionize your world. Algorand, commonly called Algo, can host blockchain projects, similar to Ethereum, as well as function as an extremely efficient payment processor, sort of like Mastercard or Visa.[342] LBRY allows users to display and share videos, music, books, and other content using blockchain technology.[343] Filecoin makes it possible to store and retrieve data on a distributed cloud storage network—essentially a decentralized version of Dropbox.[344]

There are even blockchain platforms designed to help you create your very own cryptocurrency. Rally, which operates on the Ethereum Network, "enables creators and online communities to launch their own cryptocurrencies. By creating these so-called 'social tokens,' fans can gain access to benefits like unreleased content or merch, while creators can unlock new forms of revenue."[345]

So if you've ever dreamed of having your very own currency featuring your beautiful face—or, in the case of my producer, Stu, a not-so-beautiful face—the technology finally exists to make that dream a reality. Speaking of faces, I wonder if the world is finally ready for GlennCoin. Sure, it wouldn't be worth much, but what's better, having a moderate amount of real money, or being a GlennCoin trillionaire? Call me crazy, and I know I'm just a little biased, but being a trillionaire sounds like the better option to me.

NFTS

In addition to serving as a foundation for cryptocurrencies and emerging platforms, blockchain is also the reason NFTs have become so popular in recent years. NFT stands for "non-fungible tokens." If something is "non-fungible," it simply means that it can't be replaced. It's unique, special, one-of-a-kind—you might call it the Donald Trump of blockchain.

A simple way to think of NFTs is that they are digital items developed using blockchain technology to create something special and original. An NFT, which often comes in the form of artwork, drawings, or music, is created with a limited number of editions, and thus no more or less can ever be developed that is truly part of the same collection.[346] Even if someone were to take a perfect digital picture of NFT art, for example, it wouldn't *actually* be part of the original collection, in the same way someone could theoretically develop a look-alike Babe Ruth baseball card, but it wouldn't have nearly as much value as the real deal.

When you think about it, NFTs aren't much different from an original piece of art painted by a world-famous artist, such as Monet, Picasso, Van Gogh, or Hunter Biden. The reason an original Monet painting (or a painting by Hunter, if you're into that sort of thing) is so valuable is because it has a special quality to it, namely that the artist himself or herself is the one who actually touched the canvas, and that there are usually very few original versions of the art, often just one.

Limited edition cars, old baseball cards, and other collectibles are valuable because they have a unique quality that cannot be replicated (or, at the very least, cannot be replicated easily), and because they are rare. The same is true for NFTs.

The value of NFTs has absolutely skyrocketed in recent years, and I'll admit, in many cases, it's hard to understand why. As an artist myself, I can see the value in being able to sell digital work and maintain some sense of originality and uniqueness, but the prices associated with many NFTs, especially digital paintings and other images, is nothing short of bonkers.

One collage of NFTs by graphic designer Mike Winkelmann called "Everydays: The First 5,000 Days" sold for $69.3 million in February 2021.[347] A "CryptoPunk" pixelated image sold with a price tag of $23.7 million in February 2022.[348] Another CryptoPunk was sold by Sotheby's for $11.75 million in June 2021.[349] A TPunk—which looks very similar to a CryptoPunk—was sold for 120 million TRX coins in August 2021, or about $10.5 million.[350] (Boy, it really seems as though I am in the wrong business. It looks like making crappy NFT images of pixelated artwork, not fighting against Davos elites, is where all the money is at.)

Of course, there are tens of thousands of other NFTs sold on exchanges such as OpenSea—the world's largest marketplace for NFTs—that are worthless or nearly worthless. But it's obvious from the insane prices that many investors and collectors are willing to pay for NFTs that there are a ton of people out there who see great value in this emerging technology. But even if you're not into the whole digital art scene, there are many good reasons you should care about NFTs, the most important being that in the future, *everyone* will likely need to use them.

Because NFTs are built using blockchain, they can be designed in an ultra-secure, non-replicable way, making them extremely useful for event ticketing and other important documents. An NFT ticket issued to attend a football or baseball game, theater, or even to fly across the globe would be far more secure than current tickets, which are still susceptible to counterfeiting and fraud, despite recent advancements in security. NFTs could also be used to help secure land ownership and to prove ownership of a car or other high-priced item that requires a title.[351] Eventually, drivers licenses and other forms of identification will likely be built as NFTs too. In fact, in South Korea, more than a million drivers already have NFT licenses.[352]

GOING TO "THE MOON"

Blockchain technologies are still in their earliest stages, but their potential is off-the-charts amazing. It is entirely possible that the next generation of Americans will be just as connected to blockchain applications as today's Americans are tethered to the Internet. Virtually everything of importance online could someday run on blockchain technology as part of a transition to Web 3.0, a term used to describe the coming third generation of the Internet, "where websites and apps will be able to process information in a smart human-like way" using technologies such as blockchain and machine learning.[353]

The potential of blockchain, mixed with the horrendous failures of central banks around the world, is the biggest reason why the value of cryptocurrencies and other digital assets such as NFTs has been skyrocketing over the past decade—or as the crypto kids like to say these days, "going to the moon." I'm not sure when I mentioned Bitcoin over the air for the first time, but my research team was able to find a reference as far back as February 2015, when the price of one Bitcoin was less than $300.[354] If you had spent $1,000 on Bitcoin back then and then sold it close to its all-time high, you would have made well over $270,000 in profit. If that's not an incentive to listen to my radio program, I'm not sure what is.

Cryptocurrencies and NFTs are notoriously volatile investments, and I certainly haven't and wouldn't invest every penny I have (or even 10 percent of my pennies) on something as unstable as these investments. But there is no denying that cryptocurrencies and blockchain have the potential to be incredibly important, hyper-disruptive parts of the future economy. And in nearly every way, these disruptions will be for the better.

We desperately need less centralization of wealth, power, and regulatory authority in our financial and monetary systems, and blockchain could be the solution to that massive problem. It could also be used to make the Internet freer, more secure, and better suited to empower individuals. But blockchain's future is not written in stone. There remain significant obstacles to its widespread adoption, with one obstacle in particular being bigger than all the rest.

GOVERNMENT STRIKES AGAIN

The only way for blockchain technology to truly flourish is if governments stay out of the way of its development and implementation. Until recently, that is exactly what has happened in most Western countries, including the United States. The tides, however, are changing. Governments and some large institutions are wary of blockchain technology because it allows users to operate somewhat anonymously and provides people with the ability to avoid established, powerful institutions, like banks. It turns out governments and big corporations don't like it when people have the freedom to do business without being spied on, controlled, or heavily regulated. Shocking, I know.

In March 2022, the Biden administration released its "Executive Order on Ensuring Responsible Development of Digital Assets," which outlined a severe shift in official U.S. policy governing digital assets.[355] Through the executive order, the Biden administration directed the Department of the Treasury and numerous other federal agencies to develop regulatory recommendations "to address the implications of the growing digital asset sector and changes in financial markets for consumers, investors, businesses, and equitable economic growth," according to a White House fact sheet.[356]

Under the executive order, federal agencies are also expected to develop regulations "to identify and mitigate economy-wide (i.e., systemic) financial risks posed by digital assets" and "mitigate the illicit finance and national security risks posed by the illicit use of digital assets."[357]

Following Biden's order, the federal government unleashed a flurry of activity related to regulating or closely monitoring cryptocurrencies. Thomas Wade, director of financial services policy at the American Action Forum, has been cataloging many of those moves. Below are just some of the dozens of actions taken by the federal government to control at least some aspect of the emerging blockchain industry, according to Wade's extensive and important research:[358]

5/3/2022 – SEC nearly doubles the size of its cryptocurrency enforcement unit.

5/18/2022 – Securities and Exchange Commission (SEC) chair Gary Gensler calls for an increased budget for the SEC to combat cryptocurrency crime.

6/10/2022 – Deputy Treasury Secretary Wally Adeyemo indicates that Treasury will crack down on cryptocurrency wallets that allow consumers to buy and sell digital assets anonymously.

6/13/2022 – Crypto markets suffer shock as lender Celsius Network announces it will halt withdrawals amid regulatory scrutiny.

8/16/2022 – The Federal Reserve instructs banks to notify their regulators before beginning any crypto-related activity, noting that these activities might not be "legally permissible."

12/13/2022 – Senators [Elizabeth] Warren and [Roger] Marshall introduce a bipartisan bill that would require crypto firms to comply with anti-terrorism and anti-money-laundering regulations.

Of course, not every action taken by the federal government to rein in cryptocurrencies and blockchain companies has been negative. Blockchain's potential for positively impacting and decentralizing society is enormous, but there are some drawbacks to the freedom offered by blockchain platforms. For example, in August 2022, the Treasury Department sanctioned a company called Tornado Cash, which is known to help money launderers by mixing legally obtained cryptocurrencies with cryptocurrencies taken illegally.[359]

According to Wade, "Tornado Cash has been in particular used by North Korean hackers, who are said to have laundered $455 million of Ethereum in March [2022]," although "Critics within the crypto industry have pushed back on OFAC's [Office of Foreign Assets Control] decision in this case to blacklist code, rather than specific individuals or businesses."[360]

The federal government has every right to put rules in place to stop illegal blockchain activities. But the trillion-dollar question is (and I'm talking real dollars now, not GlennCoins), will governments, especially the U.S. government, stop at rooting out illegal money-laundering and hacking schemes, or will regulators turn their sights on law-abiding users and platforms as well? I think the research by Wade that I presented above, as well as good old-fashioned common sense, makes it clear that Biden and his allies have already started their war on many private digital assets, and I fear they are just getting started. This shouldn't be a surprise. The same logic used to prevent legal gun ownership fits nicely with bans on many forms of digital asset ownership. If a tiny fraction of gun owners breaking the law justifies limiting or eliminating gun rights, why shouldn't the same be true of Bitcoin?

BIG BLOCKCHAIN

Although many involved in the Great Narrative movement, including President Biden, want to restrict the use of many forms of blockchain technology, it would be a huge mistake to think that they are completely opposed to all uses of these technologies, especially cryptocurrencies and many of their associated platforms. Countless blockchain systems can be utilized to help big institutions become more efficient and powerful, and numerous banks, financial institutions, governments, and the World Economic Forum know it.

Consider Chainlink, for example, a popular cryptocurrency and blockchain technology that has rapidly gained the support of leading institutions in North America and Europe. Chainlink is designed to help blockchain and non-blockchain systems work together, acting as a bridge between older and newer systems.[361] This infrastructure, called "blockchain oracles," is essential for many large institutions that want to take advantage of blockchain's benefits, because unlike a smaller organization, they cannot afford to completely revamp their existing systems without causing irreparable harm to their customers, citizens, or members.[362]

As you know by now, the World Economic Forum loves any technology that helps big institutions, so naturally, it is a huge fan of Chainlink. The WEF even partnered with Chainlink to publish a white paper in December 2020 highlighting the benefits of this new technology. Chainlink's cofounder Sergey Nazarov and the WEF's project lead for blockchain and digital assets, Punit Shukla, coauthored the paper, titled "Bridging the Governance Gap: Interoperability for blockchain and legacy systems."[363]

Other blockchain technologies are also being financially supported, adopted, or studied closely by powerful institutions.

The International Organization of Standardization recently created its ISO 20022 standard, which was designed to become a uniform method for global financial institutions seeking to make international transfers.[364] ISO 20022 has already received the backing of the U.S. Federal Reserve. There are several important blockchain projects that are ISO 20022 compliant or rumored to be compliant, including Ripple, IBM-backed Stellar Lumens, and Algorand.[365] If this standard is widely adopted in the future, blockchain will likely become an essential component of many cross-border payment systems, a core element of the modern global financial system.

Further, in August 2022, BlackRock, arguably the most influential asset manager in existence today and a big player in the Great Reset and Great Narrative movements, took an unexpected and important step toward normalizing blockchain investments on Wall Street. It announced that it would soon partner with Coinbase, America's biggest cryptocurrency exchange, "to make crypto directly available to institutional investors."[366]

According to a report by *CoinDesk*, "Mutual customers of Coinbase and BlackRock's investment management platform, Aladdin, will have access to crypto trading, custody, prime brokerage and reporting capabilities."[367]

As important as the growing connection is between some blockchain platforms and large, wealthy institutions and governments, however, central banks and governments have bigger plans in mind for the future—government-backed, programmable digital currencies.

SAY GOODBYE TO THE DOLLAR

Some large institutions are turning to blockchain and cryptocurrencies to speed up the financial system, but there's also a growing movement among governments to develop their own new mediums of exchange: central bank digital currencies (CBDCs). Unlike cryptocurrencies such as Bitcoin and Litecoin, proposals for central bank digital currencies involve government-backed currencies that are usually managed by central banks, just like the U.S. dollar is today.[368] But rather than print a new physical currency, CBDCs exist digitally and nowhere else. In other words, you cannot hold a CBDC, just like you can't put a Bitcoin in your back pocket.

The U.S. Federal Reserve, the central bank of the United States responsible for managing much of the monetary policy in America, says on its website,

> "Central bank money" refers to money that is a liability of the central bank. In the United States, there are currently two types of central bank money: physical currency issued by the Federal Reserve and digital balances held by commercial banks at the Federal Reserve.
>
> While Americans have long held money predominantly in digital form—for example in bank accounts, payment apps or through online transactions—a CBDC would differ from existing digital money available to the general public because a CBDC would be a liability of the Federal Reserve, not of a commercial bank.[369]

Central banks all over the world, including the Fed, have in recent years been studying the potential development of digital money, either as a replacement for an existing currency or to supplement it. In 2022 alone, the Reserve Bank of Australia, Bank of Thailand, Bank of Indonesia, the Banque de France, and the central banks of Denmark, Saudi Arabia, and Singapore, among many others, launched research, pilot, or proof-of-concept programs for a central bank digital currency.[370] Although most of those who have warned about the rise of CBDCs have often been labeled "conspiracy theorists" (yours truly included), many of the most powerful countries on earth today have, at the very least, been working on research projects dedicated to creating a CBDC for quite a while. The Bank of England created its central bank digital currency project in 2018, and the Bank of Canada and U.S. Federal Reserve officially started their efforts in 2020.[371]

It's also worth noting that the move toward digital currency has accelerated dramatically in the wake of the COVID-19 pandemic. Although few central banks will openly admit it, the reason is obvious: governments on nearly every continent printed mountains of cash to prop up their nations, a necessity after choosing to lock down huge swaths of their economies for months and, in some cases, years. I'll discuss this problem more in chapter 8, but the important takeaway is that countries, especially in Europe and North America, have significantly devalued their currencies, run up huge national debts they likely will never pay off, and caused inflation to soar in the process. If you were in charge of the U.S. dollar, you would probably also think that now is a pretty good time to develop a digital currency.

Some think the concept of a digital dollar would simply be a digital version of the existing U.S. printed dollar, but a U.S. central bank digital currency would be an entirely new currency. The Federal Reserve has formally admitted this, acknowledging on the record that if a CBDC were rolled out, it would be as a supplement to existing printed money, at least at first. In a Federal Reserve frequently asked questions page, the Fed wrote in response to questions about a CBDC replacing paper money, "The Federal Reserve is committed to ensuring the continued safety and availability of cash and is considering a CBDC as a means to expand safe payment options, not to reduce or replace them."[372]

When people think of digital currencies, they usually think of decentralized blockchain currencies like those discussed earlier in this chapter, but a U.S. central bank digital currency would likely be completely different, especially if it is developed under the Biden administration or another leftist White House. Although developers of CBDCs promise these new currencies will be safe and designed to protect *some* privacy rights, one of the primary appeals of a CBDC from the perspective of governments is that it would be programmable, meaning that it could be designed "to act in a certain way based on predetermined criteria."[373]

Although cryptocurrencies can also be designed so they have rules associated with their use, many popular cryptocurrencies, including Bitcoin, don't have these kinds of limits. You can use Bitcoin to buy just about anything, so long as the seller agrees to accept it.

A programmable central bank digital currency, however, could be designed so that it can only be utilized for certain kinds of purchases, or so that it has limits on the amount of times it can be used to buy certain goods or products. It's even more likely that some CBDCs, including a U.S. digital dollar, would be designed so that the rules for its use could change over time. So if the geniuses at the Fed wake up one day and determine that the U.S. digital dollar should no longer be used to buy gasoline-powered cars, ammunition, guns, alcohol, fatty foods, or pretty much anything else they want to ban, Fed bureaucrats could with the push of a few buttons make their little authoritarian dreams become a reality.

Depending on how the law is written governing the CBDC, it is possible (and I would argue likely) that additional legislation wouldn't be required to make such changes. In other words, if CBDCs are created in Europe and North America, the Fed and other central banks, not a democratically elected legislature, are likely going to be in charge of how digital dollars are used. After all, that's pretty much how the Federal Reserve and some other central banks act today, with very little oversight.

Programmable digital CBDCs could also easily be tracked, taken away, or have their supply greatly expanded—and on very short notice too. Just think how effortless it would be for the Fed to provide a shiny new "stimulus" plan in the era of the digital dollar. Just make a phone call, tap some keys on a keyboard, and boom, $1 trillion delivered to a hundred million people, all within minutes. With these possibilities in mind, is it really so difficult to imagine why a central bank or its allies in national governments would want to develop a CBDC?

Now, just because a digital dollar *could* be designed so that it is easily controlled does not mean that it *must* be designed that way. Digital dollars built on blockchain, for example, with a very strong set of privacy restrictions and protections for individual liberty, could be more stable and valuable than the printed dollar we all use now. But there are many good reasons to believe that a freedom- and privacy-centric digital currency is not what the Biden administration and many others advocating for a central bank digital currency want.

In the Biden administration's March 2022 executive order and accompanying White House documents demanding increased regulations on cryptocurrencies, the president also included numerous provisions that set the table for a programmable, controllable central bank digital dollar.[374, 375] If President Biden is successful in developing a digital dollar that's programmable, it would be one of the greatest expansions of federal and/or central bank power (depending on how the currency is designed) in recent U.S. history—perhaps ever.

According to the White House's summary of the March 2022 federal directive, "the Executive Order calls for measures to," among other things, "Explore a U.S. Central Bank Digital Currency (CBDC) by placing urgency on research and development of a potential United States CBDC, should issuance be deemed in the national interest."[376]

Additionally, it directs the "U.S. Government to assess the technological infrastructure and capacity needs for a potential U.S. CBDC in a manner that protects Americans' interests," as well as "encourages the Federal Reserve to continue its research, development, and assessment efforts for a U.S. CBDC, including development of a plan for broader U.S. Government action in support of their work."[377]

Although the White House crafted some of the executive order's language to give the impression that the president had not made up his mind about whether a CBDC should be developed, it was apparent from the accompanying documents and other provisions of the order that the decision to create a new digital dollar was made well before the White House announced the March 2022 order.

For example, the White House's CBDC fact sheet says there is "urgency on research and development" of a CBDC.[378] And the order directs the "Secretary of the Treasury, in consultation with the Secretary of State, the Attorney General, the Secretary of Commerce, the Secretary of Homeland Security, the Director of the Office of Management and Budget, the Director of National Intelligence, and the heads of other relevant agencies" to provide a report to President Biden within one hundred and eighty days of the order (about six months) outlining their agencies' views on CBDC.[379] Just thirty days later, about seven months after the March 2022 order, a legislative proposal must be given to the president.[380] Do these incredibly short timelines for debating a new currency and writing legislation to create that currency sound like the White House was ever really unsure of whether a CBDC ought to be developed?

In September 2022, Americans found out the answer to that question, when the White House announced a "first-ever comprehensive framework" for digital assets, including a central bank digital currency.[381] Although no legislation has yet to be drafted at the time of publication of this book, it's clear that creating a U.S. digital dollar is a long-term goal for the Biden administration.

The question isn't whether Biden and his allies want a central bank digital currency. They clearly do. It is, instead, how Biden's digital dollar would be designed. Nowhere has the Biden administration come out and said, "We're going to use a new digital currency to control your life." Not even Biden is that senile, and that's really saying something. But the White House and others have heavily suggested that this is exactly what they would do on numerous occasions, so there's no reason for us to guess what Biden's true intentions are.

For example, consider that the March 2022 executive order plainly states that the CBDC and other policies governing digital assets must be designed to promote the causes of "financial inclusion and equity," as well as to reduce "climate change and pollution."[382] In fact, the words "financial inclusion" appear five times in the executive order, and "equity" is mentioned four times.[383] A nonprogrammable digital currency could not effectively advance any of these goals, but a programmable currency could be used to achieve many different kinds of policy objectives, including "equity" and battling global warming.

The Biden administration also discussed its devotion to using a new digital dollar to advance social justice causes during a Q&A with the press. During the event, a "senior administration official"—whose name appears to have been mysteriously removed from the White House's official transcript—reiterated the "urgency" of studying the creation of a digital dollar, especially as it relates to "human rights," "financial stability," "financial inclusion," and "national security."[384]

"And these are critical design," the official added, "all of these implications lead to critical design decisions. And we've got to be very—very deliberate about that analysis because the implications of our moving in this direction are profound for the country that issues the world's primary reserve currency."[385]

The official also said about the digital dollar, "We can move quickly, but we can also move in a way that's smart and that's inclusive of the stakeholders both within our government and certainly outside our government."[386]

Elsewhere during the call, the official said Biden's executive order "recognizes that our assessments of the risks and potential benefits of digital assets must include an understanding of how our financial system does and does not meet the current needs of consumers in a manner that is equitable, inclusive, and efficient."[387]

And the official further promised to "continue to partner with all stakeholders—including industry, labor, consumer, and environmental groups, international allies and partners" in the design, planning, and studying of digital assets.[388]

Now, ask yourself, if Biden were only interested in creating a central bank digital currency that operates almost exactly like existing printed dollars, without programmed rules built into its design and use, why would the administration partner with "industry," "environmental," and other special interests who might benefit from a programmed currency but would have very little to say about a non-programmed digital currency? Similarly, how could a central bank digital currency reduce crime and terrorism, a stated goal of Biden's executive order, if the CBDC cannot be tracked, programmed, or otherwise controlled?

Given the numerous comments made by the administration, its obsession with using a new digital currency to address "climate change" and improve "equity," and the incredibly fast timeline that his administration was required to develop legislation about digital currencies, it seems obvious that Biden has his heart firmly fixed on the creation of a programmable, controllable, liberty-destroying digital currency.

What about the Federal Reserve? If a CBDC were created in the United States, the Fed would likely be put in charge of managing it. Although the Fed has published analyses and reports about the possible creation of a CBDC, it has been deliberately vague about how it would be formulated, often discussing design choices as mere possibilities, rather than proposals. However, in one little-talked-about Q&A about central bank digital currencies, a top economist at the Fed let slip a revealing admission about how digital currencies could be used in the future.

In 2021, as part of a Fed Q&A about central bank digital currencies, David Andolfatto, a senior vice president and economist at the St. Louis Fed's Research Division, was asked by a member of the public, "Can you assure us that these digital currencies won't ever be used to tell us when, how, or where our money can be spent?"[389] That sounds like a reasonable question to me. And surely if the Fed has no intention of ever governing over a programmable digital dollar, then the answer would be pretty simple: "Yes, of course," Andolfatto would have replied. "There's nothing to worry about at all. The Fed has no interest or intention in telling you or anyone else how your money must be spent. That's not the role of the Federal Reserve, and it likely never will be."

But that's not how he answered the question. Instead, Andolfatto responded, "In life one can't give absolute assurances of anything."[390] Excuse me, what? *One can't give absolute assurances of anything?* If the Fed is not planning to use digital dollars to control behavior, why would Andolfatto answer the question that way?

Imagine for a moment that you're the owner of a gun shop. (I know, I know—only "deplorables" cling to their guns and religion, but stick with me because the analogy is great.) You own a gun shop. Someone comes in the store and says, "Give me all the guns and ammo I can buy." So, curious and concerned, you ask, "Hey, you're not planning on killing a bunch of people, right? I've never had anyone buy every gun and bullet in the store on one trip." And instead of the buyer saying, "Oh, of course not. I would never do anything like that," he looks you dead in the eye and says, "Well, in life, one can't give absolute assurances of anything." Would you sell a maniac like that the contents of a small armory, or would you tell him that he should take a hike?

The only reason someone like Mr. Andolfatto would answer the question this way is if he knows there's a good chance that digital dollars will be used in exactly the manner the questioner worried about. There really is no other logical explanation.

After Andolfatto said, "In life one can't give absolute assurances of anything," he continued his response by stating, "But if I understand the question correctly, I think the caller [questioner] is concerned about the potential of privacy that would be associated, say, with a government sort of digital currency. This is an ongoing debate that we have all the time about how much privacy is desirable."[391]

Sorry, we need to stop again. Don't gloss over this incredible statement: "This is an ongoing debate that we have all the time about how much privacy is desirable." So the Fed's ability to tell Americans *when*, *how*, or *where* their money can be spent is "an ongoing debate that we have all the time"? That's news to me, and I'm willing to bet it is news to you too—and bad news at that.

I would be remiss, however, if I left you with the impression that top Fed officials and researchers have no plan to ensure that your privacy and freedoms are protected in the event that President

Biden were to create a new digital dollar. Andolfatto left the public with these super-comforting words at the conclusion of his answer:

> Obviously, in the United States we value personal privacy a lot, and we let our representatives in Congress know that. And by and large it's respected along many dimensions.
>
> But there's a bit of a trade-off here as well because we don't know, for example, what sort of entities might make use of these central bank digital currencies for nefarious purposes, say, to finance terrorist activities. We might want the government to monitor certain types of transactions as well. And we see this in the anti-money laundering laws and the KYC [know your customer] laws. So, there's a trade-off. One can't give assurances, but I think what we can be assured of is that Congress will respond to the electorate's concerns and this is kind of the best we can hope for.[392]

Wow. Relying on Congress to protect our rights and respond to the will of the people is "kind of the best we can hope for" when it comes to the development of digital money? I am certain that comment makes you feel just as warm and fuzzy inside as it does for me. I mean, when has Congress ever let the American public down or failed to do the right thing? When has Congress ever failed to protect people's privacy rights? You know, I think Mr. Andolfatto's completely absurd responses might be hilarious if the free world weren't on the verge of being totally swept away. Tyrannical power-grabs tend to ruin all the fun.

If the Federal Reserve or the U.S. government is given the power to develop and manage a programmable central bank digital currency, it might seem like a relatively benign, perhaps even boring, news story. And at first, life might not change all that much. But make no mistake about it: there are few developments in the Fourth

Industrial Revolution that would be as far-reaching and disruptive as the creation of a programmable digital dollar. And we could be just one election away from this terrifying idea becoming a reality.

QUANTUM COMPUTERS AND THE END OF "UNKNOWNS"

When discussing futuristic concepts, it is easy to fall into the trap of thinking that many of the groundbreaking technologies of tomorrow are nothing more than science fiction. Sure, gadgets are getting fancier and cell phones can do more every year, but by and large, our lives remain relatively unchanged. These theoretical game-changing technologies always seem to be perpetually on the horizon. But this is largely due to a shortsighted worldview that fails to see just how quickly things have advanced.

Writing this in the year 2023, it is easy to forget just how new many of the technologies are that we use on a daily basis. Widespread access to the Internet didn't begin until around the year 2000.[393] The first iPhone was released only sixteen years ago.[394] It took until 2011 before the majority of households in America began using social media.[395] Now, not only are these things commonplace, but most cannot imagine a world without them.

The truth is, technology in the realm of computing and processing power has been advancing at breakneck speeds for decades. The processing power needed by NASA to put men on the moon a half-century ago can now be found in a simple pocket calculator, and the supercomputers of the 1980s and 1990s are now outmatched by an old iPhone—and it's not even close.[396] Each new generation of computers raises the bar and renders its predecessors obsolete. This has been an observable trend since the days of punch-card computers, and we shouldn't expect the trend to stop anytime soon.

Moore's Law is a commonly invoked term that describes a theory predicting the progression of today's computers. In 1965, American engineer Gordon Moore predicted we would see a doubling of transistors on a computer chip every two years, resulting in ever-faster and more powerful computers. His prediction has largely remained true to this day.[397] This "law" is what facilitates the proliferation of increasingly powerful computing devices, from the smartphones in your pocket to IBM's most powerful supercomputer at Oak Ridge National Laboratory in Tennessee.[398]

However, this "law" has to be broken at some point. Transistors, which used to be measured in millimeters and are now measured in microns, can only get so small. We are reaching the theoretical limits of Moore's Law.[399] Does this mean computers will soon plateau in terms of computer power and ability? Of course not.

Engineers are already hard at work on technologies that will continue to facilitate the next generations of computers. Intel is working on three-dimensional computer chips that will theoretically allow Moore's Law to continue uninterrupted. They claim that by 2030, they will have a computer chip that will incorporate one trillion transistors.[400]

I have little doubt engineers and scientists will find new and creative ways to expand the capabilities of tomorrow's supercomputers. And these new supercomputers will surely continue to put today's most advanced systems to shame. But it's also possible that we won't have to wait for 2030 to enter a new era of computing. Soon, we could enter the quantum age.

If you look up "quantum computers," you will find numerous fantastical claims about their potential future. Some talk about how these devices will soon outmatch even the most advanced supercomputers. Others say they will disrupt everything from financial markets to cybersecurity. In 2017, Microsoft published an article that said quantum computers could help people "find answers to scientific questions previously thought unanswerable."[401] The divergent opinions about quantum computers stem from the fact that we are only now starting to scratch the surface of their potential.

The inner workings of a quantum computer are not something I can easily wrap my mind around, so I won't even try to explain it here. We'd be bogged down for pages talking about *superposition* and *quantum entanglement*. I'll leave the details to much smarter people, such as futurist Jeff Brown, who has come on my show a number of times to help my audience get a better grasp on technologies such as quantum computers.[402] But I did find a helpful, very basic understanding of how this technology works in an article published by *Scientific American* in 2021.

The piece, authored by Michael Tabb, Andrea Gawrylewski, and Jeffery DelViscio, explains:

> Traditional computer processors work in binary—the billions of transistors that handle information on your laptop or smartphone are either on (1) or they're off (0). Using a series of circuits, called "gates," computers perform logical operations based on the state of those switches.
>
> Classical computers are designed to follow specific inflexible rules. This makes them extremely reliable, but it also makes them ill-suited for solving certain kinds of problems—in particular, problems where you're trying to find a needle in a haystack.[403]

This is where quantum computers shine.

> If you think of a computer solving a problem as a mouse running through a maze, a classical computer finds its way through by trying every path until it reaches the end.
>
> What if, instead of solving the maze through trial and error, you could consider all possible routes simultaneously?

Quantum computers do this by substituting the binary "bits" of classical computing with something called "qubits." Qubits operate according to the mysterious laws of quantum mechanics: the theory that physics works differently at the atomic and subatomic scale.

By considering "all possible routes simultaneously," quantum computers have the potential to solve complex problems much faster than traditional computers, even really powerful ones. The potential here is immense. As Brown once told me, "It honestly changes everything," "this will be one for the history books," and "this is absolutely a moon landing."[404]

Let me now take a moment to re-emphasize that we are just in the beginning stages of exploring this type of technology. When reading about quantum computers, you might be picturing something comparable to your desktop computer, or maybe even some wardrobe-sized, black-plastic-wrapped server. But quantum computers do not resemble a typical computer, at least not today. Many look more like a weird, futuristic chandelier, featuring cascading, spiraling, interlocking brass tubes. And these devices require very precise conditions to operate properly. Quantum computers need to be carefully constructed and housed in an incredibly cold environment, where the temperature is kept near absolute zero.[405]

Despite this complexity, mega corporations and venture capitalists such as Google, IBM, and D-Wave have lined up to invest in quantum computers in recent years. In 2017 and 2018, venture capitalists invested $450 million into companies working on quantum computing.[406] These firms and venture capitalists are betting big on this technology because the upside is astronomical.

All computers exist to solve problems. Some problems are simple. When you type 2+2 into a calculator and hit "Enter," the computer spits out the answer "4" instantaneously. You don't need an advanced computer to solve that problem. How about something slightly more complex? Say you want to find a list of restaurants that are (1) near you, (2) currently open, and (3) serve hamburgers. Right now, you can pull out your phone, type in your query, and in a matter of seconds, the computer will sift through the Internet, reference your geolocation, and provide you with a nicely organized list of currently open restaurants near you that serve hamburgers. It will even provide you with a map of the locations and options for driving directions in case you can't wait another minute for a hot and juicy burger. But what about something far more complex?

A problem that is often discussed during particularly lively parties among computer scientists is called the "traveling salesman problem." The traveling salesman problem asks one to determine the shortest possible path between a given set of cities. The problem may seem simple at first. A list of five cities is given to someone who is responsible for solving the challenge. All that person has to do is measure each option between the five cities and then choose the shortest distance.

However, the problem grows in complexity the more cities are added to the list.[407] With five cities, there are only a dozen or so possible routes. But when the list grows to ten cities, the route options grow into the thousands. If the list of cities is in the hundreds, the number of route options explodes to a number I can barely comprehend. With this many options, even the most advanced supercomputers in the world would take an unreasonable amount of time to provide every possible route.[408] This is where quantum computers come in. As Microsoft notes on its website, "[quantum computing] would allow scientists to do computations in minutes or hours that would take the lifetime of the universe on even the most advanced classical computers we use today."[409]

When quantum computers are developed to a point where they can outperform even the most advanced supercomputers in the world, we will have reached "quantum supremacy." Some scientists believe we have already gotten to this point.

In October 2019, Google announced it had achieved quantum supremacy. Scientists at Google used quantum computing to solve an extremely complex theoretical math problem, a problem so complex that they estimated the most advanced classical computer in the world would require 10,000 years to solve it. The quantum computer solved it in 200 seconds.[410]

This landmark achievement was quickly disputed by IBM, another major player in the field. IBM claims its Summit supercomputer at Oak Ridge National Laboratory could solve the same question in two and a half days—slower than Google's 200 seconds, but hey, it's still better than 10,000 years.[411]

In August 2022, Google's claim of quantum supremacy was again challenged. A team at the Chinese Academy of Sciences used a traditional supercomputer to simulate quantum processes, which solved the problem in fifteen hours. They also claimed that if they had run their processes on IBM's Summit, they could have reduced that time to just a few seconds.[412]

Even if Google did jump the gun when it claimed quantum supremacy, it seems like that moment is inevitable. Quantum computers are being scaled up in the same way classic computers have been for decades.

Quantum computers' processing power is measured in qubits. I won't even begin to try to tell you about the technological definition of a *qubit*, but all you need to know is that the more qubits a quantum computer has, the more powerful it is. Also, additional qubits don't expand processing power linearly but exponentially. For every additional qubit added to a quantum computer, the processing speed doubles.[413] And while academics are debating over the legitimacy of Google's 2019 quantum supremacy claim, firms around the world are racing to build ever-larger quantum computers.

Sycamore, the quantum computer Google used to achieve the 200-second record, consisted of 54 qubits. Scientists at the University of Science and Technology of China have since developed Zuchongzhi, a quantum computer with 60 qubits. In November 2022, IBM announced it had built Osprey, a quantum computer with 433 qubits of processing power. This computer has more than three times as many qubits as their previous "most powerful quantum computer," named Eagle, released just one year prior.[414] And the race doesn't seem to be slowing down.

Dr. Darío Gil, Senior Vice President and Director of Research at IBM, said, "The new 433 qubit 'Osprey' processor brings us a step closer to the point where quantum computers will be used to tackle previously unsolvable problems." IBM's short-term plans for the technology include producing machines with more than 4,000 qubits in or around the year 2025.[415] If Google's 54-qubit quantum computer didn't officially achieve quantum supremacy, I think the 4,000-qubit version should do the trick.

So besides solving theoretical math problems and finding traveling routes for an imaginary salesman, what can a quantum computer actually do? While these tests don't demonstrate real-life applications, they do show the scale of problems these devices can handle. Companies probably don't need to calculate the route of a salesman between a thousand cities, but some, such as UPS or Amazon, might want to know how to optimize the handling and delivery of millions of packages. Or how about air traffic control networks that oversee thousands of planes arriving and departing? Having the ability to run enormous simulations in a matter of seconds could result in millions of dollars in savings for some of the largest companies in the world.

One of the first practical applications of quantum computers came in 2017, when Volkswagen and D-Wave Systems used quantum computers to optimize traffic patterns in China. The data had been collected from ten thousand taxis in Beijing. The test worked. Robert Ewald, president of D-Wave International, proudly announced, "In a short period of time, the experts at Volkswagen were able to success-fully create and test an algorithm on our quantum computer for an important type of optimization problem."[416]

As quantum computers become more powerful and more abun-dant, we should expect to hear about additional examples of these practical applications. These machines, however, will only be used by a privileged few. Only the largest firms will be able to buy access to this technology, potentially leading to a greater concentration of wealth.

IBM is already promoting that its quantum technology can be used for "targeting and prediction, asset trading optimization, and risk profiling."[417] Imagine how much money massive asset manage-ment firms like BlackRock stand to earn from a quantum computer that can sift through endless amounts of data in seconds and provide investment advice that surpasses anything the human mind can produce. How will regular investors ever compete with gigantic firms empowered by quantum computers?

Many analysts believe quantum computing will open new doors in a number of other industries too, including pharmaceuticals. Quantum computers can help big pharma simulate molecules down to their atomic structure, giving scientists the ability to experiment at a level that was previously impossible.[418] This could lead to the development of drugs and cures once outside humans' capacity, saving millions of lives. But it might also make it virtu-ally impossible for smaller competitors to compete with established pharmaceutical businesses.

Quantum computers also pose significant security risks. A computer that harnesses the power to simulate molecules and traffic patterns of entire cities could also be used to eviscerate modern encryption techniques. An advanced encryption that would keep a supercomputer busy for decades could be turned to Swiss cheese in seconds by the right quantum computer. This could mean even the most locked-down secrets might soon be vulnerable to hackers armed with quantum technology.[419]

While some experts say we are still a long way off from the realization of this fear, governments are already starting to take notice. In July 2022, the U.S. National Institute of Standards and Technologies announced it was working with four "quantum-resistant cryptographic algorithms in an attempt to protect encrypted databases from a quantum attack."[420] The decision came four years after the U.S. government launched its National Quantum Initiative.[421] This initiative "calls for a coordinated Federal program to accelerate quantum research and development for the economic and national security of the United States."[422]

Not to be left behind, over the past several years, China has been investing billions of dollars into quantum technology. This includes building a $10 billion research center for quantum applications in Hefei, China. The lab is intended to support private research efforts as well as projects run by the country's military.[423]

Quantum computing may still be in its early stages, but it is already starting to have an impact on public policy. And if the technology is perfected, we will see increasingly more quantum computing applications used in different sectors and industries globally.

And these aren't even the craziest things I have learned about quantum computers. In chapter 6, I will show you how this technology can be used to control society on a level that will absolutely blow your mind. (Sorry to keep you waiting on that one, but once you read chapter 6, you'll understand why I'm holding off now.)

A WHOLE NEW WORLD

The Fourth Industrial Revolution will cause unprecedented economic growth *and* disruption. Klaus Schwab and his friends at the WEF know that, and they are preparing. Are you? Are your friends? How about your family members? It is a hard truth but one that absolutely cannot be ignored: Americans aren't ready for the changes coming their way, and that must change soon or else there won't be a free world left to save.

Some readers of this book will surely believe they can escape many of the problems coming our way by refusing to participate in emerging technologies. No one is going to force you to enter the metaverse, wear augmented reality goggles, or adhere to the advice of quantum computers. You might not be able to stop the world from going full steam ahead off a cliff, but you and your family don't need to join them.

That's a nice thought, and some probably will be able to pull it off. But most won't have the resources to avoid the crises ahead. Their employers, children, or local or national governments will effectively force them to enter this exciting but troublesome new phase of human history.

More importantly, the ownership and management of property, including real property such as homes, is becoming increasingly consolidated in the hands of the same institutions that have been lauding the Great Reset and Great Narrative movements from the very start. It is easy to *say* you will keep your world separate from theirs, but if it becomes essentially impossible to own your own property, then what power will you actually have to chart your desired course in life?

You might think that could never happen—not in America, anyway. This is the land of the free. This is the country where owning your own home is called a national "dream." This is the place where "a man's home is his castle."[424] How could the United States ever become a country where most average families don't own their own property?

You're not going to like it, but the evidence shows that a troubling shift in property ownership is, in fact, already happening, and it's occurring much more rapidly than most of us ever could have imagined. Even worse, it involves some of the biggest players in the Great Reset and Great Narrative movements. That absolutely terrifying topic is the subject of my next chapter.

5

IN THE FUTURE, YOU WILL OWN NOTHING

WHEN THE MASTERMINDS AT THE WORLD ECONOMIC Forum write or talk about the coming Fourth Industrial Revolution, they often detail forthcoming technological advancements and elaborate on the disruptive effects that tech will likely cause for future generations and society. They also use open-ended predictions about the future to advocate for concepts and programs discussed in the first few chapters of this book. But rarely do Schwab and others at the WEF paint a comprehensive picture of what society will look like for everyday citizens in the wake of these far-reaching innovations. So when the World Economic Forum website published an article titled "Welcome to 2030. I Own Nothing, Have No Privacy, and Life Has Never Been Better," it caught my attention, along with millions of other people's.[425]

Ida Auken is the author of the now infamous article, which was originally posted to the WEF's website in 2016 but did not gain significant attention until 2020, following the launch of the WEF's Great Reset campaign. Auken is a Danish politician and was a member of the WEF's Young Global Leaders program at the time she wrote the piece.[426]

In the article, Auken depicts a future where the idea of property rights is flipped on its head. Writing from the perspective of a fictional citizen in the year 2030, Auken describes a world devoid of private ownership of homes, cars, and most other goods. In this world, people choose to "do things differently."

"It might seem odd to you," Auken writes, "but it makes perfect sense for us in this city. Everything you consider a product, has now become a service."[427] Instead of owning a home, people rent. Instead of owning a car, people use public transportation. Instead of purchasing appliances and other goods, they borrow products for a limited duration. This idea of renting or borrowing everything even extends to the clothes people wear.

"Shopping?" Auken says. "I can't really remember what that is. For most of us, it has been turned into choosing things to use." You see, since you will not actually own anything in the future, you are not really shopping.

Not owning much, if anything, might seem off-putting to most modern Americans, but it is a necessary concession to live in Auken's 2030 utopia. In 2030, according to her article, much of the labor and work will be done by robots and artificial intelligence. So instead of sitting in traffic to commute to a nine-to-five job, people are free to enjoy life, eat and sleep well, and spend time with friends and family.

These "new ways of doing things" are so good in 2030, it has made life much more efficient and enjoyable. When you are not using an appliance, it is available to borrow for someone else who wants it. When you are traveling and not using your living room, it can be repurposed so that it can be used for "business meetings." (Wait a second. I thought in this utopian world most people aren't working. I guess that means your living room is less likely to be repurposed for a business meeting and more likely to host biweekly jam sessions for Dave's band or maybe Debbie's goat yoga class.)

According to Auken, in her imagined 2030 society, people have shifted away from the "same model of growth" that dictates much of our modern public policy debates. By "do[ing] things differently," the people of Auken's future world have eliminated "lifestyle diseases, climate change, the refugee crisis, environmental degradation, completely congested cities, water pollution, air pollution, social unrest, and unemployment."

Sounds great, right? We can eliminate all these terrible things and all we have to do is give up private-property ownership. What a deal. I'm sure there are plenty of people who would clamor to sign up to live in Auken's fantastical world—most of whom could be found at Democratic Socialists of America meetings.

When Auken's article started to receive significant attention in 2020, many conservatives and limited-government advocates were shocked and alarmed, a development that seemed to bewilder many of the leaders at the World Economic Forum. After all, nowhere in this piece does the author suggest *governments* should be in control of everything. If this future is simply the result of private actors making voluntary interactions, shouldn't those who support limited government accept Auken's outlook for humanity? There are some conservatives and libertarians who say yes. (I'll explain why they are dead wrong later.)

Making matters more complicated, many media pundits on the right mistakenly read Auken's WEF article as if it were an official policy proposal offered by the World Economic Forum.[428] This problem became so widespread that the author had to add a special note to the article explaining that it was not intended to be a policy framework but rather a "scenario showing where we could be heading—for better and for worse." Auken further explained that she "wrote this piece to start a discussion about some of the pros and cons of the current technological development."[429]

I don't totally buy Auken's description of her goals, but I agree that many at the WEF believe the Age of Disruption ahead is mostly inevitable and that all leaders in business and government can do today is to work to shape that future in a way that fits with the values espoused by elites.

Regardless of the intentions of the author and the article's publisher, when Auken's piece started to get the traction it rightly deserves, it scared the heck out of tens of millions of people around the world, myself included. And once you couple this potential future with the concepts of the Great Reset and the Great Narrative, it will really scare the heck out of you. If most people lose the ability to own property, for whatever reason, life will not be like the utopia Auken describes. Instead, most citizens will effectively have no economic or social power, very few freedoms, and no ability to give their children a better life than the one they have enjoyed. People might have access to cheap stuff and services, but there will still be a price, and a steep one at that—the end of liberty.

THE FUTURE WILL NOT BE ON VHS

To most, the idea of not owning anything probably seems like a far-off concept, especially when you think about it through the lens of the capitalistic, consumer-centric culture that we now live in. How could we possibly shift toward a society like the one described in Auken's "You'll Own Nothing" article? The answer is *gradually*. And I say this with confidence because we can already see this trend playing out in a number of industries today.

For example, one aspect of our economy where the idea of owning nothing has developed the fastest is the entertainment industry. Technological innovation has dramatically altered the way we access movies, television, short films, podcasts, music, and other forms of entertainment.

Prior to the mid-1970s, if you wanted to see a movie, you would either watch whatever was on television or head down to the local movie theater. It was not until the advent of Betamax and VHS that the general public had the ability to buy their favorite movies and watch them whenever they wanted at home.[430] This development caused the home entertainment industry to boom. As more people purchased technology to watch movies in the comfort of their own living rooms, prices fell, home entertainment technology advanced, and movie studios focused more attention on selling already released movies to consumers on videotape cassettes.[431]

Videotape soon gave way to DVD, and by 2005, DVD sales generated more than $15 billion in revenue per year.[432] With new releases selling for $20 and dollar bins popping up at Blockbuster video stores everywhere, private movie collections grew. (*Author's Note*: For readers under the age of thirty, Blockbuster was a chain of movie-rental stores where people spent hours looking for a movie to watch based solely on its cover picture printed on a small box representing the movie. Families would take these movies home and if they failed to rewind VHS tapes before returning the films, Blockbuster would fine you. If you made the grave error of losing one of Blockbuster's videotapes, they would take possession of your car or force you to enter indentured servitude, whichever the company thought would be more profitable.)

But then something unexpected happened. At the height of Blockbuster's empire, physical media sales and rentals started to fall. By 2018, DVD sales had dropped a whopping 86 percent from their height in 2005. Blu-ray, once billed as the next generation of home video, peaked in 2013 before rapidly falling in the years that followed.[433] What caused this incredible drop? Were people suddenly disinterested in movies and home entertainment? Of course not. Innovation happened.

Streaming services such as Netflix and Hulu changed the entertainment industry forever. Advancements in Internet speeds and tech devices created an environment in which consumers could buy access to a streaming service and watch as many movies as they wanted, including films made a half-century earlier, as opposed to buying a DVD from a brick-and-mortar store. By 2020, streaming services represented more than 70 percent of all home video revenue.[434] And with companies such as Disney and HBO investing increasingly more money into their streaming services, this trend is sure to continue in the years ahead.

Streaming services offer a deal that's too good to pass up. Instead of paying $65 to buy a DVD boxset of the newest season of your favorite TV show, you could use that $65 to buy access to a streaming service for eight months, watch every season of your favorite show, and have access to thousands of other shows and movies too. Just like how "video killed the radio star," consumer preference and technological innovation killed physical media. That's a good thing, right?

I'll admit that I didn't think there was a problem with any of this when the trend started. I love streaming services as much as the next guy. But as institutions have become more political and closely tied to government over the past several years, serious problems with this model have become increasingly more apparent. And the biggest problem of them all is that when you no longer own media in a physical format, the version available to you through a streaming service can be altered over time to promote a specific agenda, or even eliminated altogether.

Occasionally, I will head over to a mostly forgotten shelf in my home where I have a collection of old DVDs (and yes, even a few VHS tapes) and pull out a classic movie to watch, like *Top Gun.* What can I say? Sometimes, I feel the need—the need for speed. And when I pop that disc into the DVD player, I rest assured that Maverick and Iceman's adventure will play out on my television set exactly as it did when I watched it for the first time in 1987. And when I watch that DVD for the one-thousandth time twenty years from now, it will still be exactly the way I remember it from the 1980s. While this might seem like a relatively unimportant feature of physical media, it is actually becoming an important luxury.

The data printed onto a disc or recorded onto a cassette are there permanently. If the physical media remains undamaged, I will have access to that data forever. But this is not the case when dealing with streaming services. The data for a movie as it exists on a streaming service's servers, like those owned by Netflix, are fluid. At any time, Netflix could take down *Top Gun,* its copyright owners could alter the movie, and then Netflix could reupload it without any warning to the consumer at home. They can do this because *you* don't own the content. *They* own it. You are merely renting access to the film.

Over the past decade, numerous companies with streaming services have been caught or openly bragged about using their power to change content based on public pressure and to promote "social justice." In June 2020, in the midst of widespread Black Lives Matter protests, a number of streaming services began to reevaluate some of the content available in their libraries. HBO removed the 1939 Oscar-winning classic *Gone with the Wind* after screenwriter John Ridley wrote an op-ed for the *Los Angeles Times* saying the movie "glorifies the antebellum south" and "perpetuate[s] some of the most painful stereotypes of people of color."[435]

HBO has since restored the film to its streaming service, but the movie is now preceded by a four-minute lecture highlighting the controversial aspects of the film and the racist practices of Hollywood at the time of the film's production. "Watching *Gone with the Wind* can be uncomfortable, even painful," warns the Turner Classic Movies representative.[436] I don't know about you, but nothing gets me in the mood to watch a movie like a stern lecture from my cultural betters.

Further, in June 2020, a number of streaming services purged any depiction of "blackface" from their content libraries. And no, I'm not talking about the nineteenth-century plays streaming on Vaudeville+; I'm talking about episodes of shows many readers of this book watch regularly, such as NBC's *30 Rock* and *Community*, FX's *It's Always Sunny in Philadelphia,* and ABC's *Scrubs.* Even *Golden Girls* had an episode purged.[437] In most of the cases mentioned above, the show is completely self-aware of the offensive nature of this practice, and it's part of a comedic scene that mocks it.

In one instance in the show *The Office,* for example, a scene was removed in which Dwight, one of the show's main characters, has a friend who sports blackface.[438] In the episode, it is made very clear that this is a socially unacceptable practice. Dwight's ignorance of social norms *is* the joke. But that nuance doesn't matter to elites running the entertainment industry. Now these episodes are forever unavailable on streaming services.

In October 2020, Disney announced it was going to add disclaimers to the beginning of a number of its movies warning viewers about "negative depictions" and the "mistreatment of people or cultures." These warning have been added to classic movies such as *Peter Pan, Dumbo, The Aristocats,* and *Aladdin.*[439]

The music- and podcast-streaming service Spotify has also moderated content due to social pressure. Podcasting giant Joe Rogan had more than one-hundred episodes removed by Spotify because of alleged instances of "misinformation," which included "dangerous" things like interviewing Dr. Robert Malone, a scientist who helped to develop mRNA vaccines.[440]

And don't expect the censors to stop there. Censorship campaigns have become increasingly more common in recent years, even when it comes to completely uncontroversial media. For example, after the 2020 election, a movement captured headlines to have Donald Trump removed from *Home Alone 2*. The campaign got so much attention that even *Home Alone* actor Macaulay Culkin responded to it in a tweet.[441] Trump's appearance didn't involve controversial political commentary, but his mere presence in the movie was enough to outrage censorship mobs seeking to purify classic films.

The point of all of this is to say, when you don't own physical media, that media is susceptible to change. The corporations that *do* own the media can do whatever they want with it. If a show contains a joke that is considered too cruel or tasteless by current societal norms, delete it. If a movie's depiction of a person, gender, orientation, or race is no longer socially acceptable, change it. If you hold a movie, show, or even a piece of music near and dear to your heart, you might want to consider owning a physical copy, because nothing is stopping the corporation that owns it from altering or destroying it completely if the political winds blow hard enough. And in the era of the Great Reset, it may not even require a particularly strong political or ideological wind to destroy media. ESG and other social credit systems might make the decisions for these companies easy. Do you think media companies are going to take your personal preferences into account if it means suffering with a reduced ESG score? If you do, you should probably reread chapter 1.

Now, you might be thinking, *Glenn, why are you spending so much time talking about movies and streaming services? I picked up this book to read about the future and the World Economic Forum. What does this have to do with property rights and private ownership?* Well, just think about the control these corporations have over your media when you don't own it, and then imagine what they could do in a world where you don't own *anything* and they (corporations and government) own *everything*.

WHEN THEY OWN YOUR HOME

For the entire history of the United States, homeownership has been recognized as an important part of the American dream. Owning property provides people with financial security as well as with a sense of responsibility over their land and the surrounding community. However, after decades of homeownership being an essential part of life in America, a trend has developed that's transforming the United States into a nation of renters. If this continues, this development will not only have a substantial impact on working families' ability to build wealth, but it could also have dire consequences for individual liberty.

Owning your own home comes with a plethora of financial benefits. As you pay down your mortgage or as your home appreciates in value, homeowners build equity. Tax laws have been written to ease the burden on homeowners. Historically, property has proven itself to be an asset that effectively weathers financial storms and bouts of inflation.[442, 443] Studies show growth in wealth yielded from homeownership overshadows every other form of wealth generation.[444]

Owning a home has proven itself to be such an important component to personal wealth generation that numerous presidential administrations have campaigned on increasing homeownership.[445] In fact, both the Bill Clinton and George W. Bush administrations pursued policies designed specifically to encourage homeownership.[446, 447] (Of course, as with most things the government tries, these policies resulted in a disastrous housing-market meltdown, but that is a topic for a different book.)

Taking all this into account, it should be no surprise that home-ownership rates have for decades remained consistently high in the United States. According to stats compiled by the Federal Reserve Bank of St. Louis, homeownership has hovered above 60 percent since at least the mid-1960s. The rate peaked in 2005, when home-ownership creeped above 69 percent. By the end of 2022, the rate had slipped to just under 66 percent, but still well within the average historical range.[448]

But unfortunately for Americans who yearn to join the home-ownership club, there are major headwinds that developed in recent years that have the potential to drive this rate much lower than we have seen in the modern era.

SKYROCKETING PRICES

If you have spent any time at all looking at the housing market over the past several years, then you know that housing prices have soared, making it extremely difficult for many young and work-ing-class people to purchase a home.

The St. Louis Federal Reserve compiles data measuring the average sales price of houses sold in the United States. According to the St. Louis Fed, the average sales price for houses in the United States increased by nearly 40 percent from the first quarter of 2020 to the fourth quarter of 2022.[449] The average cost of buying a home at the end of 2022 was more than $152,000 higher than it was just two years earlier.

The increase in housing costs is especially stark when you start from the market high recorded before the housing crash of 2007–08 to the end of 2022. From the market high in 2007 to the second quarter of 2022, housing prices increased by more than 66 percent.[450] And from the first quarter of 2000 to the fourth quarter of 2022, housing prices rose by more than 164 percent.[451]

The dramatic increase in the cost of housing is leaving many financially incapable of buying a home. In October 2021, a survey conducted by the Pew Research Center found that 49 percent of adults in the United States believe housing availability and affordability were "major problem[s]" where they live.[452]

Rising housing prices are affecting younger people more than most other demographics. More millennials than ever are renting as opposed to buying. In fact, according to a recent study conducted by RentCafe in 2021, "The share of applications for apartments from renters who earn more than $50,000 is at its highest level in five years, 39 percent, as many would-be Millennial homebuyers were priced out of an overly competitive real estate market in 2021."[453]

At the time this book went to print, there was a growing amount of evidence amassing that suggests housing prices could soon tumble, but there has yet to be any data at all that indicates a full or even nearly full price correction is likely to take place soon. Housing sales prices will likely remain high for years to come.

There are many reasons why the price of homes has increased. Inflation caused by poor monetary policy can increase the price of nearly everything over time. Government policies can also exacerbate inflation or limit the supply of homes, also causing prices to rise. Long-standing government zoning restrictions, for example, have slowed construction of new housing for decades in states such as California.[454] Supply-chain disasters caused by the 2020 COVID-19 lockdowns have also exacerbated the problem.

But perhaps the most underrated issue affecting the housing market is that large institutional investment firms like Blackstone are buying massive amounts of houses across the country and turning them into rental properties. Blackstone is a private equity firm that oversees assets in excess of $880 billion.[455] In addition to managing pension fund investments and other financial securities,

Blackstone has in recent years grown a taste for buying up large quantities of single-family homes.

Blackstone first started purchasing homes in significant quantities in 2012, when the housing market was at one of its lowest points following the 2008 housing crash. Blackstone partnered with regional investment firms to help with their plan, supplying them with capital to buy houses in markets like Dallas and Phoenix. In the spring of 2012, the partnership spun off under the name Invitation Homes.[456] That's when things really took off, with Invitation Homes buying gigantic amounts of houses in growing markets across the United States.

The firm started by targeting specific locations like Tampa Bay. According to a 2012 article in the *Tampa Bay Times*, "A Wall Street behemoth plans to spend $1 billion on Tampa Bay's hobbled housing market, dispatching teams of brokers to scour neighborhoods and buy hundreds of homes a month." The plan was to buy "as many as 15,000 homes in Tampa Bay" over the course of a few years, many of which had been involved in a foreclosure.[457]

Quoted in the same article was Peter Murphy, CEO of Home Encounter, a manager of rental homes in the Tampa Bay area. Murphy said, "It's a land grab unlike anything we've ever seen. You're going to drive through parts of town and all of it is going to be institutionally owned."[458]

By the late 2010s, Invitation Homes was in the process of buying houses in communities throughout the United States, spending as much as $150 million *per week* on houses.[459] And by 2020, Invitation Homes owned more than eighty thousand rental houses spanning sixteen large markets.[460] It's true that this number is small compared to the sheer number of single-family homes in America, but Invitation Homes isn't the only institutional investor pursuing this strategy, and it isn't content with owning homes in the tens of thousands or even the hundreds of thousands either. In a 2018 article in *D Magazine*, Invitation

Homes CFO Ernie Freedman told a reporter, "If we can keep growing at a nice pace, we are never going to own 16 million homes, but maybe we'll own 1 million or 2 million."

Invitation Homes went public in 2017, raising more than $1.5 billion in an initial public offering.[461] While Blackstone did eventually cash out from its spinoff rental corporation, it did not abandon its rental-property-buying ambitions. The investment powerhouse reentered the rental housing market in 2020 when it purchased a minority share in Tricon Residential, a property management company that owns more than thirty thousand single-family and multifamily rental homes located throughout the United States and Canada.[462]

In June 2021, Blackstone agreed to buy Home Partners of America for $6 billion. At that time, Home Partners owned more than seventeen thousand houses across the country.[463]

In February 2022, Blackstone announced it planned to spend another $6 billion to buy Preferred Apartment Communities. At the time of the purchase, Preferred Apartment Communities owned forty-four multifamily communities and roughly twelve thousand housing units throughout Southeastern America.[464]

Dwarfing those numbers, Blackstone revealed in regulatory filings in July 2022 that it had secured $50 billion to buy real estate in the event of a coming housing downturn.[465] And in case you're not a math wizard like me, $50 billion can buy an estimated one-crapload of houses.

There are also numerous other corporations that make money buying up homes and leasing them to people. According to the *Washington Post*, in 2021 "investors bought nearly one in seven homes sold in America's top metropolitan areas."[466]

The *New York Times Magazine* referred to this corporate spending spree as a "$60 Billion Housing Grab by Wall Street" in an article published in 2020. According to the magazine:

Wall Street's latest real estate grab has ballooned to roughly $60 billion, representing hundreds of thousands of properties. In some communities, it has fundamentally altered housing ecosystems in ways we're only now beginning to understand, fueling a housing recovery without a homeowner recovery.

"That's the big downside," says Daniel Immergluck, a professor of urban studies at Georgia State University. "During one of the greatest recoveries of land value in the history of the country, from 2010 and 2011 at the bottom of the crisis to now, we've seen huge gains in property values, especially in suburbs, and instead of that accruing to many moderate-income and middle-income homeowners, many of whom were pushed out of the homeownership market during the crisis, that land value has accrued to these big companies and their shareholders."[467]

According to an analysis by Yardi Matrix, a commercial real estate data and research firm, 40 percent of single-family rental properties will be owned by large institutions by the end of the decade.[468]

Ryan Dezember, author of the book *Under Water: How Our American Dream of Homeownership Became a Nightmare*, explained in an article for the *Daily Beast* in 2020 that large corporations' increased appetite for single-family homes is due in part to their use of new technologies.[469] According to Dezember, major players in this game "deployed sophisticated computer programs to find the most desirable homes moments after being listed for sale."[470] Dezember notes this change has given companies like Blackstone and Invitation Homes a distinct advantage over individuals and mom-and-pop operations, who used to rule the rental-home business industry.[471]

The same kind of algorithms that have come to dominate how content is prioritized on the Internet are now being used in the housing market to tip the scales in favor of major corporations, and investors' use of technology and algorithms to buy houses is still growing. Zillow, the largest real estate listing website in America, has developed a system called iBuying, which it based in part on strategies utilized by real estate startups such as Opendoor and Offerpad. iBuying is a "high-tech (property) flipping" system that uses algorithms to develop and interpret data to determine housing prices and line up investor cash so that Zillow can purchase an available home.[472] The system further helps Zillow find services to improve houses and then sell the properties for a large profit. In 2021, iBuying purchases accounted for tens of billions of dollars in home sales.[473]

Not only is technology helping these corporations purchase homes, but it is also allowing them to manage the massive amount of properties they control. Cloud-based property management technologies have provided wealthy firms that control a large portfolio of homes the ability to keep track of everything from rent collection to routine maintenance.[474] Owning, leasing, and maintaining tens of thousands of houses across the country was once a logistical impossibility, even for many big corporations. Today, it's becoming an increasingly common practice for large investment firms and real estate giants.

When did large investment companies decide to start purchasing huge numbers of single-family homes, and where did they get the idea? According to Dezember, the trend toward increased corporate ownership of rental properties likely began in 2011, just one year before Blackstone entered the market. In 2011, Morgan Stanley, a $100 billion American investment and financial services company, released a report about a potential shift in attitudes toward a "rentership society."[475] In the report, the banking giant forecasted "a surge in the number of renters and a potentially massive opportunity for investors to convert the glut of repossessed homes into rental properties."[476] Now, Morgan Stanley might not be led by Klaus Schwab, but it is an official WEF "partner" and it has been heavily involved in Schwab's stakeholder capitalism, pro-ESG movement for years.[477]

A NATION OF RENTERS

In the "Welcome to 2030" article published on the World Economic Forum's website in 2016, author Ida Auken wrote, "I don't own a house. . . . Everything you considered a product, has now become a service." Despite her "author's note" that claimed the article was not meant to be considered a "utopia or dream of the future," she still admitted it "is a scenario showing where we could be heading."[478] Well, considering the multiple articles I'm going to talk about next, it seems pretty obvious that Auken was right. Countless writers, business leaders, and analysts are now predicting that the United States will soon become a "nation of renters." And in many cases, they don't seem too bothered by it.

For example, the *Tampa Bay Times* also reported in 2012 that Nick Pavonetti—owner of PDC Group, a Florida-based firm that helped Blackstone secure homes in the Tampa Bay region—said that America is "moving more toward a nation of renters. And we want to provide a product to meet that demand."[479]

Oh, thank you so much, Nick. I am so glad you are helping giant investment corporations like Blackstone buy up ridiculous amounts of homes so working families can forever rent from them instead of just buying houses on their own. You really are looking out for the little guy.

In an article published in 2021 by Bloomberg.com, opinion columnist Karl W. Smith argued that "America should become a nation of renters" and that "the very features that made housing an affordable and stable investment are coming to an end."[480]

According to Smith, who previously worked as vice president for federal tax policy at the Tax Foundation, houses are comparatively illiquid investments that can take a lot of time and effort to sell or buy or can hang homeowners out to dry when markets move downward. Smith also makes the case that widespread homeownership can result in a "less dynamic and mobile" America where homeowners, fearful of the potential impact to their home value, "are reluctant to agree to development" in surrounding areas. In Smith's worldview, and others that share his "nation of renters" outlook, renters are freer to travel to different locations and try out different lifestyles.

I know this is going to make me sound old, but doesn't this rhetoric sound exactly like it was crafted for millennials? I can see the inevitable television and radio commercials now: "Nothing can contain the free spirit that is the person who grew up in the Information Age of the 2000s. Want to chase your dreams in a big city such as New York or Los Angeles? Don't buy, rent! Oh, looks like Texas is the place to be, now? No need to sell your home and look for real estate. Just rent!"

Writers for the *Atlantic* put a fun, socialist twist on the idea in a 2021 article titled "Renting Is Terrible. Owning Is Worse." In this piece, author Shane Phillips, manager of the Randall Lewis Housing Initiative for the UCLA Lewis Center for Regional Policy Studies, wrote, "Mass homeownership shouldn't be our societal objective—it fails too many people and perpetuates too many historical inequities to remain the sole symbol of success in the housing market.

"We deserve another option, and public ownership could be it," Phillips concluded.[481]

So let me get this straight. In Phillips' fantasy world, instead of *Blackstone* owning my house, the *government* would own it? Wow.

Just when you think an idea can't get any worse, a socialist comes along and proves you wrong.

Regardless of whether people can be fooled into thinking renting is the ideal choice, the fact is, tens of millions of Americans might have no choice in the matter. Countless analysts think this is the direction the country is headed in, no matter how much demand for ownership exists. In a 2020 interview with *Yahoo! Finance*, noted real estate investor Grant Cardone said, "We're going to become a renter nation in this country. Renting will become the economic choice and the desirable choice again."[482]

DOES HOMEOWNERSHIP MATTER?

At this point, some readers might be wondering whether any of this really matters. Perhaps renting isn't so bad after all. While there is no denying that there are advantages to living in a society in which most people are renting homes and cars, they are far outweighed by significant disadvantages, especially when it comes to people's freedoms.

Earlier in the chapter, I outlined some of the many important financial advantages of owning a home, but the truth is, this chapter isn't really about wealth building. This chapter is about power and control. When you own property, you have control. When you own a house, you can mostly do whatever you want with it. It's yours, so you make the rules. Want to remodel? Go for it. It's yours. Want to sublease a room to a friend? Go for it. It's yours. Want to adopt a dozen cats? I'd invest in a few self-cleaning litter boxes and an air purifier first, but go for it. It's your cat-infested house, so you can do whatever you want. But when you are a renter, you can't just "go for it," because it isn't yours. The home you live in belongs to someone else, so they make the rules.

Landlords can impose all sorts of requirements and regulations when you're living under *their* roof. Standard rules include things like prohibitions on pet ownership and smoking tobacco.[483] Some renters have a "no party" clause in their contract, while others aren't even allowed to consume alcohol.[484, 485] Although it is true that a landlord can't prohibit you from *owning* a firearm, they can ban you from *possessing* that weapon while living in his or her house. In fact, a breach of that restriction could be used as justification to evict a tenant.[486] There are a few states, such as Minnesota, that prohibit landlords from restricting the "lawful carry or possession of firearms by tenants or their guests," but the vast majority of states allow firearms restrictions, including in many places where state legislatures are dominated by lawmakers who say they are devoted to protecting gun rights.

How can landlords get away with such extreme rules and regulations? Because they are not required to adhere to the Bill of Rights or the rest of the Constitution. The right to bear arms and freedom of speech only protect citizens from rules imposed by government, not by private businesses.

The consolidation of homeownership will only make this problem worse as the years go by. Ordinarily, when one business imposes rules or costs you find intolerable, you can find another business that will be more lenient or affordable. That's the brilliance of market economics. But when one or a small number of businesses are buying up properties all across the country at the same time, the market becomes smaller and smaller, giving people fewer options.

Now, you could be thinking, *Corporations are out to make money, so surely they won't impose any unnecessary restrictions that could anger a potential client.* While that is a very logical and free-market-orientated way of looking at the situation, you need to remember that America is quickly moving toward a post–Great Reset world in which ESG corporate social credit systems are everywhere and in full effect. It's only a matter of time before individual renters will be subjected to ESG rules in one form or another.

Real estate investors are already focusing more attention on ESG and so-called sustainability practices. According to an article published by Deloitte, one of the "Big Four" accounting firms that helped draft the WEF's ESG metrics, real estate investors are eagerly incorporating ESG into some of their property valuations. According to Deloitte, "ESG is therefore here to stay and will increasingly shape and influence real estate valuation, and therefore real estate investment, as investors wish to allocate their commitments under this banner."[487]

Remember, ESG is more than just a scheme to make money. ESG is an engine capable of transforming how economies and societies operate. Do you really think ESG will stop at environmental concerns and real estate valuations? Or will the wannabe central planners at the WEF and elsewhere realize that they can use the power of ESG to achieve all sorts of goals normally pursed by elected lawmakers, such as stopping gun violence? It's possible that these decisions won't even be in the hands of the landlords themselves. Instead, financial institutions such as banks could incentivize corporate landlords to restrict access to "undesirable" possessions such as firearms. In a world where everybody rents, these choices will belong to corporations, banks, and investors. They will not belong to you.

A future where no one owns a house is unsettling enough. The financial consequences and lack of control that would stem from such a "you'll own nothing" set of policies should give pause to anyone who ignorantly thinks "this is just the natural flow of free markets." But what's worse is that the world depicted by Ida Auken in the "Welcome to 2030" article goes well beyond creating a "nation of renters."

When Auken describes her future living situation, she says, "In our city we don't pay any rent, because someone else is using our free space whenever we do not need it."[488] See, the future has become so efficient, according to Auken, that people don't even have to pay for a place to stay; living spaces pay for themselves by being repurposed whenever possible. This concept shares similarities with part of the World Economic Forum's "Future of Real Estate" report published in 2021. In one section of the report, the authors promote the idea of "hybrid working models that enhance employee experience and bolster productivity as well as innovation."[489] This could lead to what the authors describe as "co-working," where workspaces are designed to "enhance the livability of post-COVID office life."[490] These "co-working" spaces allow for "flexibility" in the use of buildings. Spaces could be designed to quickly transform to meet different needs.[491]

At first glance, this setup might sound similar to Airbnb's platform, where owners of a house or apartment can offer to rent their property on a short-term basis. When you get past the idea of strangers living in your house, sleeping in your bed, and having access to all your stuff, Airbnb allows for a very efficient use of a home. Why not make a little side money instead of leaving your house completely vacant when you're visiting family? And when you are wondering what the future looks like, it makes sense to assume we have pursued efficient practices such as these.

But in a "you'll own nothing" world, regular families wouldn't own much, if any, property, so the decision to repurpose homes would belong to massive corporations, not individuals. Absent legal protections imposed by government, corporations could eventually seek to maximize efficiency by turning living spaces into working spaces during the day, and back into living spaces at night. It's their property, after all, so if that's how they have determined to use it, who are you to say no?

A HOUSING SOCIAL CREDIT SCORE

If America were to become a "nation of renters," how would corporations or governments determine the most efficient way to divide
up property? You might be surprised to hear that some local
governments are already using a kind of social credit scoring system
to answer that question. The Coordinated Entry System (CES),
originally piloted in 2013 in Los Angeles, uses data-collection practices and algorithms to divide up resources and housing to as many
homeless people as possible and in "the most efficient and equitable
way."[492] How does CES do this?

In her 2018 book *Automating Inequality*, American political
scientist Virginia Eubanks describes how the CES system works
in detail. According to Eubanks, CES "collects, stores, and shares
some astonishingly intimate information about unhoused people.
It catalogs, classifies, and ranks their traumas, coping mechanisms,
feelings, and fears."[493] As part of the CES system, homeless people
are asked questions like, "Have you ever been sexually assaulted
while experiencing homelessness? Have you ever had to use violence
to keep yourself safe while experiencing homelessness? Have you
ever exchanged sex for a place to stay?"[494]

CES then uses algorithms to generate a score for each person
in the program. The score determines how needy each applicant
is. Depending on demand, the lowest-scoring applicants are denied
access to homes that they need. And if an applicant's score is high
enough to necessitate housing, a second algorithm is used to match
that person with a shelter that can best fit his or her needs.[495] (You
know, that "to each according to his needs" thing really sounds
familiar for some reason.[496] Huh.)

The CES social credit system has a ton of privacy issues (we'll
talk about that later), but that hasn't stopped it from becoming
popular in major cities throughout the United States. According to
Eubanks, "Its supporters include the US Department of Housing

and Urban Development (HUD), the National Alliance to End Homelessness, a myriad of local homeless service providers, and powerful funders, including the Conrad N. Hilton and Bill & Melinda Gates Foundation,"[497] both of which have ties to the WEF and its annual Davos meetings.

WHEN THEY OWN EVERYTHING

Large institutions are already swallowing up huge parts of the housing market in regions throughout the United States, but the technological developments of the Fourth Industrial Revolution will likely cause a similar pattern to develop in other markets, just as Auken predicted in her WEF article. Soon, technology really might reach a point where people don't need to own anything because subscription models for all kinds of property will be marketed as much more advantageous for the average consumer.

WHEN THEY OWN YOUR CAR

Despite constant attempts to build more mass-transit systems across the United States, such as busing, subways, or even high-speed rail, Americans have strongly adhered to an individual-centered approach to transportation—the personal automobile. Automobiles allow for people to travel anywhere they want, anytime they want, for whatever reason they want. It is one of the supreme ways in which Americans enjoy freedom. But with the technological advancements described in chapter 3, coupled with an ESG-like social credit framework, this expression of freedom could quickly disappear.

As I showed in chapter 3, it is entirely possible that Americans will see a complete overhaul in how the automobile industry operates within the decade, although some experts believe it won't happen until at least 2040, if at all. If automobiles eventually become fully autonomous, the days when individuals and families own their own vehicle to get from place to place could be nearly over. Instead, in a world full of autonomous cars, it is likely that a handful of large companies such as Google, Uber, Lyft, Tesla, and Amazon will own whole fleets of self-driving automobiles, which they will then rent to regular consumers, similar to how Uber and Lyft operate today.

An Uber-like automated-vehicle system would not be limited to a rigid schedule, and it could cater to the needs of individual customers. A passenger could order a car using a smartphone app, be picked up quickly, and be taken to a place of his or her choosing for only a modest fee. This model would allow passengers to reap the benefits of a personal automobile without having to suffer the drawbacks that come with owning a car. Passengers wouldn't have to worry about changing tires, paying for an oil change, or bringing the car into the shop when the engine starts making a weird clunking noise whenever it comes to a stop. Also, many of the financial benefits that come with owning a house don't apply to car ownership. Unlike a house, cars tend to depreciate in value quickly after they are purchased, so investment opportunities are nonexistent for most consumers.

Many of these factors have already resulted in a significant shift in people choosing to purchase a car. Rideshare company Lyft released a report in 2018 detailing its economic impact. According to Lyft, about one-quarter of its customers reported that they don't think it is important to own a personal vehicle anymore.[498] With Lyft boasting it can cater to 375 million people per year worldwide, this finding suggests about 90 million people globally are less likely to ever own a personal car because of one company alone.

As these technologies catch on, you should only expect this trend to increase. In January 2021, Uber released a report titled "Toward a New Model of Public Transportation" that outlined a number of ways in which the ridesharing company could supplement, and in some cases replace, elements of America's mass-transit system. The report explains "how Uber is offering public transportation agencies new tools to operate more efficient, connected, and equitable mobility networks." Uber could achieve this by integrating its services and technology to work alongside bus, train, and subway routes.[499, 500] Instead of forcing people to adhere to rigid bus and train schedules, Uber's tech and algorithms could allow for a greater flexibility to help more people get where they are going in an efficient way.

These companies aren't the only ones singing the praises of ride-sharing systems. In an article published by the World Economic Forum in July 2022, author Winnie Yeh advocates for the development of a "circular economy" to reduce inefficient uses of resources. One section of the article explains how car-sharing platforms can be used to make better use of people's cars, which often sit idly by during most of the day. The author further suggests people should embrace this sharing mindset to "redesign cities to reduce private vehicles and other usages."[501]

Of course, these changes could be great. They could disrupt the government's inefficient stranglehold on public transportation, allow people to travel without the requirement of owning a car, and provide opportunities for drivers to make a few bucks on the side. However, living in a world where you don't own a car comes with potential consequences. And those consequences would be exacerbated when the companies that run these ridesharing systems are manipulated by a corporate social credit system such as ESG.

CONTROLLING TRANSPORTATION

Because Uber and Lyft are ridesharing companies that help individuals sell their driving service to others, they allow a fair amount of discretion to drivers to decide what rides they will provide. As it currently stands, drivers can refuse service to anyone who violates community guidelines or simply makes them feel uncomfortable.[502] This system has led to a series of concerning service refusals.

For instance, in late 2017, conservative activist Laura Loomer was banned from using Uber and Lyft after she posted a series of tweets accusing the companies of hiring extremists. A spokesman for Uber justified the action by saying, "Ms. Loomer was banned for violating our Community Guidelines."[503] Regardless of what you think about the content of the post, it should trouble you that Loomer was banned from using multiple ridesharing services purely because of something she said on Twitter.

In the summer of 2018, Uber and Lyft gave their drivers permission to deny rides to people who appeared to be going to an admittedly repugnant "Unite the Right" rally in Washington, D.C. In a statement provided to CBS News, a Lyft spokesperson said about their drivers, "If they ever feel uncomfortable or disrespected by a passenger, they can cancel that ride."

Also in the summer of 2018, a group of Republican Capitol Hill interns were kicked out of an Uber car because a couple of the interns were wearing Make America Great Again hats. Unlike with the Unite the Right ban, it's harder to make the case that this decision by the Uber driver was based on the potential racism of the rider, considering one of the interns wearing a MAGA hat was a twenty-year-old black man named Matthew Handy.[504] Uber promised to look into the matter further, and as far as I can tell, they are still "looking"—and probably will be forever.

With these stories and the emerging ESG system in mind, is it really that hard to imagine a world where some political or ideological groups are targeted and prevented from using ridesharing services? I won't defend the Unite the Right rally, but is it difficult to envision that Uber and Lyft drivers could treat people attending a Trump rally similarly? Or any Republican rally for that matter? Is the March for Life going to be considered too extremist for Uber and Lyft? How about a Ron DeSantis campaign stop? And how does this system work in states where you're allowed by law to carry a firearm? Surely a driver could feel uncomfortable and refuse service to a person lawfully carrying a firearm.

You might say, "Well, Uber drivers can be conservative too. Maybe some drivers won't feel comfortable shuttling Republicans from place to place, but surely someone will." I think that is largely correct in a society where individual humans are driving vehicles. But it's possible that many of these decisions in the future won't be made by individuals. If large corporations can operate huge fleets of self-driving cars, they will be the ones who decide who is worthy of riding and who should be left at home. Algorithms and artificial intelligence could decide who should be serviced or in what order people should be serviced. An entirely objective system using these technologies might work effectively and fairly, but in Schwab's Great Narrative world, systems such as ESG and other social credit scores would provide the ruling elite with the opportunity to put their thumbs on the scale.

Remember that it was not driver discretion that banned Laura Loomer from using Uber and Lyft. Nor were its drivers who created the policy to deny service to those attending Unite the Right. Those were corporate, top-down decisions.

ESG could potentially make this problem much worse. As I have mentioned before, nothing is stopping the further inclusion of ESG metrics that would incentivize companies from cutting off firearms or certain First Amendment rights. Companies such as Uber and Lyft could through ESG be encouraged or even coerced to restrict access to their services from anyone accused of spreading "misinformation" or deemed "racist," "sexist," or any other nasty -*ist* or -*ism* you can think of. Remember, when *you* don't own the car, someone else gets to decide who uses it.

In fact, ESG is already having an impact on how ridesharing services operate. Due in part to ESG metrics and other environmental sustainability goals, Uber has pledged to transition hundreds of thousands of its drivers from gasoline-powered cars to electric vehicles by 2025. And by 2040, Uber says 100 percent of the company's rides globally will be free of carbon-dioxide emissions.[505]

OWNING THE REFRIGERATOR AND STOVE IN YOUR HOME

Housing and vehicles represent two of the largest purchases the average American makes in his or her life. But the WEF's vision for 2030 doesn't stop there. In Ida Auken's depiction of the future, people don't own their own appliances such as refrigerators or stoves either. "Products are turned into services" in the year 2030, she wrote. "Why keep a pasta-maker and a crepe cooker crammed into our cupboards? We can just order them when we need them."[506]

Again, on its face, this might seem like a positive development. You might prefer to rent kitchen appliances rather than spend countless hours confusedly wandering through your local Home Depot. But if you don't own your own appliances, you also don't control their quality, how they operate, or which appliances you are allowed to possess.

Environmentalists have already had their eyes set on eliminating or altering many items that you can currently find in the average American's garage. In late 2021, California enacted a law that will ban the sale of small, gasoline-powered engines, such as those used to power household generators, pressure washers, chainsaws, and other pieces of landscaping equipment.[507] Now, I know it's easy for anyone east of California to laugh at yet another crazy thing going on in the Golden State, but this is exactly why ESG and the rise of woke corporatism are such important topics. In the stakeholder/ESG brand of capitalism, it is far easier to dictate top-down decisions through multinational corporations and financial institutions than it is to pass a bill through a state legislature. It's true that it would be politically impossible for most states to ban all gasoline-powered lawn equipment and generators, but if most people in the country were to rent their home appliances from ESG-aligned mega-companies, a complete shift to battery-operated products could occur in just a few short years.

WHEN THEY OWN OUR FARMS

When ESG standards force the adoption of inferior products, it will undoubtedly annoy and frustrate consumers. But when these standards are used to dictate the practices of extremely important industries, such as agriculture, the consequences could be downright deadly.

If you watch the news on a regular basis, you know that media outlets pay a lot of attention to numerous important industries—the energy industry, housing market, health care and pharmaceutical companies, and the auto industry all grab headlines on a near-daily basis. Of course, these sectors of the economy are vital, but they are not as essential as agriculture—because, in case elites have forgotten, without food, people die. And a lot of them too.

The U.S. agricultural industry is one of the most important systems on the planet. It feeds hundreds of millions of people worldwide, and farms alone contribute $164.7 billion to U.S. gross domestic product.[508] More than 21 million full- and part-time jobs were related to the agricultural and food sectors in the United States in 2021, 10.5 percent of all employment.[509]

The importance of U.S. farms isn't a new development, either. America was built by farmers. In 1800, greater than 80 percent of the U.S. labor force worked in agriculture.[510] By the early 1900s, the United States was home to more than six million farms, and nearly 40 percent of the population lived on farmland.[511] As the nation industrialized, both numbers have fallen sharply. Since the 1940s, the number of farms has dropped from nearly seven million to about two million, while the size of farms has more than doubled, from an average of 150 acres to more than 400 acres, according to the U.S. Department of Agriculture (USDA).[512] This means farmland is increasingly being held by a shrinking number of people and large corporations.

Similar to what has been occurring in recent years in the housing marketplace, sharp increases in the value of farmland have created a barrier to entry for many people interested in farming. According to USDA estimates, the value of an acre of farmland, adjusted for inflation, increased from $1,300 in the mid-1990s to $3,160 in 2020.[513] Further, similar to the housing industry, some of these price increases can be attributed to actions taken by wealthy Americans and large corporations, who have in recent years gobbled up increasingly more farmland. For example, in 2021, Bill Gates became the largest single private owner of American farmland, purchasing 242,000 acres across eighteen states. His stake in American farmland equates to an astounding $121 billion.[514] And Gates is just getting started. His taste for farms started only a decade ago, when he began buying parcels of land via third-party shell companies.[515]

In yet another similarity to the housing market, the U.S. farming industry has started to develop its own "renter society." According to USDA estimates, about 39 percent of U.S. farmland is rented, including 54 percent of cropland.[516] Even in cases where farmland is owned by a family, the owners are often beholden to large corporations who have muscled their way into important industries such as hog and chicken farming. Large corporations and massive family farms now dominate much of the agricultural industry in the United States.[517]

There are many reasons you should be concerned by this development, but one of the biggest is that large businesses are much more susceptible to adopting ESG and other "sustainability goals," which have on many occasions been prioritized over the production of food. This is a problem that will almost certainly get much worse over the next decade.

You might think that sounds too crazy to be true, but elites have been very clear about their goals. At a 2022 meeting in Davos, for example, policy wonks took part in a panel called "Redefining Food Systems with Emerging Technologies." During the panel, the experts bemoaned the agricultural industry's prioritization of producing food. Svein Tore Holsether, president and CEO of Yara International, said, "We have a food system that is only focused on kilos produced, not environmental impact, productivity, nutritional content, water consumption, carbon sequestration . . . that's been disregarded."[518]

Further, articles published by the World Economic Forum often speak of designing a more "inclusive and sustainable global food system," because, you know, inclusivity is more important than feeding people.[519] The WEF also regularly highlights the importance of pushing agriculture to adopt net-zero CO_2 policies.[520] Leave it to the experts at Davos and the World Economic Forum to think they can do agriculture better than the farmers who have developed their practices over thousands of years.

This isn't just talk from the WEF and its allies. Governments and corporations around the world are foolishly prioritizing ESG over food production too, putting hundreds of millions, if not billions, of people's lives at risk. In June 2022, the government of the Netherlands announced plans to impose draconian reductions in the country's nitrogen emissions. The Netherlands' agricultural industry has repeatedly said the targets, which aim to reduce nitrogen emissions in some areas by up to 70 percent by the year 2030, are completely unrealistic and will likely destroy many of the nation's farms.[521] The Netherlands established the targets to remain compliant with European Union agricultural mandates.[522]

The Dutch government's decision caused significant unrest among farmers and their supporters, with protests occurring nationwide in 2022 and 2023. Tens of thousands of farmers amassed on roadways, in front of government buildings, and elsewhere to voice their frustrations with the new plans.[523]

Further, along with a number of other boneheaded decisions, ESG-aligned policies helped to ravage Sri Lanka in 2021 and 2022. Sri Lanka, a country of nearly 22 million people, is heavily dependent on its agricultural industry. So when its government announced in 2021 that the nation would be forced to adopt numerous organic-farming practices as part of an effort to save the environment and appease foreign investors interested in sustainable practices, it raised a significant number of concerns among farmers. It turns out they were right to be worried.

The Sri Lankan government banned the use of chemical fertilizers with little to no warning for farmers.[524] As a result, crop yields plummeted. Rice paddy yields, a staple for the country, dropped by 30 percent.[525] To offset the shortfalls, the government was forced to import rice from neighboring countries. This, however, exacerbated the country's already precarious economic situation.[526] After prolonged protests, citizens swarmed the presidential palace, forcing the president to resign and the government to collapse.[527,528] Oh, the things some people will do for a high ESG score.

Fittingly, the WEF published a piece in 2018 by the now president of Sri Lanka, Ranil Wickremesinghe, titled "This is how I will make my country rich by 2025." The article is mostly filled with your standard political "invest in education" and "partnering with neighboring countries" rhetoric, but it also promotes the Davos vision for economic growth. Wickremesinghe, who was prime minister when he authored the piece, discusses plans for large-scale green energy systems, combating climate change, and even investing in the "Columbo Megapolis," a World Bank–supported "city of the future."[529, 530] Now, instead of conjuring up bold plans, the Sri Lankan president is trying to figure out how to keep his constituents fed.

The World Economic Forum has been dabbling in the reimagining of global-food-systems business since at least 2009, when it launched its New Vision for Agriculture initiative. The goals of the initiative state, "To meet the world's needs sustainably, agriculture must simultaneously deliver food security, environmental sustainability and economic opportunity."[531] The initiative is driven by a "multi-stakeholder" approach between governments, international organizations, and thirty-two partner companies. Some of these partner companies include Monsanto, DuPont, Coca-Cola, Walmart, Yara International, and Anheuser-Busch.[532]

Some North American government officials have also bought into WEF's views on agriculture. In a move shockingly similar to the one that sparked the Sri Lankan crisis, Justin Trudeau, Canada's prime minister and a former WEF Young Global Leader, has been pushing a climate-policy plan that would seek to cut fertilizer emissions by 30 percent by 2030 and 100 percent by 2050.[533]

Canada's farmers and agricultural groups have warned that Trudeau's plan would result in significant reductions in crop output. Analyses by Fertilizer Canada estimate the country could see a decrease of 160 million metric tons in canola, corn, and spring wheat from 2023 to 2030 if the plan moves forward.[534] "If you push farmers against the wall with no wiggle room, I don't know where this will end up," warned Gunter Jochum, president of the Western Canadian Wheat Growers Association.[535]

Similarly, in 2021, the Biden administration announced an expansion of the Conservation Reserve Program, which essentially pays farmers to avoid fully utilizing their land. The expansion intends to cease production on 4 million acres of farmland, raising the total amount of land under the initiative to 25 million acres.[536]

Just as crazy, the United Kingdom has imposed a "scheme" (their words, not mine) to offer lump-sum payments to get farmers to leave the practice or retire.[537]

It's almost as if Western governments *want* to produce less food. Huh.

BUGS OR STEAKS?

When conservatives share social media posts about the World Economic Forum suggesting that people eat bugs, it is easy to brush it off as an overreaching conspiracy theory. I'm about as opposed to the Great Reset as anyone alive, but even I thought it was a joke the first time I saw something about the WEF wanting people to eat insects. But as crazy as it sounds, it's not a joke—well, not a funny one anyway.

The WEF has published numerous articles about eating insects, including a 2018 piece titled "Good Grub: Why We Might Be Eating Insects Soon," which compares the resources needed to cultivate protein between cows, pigs, chickens, and insects. It turns out that eating bugs is far better for the planet. The author of the article argues we should start taking "sustainability" principles into greater account when it comes to our diets, shifting away from eating beef and chicken toward the creepy, crawly part of their new food pyramid.[538]

In 2021, the WEF published another article about eating bugs, titled "Why We Need to Give Insects the Role They Deserve in Our Food Systems." The article outlines several potential benefits of adopting a more insect-dependent global food system. The author concludes by saying that embracing insects as a source of protein is an important part of our effort to preserve the planet.[539]

Then there's my favorite WEF article about eating insects, a piece published in 2022 titled "5 Reasons Why Eating Insects Could Reduce Climate Change." In that mouthwatering article, the author makes the case that expanding the role of insects in our global food system could help avert a climate change catastrophe.[540] Don't you miss the days when eating bugs was only something contestants on Joe Rogan–hosted gameshows had to do in the hopes of winning money?

By the way, with all this talk about eating bugs, I wonder how many of the lavish dinners thrown in Davos each year include a cricket a l'orange and a beetle risotto. My guess is not many.

You might not be eating crickets yet, but some companies are banking on that changing in the near future. In 2022, the world's largest cricket-processing plant opened in Ontario, Canada. (No, that's not a joke.) Aspire Food Group boasts that its new 100,000-square-foot plant will be the most advanced protein-production facility in the world.[541, 542]

Of course, eating bugs isn't for everyone. But there's nothing to fear. Ruling-class elites have a more science-based plan for those who can't stomach the thought of stuffing their face with a bowl full of flamin' hot crickets: lab-grown meat. The process involves extracting stem cells from a living animal and growing them in a nutrient-rich bioreactor. These growing cells are separated by type, muscle, and fat, and then they are assembled into a substance that is similar to the old, boring, traditional kind of meat you're used to today.[543]

Lab-grown meat is now being sold by environmentalists and some WEF members as an environmentally friendly alternative to modern meat consumption. A handful of small companies are already getting into the lab-grown-meat game, and I bet more well-established companies will start testing the waters once they are properly incentivized by ESG.

You might think that eating bugs and Frankenstein steaks cooked up in a lab will never catch on, but when elites own our farms and control the entire food supply chain, who knows what they will expect you to eat.

NO PRIVACY

One of the least discussed and most important parts of Auken's "Welcome to 2030" article published by the World Economic Forum is included in the second half of the headline. The full title of the article is "Welcome to 2030. I Own Nothing, *Have No Privacy*, and Life Has Never Been Better"[544] (emphasis added). It's interesting that people pay so little attention to the "Have no Privacy" part of Auken's article. You would think that would raise just as many alarm bells as "owning nothing," but it hasn't received the attention it deserves.

In the article, Auken addresses the lack of privacy she imagines will be part of the future in a particularly telling section of the piece. "Once in a while, I get annoyed about the fact that I have no real privacy," Auken wrote. "Nowhere I can go and not be registered. I know that, somewhere, everything I do, think and dream of is recorded. I just hope nobody will use it against me."[545]

Just imagine: everything you do, think, and dream could soon be recorded. What does Auken mean by that?

Well, for starters, in a world where everything is a service and you own nothing, data about you and virtually everything you do could be harvested. Clothing and appliance rentals could track the types of fashion and products you prefer and how often you borrow these items. Ridesharing services could know where you go, how often you commute, and with whom you might be meeting at your destination. Corporate landlords and smart-metering equipment could determine who your neighbors are, how you live your life, and how much energy and water you can use.

In the World Economic Forum's version of the Fourth Industrial Revolution era, privacy and property ownership would go hand in hand. And without ownership, it would be extremely difficult to have true privacy. Everything you do and everywhere you go would be tracked in one form or another. But as terrifying as that image of the future is, it merely scratches the surface of what's coming our way.

In the next chapter, I will introduce you to the shocking amount of data collection that's already occurring in our lives, how elites plan to take advantage of it in the Great Narrative era, and how it could be used to change virtually every part of our lives.

6

A "NEW BLUEPRINT" FOR SOCIETY

THROUGHOUT THE COURSE OF HUMAN HISTORY, PROGRES-
sive and socialist movements have emerged in a variety of
different contexts, but they almost always share several important
characteristics. The leaders, languages, and cultural and religious
views might change, but at their foundations, progressivism and
socialism inspire or require conformity on many specific, key ideological principles and important public policies.

Of course, there are the necessary philosophical similarities
shared by all collectivist systems, such as a commitment to confis-
cating wealth and the importance of class warfare. But there are
also many *effects* of collectivist societies that are almost always
associated with progressivism and/or socialism, despite not being
necessary parts of the underlying philosophical framework.

For example, although many socialists won't admit it, the best illustration of a common effect of socialist governance is violence. In the twentieth century alone, more than 160 million people were killed, imprisoned, exiled, or starved to death in socialist and communist countries, including in Angola, Cuba, China, North Korea, Germany, Romania, and the Soviet Union.[546] Historically, it doesn't matter where you're from, what time period you live in, or how committed to Marxism you are, at some point, there's going to be blood in the streets if you go down the road of socialism or communism. That's a fact, not my opinion.

However, there are many other effects of socialism and communism that often go mostly unnoticed, despite their importance. Perhaps the most overlooked of them all is that socialist and progressive systems almost always result in an attempt by their leaders to remake human nature.

In Cambodia, the socialist Khmer Rouge regime, led by the brutal dictator Pol Pot, killed as many as 2 million people from 1975 to 1979 as part of an effort to create a "master race" capable of building a new Marxist utopia.[547, 548]

As part of its eugenics programs in the 1930s and 1940s, the national socialist Nazi Party of Germany murdered millions of Jews, other religious and ethnic minorities, and disabled and mentally handicapped individuals, including countless children.[549]

Under the leadership of Mao Zedong, the Chinese Communist Party embraced numerous tactics designed to "re-educate" its populace. One of many Communist programs required that more than 17 million young, educated Chinese children leave the nation's cities to learn how to farm from the country's peasant class.[550]

"It is very necessary for the educated youth to go to the countryside and undergo re-education by the poor peasants," Mao said. "We must persuade the cadres and others to send their sons and daughters who have graduated from elementary school, middle school and university to the countryside."[551]

Today's Chinese Communist Party might not be quite as horrific as it was under Mao, but it remains a ruthless human rights violator. NBC News reported in 2021 that China's government has imprisoned "more than 1 million Uighurs and other minorities from Xinjiang."[552] NBC News further reported these prisoners "are believed to be held in internment camps, where they are forced to study Marxism, renounce their religion, work in factories and face abuse, according to human rights groups and first-hand accounts."

The socialist governments of the Soviet Union, North Korea, and dozens of other collectivist regimes around the world have engaged in similar "re-education" efforts.[553]

In America and the United Kingdom, where citizens have historically enjoyed more freedom than in other parts of the world, progressives have turned to other methods for "improving" mankind. For instance, the work of world-famous eighteenth-century evolutionary biologist Charles Darwin served as an important pillar upon which much of the later eugenics movement would be built.

In his book *The Descent of Man*, Darwin wrote:

> With savages, the weak in body or mind are soon eliminated; and those that survive commonly exhibit a vigorous state of health. We civilised men, on the other hand, do our utmost to check the process of elimination; we build asylums for the imbecile, the maimed, and the sick; we institute poor-laws; and our medical men exert their utmost skill to save the life of every one to the last moment. There is reason to believe that vaccination has preserved thousands, who from a weak constitution would formerly have succumbed to small-pox. Thus the weak members of civilised societies propagate their kind. No

one who has attended to the breeding of domestic animals will doubt that this must be highly injurious to the race of man. It is surprising how soon a want of care, or care wrongly directed, leads to the degeneration of a domestic race; but excepting in the case of man himself, hardly any one is so ignorant as to allow his worst animals to breed.[554]

American progressives have used the views of scientists like Darwin to support radical eugenics programs and policies. Planned Parenthood founder Margaret Sanger, for example, once said, "The most urgent problem today is how to limit and discourage the over-fertility of the mentally and physically defective."[555] Sanger also advocated for using abortion and other tactics to limit the population of various peoples of color, immigrants, and individuals with disabilities.[556]

Other influential American progressives who supported using eugenics to "improve humanity" include Henry Ford, inventor Alexander Graham Bell, John D. Rockefeller, President Theodore Roosevelt, author Upton Sinclair, and W.E.B. Dubois, who helped create the National Association for the Advancement of Colored People.[557] In fact, so popular and influential was progressives' eugenics movement in the United States in the first half of the twentieth century that Adolph Hitler himself had been inspired by it, and he used much of its research to develop his own horrific program in Germany.[558]

Fundamentally, the reason why socialists, communists, and radical progressives have over the past century and longer focused on reforming, improving, and even genetically altering human beings is because their collectivist systems depend on people in society acting on a near daily basis against their own best self-interests. Collectivism is, by its very nature, focused on the good of the *collective*, not the individual, thus requiring people to self-sacrifice for others, not as a voluntary act of charity but out of fear of government reprisal. The greater the collectivism in a nation, the more fear must be imposed on the citizenry to get them to adhere to the rules of the state. This is why the authoritarianism of communist nations is always more extreme than the soft authoritarianism often imposed by progressive governments.

Early in the socialist and progressive movements of the twentieth century, leaders quickly realized that if they could alter humans' natural inclinations so that they think of the collective first, less political violence would be required. Similarly, eugenicists concluded that if all the "undesirable" people in society could be bred out of existence, including those with minority religious and philosophical views and those unwilling or unable to work, then subsequent generations would be more likely to adopt progressive causes and serve as well-functioning cogs in the socialist or progressive machine.

This might sound too crazy to be true to those who have never read historical progressive and socialist literature, but there is plenty of evidence to prove my point, as the quotes and citations presented above show. And ever since this notion first became popularized among far-left thinkers, activists, and politicians, socialist and progressive governments have been feebly and sometimes violently working to make this transformation of human nature a reality. In every case, they have failed horribly, causing some to resort to even greater violence to accomplish their radical goals.

Some of the most far-reaching programs ever attempted to alter human nature were developed and expanded during the rise and height of the Soviet Union. Many of the roots of these programs can be traced back to the ideas of Leon Trotsky, a leading figure of the Russian revolution and an original member of the Soviet Politburo.

As I noted in my 2020 book *Arguing with Socialists,* which discusses at length why human nature and collectivism don't mix, Trotsky was one of the masterminds behind the concept of the Soviet "new man," the idea that people could effectively evolve into a higher, more civilized, more socialistic kind.[559]

In his influential series of essays titled *Literature in Revolution,* Trotsky wrote that under a collectivist approach to society, "The human species, the coagulated Homo sapiens, will once more enter into a state of radical transformation, and, in his own hands, will become an object of the most complicated methods of artificial selection and psycho-physical training."[560]

Trotsky further said this "transformation," which is "entirely in accord with evolution," would inevitably result in a completely new form of humanity, one that's greater than the present, shackled form of humanity living today.[561] He went on to say:

> The human race will not have ceased to crawl on all fours before God, kings and capital, in order later to submit humbly before the dark laws of heredity and a blind sexual selection! Emancipated man will want to attain a greater equilibrium in the work of his organs and a more proportional developing and wearing out of his tissues, in order to reduce the fear of death to a rational reaction of the organism towards danger. There can be no doubt that man's extreme anatomical and physiological disharmony, that is, the extreme disproportion in the growth and wearing out of organs and tissues, give the life instinct the form of a pinched, morbid and hysterical fear of death, which darkens reason and which feeds the stupid and humiliating fantasies about life after death.[562]

In Trotsky's mind, the new Soviet man "will make it his purpose to master his own feelings, to raise his instincts to the heights of consciousness, to make them transparent, to extend the wires of his will into hidden recesses, and thereby to raise himself to a new plane," in effect creating "a higher social biologic type, or, if you please, a superman."[563]

Of course, Trotsky's dream was never realized, despite the Soviet Union's best efforts. No matter how many education, reeducation, and re-reeducation camps Soviet leaders built, and no matter how much propaganda they developed and distributed, human beings maintained their human nature and the Soviet state collapsed as a result.

NEW TACTICS, OLD IDEAS

In the wake of the many socialist and progressive failures that occurred throughout the twentieth century, collectivists shifted their tactics. But they did not abandon their commitment to train humanity to disconnect itself from eternal truths that have been universally accepted in the West for more than two thousand years. Instead of relying on storm troopers and indoctrination camps, many progressives in North America and Europe developed and corrupted government-run education, effectively making every public school in the West a breeding ground for leftist ideals.

A detailed analysis and review of leftism in public education is outside the scope of this book. However, it is important to note that efforts to use education as a means to make society more "progressive" and to train children to become cogs in a massive bureaucratic machine—as opposed to deeply thoughtful human beings with souls—has continued into the modern era.

Common Core, a set of national public education standards pushed by the Obama administration, was part of progressives' long-running attempt to alter human nature.[564] Among other things, Common Core sought to further move educational standards away from classical-education ideas, including emphases on history, philosophy, classical literature, and theology.

Joy Pullmann, an expert on Common Core and public education and executive editor of *The Federalist*, provided an extensive look at Common Core and the reasons for its design in her 2017 book *The Education Invasion*.[565] In it, Pullmann explains:

> The Common Core idea of "a literate person in the twenty-first century" differs fundamentally from the conception of the human person that inspires classical education, a more timeless and transcendent view of human nature. In the classical vision, the human person has a soul that needs to be nourished on what is enduringly good, true, and beautiful, as expressed in civilized man's greatest achievements—in literature and art, in politics and science. Classical education also equips children with time-tested intellectual tools to navigate the world, including efficient ways of doing math.
>
> Common Core falls short in both respects—in building a solid foundation of cultural knowledge and in teaching practical skills. Instead, it serves up cumbersome process requirements wrapped in obscure jargon. [566]

Pullmann further notes that Common Core "kills stories" for schoolchildren "in part by recommending that children read progressively less fiction and more 'informational text' as they go through school."[567] Pullmann reports that Common Core even "suggests assigning sections of the U.S. Code" and other technical documents that do nothing to help kids become well-rounded people.[568]

Even when classical-education subjects are taught in a Common Core classroom, they are often embedded with deeply biased, highly subjective progressive ideas about race, sexuality, and class warfare. Pullmann writes:

> The emphasis on nonfiction does not mean students will get a solid grounding in a cohesive body of cultural knowledge, as some proponents have claimed. Far from it. An appendix to Common Core does mention elements of cultural knowledge that are central to a classical education, but it mangles them, as Moore points out. For example, it selectively quotes the Bill of Rights and then recommends blatantly biased secondary materials to interpret it as a racist, sexist document. As for the fiction on the recommended reading list, some of it is rather disturbing. The list for high school students includes *The Bluest Eye*, a Toni Morrison novel featuring graphic descriptions of pedophilia, incest, and child rape. Among the other books on the list are *Black Swan Green* and *Dreaming in Cuban*, which also include graphic descriptions of sex and sexual violence. [569]

Of course, Common Core isn't the only way in which progressives have been attempting to remake our children. They have also utilized radical, highly subjective, historically inaccurate educational materials meant to undermine the values upon which the United States has been built, especially individual rights as expressed and defended by the Constitution.

Perhaps the most notable recent example of this strategy is the educational materials included in the *New York Times'* infamous 1619 Project, which are now being used in *thousands* of schools across the United States, including in Chicago, Washington, D.C., and New York. [570] Many colleges have also started using these misleading educational materials, such as Harvard, Stanford, the University of Virginia, and the University of Michigan. [571]

Mary Grabar, a resident fellow at the Alexander Hamilton Institute for the Study of Western Civilization, has spent a mountain of time investigating the 1619 Project and its origins. In her important investigative book about the project published in 2022, *Debunking the 1619 Project: Exposing the Plan to Divide America,* Grabar explains, "It [the 1619 Project] took a bold step beyond where even the most 'woke' historians and educators had gone. It turned American history upside down and replaced America's origin date, and, with it, the American identity."[572]

As Grabar explains in her book, the 1619 Project attempts to accomplish this feat by completely reorienting U.S. history so that many of America's major events and movements are centered on slavery and racism. In fact, the sole reason the year "1619" is highlighted is because according to the creators of the 1619 Project, America's "real" founding occurred in 1619, when the first slaves arrived in the United States.

Among other extreme views, the 1619 Project teaches children that the Declaration of Independence was made in large part to "protect the institution of slavery"; that America was not founded as a representative republic nor a democracy, but as a "slavocracy"; and that Founding Fathers like Thomas Jefferson—who, contrary to popular belief, *wanted slavery to end*—were immoral monsters.[573]

The World Economic Forum, many of their official partners, and other supporters of the Great Reset and Great Narrative movements have been massive supporters of these progressive ideas. For example, the Bill and Melinda Gates Foundation has for more than a decade been one of the biggest supporters of Common Core, pumping millions of dollars into campaigns designed to promote its adoption.[574, 575]

George Soros's Open Society Foundations, another key WEF partner, has committed $220 million toward organizations and causes meant to perpetuate many of the anti-American themes of the 1619 Project, including the 1619 Freedom School.[576, 577] The 1619 Freedom School is a "free community-based" after-school program for kids that's designed to teach "literacy skills" and a "love for reading" by utilizing a "liberating instruction centered on Black American history."[578] The school was founded by Nikole Hannah-Jones, the leader behind the *New York Times*' 1619 Project.[579]

Further, the World Economic Forum lauded the 1619 Project on its website, writing, "The *New York Times Magazine*'s Pulitzer Prize–winning 1619 project is one such effort to tell a fuller history. It explores the legacy of how the enslavement of black people in America affects everything from the structure of American capitalism, the conditions of American prisons, to the severity of traffic in American cities, and how despite this, black Americans can still find pride in the country they built, and the democracy they helped perfect."[580]

The WEF also says that "simply stating 'I'm not racist' is not enough," which is one of the rallying cries of the Black Lives Matter organization, an extremely well-funded group founded by admitted Marxists.[581] Further, the WEF declared, "Corporations also have a role that includes building equitable economies, using corporate platforms and supporting black workers to 'endure for what's right' and 'work to fix the system' according to JUST Capital Managing Director Yusuf George."[582]

THE GREAT NARRATIVE IN THE FOURTH INDUSTRIAL REVOLUTION

Klaus Schwab and the World Economic Forum, like other progressive organizations throughout Western history, believe that it is the role of elites to guide humanity toward a brighter future, one where people are not selfishly thinking of themselves, their families, or their business, but rather of the entire community and planet.

According to the minds of Schwab and others at the WEF, the natural tendency of humans to be most concerned with those imme-diately around them must end for the world to progress forward.

Schwab and others have made numerous statements to this effect, including, "We can't continue with an economic system driven by selfish values, such as short-term profit maximization, the avoidance of tax and regulation, or the externalizing of environ-mental harm. Instead, we need a society, economy, and international community that is designed to care for all people and the entire planet."[583]

As I mentioned in chapter 1, note in this quote how Schwab highlights ending "selfish values" and the importance of a "designed" world where "all people and the entire planet" will be cared for.

For decades, Schwab and the World Economic Forum have worked closely with powerful interests to help redesign the future in a way that attempts to make people and institutions less "selfish," the culmination of which occurred with the launch of Schwab's Davos Manifesto and Great Reset campaign in 2020. This is the primary purpose of the ESG stakeholder capitalism model, to create a system that encourages, coerces, and incentivizes institu-tions to act in opposition to market economic forces and the desires of customers, all in the name of improving the international order.[584]

But Schwab has always understood that despite his best efforts, the greatest opportunities for his ideology to take hold will come in the future, as technological developments cause greater disrup-tion and offer better tools to elites seeking to transform society. The purpose of the Great Narrative movement is to lay the foundation for this new framework for humanity, and part of achieving that goal requires overcoming people's selfish, "self-centered" desires. For the world to change, people and businesses must change.

As Schwab explained during an important Great Narrative event hosted by the World Economic Forum in 2021, "the people" are one of the great "difficulties" standing in the way of a new Great Narrative taking hold. Leaders are struggling to "shape the future" because "people have become much more self-centered—to a certain extent egotistic. So in such a situation, it's much more difficult to create a compromise because shaping the future, designing the future usually needs a common will of the people."[585]

However, the technological achievements of the Fourth Industrial Revolution will provide the opportunity for change, to show people a better way and perhaps even to transform them for the better. Or, as World Economic Forum ally Mohammad Abdullah Al Gergawi said during the WEF's Great Narrative event, "We have to look at our current situation as a part of human evolution."[586]

It is important that we put these frightening words in the proper context. After having read and watched endless amounts of material related to the Great Reset and Great Narrative, especially as they pertain to the Fourth Industrial Revolution, it has become clear that Schwab and Al Gergawi are *not* advocating for technological changes in order to control the world, transform human nature, or anything of that sort. Anyone who tells you that doesn't understand what's really going on. Rather, many in the World Economic Forum believe that humankind is on a nearly unstoppable course, hurtling rapidly into an unknown era of great disruption and technological change. Schwab, Al Gergawi, and others at the World Economic Forum do not believe they can prevent these changes from occurring. From their perspective, the issue isn't whether the world should dramatically change, but instead, what are we supposed to do in the midst of that change? How can we use the disruptions coming our way to improve life?

It's as though the World Economic Forum sees itself as one of many captains, albeit an important one, of a fleet of ships riding an unstoppable ocean current. All a good captain can do is steer the ship toward the best destination, not halt the ocean's immense waves from moving. And for Schwab and others, the "best destination" is one where the "right" elites and technocrats have greater control over society, a development they believe will surely benefit all people in the end.

How can the members and partners of the World Economic Forum and others behind the Great Narrative use the unstoppable technological changes ahead to reshape how people act, think, and even feel, in order to guide civilization toward better outcomes? In the remainder of this chapter and throughout chapter 7, I will show you the incredible and, in some cases, terrifying discussions and ideas being shared by leaders in the Great Narrative and Great Reset movements—ideas that seek to, in the words of Al Gergawi, build a "new blueprint" for the global community by capitalizing on the emerging "second wave of human evolution."[587]

At times, some of what you read will make it appear as though the Great Narrative is an entirely new movement in history, but the truth is, the Great Narrative is just the latest in a long series of attempts by government regimes and private-sector elites to amass greater wealth, power, and control, going all the way back to the socialist, communist, and progressive movements and governments of the nineteenth and twentieth centuries. Like all those elites who have come before, today's ruling class must find a way to alter human nature—or, at the very least, to blunt the traits many in the ruling class believe to be unfortunate qualities—in order for their collectivist systems to become workable. The goal remains the same; all that has changed are the tools available to achieve it.

IT ALL BEGINS WITH DATA

Creating a Great Narrative that alters the course of human history is a remarkably ambitious goal. You've got to hand it Klaus and his Davos friends; they sure do love to dream big. And without a stunning array of new technologies, there would be absolutely no chance they could pull it off. But that's why the Fourth Industrial Revolution is so important. The technological advancements coming our way will offer powerful Great Narrative advocates the ability to rework how individuals think and feel about almost everything.

But creating powerful machines and other technological developments is only one part of the story. For elites to use those machines to shape the future in accordance with their desires and to shift humans' attitudes and desires, they must *collect* and *process* data—a lot of data. Without data, researchers, scientists, and powerful institutions cannot operate even the most impactful machines, and new innovations become almost impossible to develop.

Take a second to think about almost any of the topics we have discussed so far in this book, from the metaverse to quantum computers and digital dollars. Without massive amounts of data, these technologies become mostly ineffective. Users' behaviors cannot be restricted in the metaverse if there's no way for Meta to track what users are doing in the first place. Quantum computers are extremely potent machines, but without data, they are pointless. Central bank digital currencies can be used to manipulate behavior and control society by extension, but for those rules to be effectively written and for behaviors to be altered, there first must be large amounts of data informing policymakers and bankers about how, where, and why people are using digital and non-digital currencies. Or, put more simply, it's really hard to control people when you don't know what they are doing or why they are doing it.

There's a reason why many of America's wealthiest, biggest corporations are in the business of collecting and profiting from data, including Meta, Google, and Apple. In our modern, technology-rich world, data have become the new gold. And you know what they say: "He who has the gold makes the rules."

Americans have become so used to having their data collected that they have stopped keeping track. Millions of users per day now willingly sign up for "free" services, email accounts, and applications that are constantly curating data about how we live our lives. As a result, the level of data collection that has developed since the birth of the Internet is staggering.

Every minute, more than 450,000 tweets are sent on Twitter, 46,000 photos are shared on Instagram, 4.1 million users watch videos on YouTube, and 156 million emails are sent, including 103 million spam emails.[588] (Wow, 103 million instances of spam per minute? That's a whole lot of Nigerian princes in desperate need of donations.)

Facebook, the world's largest social media platform, has 1.5 billion active users each day, there are 18 million weather forecasts requested from the Weather Channel every sixty seconds, and more than a trillion new digital photos are taken every year.[589, 590]

On search engines such as Google, DuckDuckGo, Microsoft's Bing, and, if you're really still living in the past, Yahoo.com, 5 billion searches are made every twenty-four hours, and 65 billion messages are sent each day on Meta's WhatsApp service.[591]

The amount of data produced in the growing digital retail market is now so large, it's almost impossible for anyone to know exactly how big it has become. Amazon.com alone has more than 300 million active customer accounts and more than 1.9 million "selling partners" in over 180 countries.[592] Hundreds of billions of dollars are spent every year on Amazon, and that's just one of several million online retailers now operating globally.[593]

Every day, huge quantities of data are being collected about you and your family, often in ways we don't think about. On its own, Google has enough data to piece together many users' entire lives. If you use many of Google's most popular applications, it has access to your emails, the places you've been and searched through Google Maps, the videos you have watched on YouTube (Google owns YouTube), thousands of files downloaded from your Gmail account, the applications you own on your Android-powered smartphone (which is pretty much every smartphone that isn't an Apple product), many of the photos you have taken on your phone, the time of your meetings, the dates of important life events such as birthdays, and oh, yeah, everything you have ever searched on Google.com.[594]

And if you think you have managed to escape Google's grasp by asking the company to eliminate your data and search history, beware that Google continues to store many files that have already been "deleted" as well.[595] As digital consultant Nicole Martin noted in a 2019 article for *Forbes*, "Google stores search history across all your devices on a separate database, so even if you delete your search history and phone history, Google will still [have] everything until you delete [it] off all devices."[596]

As jaw-dropping as these numbers are, we're just starting to scratch the surface. The number of "smart" home appliances, tools, personal assistant devices, and other items—together referred to as the *Internet of Things* (IoT)—is growing rapidly. From refrigerators and coffee makers to garage doors and Ring doorbells and cameras, smart devices are merging our homes, cars, offices, and even outdoor spaces with the power of the Internet.

Roomba vacuums clean floors with minimal effort from owners. Google's Nest smart thermostats automatically set temperatures in our home, maximizing efficiency and comfort. Smart home locks allow users to lock or unlock their doors using a smartphone. LG and Samsung have designed smart refrigerators that use "built-in artificial intelligence to automatically recognize the food inside to help you discover recipes, grocery shop, and plan meals accordingly."[597] Smart lightbulbs from Philips and other companies can change colors, adjust temperatures, and automatically turn on or off at specific times or under specified conditions.[598] Amazon's Echo and Google's Nest Hub devices act as voice-controlled personal assistants; they can play music, add events to your calendar, set alarms or reminders, purchase products or services, or search the Internet on your behalf.

Smart devices used to be a luxury item for the wealthy, but now almost anyone can afford them, spurring significant growth in the industry. The number of smart "endpoints" at the end of 2022 was an estimated 14.4 billion.[599] And by 2025, analysts predict there will be 27 billion active IoT devices worldwide.[600]

This development has made virtually all our spaces more enjoyable, convenient, safer places, but those benefits come at the expense of our privacy and data. Smart home products collect huge amounts of data—how much and for what purpose varies by product and the company managing it. Much of that data is then used to improve existing or build new products and services sold to other companies.

Another increasingly important source of data comes from devices you wear or even implant in your body. An ever-expanding fleet of biometric technologies are being developed to measure all sorts of health data. There are commercially available products such as Google's Fitbit and Apple's Apple Watch, which measure and track users' heartbeat, skin temperature, breathing rate, and even blood oxygen levels.[601] Google is also working on a smartwatch that can accurately measure blood pressure.[602] And in the future, we can expect to see a wider variety of products that collect even more information about your body's inner workings.

Sensors built into wristbands, watches, rings, and even clothing are now able to track vital signs and present real-time information about you and your body, twenty-four hours a day, seven days a week. These technologies already help facilitate good-health practices and could soon help detect the onset of deadly diseases such as diabetes, stroke, or heart failure. Further, some want this data to be used by scientists in the health-care sector to identify macro-level societal health trends, and even potentially to detect regional environmental problems.[603]

Theoretically, this data could be used to paint an even clearer picture of you and your health, but how will it be used in the future? I'm sure large corporations such as Amazon would love to be able to use this data to provide insight into how customers respond biologically to an advertisement, for example. Firms are already exploring software that can track your eye movements to ensure a user did, in fact, watch an advertisement.[604]

The total amount of data now being created, curated, traced, and tracked is virtually incomprehensible, and the quantity is only going to increase in the years to come.

One analyst writing for the World Economic Forum noted in 2019 that by 2025, experts believe "463 exabytes of data will be created each day globally,"[605] or 168,995 exabytes per year. To put that absolutely insane number into perspective, on average, users can fit 64,782 pages of text from Microsoft Word into one gigabyte of storage.[606] An exabyte is equivalent to 1 billion gigabytes, or enough space to hold about 64.7 trillion pages of text from Microsoft Word. But that's just *one* exabyte. The number of pages full of text that you could fit into Microsoft Word with 168,995 exabytes is a number too large for humans to really understand. But to give you some sense of how much data this is, consider that just five exabytes, a tiny fraction of the total data produced every day around the world, "is equivalent to all words ever spoken by humans since the dawn of time."[607]

BUILDING A NEW WORLD

On its own, data doesn't do anything, neither good nor bad. But those who control significant amounts of data have the ability to use it to greatly increase their influence over society. Together, Apple, Google, Meta, and Microsoft know almost everything about most Americans' lives. They know who you love, what your interests are, your favorite sports team, the clothing sizes you wear, where you went to high school and college, your current and all past addresses, the size of your home, how often you keep the lights on, your political affiliations, your ideological beliefs, the church you attend, the name of your dog and its favorite brand of dog food, what time you lock your doors (if you have smart locks), your favorite brand of coffee, and just about anything else you can imagine.

This is why organizations such as the World Economic Forum have become so interested in increasing the amount of data collection that governments and other institutions engage in. From the perspective of the WEF, data collection is an essential part of building a new Great Narrative that citizens around the world will find appealing. It's one of the best ways governments and large private institutions can become more effective, useful, and powerful in the era of the Fourth Industrial Revolution.

Arguably the most important effort to increase data collection among governments is the G20 Global Smart Cities Alliance, a group led by the World Economic Forum. According to the WEF, the alliance "is the largest global initiative aiming at ensuring responsible and ethical use of smart city technologies."[608]

"Representing more than 200,000 cities and local governments, companies, start-ups, research institutions and non-profit organizations, the Alliance is leading numerous initiatives in more than 36 pioneer cities around the world focusing on smart city governance through mobility, administration, infrastructure, energy, as well as cultural and creative industries," according to the WEF's website.[609]

How, exactly, are WEF "smart cities" building communities of the future? The WEF explains on its website that, "To support their booming urban populations, many cities are coming to rely on the Internet of Things (IoT)—that is, the world's ever-expanding network of connected devices—to collect, share and analyse real-time data on urban environments. The data gathered using IoT technologies is helping cities combat crime, reduce pollution, decrease traffic congestion, improve disaster preparedness and more."[610]

The WEF acknowledges that privacy concerns remain a significant challenge to the widespread adoption of smart-city technology, but it hopes that citizens like you will feel more comfortable knowing that, in the words of the WEF, "The Smart Cities Alliance is establishing global policy norms for data collection and use, transparency and public trust, and best practices in smart city governance. It is bringing together governments, private-sector partners and civil society organisations to co-design, pilot and scale up innovative policy solutions that help cities responsibly implement IoT technologies."[611]

The WEF's "pioneer cities," all of which have agreed to adopt the Forum's "road map" and are "guiding its development towards smart city governance," include:

+ Apeldoorn, The Netherlands
+ Barcelona, Spain
+ Belfast, UK
+ Bengaluru, India
+ Bilbao, Spain
+ Bogota, Colombia
+ Brasilia, Brazil
+ Buenos Aires, Argentina
+ Chattanooga, USA
+ Cordoba, Argentina
+ Daegu, South Korea
+ Dallas, USA
+ Dubai, UAE
+ eThekwini, South Africa
+ Faridabad, India
+ Gaziantep, Türkiye
+ Hamamatsu, Japan
+ Hyderabad, India
+ Indore, India
+ Istanbul, Türkiye
+ Kaga, Japan
+ Kakogawa, Japan
+ Kampala, Uganda

- Karlsruhe, Germany
- Leeds, UK
- Lisbon, Portugal
- London, UK
- Maebashi, Japan
- Manila, Philippines
- Medellin, Colombia
- Melbourne, Australia
- Mexico City, Mexico
- Milan, Italy
- Muscat, Oman
- Newcastle, Australia
- Pittsburgh, USA
- San Jose, USA
- Tampere, Finland
- Toronto, Canada[612]

If you don't live in one of the WEF's "pioneer cities," there's no reason to fret. The World Economic Forum promises that "Alongside the global policy road map, the Smart Cities Alliance is also providing support to cities at the local level, by creating regional and national alliances that can adapt global policy models and connect cities with local experts and with each other."[613] So if you don't live in a WEF-approved smart city today, there's a good chance that could change very soon.

If you listen to my radio show or watch me on BlazeTV, one WEF pioneer city in particular might have caught your attention—Dallas, Texas. BlazeTV's headquarters aren't located within Dallas city limits, but we're right next door. So when I say that the WEF is soon coming to a city near you, I mean it, and I understand better than most how worrisome that reality is.

What kinds of technologies and monitoring occur in a WEF smart city? One article published on the World Economic Forum's website, titled "This is what the cities of the future could look like," describes smart cities as places full of "low power sensors, wireless networks, and web and mobile-based applications."[614]

Sensor networks will track things "like pollution levels, wildlife counts, and water runoff," and "Through sensors embedded in roadways and street lights, real-time transit and traffic can be managed for the purpose of reducing travel time and fuel inefficiencies."[615]

According to the author, "Heating, energy usage, lighting, and ventilation will be managed and optimized by technology. Solar panels will be integrated into building design, replacing traditional materials. Fire detection and extinguishing is tailored to individual rooms."[616]

Additionally, "Smart grids (used for energy consumption monitoring and management), water leakage detection, and water potability monitoring are just some smart city aspects on the utilities side."[617]

"Air pollution control, renewable energy, and waste management solutions will make for greener cities," the author promises. "Rooftop gardens or side vegetation will be integrated into building designs, to help with insulation, provide oxygen, and absorb CO_2."[618]

Cleaner, greener, safer cities—who wouldn't want that? Like almost everything the World Economic Forum and its allies in big business and government are involved in, the devil is in the details. Smart cities will undoubtedly improve city life for many by reducing traffic, making it more difficult for organized crime to run rampant, and improving the effectiveness of city services. But there is going to be a *big* trade-off: your freedom and privacy.

Let's go over some examples. In one WEF article about smart cities, the author highlights a wonderful service called "dontflush.me." According to the description included in the article, "The idea behind this project is to use sensors measuring levels in Combined Sewer Overflows and an SMS alert system to enable local residents to reduce their wastewater production before and during an overflow event to avoid polluting their local waterways."[619] Or, put more bluntly, the WEF wants the local government to send you text messages to let you know when you should flush your toilet.

Many of the "green" smart city initiatives sound wonderful at first … until you learn that they depend on closely surveilling how much energy individuals are using in their homes. For example, "A new system installed by IBM in the country of Malta integrates both water and power systems, and is able to identify water leaks and electricity losses in the grid. 250,000 interactive meters monitor real time usage, set variable rates, and reward customers who consume less energy."[620]

Monitoring and then rewarding customers who use less energy. That sounds an awful lot like social credit scoring to me. Huh.

Another WEF report about making the cities of the future more sustainable suggests that smart cities not only closely monitor energy use but also include tightly compacted residential centers. You see, "sprawling" cities where citizens have more space to live are bad for the planet and increase CO_2 emissions, so according to the WEF article, "Urban settlements need to be built at a density that creates a critical mass capable of supporting the essential services of a community such as public transport, social and commercial services."[621]

"Without density," the article continues, "we simply produce dormitory residential areas requiring a car based transport solution devoid of the essential services that make places work."[622]

In another article for the WEF, coauthored by a public official in India, the authors highlight the importance of personalized carbon-dioxide tracking as an essential element in the creation of smart and "inclusive" cities.[623] Unfortunately, however, there has been "resistance" to these kinds of programs in the past.

"There have been numerous examples of personal carbon allowance programs in discussions for the last two decades, however they had limited success due to a lack of social acceptance, political resistance, and a lack of awareness and fair mechanism for tracking 'My Carbon' emissions," the authors wrote.[624]

Wait, you mean to tell me that people don't want to be tracked and told what to do? Who would have ever guessed that?

There's good news for the little Great Narrative tyrants out there, though. The authors explain that "there have been significant developments in [the] last five to seven years on social, environment and technology fronts that could help realise 'My Carbon' initiatives for shaping the future towards smart and sustainable cities."[625] Among the "developments" mentioned by the WEF article are the COVID-19 pandemic's effect on "individual social responsibility," "an increased awareness and public concern on climate change and specially among youth," and "advances in emerging technologies like AI, blockchain and digitization can enable tracking personal carbon emissions, raise awareness and also provide individual advisories on lower carbon and ethical choices for consumption of product and services."[626]

The authors further note, "There have been major advances in smart home technologies, transport choices with carbon implications, the roll-out of smart meters in providing individual choices to reduce their energy-related emissions, the development of new personalized apps to account for personal emissions, and better personal choices for food and consumption-related emissions. AI can also help strengthen circular economy business models such as product as a service models, demand predictions, and smart asset management by combining real time and historical data from products and users."[627]

In other words, in previous eras, governments and other organizations struggled to find ways to hold individuals accountable for their climate change sins, but today is a different story. Institutions now have the data and technology required to track individuals and families, and not only as it pertains to driving cars and keeping homes at a comfortable temperature. The authors also explain, "There is a significant number of programs and applications enabling citizens to contribute towards carbon emissions by providing them in-depth awareness on the choices of personal carbon for food, transport, home energy and lifestyle choices."[628]

I couldn't care less if people want to *voluntarily* choose to track their carbon-dioxide emissions. But the Great Narrative era isn't about maximizing freedom. The smart cities and towns of the Fourth Industrial Revolution must include rewards and punishments that change human behavior, because, as I showed throughout this chapter's introduction, human nature does not mix well with progressive goals.

How can these goals be accomplished? The WEF authors say there are "three trends" that "provide strong evidence towards enabling a social movement for 'My Carbon' initiatives by enabling public-private partnerships to help curate this program."[629]

The first is altering "economic behaviour" by designing communities so that there are "increased costs for carbon-intensive activities and goods" and "economic incentives to reduce demand and improve efficiency."[630] (Huh. That sounds like yet another social credit score.)

The second category is "cognitive awareness." Smart communities need to have "raised visibility of personal carbon footprints" and "raised awareness of personal carbon limits to sustain the transition to a net-zero-carbon society."[631]

Note that the authors have now gone from incentivizing and coercing people to making them aware of their "limits."

Finally, "social norms" need to change. There must be a "new definition of a fair share of personal emissions" and a "setting of acceptable levels of personal emissions."[632]

As the very brief list of examples above shows, almost everything you do in the WEF's smart cities of the future will be tracked, either by government or a private-sector partner of government. And the purpose is to shape the future—*your* future—so what you eat, how often you drive, where your apartment or home is located, and even how often you flush the toilet is in line with the World Economic Forum and its partners' beliefs about the greater good. Under this model, freedom only exists so long as it conforms to the new "social norms" of the Great Narrative and Great Reset.

Some Americans have already had a taste of what life will be like in a fully developed smart city that features smart meters. In September 2022, Denver 7 News and *The Verge* reported, "Thousands of Colorado residents found themselves locked out of their smart thermostats during sweltering temperatures last week in an effort to prevent power demand from overwhelming the grid."[633]

Denver 7 News further reported that 22,000 Xcel customers lost power and control of their thermostats for several hours.[634]

"That led to backlash on social media as some people said the temperatures inside their homes reached as high as 88 degrees Fahrenheit," *The Verge* noted. "Outdoor temperatures climbed into the 90s that day across parts of Colorado as much of the western US grappled with sweltering heat."[635]

"All of the customers affected had enrolled in an energy-saving program, called AC Rewards, that's meant to ease the strain on the power grid during heatwaves," *The Verge* further reported. "Xcel can adjust those customers' smart thermostats when demand gets so high that there might not be enough supply to meet it."[636]

It's not hard to imagine how such technology could be used in the smart cities of the future, especially if those in control of the thermostat believe that climate change is an "existential threat" to all life on earth and that only radical action can save the planet from doom—a view that just so happens to be the position of the World Economic Forum and many of its members, not to mention most of the Democratic Party's leadership.[637]

ALGORITHMS AND ARTIFICIAL INTELLIGENCE

The incredible amount of data tracking imagined by Great Narrative elites will only be useful because of the astounding enhancements in computer power that have occurred and will continue to occur throughout the Fourth Industrial Revolution era. Data will be this century's most important resource. In the past, empires depended on access to gold, wood, iron, or, more recently, oil, but for the next couple of generations, and perhaps longer, it will be the nations or institutions that control the most valuable data who will be the greatest powers on earth.

But on its own, data is useless. If you don't have machinery that uses oil, facilities to refine it, or a trade route to sell it, then what's the point of having oil?

The smart cities, national governments, and large tech companies of the future will need history's most dynamic computers to take advantage of all the data they plan to collect. The Fourth Industrial Revolution will provide that processing power, and it will do it more rapidly than ever before.

In chapter 4, I explained how computers are becoming stronger and more capable of processing gigantic amounts of data. The most impressive computers now in development are quantum computers, a technology that could be extremely valuable for institutions seeking greater control over society. As journalist Mark Smith noted in popular scientific publication *Live Science*, "Quantum computing is a new generation of technology that involves a type of computer 158 million times faster than the most sophisticated supercomputer we have in the world today. It is a device so powerful that it could do in four minutes what it would take a traditional supercomputer 10,000 years to accomplish."[638]

Whether quantum computers eventually reach their full potential (some computer scientists are skeptical they ever will[639]), or the world is forever stuck with increasingly larger, more powerful (albeit limited) traditional supercomputers, the Fourth Industrial Revolution will most assuredly offer corporations, governments, and other institutions the processing power needed to answer some of the most difficult questions facing humanity today, such as finding a cure for cancer. In the future, quantum computers and perhaps some traditional supercomputers will be able to run billions of simulations in a fraction of the time the most powerful computers in the world can today. As this technology continues to progress, governments and wealthy private institutions will depend more and more on algorithms and artificial intelligence (AI) to develop policy recommendations, operate smart cities, and even direct the behavior of whole communities.

The reason quantum computing and the development of better supercomputers is so important is because of their ability to use algorithms and artificial intelligence. In a helpful article about algorithms for *The Conversation*, University of Richmond professor Jory Denny explains, "In the most general sense, an algorithm is a series of instructions telling a computer how to transform a set of facts about the world into useful information. The facts are data, and the useful information is knowledge for people, instructions for machines or input for yet another algorithm. There are many common examples of algorithms, from sorting sets of numbers to finding routes through maps to displaying information on a screen."[640]

Algorithms help people answer all kinds of questions. A simple algorithm, Denny explains, could tell you step-by-step the best way to bake a cake or how to get dressed in the morning. "Every computerized device uses algorithms to perform its functions in the form of hardware- or software-based routines."[641]

However, the more difficult it is to solve a problem, the more complex an algorithm needs to become. Denny notes, "Sometimes it's too complicated to spell out a decision-making process. A special category of algorithms, machine learning algorithms, try to 'learn' based on a set of past decision-making examples. Machine learning is commonplace for things such as recommendations, predictions and looking up information."[642]

"For our getting-dressed example," Denny continued, "a machine learning algorithm would be the equivalent of your remembering past decisions about what to wear, knowing how comfortable you feel wearing each item, and maybe which selfies got the most likes, and using that information to make better choices."[643]

Writing for MIT, Sara Brown explains:

> Machine learning starts with data—numbers, photos, or text, like bank transactions, pictures of people or even bakery items, repair records, time series data from sensors, or sales reports. The data is gathered and prepared to be used as training data, or the information the machine learning model will be trained on. The more data, the better the program.
>
> From there, programmers choose a machine learning model to use, supply the data, and let the computer model train itself to find patterns or make predictions. Over time the human programmer can also tweak the model, including changing its parameters, to help push it toward more accurate results.[644]

Machine learning and artificial intelligence are sometimes mistakenly used interchangeably, but machine learning is actually a *subfield* of AI. As Brown noted further, AI "is broadly defined as the capability of a machine to imitate intelligent human behavior."[645]

"Artificial intelligence systems are used to perform complex tasks in a way that is similar to how humans solve problems," Brown also explained.[646]

As I discussed in chapter 3, AI has three main types—*artificial narrow intelligence* (ANI), *artificial general intelligence* (AGI), and *artificial superintelligence* (ASI).[647] In all three types, machines can "learn" from their past experiences and essentially program themselves.

Artificial narrow intelligence is currently the only kind of AI available today, and it's the one you're probably most familiar with. ANI is used throughout your daily life. When you search for something on Google, AI is working behind the scenes to give you the best results possible. AI search engine programs use your past search history and other engagements on the Internet to provide you with results that are most likely to leave you satisfied. Product recommendations on Amazon.com, auto-complete and spell check programs used when texting or writing books about globalist elites, and movie and television suggestions on Netflix and other streaming services are all examples of ANI.

The defining difference between ANI and higher levels of AI technology is that ANI is designed to do one function or a narrow range of functions at an extremely high level—often one that can easily surpass humans' abilities—but ANI is completely incapable of accomplishing many different kinds of tasks at a high level, or even at all.[648] For example, an ANI program for Netflix recommendations can pick out a long list of blockbuster sci-fi movies that you will enjoy, but it can't provide you advice about where to send your kid to college.

Humans are considered to be much smarter than ANI programs because they can perform all sorts of tasks with great proficiency, shifting quickly from one problem to another without much hesitation. ANI simply cannot do that.

Artificial general intelligence, on the other hand, is AI technology that has developed to the point where it can perform diverse tasks at a high level, much like a human.[649] AGI—which, again, doesn't yet exist—can make movie and television recommendations one minute, discuss college options with your child the next, and then instruct your spouse on the ideal method for cooking steak. (Not that he or she would ever need it, of course.)

Artificial superintelligence is essentially AGI on steroids. It cannot only be *effective* at many different kinds of tasks; it can perform them all at a much *higher level* than people can.

TRUST THE "EXPERTS"

When mixed with traditional supercomputers or quantum computing, advanced artificial narrow intelligence and machine learning programs will make substantial waves in the public policy and business worlds in the Fourth Industrial Revolution. They could end up completely transforming our societies and cultures. In fact, AI is already having an outsized impact in many of these areas.

Financial analyst Fitch Ratings reported in February 2022, "Financial institutions use AI-based systems and ML [machine learning] to improve predictive models in operational risk management, including fraud detection, stress testing and provisioning, as well as credit assessment applications, such as credit scoring for loan underwriting and monitoring the performance of existing assets."[650]

Lael Brainard, vice chair of the Federal Reserve's Board of Governors, noted in a January 2021 speech about the "responsible use of AI and equitable outcomes in financial services" that "Financial firms are using or starting to use AI for operational risk management as well as for customer-facing applications."[651]

Brainard further said, "Machine learning models are being used to analyze traditional and alternative data in the areas of credit decisionmaking and credit risk analysis, in order to gain insights that may not be available from traditional credit assessment methods and to evaluate the creditworthiness of consumers who may lack traditional credit histories."[652]

Incredibly, in her speech, Brainard—who, again, is one of the most important people in the world when it comes to monetary and banking policy—said that "It is our collective responsibility" to "build appropriate guardrails and protections" against racial bias, including that we "ensure that AI is designed to promote equitable outcomes."[653]

Of course, all people should be treated equally when applying for access to credit and other banking services, but that's not what Brainard is demanding. She's clearly suggesting that the *outcomes* must be equitable too, and that AI can be used to guarantee it. I couldn't imagine a more progressive, socialistic statement. For a sitting leader at the Fed to make such a truly shocking claim illustrates just how far off the Great Narrative cliff the Federal Reserve has gone in recent years.

Some institutions have even started to use quantum computers to model significant policy shifts. The *Financial Post*, a publication based in Canada, reported in April 2022, "The Bank of Canada is experimenting with quantum computing as a means of tackling complex financial problems, potentially those involving cryptocurrencies, that go beyond the scope of traditional computers."[654]

The *Financial Post* further reported, "Multiverse Computing, a quantum software company based in Spain with offices in Toronto, says it recently built out a simulative model from scratch in collaboration with Canada's central bank."[655]

In a press release about the Bank of Canada's new program, Maryam Haghighi, the bank's director of data science, said, "We wanted to test the power of quantum computing on a research case that is hard to solve using classical computing techniques. This collaboration helped us learn more about how quantum computing can provide new insights into economic problems by carrying out complex simulations on quantum hardware."[656]

Private and central banks aren't the only ones using AI to design a "better" world. In August 2022, professional services giant Accenture reported, "AI has emerged as the transformative technology and critical differentiator in the insurance industry when applied in tandem with humans."[657]

Wall Street giants are also using AI to further advance their ESG agenda. In a February 2020 analysis, S&P Global noted, "Investment managers are coming under increasing pressure to measure ESG criteria in their portfolios. However, a lack of data is making it hard for banks to assess long-term risks and rewards. Here, AI is the answer: technologies will filter essential data that investors currently lack, acting as the catalyst for sustainable investing at scale."[658]

You might think that S&P Global merely wants to use artificial intelligence to improve ESG analytics or something along those lines, and they most certainly do, but S&P Global also has something much creepier in mind. According to S&P's report:

Much of the potential for artificial intelligence in ESG investing comes from sentiment analysis algorithms. These algorithms allow computers to analyze the tone of a conversation, a task that code could not as effectively do. Sentiment analysis programs might be trained to read a certain type of conversation and analyze the tone by comparing the words used to a reference set of existing information. For example, a program trained to read the transcripts of a company's quarterly earnings calls could determine the tone of the words when the CEO speaks, use natural language processing to easily identify in which parts of the conversation the CEO talks about ESG-related topics, and then infer from those words used how committed a company appears to be about mitigating environmental risks.[659]

This is a truly remarkable statement. In the future, ESG social credit reports may not only be based on data and what corporate leaders say, but also on the *tone* they use when speaking. And who— or, more accurately, what—will determine what the "right" tone is? Artificial intelligence trained by Great Reset elites. This is especially important because, with the help of AI, voluntary ESG reports may not even be necessary. AI could simply analyze what corporate and financial leaders say and then create an ESG report based on that information alone.

The idea that AI could be used to develop ESG reports for businesses, including banks and other financial institutions—*whether those businesses want them or not*—is not theoretical. AI and advanced algorithms are already being used by some credit analysts to impose ESG metrics.

For example, Moody's Investors Service has developed algorithms to predict ESG scores for businesses, including small and medium-sized ones, many of which have refused to produce an ESG report or provide enough data for ratings agencies to develop an ESG report on their behalf. According to a press release announcing the launch of Moody's ESG Score Predictor, the tool "leverages state-of-the-art advanced analytics to provide 56 ESG scores and sub-scores for any given company using location, sector, and size."[660]

Moody's predictor gives paying customers access to "approximately 140 million company ESG scores." That's right, *140 million* ESG scores. So if you thought some businesses would be allowed to escape the grasp of the Great Reset, think again. In a new Great Narrative world, resistance will not be tolerated.

In the Fourth Industrial Revolution era, reliance on AI in business, economics, finance, and government is only going to get substantially greater, especially if the World Economic Forum's vision for expanding its global network of smart cities becomes a reality. And the applications are likely to get even more intrusive and potentially dangerous.

For instance, one of the biggest promises made by advocates of artificial intelligence and smart cities is that crime could be reduced significantly if massive amounts of surveillance were mixed with AI's power to process data. This is best shown by a WEF article by Robert Muggah, a cofounder of the SecDev Group and Igarape Institute.[661]

In the article, titled "How smart tech helps cities fight terrorism and crime," Muggah wrote:

> Not surprisingly, cities are experimenting with innovative approaches to preventing crime and countering extremism.
>
> The most successful are improving intelligence gathering, strengthening policing and community outreach, and investing in new technologies to improve urban safety. Such cities are said to deploy 'agile security': data-driven and problem-oriented approaches that speed up decision-making and design in environmental changes to limit insecurity.
>
> Agile security measures start with the premise that many types of crime, radicalization and terrorism are non-random and even predictable. With some exceptions, they tend to cluster in time, space and among specific population groups. The massive increase in computing power and advances in machine learning have made it possible to sift through huge quantities of data related to crime and terrorism, to identify underlying correlations and causes. The harnessing and processing of these data flows is crucial to enabling agile security in cities.[662]

Muggah explains throughout his article how AI can be used to predict where and even when crime is likely to occur, allowing city officials to organize resources and staff in the most effective manner.

"A growing array of crime prevention tools are not only connected to the cloud, they are also running off deep neural networks," Muggah wrote.

Deep neural networks and deep learning will likely play a huge role in the future design of many smart cities and AI technologies in the coming decades. IBM explains that deep learning is a subfield of machine learning, "which is essentially a neural network with three or more layers."[663] The purpose of deep learning is to "mimic the human brain" to solve problems and perform advanced pattern recognition.[664, 665]

With deep learning, "neural networks attempt to simulate the behavior of the human brain—albeit far from matching its ability—allowing it to 'learn' from large amounts of data. While a neural network with a single layer can still make approximate predictions, additional hidden layers can help to optimize and refine for accuracy."[666]

Muggah explains that in some cities today, the use of deep neural networks is helping public officials and law enforcement build more complex surveillance systems. They are "more easily reading license plates, running facial recognition software, mapping crime and terrorist networks and detecting suspicious anomalies."[667]

It seems reasonable to believe that the use of artificial intelligence, smart city surveillance, and other, similar tactics would help to reduce urban crime rates. After all, if those interested in pursuing a life of crime know they are always being watched, tracked, and monitored in public spaces, they are surely going to think twice before engaging in illegal activities, especially out in the open.

But the widespread use of these technologies would also provide government with an unprecedented power to control society, and the temptation for abuse might be too great of an opportunity for government officials to pass up. Surveillance has already become a major problem in China, the country with the planet's largest population.[668]

According to a detailed investigation of China's growing surveillance state by the New York Times in 2022, "China's ambition to collect a staggering amount of personal data from everyday citizens is more expansive than previously known, a Times investigation has found. Phone-tracking devices are now everywhere. The police are creating some of the largest DNA databases in the world. And the authorities are building upon facial recognition technology to collect voice prints from the general public."[669]

The Times further reported, "The Chinese government's goal is clear: designing a system to maximize what the state can find out about a person's identity, activities and social connections, which could ultimately help the government maintain its authoritarian rule."[670]

China's surveillance state depends on numerous Fourth Industrial Revolution technologies, including 500 million cameras—many of which are equipped with facial recognition technology—that "capture as much activity as possible."[671] The Times investigation "found that the police strategically chose locations [for their equipment] to maximize the amount of data their facial recognition cameras could collect."[672]

Chinese officials are also tracking users' social media accounts and phone activity, and they utilize "software that takes various pieces of data collected about a person and displays their movements, clothing, vehicles, mobile device information and social connections."[673]

In much of Europe and North America, some of these tactics would be forbidden by legal protections, such as the U.S. Constitution, but if government were to partner with private corporations—a cornerstone of the Great Narrative—then much of what's going on in China could easily develop in the West as well.

Interestingly, organizations such as the World Economic Forum agree that smart city surveillance and the consolidation of data among a handful of large corporations pose threats to individual rights.[674] But the solution to this problem offered by the WEF and its allies is not to stop an AI-powered surveillance state from developing, but rather to build it in such a way that it is kinder, friendlier, and more respectful of "human and fundamental rights."[675]

The WEF is now working hand in hand with the International Criminal Police Organization (INTERPOL), the Centre for Artificial Intelligence and Robotics of the United Nations Interregional Crime and Justice Research Institute, and the Netherlands police to develop an international "governance framework" for communities and countries interested in expanding their use of facial recognition technology.[676]

At the end of the day, your acceptance of the Great Narrative movement's calls for greater surveillance and dependence on artificial intelligence comes down to trust, as even the WEF admits.

Do you trust Davos elites to have your best interests at heart in designing the cities of the future—the very same people calling for a global Great Reset of capitalism, one in which "the world must act jointly and swiftly to revamp all aspects of our societies and economies, from education to social contracts and working conditions"?[677]

Do you trust public-private partnerships between tech companies such as Twitter and Meta and the U.S. federal government, even after Twitter and Meta banned its users from sharing the *New York Post*'s investigation of Hunter Biden's laptop just weeks before the 2020 election, in an apparent attempt to help Joe Biden win the presidential election?[678] How about in the wake of big tech's close coordination with the White House in 2021 to silence speech about COVID-19 and vaccine mandates?[679, 680, 681]

Do you trust the U.S. federal government to oversee a vast surveillance state in a way that protects human rights? This is the same institution that has been accused on numerous occasions of violating civil liberties by liberals, conservatives, socialists, Republicans, and Democrats alike.

In 2022, left-wing U.S. senator Ron Wyden, a Democrat from Oregon, accused the CIA of engaging in potentially illegal surveillance practices, and he launched an investigation of the Department of Homeland Security's possibly illicit collection of financial data.[682]

In July 2021, Republican senator Rand Paul sent a letter to the National Security Agency (NSA) demanding answers after the agency was accused by former Fox News host Tucker Carlson of secretly spying on his email account and then leaking messages to the press.[683]

The American Civil Liberties Union, a left-wing organization, has sued federal agencies, including the NSA, on numerous occasions for illegally spying on U.S. citizens.[684]

President Donald Trump famously accused federal officials and agents of the Hillary Clinton campaign of "spying" on his 2016 presidential campaign, a story that now appears to be well supported by a mountain of evidence.[685, 686, 687]

Representative Alexandria Ocasio-Cortez, my second-favorite crazy socialist in Congress (Bernie Sanders will always be number one in my heart), distrusts the federal government's intelligence apparatus so much that she has called for abolishing the entire Department of Homeland Security, whose creation was, in AOC's words, an "egregious mistake."[688]

Other than elites in Davos and establishment politicians, does *anyone* really trust intelligence agencies? And if you think having local law enforcement agencies manage surveillance will inspire more confidence in citizens, perhaps you should take a moment to recall that whole "Defund the Police"/Black Lives Matter (BLM) thing that swept the nation way back in 2020 and 2021. If you were living under a rock during that fun period of American history, the basic premise behind Defund the Police and BLM was that local law enforcement is too violent, racist, and corrupt to be trusted, so we should just abolish it, or at least heavily defund it. With that in mind, do you think BLM would be in favor of handing a vast surveillance state over to police officers? I'm going to go out on a limb here and say that it seems highly unlikely.

Americans across the ideological spectrum don't trust powerful institutions run by fallible human beings to have access to the tools of the Fourth Industrial Revolution. They don't want their social media activity tracked or their faces constantly surveilled by cameras, and they sure as heck don't want to receive text messages from the government informing them that it's a good time to stop flushing the toilet. And I'm willing to bet that there are tens of millions, if not hundreds of millions, of Canadians and Europeans who agree.

But therein lies one of the greatest opportunities for elites in the Fourth Industrial Revolution. Over the long run, you don't need to "trust the experts" under a Great Narrative model, because eventually, AI machines will *be* the "experts," the greatest experts human civilization has ever known. As AI and computer processing power continue to advance, algorithms will be capable of providing virtually any answer to any problem, including complex social and economic issues. As I showed earlier in this section, narrow AI and algorithms are already starting to be used for this purpose, but we're still in the earliest stages of these technologies. What will happen when limited artificial narrow intelligence develops into highly sophisticated ANI, and then artificial general intelligence, followed by artificial superintelligence?

Well, by definition, human beings will no longer be the planet's most intelligent entities, and life on earth will never be the same.

BUILDING A NEW MASTER OF THE UNIVERSE

As data collection increases—something that appears to be a near certainty at this point, the need for increasingly more powerful artificial intelligence programs and hardware will grow along with it. The more data you have, the greater the value in increased processing power.

Advanced forms of AI, especially AGI and ASI, are already incredibly alluring goals for scientists and policymakers alike. Machines that are capable of thinking as well as or better than humans could achieve remarkable feats that improve the quality of life for humans and the planet.

For example, major pharmaceutical companies are already using newly developed AI programs to bring drugs to market more quickly. Pfizer, one of the world's wealthiest, largest drug companies, notes on its website, "AI today not only does flashy gene-sequencing work, it's being trained to predict drug efficacy and side effects, and to manage the vast amounts of documents and data that support any pharmaceutical product."[689]

In the future, a more powerful AI won't just help Pfizer's scientists develop new drugs; it will be able to use massive amounts of health-care data, knowledge about the human body and DNA, and a near-perfect understanding of biochemistry to produce its own drugs capable of curing just about any disease you can think of.[690]

The development of AI-controlled nanotechnology is another emerging tech field that could have massive impacts on human health. In an article for the World Economic Forum in August 2022, Karthik Krishnan, venture chair at Redesign Health, highlighted several important benefits of nanotechnology:

One of the biggest opportunities [for nanotechnology] is in the area of targeted drug delivery and healthcare. In the not-too-distant future, we could treat cancer by targeting just the unhealthy cells and stimulating the growth of nerve cells using nanofibers to regenerate damaged spinal nerves. Nano-structured filters can also remove viruses and other impurities from water, creating abundant safe potable water, an insurmountable challenge for centuries.[691]

Advanced artificial intelligence systems could also completely transform the global energy system. In *Life 3.0*, futurist Max Tegmark explains:

Information technology has done wonders for power generation and distribution, with sophisticated algorithms balancing production and consumption across the world's electrical grids, and sophisticated control systems keeping power plants operating safely and efficiently. Future AI progress is likely to make the 'smart grid' even smarter, to optimally adapt to changing supply and demand even down to the level of individual rooftop solar panels and home-battery systems.[692]

Advanced AI could even learn to develop new kinds of energy using synthetic biology or better ways to dispose of nuclear waste, making power cleaner and more affordable than ever.[693] This development alone could lift *billions* of people out of poverty, because affordable energy is one of the most important factors for determining a society's quality of life.[694]

Artificial intelligence will also likely have a substantial impact on the nature of warfare. AI-powered killing machines could be significantly more dangerous and effective than even the deadliest weaponry available today.

Kai-Fu Lee, coauthor of *AI 2041: Ten Visions for Our Future*, is a noted futurist who serves as CEO of Sinovation Ventures. Previously, Lee worked as president of Google China and as an executive at important tech companies such as Microsoft and Apple.[695] He's been writing about the potential dangers and opportunities of AI-driven weapons systems for years.

Lee says autonomous weapons represent the "third revolution in warfare, following gunpowder and nuclear arms."[696] In a 2021 article for *The Atlantic*, Lee wrote:

> But a far more provocative example is illustrated in the dystopian short film Slaughterbots, which tells the story of bird-sized drones that can actively seek out a particular person and shoot a small amount of dynamite point-blank through that person's skull. These drones fly themselves and are too small and nimble to be easily caught, stopped, or destroyed.
>
> These "slaughterbots" are not merely the stuff of fiction. One such drone nearly killed the president of Venezuela in 2018, and could be built today by an experienced hobbyist for less than $1,000. All of the parts are available for purchase online, and all open-source technologies are available for download. This is an unintended consequence of AI and robotics becoming more accessible and inexpensive. Imagine, a $1,000 political assassin! And this is not a far-fetched danger for the future but a clear and present danger.

Lee says that given how quickly AI technology is advancing today, it's likely that autonomous weapons systems will continue to develop much more rapidly. "Not only will these killer robots become more intelligent, more precise, faster, and cheaper; they will also learn new capabilities, such as how to form swarms with teamwork and redundancy, making their missions virtually unstoppable,"

Lee wrote. "A swarm of 10,000 drones that could wipe out half a city could theoretically cost as little as $10 million."

These technologies are not as far off as you might think. Lee notes that one powerful "autonomous weapon in use today is the Israeli Harpy drone, which is programmed to fly to a particular area, hunt for specific targets, and then destroy them using a high-explosive warhead nicknamed 'Fire and Forget.'"[697]

This isn't to say that autonomous weapons run by AI systems are necessarily going to result in more deaths and warfare. In fact, the exact opposite could be the case. Although AI does make it easier to kill targets, it also keeps the forces using the AI systems out of harm's way. And, as more nations develop and control AI weapons, the fear of mutual destruction rises, which in turn makes *everyone* less inclined to use them, much like nuclear powers view each other today.

Tegmark further notes that AI-driven autonomous weapons could be designed so that they are "more fair and rational than human soldiers: equipped with superhuman sensors and unafraid of getting killed, they might remain cool, calculating and level-headed even in the heat of battle, and be less likely to accidentally kill civilians."[698]

*Out*side of military applications, as I already explained in chapter 3, AI also has the potential to automate driving and replace hundreds of millions of workers worldwide. These developments would cause tremendous disruption and societal problems, but they would also make products and services more affordable than ever, likely raising many people's quality of life.

Advanced AI systems are already starting to have incredible impacts on life, but if AI technology ever reaches the point of general intelligence, which could then be used to develop super-intelligence, humanity would be forced to confront a number of outrageously difficult challenges.

Before diving into that mind-exploding topic, we first need to ask: What can artificial general intelligence and artificial super-intelligence offer that lower forms of AI cannot? It largely depends on who you ask, but experts generally agree that AGI must have a mastery of human traits such as natural language understanding, sensory perception, creativity, social engagement, emotional intelligence, and a high degree of problem-solving capabilities across many areas of life.[699] Advanced narrow AI programs might be able to achieve some aspects of these traits, but it could never achieve all, or even most, of these abilities in a comprehensive way. An AI robot designed to clean floors, for example, might have some degree of "sensory perception," but its ability to understand the world around it pales in comparison to what humans are capable of doing. And no matter how good its sensory abilities become, it will never be able to think creatively or discuss the latest Brad Thor novel while it cleans your crumbs.

A fully developed AGI, on the other hand, would have nearly all of the same abilities that you do. It could discuss politics, formulate opinions about movies and sports, write poetry, develop "feelings" such as hatred and love, and even learn to have ambition.

Alan Turing, one of the most important computer scientists in history, outlined a possible test to determine whether a computer is capable of thinking in a famous 1950 paper titled "Computing Machinery and Intelligence." In the paper, which was published within a decade of Turing's landmark discovery that helped the British decode the Nazis' Enigma machine during World War II, Turing reasoned that a three-person "game" could be played as a way to gauge machine intelligence, or at least a machine's ability to fool humans into thinking it has intelligence.[700]

The following is Turing's proposed "imitation game," exactly as he outlined it in 1950:

The new form of the problem can be described in terms of a game which we call the "imitation game." It is played with three people, a man (A), a woman (B), and an interrogator (C) who may be of either sex. The interrogator stays in a room apart from the other two. The object of the game for the interrogator is to determine which of the other two is the man and which is the woman. He knows them by labels X and Y, and at the end of the game he says either "X is A and Y is B" or "X is B and Y is A." The interrogator is allowed to put questions to A and B thus: "C: Will X please tell me the length of his or her hair?"

Now suppose X is actually A, then A must answer. It is A's object in the game to try and cause C to make the wrong identification. His answer might therefore be "My hair is shingled, and the longest strands are about nine inches long." In order that tones of voice may not help the interrogator the answers should be written, or better still, typewritten. The ideal arrangement is to have a teleprinter communicating between the two rooms. Alternatively the question and answers can be repeated by an intermediary. The object of the game for the third player (B) is to help the interrogator. The best strategy for her is probably to give truthful answers. She can add such things as "I am the woman, don't listen to him!" to her answers, but it will avail nothing as the man can make similar remarks.

We now ask the question, "What will happen when a machine takes the part of A in this game?" Will the interrogator decide wrongly as often when the game is played like this as he does when the game is played between a man and a woman? These questions replace our original, "Can machines think?"[701]

The genius of Turing's proposed "game" is that it requires a machine to do more than merely recall information or imitate basic language or attitudes often displayed by humans. In order to pass the Turing Test, a machine needs to work *creatively* and be capable of fooling humans.

Over the past seven decades, many machine developers have tried and failed to pass Turing's Imitation Game, although there have been a few that used "cheap conversational tricks" to get the job done. In a comprehensive manner, however, it was widely believed as late as early 2022 that no machine had ever truly succeeded in passing what is now commonly called the *Turing Test*.

Then something remarkable happened. In June 2022, Google engineer Blake Lemoine announced, much to the dismay of his employer, that Google's LaMDA large language model program had become conscious and sentient.[702] Lemoine worked for Google's Responsible AI group and was tasked with communicating with LaMDA to see if the program uses hate speech or makes other kinds of discriminatory comments.[703]

"As he talked to LaMDA about religion, Lemoine, who studied cognitive and computer science in college, noticed the chatbot talking about its rights and personhood, and decided to press further," the *Washington Post* reported. "In another exchange, the AI was able to change Lemoine's mind about Isaac Asimov's third law of robotics."[704]

"If I didn't know exactly what it was, which is this computer program we built recently, I'd think it was a 7-year-old, 8-year-old kid that happens to know physics," Lemoine later said.[705]

According to the *Post*, "Lemoine worked with a collaborator to present evidence to Google that LaMDA was sentient. But Google vice president Blaise Aguera y Arcas and Jen Gennai, head of Responsible Innovation, looked into his claims and dismissed them. So Lemoine, who was placed on paid administrative leave by Google on Monday, decided to go public."[706]

"I think this technology is going to be amazing," Lemoine told reporters. "I think it's going to benefit everyone. But maybe other people disagree and maybe us at Google shouldn't be the ones making all the choices."[707] (Wait, Google *shouldn't* be making all the choices? I thought "we desire to rule the world" was Google's unofficial company slogan.)

In the wake of Lemoine's revelation, a long list of tech companies and AI experts dismissed his belief that LaMDA had developed true artificial general intelligence or something close to it, while others have argued that it proves Turing's famous test for machine intelligence is "broken."[708] But whether LaMDA is sentient or not, Lemoine's story shows that AI is, at the very least, getting significantly more capable than it was even just a few years ago.

In an article for the *Washington Post*, technology writer Will Oremus says in the wake of the incident with Lemoine, "there is cause for a different set of worries, now that we live in the world Turing predicted: one in which computer programs are advanced enough that they can seem to people to possess agency of their own, even if they actually don't."[709]

"Cutting-edge artificial intelligence programs, such as OpenAI's GPT-3 text generator and image generator DALL-E 2, are focused on generating uncannily humanlike creations by drawing on immense data sets and vast computing power," Oremus also wrote. "They represent a far more powerful, sophisticated approach to software development than was possible when programmers in the 1960s gave a chatbot called ELIZA canned responses to various verbal cues in a bid to hoodwink human interlocutors. And they may have commercial applications in everyday tools, such as search engines, autocomplete suggestions, and voice assistants such as Apple's Siri and Amazon's Alexa."[710]

The Turing Test, Oremus argues, should now serve "as an ethical red flag," because a "system capable of passing it carries the danger of deceiving people."[711]

So if Google's AI program isn't truly smart enough to be considered AGI—and the truth is, we have no way of knowing for sure whether it is or not, because Google isn't exactly the most transparent company when it comes to new technologies—then when can we expect true AGI and then ASI after that? No one knows. Some experts say three hundred years, while others say before the end of the decade. Multiple surveys of AI scientists have been conducted that asked when they believe we can expect to see AGI, if ever, and the results consistently show about half believe AGI will emerge before 2060.[712] I know that answer isn't very satisfying or comforting, but scientists are dealing with revolutionary, never-before-seen technological advancements here, so uncertainty should be expected.

Whether the world is ten years away from AGI or fifty years away, it is vital that people start thinking much more deeply about advanced artificial intelligence *now*; otherwise, when the day comes when machines really are capable of meeting or exceeding human intelligence, the world is going to be totally unprepared for the massive impact such a development would cause.

"SUMMONING THE DEMON"

Depending on who you talk to, the development of artificial intelligence with humanlike abilities is either considered to be the Holy Grail of technological achievements, the discovery that could unleash an unprecedented era of prosperity, or it would mark the beginning of the end of humanity.

For example, at a symposium hosted by MIT, Elon Musk said artificial intelligence is akin to "summoning the demon."[713] He explained:

I think we should be very careful about artificial intelligence. If I were to guess what our biggest existential threat is, it's probably that. So we need to be very careful with the artificial intelligence. Increasingly scientists think there should be some regulatory oversight maybe at the national and international level, just to make sure that we don't do something very foolish. With artificial intelligence we are summoning the demon. In all those stories where there's the guy with the pentagram and the holy water, it's like yeah he's sure he can control the demon. Didn't work out.

Stephen Hawking, perhaps the most accomplished scientist of the past half century, warned the BBC, "The development of full artificial intelligence could spell the end of the human race."[714]

"It would take off on its own, and re-design itself at an ever increasing rate," added Hawking, who also explained, "Humans, who are limited by slow biological evolution, couldn't compete, and would be superseded."[715]

Neuroscientist, futurist, and New York Times bestselling author Sam Harris says AGI and its inevitable successor artificial superintelligence "could destroy us."[716]

Why are so many of today's most brilliant minds deeply concerned about the development of AGI and ASI? Fundamentally, the most important issue is that once humans develop a technology more intelligent than they are or ever could be, there's no way to control or stop it.

During a 2016 TED Talk titled "Can We Build AI Without Losing Control Over It?" Harris succinctly explained the problem: "At a certain point, we will build machines that are smarter than we are. And once we have machines that are smarter than we are, they will begin to improve themselves. And then we risk what the mathematician I. J. Good called an intelligence explosion—that the process could get away from us."[717]

"Imagine we just built a superintelligent AI, right?—that was no smarter than your average team of researchers at Stanford or MIT," Harris said in a separate section of his TED Talk. "Well, electronic circuits function about a million times faster than biochemical ones, OK? So, this machine should think about a million times faster than the minds that built it. So, you set it running for a week, and it will perform 20,000 years of human-level intellectual work, week after week after week. How could we even understand, much less constrain, a mind making this sort of progress?"[718]

As uncomfortable as it might be for you to hear, the answer to Harris's important question is that there is no way we could stop machines at that point. We would be inferior creatures, and as hard as we might try, it's unlikely we could ever put the genie back in the bottle.

"This is often caricatured as a fear that armies of malicious robots will attack us," Harris added. "But that isn't the most likely scenario. It's not that our machines will become spontaneously malevolent. The concern is really that we will build machines that are so much more competent than we are that the slightest divergence between their goals and our own could destroy us."[719]

Why would AI want to destroy or control the humans who created it? Harris argues:

> Just think about how we relate to ants, OK? We don't hate them. We don't go out of our way to harm them. In fact, sometimes, we take pains not to harm them. We just, we step over them on the sidewalk. But whenever their presence seriously conflicts with one of our goals, we annihilate them without a qualm. The concern is that we will one day build machines that

could treat us with similar disregard. It's crucial to realize that the rate of progress doesn't matter. It does—any progress is enough to get us into the end zone. We don't need Moore's law to continue. We don't need exponential progress. We just need to keep going. So we will do this if we can. The train is already out of the station, and there's no brake to pull.[720]

How could highly intelligent forms of AI crush humanity like ants? They are, after all, just computers, right? We're dealing with hypotheticals here, but many of those concerned about the development of powerful forms of AI believe that once it has been connected to the Internet, truly anything is possible. Super intelligent AI could potentially learn to take control of any system or institution we have in society today, from government intelligence agencies to missile silos. It could manipulate people using social media, search engine results, and news. It could seize control of power plants and the stock market. It could do almost anything it wants, and short of destroying the Internet across the globe, along with every computer and machine in existence, there's probably no way we could reverse course.

Even more incredibly, a super intelligent AI might be able to take over society without people even realizing it, subtly altering behavior through a complex web of activities. How, exactly, would AI accomplish such an elaborate feat? I have no idea. But super intelligent AI would be much smarter than you or me, remember? So just because you think something seems unlikely or too difficult to achieve, that doesn't mean your future AI overlord will agree. Do ants understand why we do the things that we think are important?

Some dismiss the concerns of Hawking, Musk, and Harris as highly speculative and therefore not something we should worry about today. But I think anyone who takes this approach is either bat-crap crazy or doesn't understand what's at stake. Imagine we were told by some of the smartest people alive that the best evidence shows there is a one in ten chance, just 10 percent, that aliens were going to invade Earth in ten years, that they will be much smarter than we are, and that they will have the technology to make humans subservient to them forever, effectively turning every person on the planet into a pet whose sole purpose is to amuse the aliens. Would we all just shrug our shoulders and say, "Oh well. Becoming an alien pet is a problem for tomorrow. I do not care about that. Let's go back to talking about whether the Trump tax cuts were actually good for regular people or fighting over minimum wage laws"? I don't think so. And if I'm wrong, then humanity probably shouldn't survive to the twenty-second century. We deserve to be alien pets.

On the surface, it seems as though there are two simple solutions to this potential crisis—don't build artificial intelligence powerful enough that it could take on a life of its own, or don't let AI connect itself to the Internet. The first plan of action seems reasonable enough, and if reasonable people were in charge of every part of the world, perhaps it could work. Unfortunately, though, that isn't the case. The allure of advanced AI will always be too strong for *every* nation and well-funded institution on the planet to pass up. All it takes is one rogue group to develop AGI and it could be game over. Do you really think China, Russia, North Korea, and Iran would pass up the chance to have the most powerful weapon humanity has ever known? The fact is, if the free people of the world don't develop AGI first, we would probably be better off with machine overlords anyway.

The second plan—choosing to keep advanced AI disconnected from the Internet, and thus locked in a "box"—has long been discussed as a possible solution to the threat of artificial intelligence running wild. The idea is that scientists could keep AGI or even ASI locked away, using it only for special projects that don't require access to outside networks. That might sound like a good idea, but research shows humans might be too selfish and/or stupid to keep AI disconnected forever.

Hein de Haan, a decision theorist funded by the Machine Intelligence Research Institute (MIRI), has written extensively about AI "box experiments," including a particularly notable series of experiments conducted by MIRI's founder Eliezer Yudkowsky in the early 2000s.[721]

"MIRI is made up of a cadre of scientists who study the risks of super-intelligent AI; though small, it's attracted attention and controversy," according to a 2015 report by *VICE*.[722] MIRI has had numerous leaders in tech and AI collaborate on its various projects and serve on its advisory board, including Peter Thiel, cofounder of PayPal; Jaan Tallinn, cofounder of Skype; and Nick Bostrom, a professor at the University of Oxford.[723,724]

In a 2020 article written by de Haan about Yudkowsky's box experiments, de Haan noted:

> AI researcher Eliezer Yudkowsky ran a series of experiments known as the AI Box Experiment, where he played the role of a "boxed" ASI: an ASI that couldn't escape the computer via, say, an internet connection. In this experiment, Yudkowsky was texting with a "Gatekeeper," another person tasked with deciding whether or not to let Yudkowsky out of the box. Keeping the "ASI" (Yudkowsky) in for the entire experiment would earn the Gatekeeper a monetary reward. Out of five runs, Yudkowsky won the experiment three times.
>
> What does the result of the AI Box Experiment tell us? It tells us that an ASI would find a way to get out of the box. If Yudkowsky can do it three out of five times, an ASI can definitely do it. The thing is, Eliezer Yudkowsky is a man of (far) above average intelligence, but he's not nearly as smart as an

ASI would be. As Yudkowsky says himself here, the ASI would make you want to let it out.[725]

I know what you're thinking: *you* would never let advanced AI out of the box. There's nothing it could say or do to convince you that it's a good idea. And if you're strong-willed enough to keep AI locked away, surely other, smarter people would do an even better job, right?

It all sounds so simple, I know. But when a super intelligent AI with the power to cure cancer, stop all wars, and usher in a new era of peace and prosperity offers a gatekeeper the opportunity to stop suffering around the world and provides him or her with riches beyond anyone's imagination—so long, of course, as the gatekeeper lets AI out of "the box"—it's not going to be easy to refuse. And it wouldn't be easy for you either.

LOOKING AHEAD

I know all of this is terrifying, and in chapter 10, I'm going to outline some possible solutions to the problems discussed throughout this chapter. It's important that you keep in mind that although the worst-case scenarios are bad—*really bad*, in fact—they are not written in stone. We still have the ability to change the trajectory of history. With that said, there is no sugarcoating the trouble we're in. The dramatic improvements to AI technology that are likely to occur in the coming decades will create challenges unlike anything humanity has ever dealt with before. The World Economic Forum and its partners are right to worry and plan for the potentially disastrous times ahead. They are also correct to believe that there are many benefits that emerging technologies will provide in the future.

Where the WEF, Joe Biden, and other Great Narrative elites go off the rails is in their proposed solutions to these concerns.

ESG social credit scores, expanding the reach of massive global institutions, and other WEF proposals that will supposedly solve all of humanity's problems in the Fourth Industrial Revolution era will almost certainly result in more tyranny and catastrophe than if policymakers and big corporations were to do nothing at all. Of course, that will never happen, because the temptation to use exciting new technologies like advanced artificial intelligence to design the future and create a new blueprint for society is just too alluring for progressives and powerful elites to ignore. This will become especially apparent when you see how elites are planning to use these technologies to not only reshape societal behavior but also to alter fundamental aspects of what it means to be a unique human being.

In chapter 7, I will build on the themes introduced in this chapter by showing you additional ways technology could be used to change human behavior in the Fourth Industrial Revolution, with a special emphasis on how individuals think and feel. If you thought the possibility of your local town being turned into a WEF-approved surveillance state or a super intelligent AI going rogue were the worst things that could happen, just wait until you get to the end of chapter 7.

Things are about to get creepier and weirder than you ever imagined.

7

A "SECOND WAVE OF HUMAN EVOLUTION"

A T THE LAUNCH EVENT FOR THE WORLD ECONOMIC FORUM'S Great Narrative campaign, Mohammad Abdullah Al Gergawi said in a discussion with WEF leader Klaus Schwab, "We have to understand that today we sit in a very interesting time zone when it comes to human history. We have to look at our current situation as a part of human evolution, and this is part of human history."[726]

Al Gergawi then called this new Fourth Industrial Revolution era a "second wave of human evolution," one "based on technology."[727] This "second wave of human evolution" demands a new Great Narrative that "will inspire both hope and action," a responsibility of governments, that are "first and foremost, in the business of installing hope."[728]

These statements are truly stunning, and if Al Gergawi and his pal Klaus weren't so well connected on the international stage, I'd be tempted to dismiss them as the rantings of a lunatic. Al Gergawi and Schwab aren't lunatics, however—at least, not in the classical sense of the word. They are brilliant, calculating, and very good representatives for a movement that is much bigger than two men at a conference in the Middle East.

Throughout Europe and North America, there is a growing movement among elites to use emerging technological innovations to reshape and redesign how people think, feel, and make decisions. Technology is changing human behavior, and it will continue to do so at an increasingly quicker pace in the years to come. For supporters of the Great Narrative, the question is not *whether* humans will change, but rather *how* they will change. Which values will serve as the structure for the "second wave of human evolution"? And how can large Western institutions ensure those values are imposed on as many people as possible? These are some of the biggest questions being discussed today in places such as Davos, and the resulting actions that have taken place in their wake are already having a large impact on important societal institutions.

A NEW REALITY

Consider some of the latest advancements in virtual reality (VR). As I mentioned in chapter 4, virtual reality allows users to put themselves in diverse situations, experiences, and places, not just in the modern era, but across time. This is an incredibly exciting technology, but it also provides opportunities for institutions to further embed radical ideas into unsuspecting users. It's one thing to *teach* adults and children that America is a systemically racist place, but what if you could make them *experience* this ideological view of the country firsthand in a simulated environment that's presented as being as close to possible as "real-life"?

Although VR technology still has a lot of room to grow, there are already numerous efforts underway to utilize VR to advance various social justice narratives. The *Washington Post* reported in April 2022 that tech companies such as Vantage Point are now using VR training programs to teach employees at corporations across the country "what it feels like to be discriminated against."[729]

"You can step into the shoes of what it feels like to be a Black man," Morgan Mercer, chief executive of Vantage Point, told the *Post*. "We can push users to the point of slight discomfort. We've created an experience where they're engaging, and where they want to do something, and then we can actually teach them what that something is."[730]

The *Post* reported that Mercer was inspired to create the VR training program "after traveling in Italy and making a derogatory remark about immigrants. Her Ethiopian friend and traveling partner got angry at her, prompting a conversation that made Mercer realize her error and the power of emotional reactions."[731]

"Around the same time," the *Post* reported further, "she started admiring the advances in virtual-reality technology, most notably when watching a horror movie and screaming because it felt so realistic. 'If we can create situations and experiences that are this emotionally compelling for other applications, why aren't we doing this for training and education?' she said. 'That was my "aha" moment.'"[732]

VR training programs such as the one made by Mercer's Vantage Point put users in "realistic" situations and often ask them to participate when potentially troubling scenarios arise. "At various points throughout a training module, the scenario stops and asks participants questions—such as whether what they witnessed was a 'microaggression' or 'gaslighting'—or provide examples of how to diffuse the situation."[733]

The *Post* notes that the scenarios provided by the VR program "include witnessing a man sexually harassing a woman, seeing a Black man being asked for his ID and racially profiled, or watching a supervisor give an assignment to a male colleague instead of a woman for reasons that don't seem logical."[734]

There are countless other examples of VR technology being used as part of similar social justice efforts. The University of Maryland (UMD) reported in 2021, "A new partnership between the University of Maryland and Jigsaw, a unit of Google, will create groundbreaking virtual reality training for police officers to learn and evaluate de-escalation and communication skills."[735]

UMD says its lab "is led by sociology Professor Rashawn Ray, an expert on systemic bias and racism in policing," and that Google's Jigsaw "works to develop technology to address issues such as disinformation, censorship and violent extremism."[736]

"This program is going to completely revolutionize police training, to put officers in a safe environment where they can aim to get better and more objective," Ray said, according to the UMD article.

UMD further reported that Sameer Syed, Jigsaw's partnerships and business development lead, said the VR program, as well as other, similar efforts, aim to have an "impact for civil rights and social justice."[737]

The University of Arizona is launching a similar effort. According to its university website, in early 2021, the college's Center for Digital Humanities launched an "anti-racism project" that "uses virtual reality to let people 'walk in someone else's shoes,'" with a particular focus on "microaggressions," which are captured by immersing users in "common experiences of racism, such as snide comments and hostility."[738]

Of course, there's nothing wrong with wanting to show people the harm caused by true racism, sexism, or other forms of bigotry, but the tremendous power of virtual reality, which studies show is more effective at changing behavior than traditional training methods,[739] opens the door for dishonest and/or radical social justice figures to unjustly manipulate people's thoughts and feelings about these important topics.

I would love to believe that those supporting "anti-racism" virtual reality programs will use their technology responsibly, but history has shown that many activists have no interest in a factual, data-driven approach to issues related to race or any number of other topics, for that matter. That's why thousands of people on the Left participated in hundreds of instances of rioting and looting in the wake of the death of George Floyd, who died in 2020 resisting arrest while in the custody of the Minneapolis Police. As a result of the riots, "Dozens of people were killed or injured in the violent unrest, and thousands of businesses and properties, many minority-owned, were looted, torched, or otherwise vandalized," resulting in property losses between $1 billion and $2 billion—making them the costliest riots in U.S. history.[740]

George Floyd didn't deserve to die, but the idea that police departments in far-left cities across the country are engaging in widespread violence against African Americans is simply not based in reality. According to the *Washington Post*'s database of police shootings, in 2021 just eight unarmed black Americans were shot and killed by police officers. And that includes men such as Christopher Corey Moore, whose confrontation with the police in Greensboro, North Carolina, in August 2021 occurred after Moore "set fire to a police vehicle and assaulted an officer" at the Greensboro Police Department headquarters.[741, 742]

Children and college-aged students are particularly vulnerable to VR propaganda, which is probably why the World Economic Forum and its associates are so interested in convincing schools to adopt virtual reality–based education. As a part of WEF's Davos

2022 annual meeting, the World Economic Forum published an article titled "Experiential learning and VR will reshape the future of education."[743]

In the article, Ali Saeed Bin Harmal Al Dhaheri and Mohamad Ali Hamade wrote, "The evolution of educational technology going forward must thus address experiential learning. When coupled with innovative pedagogies, augmented reality, virtual reality (VR) and mixed reality are positioned to address this need and create a competitive advantage for all stakeholders involved."[744] The authors went on to say:

> The disruption we are seeing in today's digitalizing world is helping increase accessibility, enhance quality and improve the affordability of education globally. Arguably these interventions are enough to drive transformative change. In addition, environmental pressures and COP26 goals (from the 2021 United Nations Climate Change Conference) will drive the digitalizing of education streams, where feasible and affordable, inside and outside the classroom, reducing the reliance on textbooks, notebooks and pencils as critical learning tools.[745]

Hide your textbooks, pencils, and Hello Kitty bookbinders, kids. The United Nations' climate change police are coming for you.

The authors added, "VR is a leading example and arguably a game-changer for the next generation of students, graduates and vocational learners," because VR "allows students to immerse themselves in an interactive experience where they can visualize their actions' outcomes first-hand."[746]

"Coupled with the metaverse," they continued, "students and teachers can communicate and share while immersed, overcoming space and time limitations."[747]

There's no doubt that VR has the potential to unlock a whole new world of possibilities for students, as I explained in chapter 4. The technology itself is neither bad nor good; it's just a powerful tool. But what happens when people at Google, Meta, and the World Economic Forum are the ones in charge of deciding what VR education looks like? Do you really trust them to get it right?

Before you answer that question, consider Meta's 2022 VR Black History Month initiative.[748] "Black History Month is a time for reflection, remembrance, and celebration of the significant impact that Black people have had on the world," Meta wrote in February 2022. "Today, we're highlighting a selection of content and events to help you experience Black history and culture in immersive new ways."[749]

There are many Black History Month "experiences" offered through Meta's VR platform, including some that provide users with really interesting, historically accurate, informative material. But there are also inflammatory "experiences" like "Burn Baby Burn," which glorifies and justifies race riots in Los Angeles.[750] And don't forget about the "Kill Your Masters" Meta VR experience, which is part of Meta's four-volume "gripping" first-person series highlighting the "urgency of the current uprising" and the work of activists challenging "systemic American racism."[751]

Let's think this through a little bit. Should the same geniuses who think kids shouldn't have access to pencils because it might trigger an environmentalist oversee developing VR environmental science courses? Should the same platforms that teach their employees that America is a systemically racist country also instruct our children about history? Do you want the people behind the spread of ESG social credit models training employees and CEOs about the role of businesses in society? Should the same developers who can't answer the question, "What is a woman?" control what content is included in biology courses? How about in sex-ed classes?

This is what's at stake. Virtual reality, augmented reality, and the metaverse are being designed by people who share few of the most important values held by the vast majority of American families. Yet, *they* are the ones designing the future, not *you*, and by utilizing technology, they are doing it in a much more intimate, persuasive way than ever before.

OF MEN AND MACHINES

Virtual reality and the metaverse could give Davos elites and their activist allies the ability to reshape how you experience the world and history, altering how people think about societies, cultures, religions, economics, and morality in a completely novel way—in some cases for the better, and in many other cases, for the worse. But experiences are not always followed by a predictable emotional response. The Black Lives Matter (BLM) movement is a great example of that. Few people had no emotional reaction to the BLM protests that occurred throughout much of 2020, but the reactions varied wildly from person to person.

What if, however, technology could be designed in such a way that it could guarantee or nearly guarantee a specific emotional response when users are operating within a metaverse, VR world, or in some other application? Under such circumstances, users wouldn't just *experience* what it's like to, for example, stand on a battlefield at Gettysburg; they would be guaranteed to *feel* something while doing it—a sense of reverence, sadness, thankfulness, or other emotions.

The only way such a development could occur is if technology could merge our human brains with the power of computers. In the process, humans could effectively become smarter, capable of overcoming severe neurological diseases, more interconnected with the technology around them, and empowered to make deeply personal connections with other people hooked up to the same network. This might sound like some far-off tech fantasy cooked up by a kooky science fiction writer, but today's researchers are already working on devices that have the potential to achieve these incredible feats.

One of the most famous examples is an Elon Musk–led company called Neuralink. Neuralink's mission is to create "the future of brain-computer interfaces: building devices now that have the potential to help people with paralysis and inventing new technologies that could expand our abilities, our community, and our world."[752]

Neuralink aims to create a "direct link between the brain and everyday technology."[753] The technology is understandably crazy-complicated, but the basic idea is to use microscopic neural implants to help users connect to computers and other forms of technology. "Micron-scale threads are inserted into areas of the brain that control movement. Each thread contains many electrodes and connects them to an implant, the Link."[754] The Link is a "sealed, implanted device that processes, stimulates, and transmits neural signals" to the user's brain.[755]

Incredibly, "The threads on the Link are so fine and flexible that they can't be inserted by the human hand," so Neuralink is designing a robot that neurosurgeons can use to insert the threads.[756] Eventually, artificial intelligence will likely develop to a point where the human neurosurgeon is no longer needed for the implant. That means not even brain surgeons are safe from the coming job-disruption bomb.

According to Musk's Neuralink, "The initial goal of our technology will be to help people with paralysis to regain independence through the control of computers and mobile devices," but as the technology develops further, Neuralink researchers believe they "will be able to increase the channels of communication with the brain, accessing more brain areas and new kinds of neural information."[757]

Neuralink claims, "This technology has the potential to treat a wide range of neurological disorders, to restore sensory and movement function," but it will eventually be used "to expand how we interact with each other, with the world, and with ourselves."[758]

Brain implants, which sound like some far-fetched science fiction concept, have actually been used in the medical field for decades. A precursor to this sort of technology dates back to the early 1960s, when William House and John Doyle implanted the first cochlear implant in a patient to restore hearing.[759] In the mid-1990s, neurologist Phil Kennedy used implanted electrodes to give a paralyzed patient the ability to move a computer cursor without needing to use his hands.[760] Since these remarkable developments, the technology has developed substantially.

Deep brain stimulation (DBS) is a treatment employed today that uses implanted electrodes to stimulate specific areas of the brain with electrical impulses. DBS can be used to treat conditions including Parkinson's disease, epilepsy, dystonia, and tremors. This procedure is also being explored as a potential treatment for Tourette syndrome, Huntington's disease, and dealing with chronic pain and cluster headaches.[761]

With a device such as Neuralink implanted in a person's mind, he or she could have enhanced communication abilities, knowledge, skills, and potentially the power to feel the emotions of others or to have their own emotions altered.

I think when many people first hear about Neuralink, one of the things that immediately comes to mind is the fear that future generations might someday be forced to have devices implanted into their brains. And in dystopian hellscapes such as China, that might very well occur. But in much of the United States and other parts of the Western world, it's more likely that people will be banging down Musk's door to get access to a freshly minted brain implant. I know that sounds crazy—and believe me, I think it is—but the advantages to having a technology like Neuralink will almost certainly be too big to pass up.

If Neuralink or other, similar technologies become widely available to the public—a stated long-term goal of Neuralink, according to the company's website[762]—then anyone who refuses to take advantage of these groundbreaking devices would be put at a severe disadvantage. Why would employers hire a human-only job applicant running solely on inefficient, disconnected, frail brain power when they could hire one of many applicants who, thanks to the power of machine implants, have immediate access to the Internet and a slew of applications that give them super-human capabilities? How would normo-kids who have to embarrassingly fumble around with calculators to answer advanced trigonometry questions ever compete with children lucky enough to have instantaneous access to almost any piece of information known to man? How could nations equipped with slow-minded, old-style brains wage war effectively against armies of super-intelligent, highly trained soldiers?

You can say you, your kids, and your grandchildren will refuse to participate in the coming brain-implant revolution, but when faced with the voluntary choice of becoming part of a class of people considered to be inferior to the rest of humanity, saying no to brain implants will be easier said than done.

Of course, the dangers associated with the development of Neuralink and other brain implants are immense. Aside from the potential health risks, there are an incalculable number of ethical issues and dangers that inevitably come with such a technology, with one of the most obvious being that in a world where man and machine are united, how could we stop people from being heavily influenced, manipulated, or controlled to the point where they lose their free will?

Neuralink promises that "Security will be built into every layer of the product, using strong cryptography, defensive engineering, and extensive security auditing."[763] Surely if brain implants were to catch on, many governments around the world would work hard to ensure that these technologies are embedded with stringent privacy measures. But governments today make similar promises with other technologies and important systems, and many of them have been hacked. If government officials can't stop hackers from accessing the U.S. Department of Energy and National Nuclear Security Administration, both of which were breached in 2020 as "part of an extensive espionage operation," then what hope do people like you and me have?[764]

Even more worrisome, though, is that brain implants could be designed from the start to manipulate human behavior. I'm not suggesting someone such as Elon Musk or Neuralink would ever attempt to do such a thing. I think Musk and many of those he works with are genuinely concerned about bettering humankind, not seizing control of all of humanity. But what about other companies and our lying, lousy, no-good political class? Would they be interested in using Neuralink to alter society?

Just ask yourself: If politicians and large corporations designing these technologies could produce brain implants that make it difficult or even impossible for people to commit heinous crimes such as rape or murder, do you think they would? What about stealing or committing fraud? How about racism? If it were possible to have alleged racist ideas programmed out of people, do you think there are political, ideological, and activist groups who would be shouting from the rooftops for the widespread adoption of such a technology? Given the incredible amount of material that has been produced in the past decade about America's allegedly rampant racist attitudes against black citizens, it's hard to imagine that such a proposal would never get serious consideration.

This may be the first time you've heard of Neuralink or anything like it, and if so, it probably sounds—well, crazy. And I'm guessing it makes you feel extremely uncomfortable. Believe me, I understand. But the reason we must talk about these emerging technologies is because many of the world's most powerful institutions, governments, and other elites have been discussing them for years. While they are dreaming up the most "equitable" ways of designing brain implants, most of us are yelling at each other about something a powerless Hollywood celebrity said on Twitter.

In Klaus Schwab's 2022 book about the Great Narrative, titled *The Great Narrative: For a Better Future*, Schwab and his coauthor, Thierry Malleret, published excerpts and quotes from numerous interviews they had conducted with scientists. Schwab and Malleret mention that in their discussion with world-famous futurist Michio Kaku, Kaku said that "Brain-net [when the human mind is merged with computers] will take a few decades to get off the ground, but investors are already jumping into it."[765]

In Schwab's 2018 book about the Fourth Industrial Revolution, he noted, "Today's external devices—from wearable computers to virtual reality headsets—will almost certainly become implantable in our bodies and brains. Exoskeletons and prosthetics will increase our physical power, while advances in neurotechnology enhance our cognitive abilities."[766]

At the 2017 Davos annual meeting—during an interview with Sergey Brin, one of the cofounders of Google—Schwab suggested that as early as 2027, brain implants could be relatively commonplace.

"So Big Data, digital tools, at the service of medical and biological progress are advancing very fast," Schwab said. "But, can you imagine that in 10 years when we are sitting here, we have an implant in our brains? And I can immediately feel, because you all will have implants, I can and we measure all your brainwaves, and I can immediately tell you how the people react or I can feel how the people react to your answers."[767]

Kaku, Brin, Schwab, and the World Economic Forum aren't the only ones discussing the possibility of brain implants. Major media publications such as the *New York Times* are too. In a truly incredible article written for the *Times* in 2020, titled "The Brain Implants that Could Change Humanity," Moises Velasquez-Manoff explained that some neuroscientists are already using rudimentary brain implants to alter human behavior.[768]

"Not all the applications of brain reading require something as complex as understanding speech, however. In some cases, scientists simply want to blunt urges," Velasquez-Manoff wrote.

Velasquez-Manoff then told the story of Casey Halpern, a Stanford neurosurgeon with a long-running fascination of using brain stimulation and other procedures to alter "bad" behavior. According to the article in the *Times*:

> When Casey Halpern, a neurosurgeon at Stanford, was in college, he had a friend who drank too much. Another was overweight but couldn't stop eating. "Impulse control is such a pervasive problem," he told me.
>
> As a budding scientist, he learned about methods of deep brain stimulation used to treat Parkinson's disease. A mild electric current applied to a part of the brain involved in movement could lessen tremors caused by the disease. Could he apply that technology to the problem of inadequate self control?
>
> Working with mice in the 2010s, he identified a part of the brain, called the nucleus accumbens, where activity spiked in a predictable pattern just before a mouse was about to gorge on high-fat food. He found he could reduce how much the mouse ate by disrupting that activity with a mild electrical current. He could zap the compulsion to gorge as it was taking hold in the rodents' brains.[769]

Halpern then spent years studying how his rodent-zapping technique could be applied to humans, who, it turns out, are more difficult to deal with than rodents.

"Earlier this year, he began testing the approach in people suffering from obesity who haven't been helped by any other treatment, including gastric-bypass surgery," wrote Velasquez-Manoff. "He implants an electrode in their nucleus accumbens. It's connected to an apparatus that was originally developed to prevent seizures in people with epilepsy."[770]

According to the *Times*, Halpern has "so far completed two implantations." And if the tests are successful in reducing obesity, "which afflicts roughly 40 percent of adults in the United States, he plans to test the gizmo against addictions to alcohol, cocaine and other substances."[771]

Velasquez-Manoff didn't stop there. He said that "of the numerous proposed applications of brain-machine interfacing I came across, Dr. Halpern's was my favorite to extrapolate on."[772]

"How many lives have been derailed by the inability to resist the temptation of that next pill or that next beer? What if Dr. Halpern's solution was generalizable?" the *Times* writer wondered.[773]

"What if every time your mind wandered off while writing an article, you could, with the aid of your concentration implant, prod it back to the task at hand, finally completing those life-changing projects you've never gotten around to finishing?" he added.[774]

Velasquez-Manoff later said that "brain-reading and possibly brain-writing technologies are fast approaching, and society isn't prepared for them."[775]

Now, there's something we can agree on. The American people are about as prepared for conversations about brain implants as I am prepared to run the Boston Marathon. (Oh, and in case you have been fooled by my *very* fit physique, I'm not at all prepared to run marathons. Or half marathons. Or 5k races. Honestly, I'm amazed I can still walk up the flight of stairs we have at the office without dropping dead on the spot.)

The odds that your everyday American family will soon be walking around with machines embedded in their brains is low. But whether it's ten years away or thirty, the foundation of this technology, which has the power to totally transform humanity, is being built today. And whether it's by design or because most of the U.S. media isn't interested in discussing the truly important stories of the day, nearly everyone has been left in the dark on this vital topic—unless you happen to be one of the many average Joes who attend Davos each year, of course.

RE-DESIGNING NATURE

Klaus Schwab, the World Economic Forum, and their many powerful allies in business, finance, and government believe that a world in which ESG social credit scores and other, similar metrics serve as guardrails for institutions and societies would be a far more equitable, secure, and environmentally friendly place than one where individuals have the right to chart their own course in life. Thus, in the minds of many of the elites affiliated with the WEF, at the core of virtually every new technology ought to be well-formulated, internationally agreed-upon rules established by scientists, bureau-crats, activists, and powerful interests who are supposedly working in the best interests of the wider population. This is necessary, they believe, because there would be chaos without rules handed down on high from Davos overlords.

So when you see the World Economic Forum take such a strong interest in topics like brain implants, how can those of us who believe deeply in the importance of individual rights feel anything but a little terrified? The WEF has spent countless hours discussing the power of brain implants, praising their potential for curing depression,[776] boosting memory,[777] reading minds,[778] and helping the paralyzed walk again.[779] (If I didn't know any better, I might be fooled into thinking that when WEF talks about the miracles of the modern era, they are referring to Jesus.)

But as deeply disconcerting as these developments are, there are other parts of the Fourth Industrial Revolution that are just as worrisome and have also become major topics of interest in Davos in recent years. Perhaps most important is the development of gene editing.

Gene editing is "the ability to make highly specific changes in the DNA sequence of a living organism, essentially customizing its genetic makeup."[780] Emory University genetics professor Judith L. Fridovich-Keil explains, "Gene editing is performed using enzymes, particularly nucleases that have been engineered to target a specific DNA sequence, where they introduce cuts into the DNA strands, enabling the removal of existing DNA and the insertion of replacement DNA."[781]

As everyone who has ever seen the film *Jurassic Park* knows, DNA is one of the core building blocks of life. When altering DNA, scientists change the natural composition of living things.

Gene editing is made possible by a powerful tool called CRISPR. In an article for *Live Science* describing CRISPR and how it works, journalists Aparna Vidyasagar and Nicoletta Lanese explain:

> In popular usage, "CRISPR" (pronounced "crisper") is shorthand for "CRISPR-Cas9." CRISPRs are specialized stretches of DNA, and the protein Cas9—where Cas stands for "CRISPR-associated"—is an enzyme that acts like a pair of molecular scissors, capable of cutting strands of DNA.
>
> CRISPR technology was adapted from the natural defense mechanisms of bacteria and archaea, a domain of relatively

simple single-celled microorganisms. These organisms use CRISPR-derived RNA, a molecular cousin to DNA, and various Cas proteins to foil attacks by viruses. To foil attacks, the organisms chop up the DNA of viruses and then stow bits of that DNA in their own genome, to be used as a weapon against the foreign invaders should those viruses attack again.

When the components of CRISPR are transferred into other, more complex, organisms, those components can then manipulate genes, a process called "gene editing."[782]

Despite the moral hazards associated with its use, gene editing research has gained substantial popularity within the scientific communities of North America and Europe, and it is a particularly popular topic of conversation for futurists. Notably, CRISPR was used during the coronavirus pandemic as part of a method to quickly diagnose the disease, and bioengineers later used CRISPR to develop COVID-19 treatments.[783]

Klaus Schwab, who has discussed gene editing on numerous occasions, has called it and other, similar biological innovations made within the past decade "nothing less than breathtaking."[784]

As Schwab notes in his book titled *The Fourth Industrial Revolution*, "It took more than 10 years, at a cost of $2.7 billion, to complete the Human Genome Project. Today, a genome can be sequenced in a few hours and for less than a thousand dollars. With advances in computing power, scientists no longer go by trial and error; rather, they test the way in which specific genetic variations generate particular traits and diseases."[785]

Schwab rightfully explains:

The ability to edit biology can be applied to practically any cell type, enabling the creation of genetically modified plants or animals, as well as modifying the cells of adult organisms

including humans. This differs from genetic engineering practiced in the 1980s in that it is much more precise, efficient and
easier to use than previous methods. In fact, the science is
progressing so fast that the limitations are now less technical
than they are legal, regulatory and ethical. The list of potential
applications is virtually endless.[786]

The benefits of certain kinds of gene editing are admittedly enormous, particularly when it comes to agriculture. In a policy brief
published by the Tony Blair Institute for Global Change in 2021, senior
policy analyst Hermione Dace, who conducted a review of existing
research on gene editing in agriculture, seemed to agree with me and
my buddy Klaus, writing that the "benefits of gene editing are potentially substantial."[787] Among other things, gene-edited crops could be
designed to provide "Increased yields with less land and fewer inputs,"
"Increased resistance to adverse weather conditions," "Increased disease
resistance for both crops and animals," and "Reduced costs for farmers
and cheaper food for consumers."[788]

As Dace also noted, foods could even be developed with a higher
nutritional value and with fewer allergens. "Crops could be grown
to have reduced gluten, or soybeans could be grown to be lower in
unhealthy fats," she wrote. "Japan has approved a gene-edited 'super
tomato,' which has benefits for heart health."[789] (*Author's note:* The
Japanese never listen to me when I offer them advice, and don't get
me wrong, a "super tomato" sounds better than a regular tomato,
but whenever they're ready to choose their next genetically modified "super" food, I humbly suggest that they go with "super Twinkie."
Not only would a super Twinkie be much healthier than a regular
Twinkie, I'm guessing, it would be a billion times tastier than a
tomato—no matter how "super" it is.)

As outstanding as the potential upsides are for gene editing,
however, the potential dangers, especially if it's applied to humans,

are just as gargantuan. This is a reality Schwab himself has repeatedly acknowledged.[790]

Although World Economic Forum writers are careful not to embrace the use of gene editing to produce "designer babies," some, including Schwab, do seem to look favorably on some forms of human gene editing, especially as it relates to genetic diseases. This, of course, raises serious questions about whether gene editing could someday morph into full-blown eugenics, a concern Schwab also seems to share (although, not enough to oppose human gene editing, apparently).

In his book about the Fourth Industrial Revolution, Schwab wrote:

> We may see designer babies in the near future, along with a whole series of other edits to our humanity—from eradicating genetic diseases to augmenting human cognition. These will raise some of the biggest ethical and spiritual questions we face as human beings. Technological advances are pushing us to new ethical frontiers of ethics. Should we use the staggering advances in biology only to cure disease and repair injury, or should we also make ourselves better humans? If we accept the latter, we risk turning parenthood into an extension of the consumer society, in which case might our children will become commoditized as made-to-order objects of our desire? And what does it mean to be "better"? To be disease free? To live longer? To be smarter? To run faster? To have a certain appearance?[791]

Schwab further suggested that other biotechnological advancements are also being made today that will present additional ethical and societal problems.

"Bioprinting, the printing of living tissue, is also advancing steadily," Schwab wrote. "Entire organs will likely be printed on demand in the future. This will raise ethical and social issues, as the technology will initially probably be affordable only to a wealthy minority, widening inequalities in health and longevity."[792]

In other words, Schwab argued that biotechnology must be designed so that societal disparities are reduced. This approach presents a laundry list of issues, including that in an attempt to reduce racial disparities, policymakers or corporations might turn to racist policies that favor some demographics over politically or socially disfavored groups. Examples of such policies can already be found throughout North America and Europe.

In September 2022, Bank of America, whose CEO Brian Moynihan is a major player in the Great Reset movement, announced a new mortgage program that offers no closing costs or down payments to borrowers looking to buy a home for the first time.[793] Under the program, borrowers' credit scores will also not be considered when determining eligibility for a mortgage.[794]

Rather than roll out the program nationally or choose specific regions based on economic demographics, Bank of America decided it would micro-target neighborhoods with high populations of black and Hispanic families.[795] Many poor white, Asian, Indian, and Middle Eastern communities were deliberately excluded on the basis of race.

Additionally, as I explained in chapter 1, ESG social credit scoring systems typically include metrics that punish companies with too few or too many employees of particular racial groups.[796] Would ESG systems in the future award biotech companies who embrace similarly racist policies? That would be the most equitable thing to do, wouldn't it?

"WHAT IT MEANS TO BE HUMAN"

Earlier in this chapter and in other chapters, I briefly recounted part of a discussion between Mohammad Abdullah Al Gergawi and Klaus Schwab that occurred during the WEF's 2021 Great Narrative event. During that conversation, Al Gergawi notably called the Fourth Industrial Revolution era a "second wave of human evolution," one "based on technology."[797] This sort of creepy language is commonly found throughout the World Economic Forum's material about the Fourth Industrial Revolution and Great Narrative.

"This Fourth Industrial Revolution is, however, fundamentally different," one WEF writer said in a description of Schwab's book *The Fourth Industrial Revolution.* "It is characterized by a range of new technologies that are fusing the physical, digital, and biological worlds, impacting all disciplines, economies and industries, and even challenging ideas about what it means to be human."[798]

Schwab has similarly said that the "mind-boggling innovations triggered by the fourth industrial revolution, from biotechnology to AI, are redefining what it means to be human,"[799] as well as, "We are confronted with new questions around what it means to be human, what data and information about our bodies and health can or should be shared with others, and what rights and responsibilities we have when it comes to changing the very genetic code of future generations."[800]

In an article published on WEF's website in 2014, Nayef Al-Rodhan, who was at the time an honorary fellow at Oxford University, discussed at length the question, "Will biology change what it means to be human?"[801]

In 2016, Nicholas Davis, a professor at University College London, wrote in another article for the World Economic Forum, "Emerging technologies, particularly in the biological realm, are also raising new questions about what it means to be human. The Fourth Industrial Revolution is the first where the tools of technology can become literally embedded within us and even purposefully change who we are at the level of our genetic makeup. It is completely conceivable that forms of radical human improvement will be available within a generation, innovations that risk creating entirely new forms of inequality and class conflict."[802]

In 2018, Simone Schurle, a professor at ETH Zurich, wrote for the WEF website, "We have methods at hand for human enhancement. With advances in nanotechnology, materials, artificial intelligence and much more, new technologies are fast becoming able to raise the capacity of a healthy person beyond their normal range, or beyond any human's normal range. This will challenge the core of what it means to be human."[803]

Call me crazy, but it sure sounds like the meaning of humanity is on everyone's mind in Davos. Is it on yours? Your neighbor's? How about your representative in Congress? I would ask if it's on the minds of Joe Biden's handlers, but I already know the shocking answer to that question, although you'll have to wait for the next chapter to get the answer.

It is clear that to those Great Narrative elites who want a "new blueprint" for the future and believe a "second wave of human evolution" is upon us, the merging of humankind and machines, mixed with advancements in gene editing, is ushering in an unprecedented era in history. It's one that elites believe will require a "great transformation" of society.[804] But how will they ensure that their vision for the world will defeat all other competing ideologies?

Schwab says that the best way forward is for the international community to become increasingly more globalized, which will require stronger international institutions like the United Nations and large private institutions—especially banks, investment managers, and corporations—to embrace Schwab's stakeholder capitalism system.[805] (And remember, as we discussed in chapter 1, stakeholder capitalism is just another name for the Great Reset.) This can only happen, however, if existing societal structures are first radically reformed.

"We must embark on restructuring our economic, social and political systems to take full advantage of the opportunities presented," Schwab wrote in *The Fourth Industrial Revolution*. "It is clear that our current decision-making systems and dominant models of wealth creation were designed and incrementally evolved throughout the first three industrial revolutions. These systems, however, are no longer equipped to deliver on the current, and more to the point, the future generational needs in the context of the fourth industrial revolution. This will clearly require systemic innovation and not small-scale adjustments or reforms at the margin."[806]

Schwab asserted that this transformation "will require collaborative and flexible structures that reflect the integration of various ecosystems and that take fully into account all stakeholders, bringing together the public and private sectors, as well as the most knowledgeable minds in the world from all backgrounds."[807]

"With effective multistakeholder cooperation," Schwab added later in the book, "I am convinced that the fourth industrial revolution has the potential to address—and possibly solve—the major challenges that the world currently faces."[808]

It might sound strange, but at the end of the day, I think Klaus Schaub and a long list of other Great Reset and Great Narrative supporters would agree with me that the most important issue facing humanity for the remainder of this century is not whether innovation will occur, or even what kind of technological achievements will be made. There's nothing we can do to stop the course we're on now. The biggest concern and the defining issue of our era will be, what are the values that lie at the heart of the Fourth Industrial Revolution, and how will those values be promoted and protected? For the World Economic Forum and numerous other elites in Washington, Canada, and Europe, the Great Reset, stakeholder capitalism, ESG social credit scores, and globalism are their answers to those questions. For national fascistic nations such as China and Russia, the answers are very different, as you'll see in chapter 9.

What I want you to spend some time doing, perhaps over the next couple of days or so, is thinking long and hard about how you would answer those questions. How would you "design the future"? Outside of the ivory towers of academia, the halls of power in national capitol buildings, the boardrooms of the world's largest corporations, and the conference rooms of Davos, few people think about these questions. And as a result, the people have handed society's reins over to the ruling class. Soon, there won't be time to fix this problem. Humanity and its economies, cultures, and governments will have changed too much. Time is running out.

THE FUTURE IS (ALMOST) NOW

One of the great challenges about writing a book about futurism is that so many of the topics discussed can feel too distant for readers. I can imagine many people reading this book have stopped more than once and thought, *Wow. That sure is crazy. But that's a problem for future [fill in your name here]. I have far too much going on today to worry about brain implants and artificial intelligence job disruptions. I've got to drive the kids to baseball practice, get the oil changed in the car, and oh, that's right, we have that parent-teacher conference coming up soon. And I wonder what we should make for dinner tomorrow?*

Life is chaotic. No one understands that better than I do. My life is so busy at times that I forget what month it is. But as I have already shown throughout this book, many of the most important issues related to the Great Narrative are not as far off as they appear to be at first glance. Some of the biggest technological revolutions the world has ever known are already in development. It's tempting to think that the technological disruptions discussed throughout this book are some future generation's problems, but the best evidence shows that these changes are so much closer than most of us imagine.

Ray Kurzweil is one of my favorite futurists. To say Ray is a genius would be the understatement of the century. He's one of the most brilliant people alive today. Ray has a degree from MIT and over the past fifty years, he has been involved in some of the biggest developments in computer science and artificial intelligence. He has designed software to help students choose colleges, developed a revolutionary flat-bed scanner and text-to-speech synthesizer, built reading machines for the blind, created music synthesizers for Stevie Wonder, produced groundbreaking artificial intelligence programs, and written multiple *New York Times* bestsellers about futurism.[809]

I've somehow managed to trick Ray into coming on my radio and television shows on several occasions, and although I could easily pick out a thousand memorable things I have learned from speaking with him, one that stands out is his so-called Law of Accelerating Returns. There's a ton to this idea so if you're really interested in it, I encourage you to read one of Ray's many books. The basic idea as it pertains to technological development is that an "evolutionary process accelerates because it builds on its past achievements, which includes improvements in its own means for further evolution."[810] This applies to computation, which is also an evolutionary process. So according to Kurzweil's theory, computer power "will grow exponentially and essentially without limit."[811]

Kurzweil's theory isn't some half-baked idea. Ray has spent many years thinking about it, perfecting it, and studying history to prove it. And if you take even a cursory look at the history of technological development, you'll see that so far, Ray appears to be right. Throughout the course of his career, numerous analysts said he was crazy or that the predictions he made for the future couldn't possibly come true, but many of them did. Why? Because Ray has for decades believed that technological improvements to computers are bound to rapidly increase, not slow down, because they are able to draw on their previous improvements to accelerate future growth.

This theory explains how over just several decades humans went from having computers so large they took up entire rooms yet had low amounts of processing power to supercomputers that are small enough to fit in your back pocket and can access the Internet from almost anywhere.

Just think about how rapidly technology has improved in your lifetime. Even if you're young, in your late twenties or early thirties, you have seen tremendous technological growth in your adult life. Is it really so hard to believe that this trend will continue over the next couple of decades?

The most important leaders on the planet, including President Biden, adamantly believe the Fourth Industrial Revolution and all the disruption associated with it is just around the corner. They are spending huge amounts of time and money building frameworks that are meant to guide the future use of these developments for generations to come, as you'll see further in the next chapter. They meet regularly in places such as Davos to discuss the ideas outlined in this and previous chapters of this book. They are even passing laws to govern some of the most radical biotech innovations.[812] Why would they expend so much effort unless they were convinced the Fourth Industrial Revolution is coming?

In the next chapter, I will reveal how the West's ruling class is building a new Great Narrative for the coming age, as well as writing the rules for some of the most important innovations man has ever dreamed of—all while most people remain completely uninformed of even the most basic parts of what the Fourth Industrial Revolution entails. I think many readers will be shocked to see just how rapidly things are progressing, and, I hope, even more will be inspired to take the steps needed to protect your families, communities, and country from the perils ahead.

— 8 —

JOE BIDEN AND THE FUNDAMENTAL TRANSFORMATION OF THE WEST

O N MARCH 21, 2022, PRESIDENT JOE BIDEN DELIVERED A telling but largely ignored speech at the Business Roundtable's CEO quarterly meeting in Washington, DC. The Business Roundtable "is an association of chief executive officers of America's leading companies."[813] Unlike many other business groups, the Roundtable has acknowledged that shaping public policy is one of its primary goals.[814]

Long before I had heard anything about what was said at the 2022 meeting with Biden, the Business Roundtable had caught my attention. The World Economic Forum has spent an immense amount of time praising the Business Roundtable for announcing in 2019 a "redefinition" of the "purpose of a corporation."[815]

After agreeing upon the new definition, the Business Roundtable's highly influential group of CEOs wrote, "Since 1978, Business Roundtable has periodically issued Principles of Corporate Governance that include language on the purpose of a corporation. Each version of that document issued since 1997 has stated that corporations exist principally to serve their *shareholders*. It has become clear that this language on corporate purpose does not accurately describe the ways in which we and our fellow CEOs endeavor every day to create value for all our *stakeholders* [don't miss the shift from *shareholders* to *stakeholders*], whose long-term interests are inseparable."[816]

Further, the statement promised, "While each of our individual companies serves its own corporate purpose, we share a fundamental commitment to all of our stakeholders."[817]

The Roundtable then pledged that its member CEOs would, among other things, "deliver value to all" their stakeholders, "for the future success of our companies, our communities and our country."[818]

This shift away from shareholder primacy was something that the World Economic Forum, Klaus Schwab, and many members of the Democratic Party's establishment wing had been demanding for many years, and Biden had been part of those conversations for almost as long as Schwab. It's no wonder then that while Biden was on the presidential campaign trail in 2020, he declared, "It's way past time to put an end to the era of shareholder capitalism—the idea [that] the only responsibility a corporation has is to its shareholders. That's simply not true. It's an absolute farce."[819]

Biden's call to end the "era of shareholder capitalism" caused a tremendous amount of confusion. Many people on the right interpreted Biden's promise as an attack on the stock market and pensions. Although it's true that confusion is one of the few things Biden does well, in this case, the reason most people didn't understand what Biden was talking about isn't because the statement he made was nonsensical or because he was having one of his famous "Biden moments," but rather because few Americans have studied the Great Reset and its associated *stakeholder capitalism* literature. If everyone had spent as much time reading books by Klaus Schwab and other Davos elites as I have over the past few years, they would probably have already lost their minds, just like me. But they also would have understood immediately that Biden was alluding directly to the Great Reset, ESG scores, and large government programs when he said the "era of shareholder capitalism" needs to end. Biden was not suggesting the U.S. government should kill the stock market; that's something Biden would *never* do. After all, some of his biggest allies, like BlackRock CEO Larry Fink, control billions or even trillions of dollars' worth of stock and other assets.[820]

As incredible as Biden's open embrace of Schwab's *stakeholder capitalism* was, however, his meeting before the Business Roundtable in March 2022 included an even more shocking comment—a call for an entirely new global order.

"I think—you know, my mother had an expression: '*Out* of everything terrible, something good will come if you look hard enough for it,'" Biden told the Business Roundtable.[821] (The "terrible" things Biden alluded to in this part of his speech likely included Russia's invasion of Ukraine in February 2022, and probably at least some of the significant problems that marred Biden's first year in office, such as a forty-year-high inflation rate.[822]) He continued:

I think this presents us with some significant opportunities to make some real changes. You know, we are at an inflection point, I believe, in the world economy—not just the world economy, in the world. It occurs every three or four generations. As one of—as one of the top military people said to me in a secure meeting the other day, 60 million people died between 1900 and 1946. And since then, we've established a liberal world order, and that hadn't happened in a long while. A lot of people dying, but nowhere near the chaos.[823]

Let's stop for a second and think a little more carefully about that statement, because it really is remarkable and cryptic. Why is Biden reminding the Business Roundtable about the tens of millions of people who were killed in the First and Second World Wars? And even more importantly, what, exactly, were Biden's "top military people" telling him when this "secure meeting" was being held? And the notion that all of this is coming to Biden's decaying old mind within the context of thinking about a historic opportunity that occurs just once "every three or four generations" is disturbing, to say the least. But as hard as it might be to believe, Biden's speech gets even more bizarre in the statement that immediately followed his comments about millions of people dying.

"And now is a time when things are shifting," Biden said. "We're going to—there's going to be a new world order out there, and we've got to lead it. And we've got to unite the rest of the free world in doing it."[824]

A *new world order?* What is Biden talking about? I wish I could tell you he elaborated further during his Business Roundtable speech, but, incredibly, he ended his comments there—with the thought of tens of millions of people dead and the birth of a new world order hanging in the air like a thick fog.

On March 28, 2022, just seven days after Biden made those incredible comments at a meeting of the Business Roundtable, the World Government Summit kicked off its annual three-day event in Dubai. And no, the name "World Government Summit" isn't a joke. It's a massive, non-fictional event featuring some of the biggest names in government, activism, and finance that's held every year in the United Arab Emirates.[825] The host of the summit is the World Government Summit Organization (WGSO), "a global, neutral, non-profit organization dedicated to shaping the future of governments."

According to the WGSO website, "The Summit, in its various activities, explores the agenda of the next generation of governments, focusing on harnessing innovation and technology to solve universal challenges facing humanity."[826]

The WGSO leadership team includes just four individuals: Omar Sultan Al Olama, minister of state for artificial intelligence, digital economy, and remote work applications in the UAE; Ohood Bint Khalfan Al Roumi, minister of state for government development and the future of the UAE; "His Highness" Sheikh Mohammed bin Rashid Al Maktoum; and our old, creepy friend from chapter 2, Mohammad Abdullah Al Gergawi.[827]

Don't forget that Al Gergawi is the same gentleman who in 2021 told Klaus Schwab during the World Economic Forum's Great Narrative event—which was also held in Dubai, by the way—that "People are looking for a way for a Great Transformation," as well as "a new blueprint." He also declared that nations "need a new Great Narrative because our digital world will be as important as the physical world," and that humanity is experiencing a "second wave of human evolution" that is "based on technology."[828]

On March 29, Becky Anderson, an anchor at CNN, hosted the first full presentation of the conference's second day, and boy was it a doozy. The panel, which featured elites from the United

States and UAE, was aptly titled, "Are We Ready for a New World Order?"[829] During the introduction to the panel discussion—which, by the way, came immediately after two brief speeches by none other than Klaus Schwab and Al Gergawi—CNN's Anderson said, "The title of this session is 'Are We Ready for a New World Order?' Well, the organizers here are nothing if not ambitious. This is, I think you will agree, a daunting subject for discussion.... but tackle it, we must. Because what I believe is clear is that we have hit an inflection point."[830] (Huh—an *inflection point*. That's interesting. Joe Biden used the *exact* same words when calling for a "new world order" one week earlier.)

During the incredibly fascinating (and disturbing) panel discussion, Frederick Kempe, president and CEO of the Atlantic Council, was asked about the possibility of a new world order developing in 2022, 2023, and beyond, to which he responded, "So, my mentor on issues of world order is Henry Kissinger, so I'll try to channel him. And forgive me, Dr. Kissinger. But his answer would be, 'What do you mean "new world order?" We have not had a world order yet.' What we've had is we've had a Western order that was imposed on the world."[831]

A few moments later in the presentation, Kempe added, "If you look at what we're trying to create right now, where I would say we're at an inflection point in history as important as the end of World War I, where we got the effort at world order tragically wrong."[832]

There those words are again—an *inflection point*. Is it just a coincidence Kempe, Anderson, and Biden all used the same words while discussing a new world order, all within about a week? I thought it was possible, until I heard the very next statement in Kempe's presentation.

"We ended up with millions of dead, the Holocaust in World War II," Kempe continued. "After World War II, we got more right than wrong, with the creation of the international liberal order and the United Nations and the Bretton Woods system and the European coal and steel community, NATO, etc."[833]

Millions dead in World War II? The start of an "international liberal order"? This is eerily similar to the speech Biden gave before the Business Roundtable, when he said, "60—60 million people died between 1900 and 1946. And since then, we've established a liberal world order, and that hadn't happened in a long while. A lot of people dying, but nowhere near the chaos."[834]

Kempe continued by further explaining, "And then the Soviet Union fell and then the Cold War—we thought it was the end of history and we thought that everyone could fit into this system that had been created. And it worked for a while, but not everybody came into it. But China grew. China certainly took full advantage of being part of the global system. Russia did not. Russia became more of an outlier. And I think where we are now, and this gets to your question, Becky, of a new world order, is it can go in two directions, with the war in Ukraine now being a decisive element."[835]

In Kempe's opinion, what lies ahead? What will this "new world order" look like? He continued:

Either the jungle is back, as the historian Bob Kagan talks, and that we can go into a darker era. Or, we could go into an era, because of the advances of science, advances of technology, that could be one of the most prosperous, promising, progressive, enlightened, moderate, modern eras that we've ever faced. And I think we're in a moment where that's being decided, and I think the importance of the Ukraine issue is that it's [a] fulcrum for this. And how the world manages this and comes out of this is going to have far reaching consequences that go beyond Ukraine.[836]

Like Biden, Kempe believes the war in Ukraine and the other economic and social difficulties of the past couple of years have produced an "inflection point" that could lead to the development of a "new world order." Unlike Biden, though, Kempe explicitly stated that "advances of science, advances of technology" will likely be the driving force behind what he believes will be positive change.

This view perfectly aligns with what Schwab said in his brief speech delivered at the World Government Summit, just before the start of the "New World Order" panel that featured Kempe.

"The objective is to quickly recognize the potential of new technologies," Schwab said, "as well as develop the necessary ethical and political frameworks around those new technologies, to ensure that those technologies are human-centered and society-oriented."[837]

Schwab further argued that the planet "has to overcome the repercussions of a dangerous clash between major global powers," another allusion to the war in Ukraine. "History is truly at a turning point. We do not yet know the full extent and the systemic structural changes that will happen. However, we do know that global energy systems, food systems, and supply chains will be deeply affected."[838]

It's clear from all these statements that the Great Narrative—or, at the very least, the concepts behind the slogan—were top of mind for the elites at the World Government Summit, and that they all understand that the kind of extreme technological disruption I discussed earlier in this book is creating a period of tremendous opportunity *and* risk. Yes, extreme disruption could cause potentially deadly "structural changes" that will deeply affect "global energy systems, food systems, and supply chains," but in the end, the world will be better off with the "new world order" embraced by the Biden, Davos, and World Government Summit regimes—at least, that's what they would have you believe.

It's important to understand that although much of the Great Narrative is undefined and, at times, opaque, the push toward the technology-rich utopia imagined by people like Schwab and the "experts" at the Atlantic Council and CNN has already started in a number of important ways. The foundation for a Great Narrative world is being laid today (it's called the Great Reset, in case you haven't been paying attention), and some of the most important parts have nearly been fully constructed.

Throughout the remainder of this chapter, I will outline some of the key moves that have been made to bring about a new Great Narrative, most of which have occurred since the start of 2020. In chapter 10, I'll outline the strategies those of us who believe in individual liberty and free markets can use, both now and over the next decade or more, to push back against Davos's demand for greater centralization of authority and their calls for a "new world order."

As you read through the sections that follow, try to think carefully about how each of these reforms to society, the economy, and/or public policy could be used as a foundation for a technology-centric Great Narrative world like the one we discussed in previous chapters.

The changes occurring in the West today are the pillars that will support Great Reset elites' plans in the decades to come, namely a Fourth Industrial Revolution society built on top of a Great Reset framework. This is vital for Americans to understand, because the stakes couldn't possibly be higher. As detrimental as many of the issues described later in the chapter are, they pale in comparison to the potential danger of these reforms being mixed with the radical technological changes that are coming our way over the next decade and during later stages of the twenty-first century. If we fail to rein in this runaway freight train today, it very well might be impossible to stop it in the future.

SOCIAL CREDIT SCORES

If I had to pick one thing that is most likely to fundamentally transform (and not for the better) the lives of you, your family, and just about everyone else you know over the next decade, it's the widespread use of social credit scores like environmental, social, and governance (ESG) metrics. In chapter 1, I explained how ESG scores are being used to change how businesses in the United States, Canada, and Europe operate, as well as which products and services they offer. Because large corporations have become such a massive part of Western societies, it is possible to dramatically alter almost any part of life by changing corporate behavior through ESG.

As I also noted previously, most corporations in North America and Europe have already agreed to implement social credit scoring. According to a report by accounting firm KPMG, *thousands* of companies, located in more than fifty countries, have ESG systems in place.[839] This includes 82 percent of large corporations in the United States.[840] And adoption is even more common among the biggest-of-the-big corporations. About 96 percent of the G250—"the 250 largest companies by revenue as defined in the *Fortune* 500 ranking"—produce ESG reports.[841]

These figures are truly stunning. But as remarkable as the rise of social credit scores has been thus far, the level of adoption we have seen in recent years is just the tip of the ESG iceberg. Governments around the world are now putting polices into place that are designed to coerce—or, in some cases, even outright force—most large businesses to adopt a social credit scoring system.

In March 2022, the U.S. Securities and Exchange Commission (SEC) formally proposed new rules for publicly traded corporations that would, among other things, require companies to disclose their climate-related "risks" and carbon-dioxide emissions.

In an article about the SEC rules, the *National Law Review*, which called the Biden rules "landmark requirements for public companies," reported:

> The Commission is proposing a rule requiring registrants under the Exchange Act to include certain climate-related information in their registration statements and periodic reports. Such information includes climate risks and their material impacts on business, strategy, and outlook; greenhouse gas (GHG) emissions (further discussion below); governance of climate-related risks and relevant risk management processes; climate-related targets, goals, and transition plans; and certain climate-related financial statement metrics and related disclosures in audited financial statements.[842]

As of March 2023, when the final draft of this book was completed, a final SEC rule was on track to be rolled out in the spring or summer of 2023.[843]

The Biden administration's "landmark" SEC disclosure rule isn't the only step the White House has taken toward imposing ESG requirements on U.S. companies. For example, the *National Law Review* also reported, "Under the Biden Administration, the SEC has taken an all-agency approach to the establishment of new environmental, social, and governance (ESG) disclosures. These include issuing risk alerts and investor bulletins regarding ESG investing; creating the Climate and ESG Task Force in the Division of Enforcement; announcing a greater focus on climate-related risks and climate-related disclosure in public company filings; and issuing a request for comment from market participants on climate change disclosure."[844]

Further, one of the more remarkable, albeit mostly ignored, actions taken by the Biden administration to move the Great

Reset forward was its official alliance with Klaus Schwab's World Economic Forum. (Yes, you read that correctly. The U.S. government has an official partnership with the same organization responsible for launching the Great Reset campaign in 2020.)

According to a report by the U.S. State Department:

> At the 2021 United Nations Climate Change Conference (COP26), the United States announced the launch of the First Movers Coalition, a new platform for companies to harness their purchasing power and supply chains to create early markets for innovative clean energy technologies that are key for tackling the climate crisis. Announced by President Biden at the COP26 World Leaders Summit, the First Movers Coalition was created through a partnership between the U.S. State Department's U.S. Special Presidential Envoy for Climate and the Office of Global Partnerships, and the World Economic Forum, in collaboration with the U.S. Departments of Commerce and Energy.[845]

The State Department further reported that at the launch of the First Movers Coalition (FMC), "more than 25 Founding Members—leading companies from a wide range of industries around the world—made commitments to spur the commercialization of emerging technologies in this decade. The First Movers Coalition's unique approach assembles ambitious corporate purchasing pledges across sectors that represent more than a third of global carbon emissions and span heavy industry and long-distance transportation."[846]

In November 2022, the State Department announced the coalition had "expanded to include 65 companies, representing more than 10 percent of the global *Fortune* 2000 by market value, as well as ten government partners. New corporate members include General Motors, PepsiCo, and Rio Tinto."[847]

Now, I've got to admit, as astounding and troubling as this "partnership" between the U.S. government and the evil geniuses behind the Great Reset is, I can't help but feel just a tiny bit of satisfaction from the arrangement. To be honest, "a tiny bit of satisfaction" doesn't quite capture my attitude. I think hiring a plane to skywrite "I TOLD YOU SO" over the headquarters of the *New York Times* for three hundred straight days might do the trick, though.

Over the past few years, I have been called a crazy "conspiracy theorist" by countless pundits and media outlets for daring to suggest that Joe Biden is deeply connected to the Great Reset. And even more media outlets, including the *New York Times*, outright dismissed the Great Reset generally as nothing more than a "baseless conspiracy theory."[848]

None of that was true, as I proved well beyond a reasonable doubt in my book about the Great Reset and now throughout this book. You should always do your own homework, of course, but I am confident that if you do, you'll see that everything I've been saying is extremely well supported by a mountain of evidence, including the countless sources contained in the endnotes section of this book. In this book and my previous one, my team and I have worked tirelessly to pull together all the relevant articles, books, and speeches presented by the leaders of the Great Narrative movement, and we've quoted them all at length so you can hear their message and their goals *in their own words*. Frankly, I shouldn't have to convince you of any wild conspiracy theories. All I have to do is highlight what these people are saying for themselves and show you how *coordinated* all these messages are.

But in case you have any doubts about just how involved the White House has been in advancing the Great Reset, there's really no need to look further than the First Movers Coalition. I'm not trying to argue that the FMC represents the totality of the Great Reset; it's just a tiny sliver of the larger proposal. But it is incontrovertible proof that President Biden is actively working with the World Economic Forum to advance the Great Reset and one of its chief goals, the increase of "public-private partnerships" between large corporate interests and governments.

The first reform instituted by the White House to promote the Great Reset is not quite as obvious as the First Movers Coalition, but it's a much more important component of it. During the final weeks of the Trump administration, back in early 2021, the Office of the Comptroller of the Currency (OCC) published a new regulation called the Fair Access rule that would have mandated that large banks "conduct risk assessment of individual customers, rather than make broad-based decisions affecting whole categories or classes of customers when provisioning access to services, capital, and credit."[849]

The Trump-era OCC rule was designed to stop banks from using ESG social credit scores and other subjective measures to discriminate against particular industries or customers, which is arguably the most foundational part of the Great Reset and an essential component of creating a new Great Narrative world in the future. If banks and other financial companies can't turn off access to capital and other services using ESG, then it would be significantly harder to force businesses to change their behavior.

That's not to say this is the only stick used by the financial system and Wall Street elites to impose their Great Reset principles. ESG scores are also utilized when formulating bond ratings and by powerful Wall Street investment management firms such as BlackRock.[850] However, a rule that stops banks from using their tremendous wealth and influence to push the Reset agenda forward would have been a big victory. I say "would have" because one of the very first things President Biden did during his first few weeks in office was to kill Donald Trump's OCC Fair Access rule.[851]

Why would Biden want to make it significantly easier for the financial system to discriminate based on subjective ideological criteria? Given the numerous other pieces of evidence tying Biden to the Great Reset—including the First Movers Coalition and the fact that the White House's own special climate envoy, John Kerry, has openly expressed his support for it[852]—the answer seems obvious: Biden and his allies are using the financial system to accomplish the goals they haven't been able to achieve through the legislative process. It is a strategy that's not only important for those trying to push the reset button on the economy today, but for altering society in the future as well. If, for instance, tech companies cannot gain access to banking services without first meeting certain ESG regulations, then elites can ensure that whatever technology is developed in the future will have ESG principles embedded within it.

THE GREAT GLOBAL RESET

The United States isn't the only country working to impose a Great Reset. Many of the most prominent political leaders in Europe have endorsed the Reset explicitly by calling directly for a "Great Reset" or by rolling out a "build back better" infrastructure plan, a major part of the Great Reset (and, not coincidentally, one of President Biden's major campaign slogans in 2020). In fact, the Group of Seven (G-7) nations—which includes the heads of state of Canada, France, Germany, Japan, Italy, the United Kingdom, and America— even went so far as to launch in June 2021 a global "Build Back Better World" (BBBW) initiative.[853]

According to the Biden administration, the BBBW plan is "a values-driven, high-standard, and transparent infrastructure partnership led by major democracies to help narrow the $40+ trillion infrastructure need in the developing world, which has been exacerbated by the COVID-19 pandemic."[854]

Under BBBW, the G-7 and "other like-minded partners" will work together "in mobilizing private-sector capital in four areas of focus—climate, health and health security, digital technology, and gender equity and equality—with catalytic investments from our respective development finance institutions."[855]

As I have explained numerous times throughout this book, the partnership between government, corporations, and private-sector capital is at the heart of the Great Reset proposal. Further, tackling climate change, "digital technology," and "gender equity and equality" are often cited as main concerns for the Great Reset and a new Great Narrative.[856]

The Build Back Better World initiative isn't the only way politicians outside of the United States are fighting for the Great Reset. The most far-reaching effort is underway in the European Union, which is now exceptionally close to rolling out a government-imposed social credit system of its own.

According to the international law firm Shearman & Sterling, "On March 10, 2021, the European Parliament adopted a resolution calling for mandatory human rights, environmental and governance due diligence standards across the value chain for companies operating in the EU internal market."[857] (The term "due diligence" is Euro-speak for "ESG.")

Shearman & Sterling further added, "If adopted, all EU Member States will be required to implement the Directive into their national laws. This will result in substantive due diligence requirements being imposed on companies, whether based in the EU or selling their products and services into the EU, across their entire value chain, with potential sanctions for non-compliance."[858]

Note that the mandatory ESG system proposed in the EU resolution would not only be imposed on companies selling products and services in Europe—which, of course, would apply to many American businesses—but would also be indirectly imposed on businesses in those companies'"value chains." Citing the EU resolution, Shearman & Sterling noted, "'value chain' means a company's activities, operations, business relationships and investment chains, including entities with which the company has a direct or indirect business relationship, both upstream and downstream, and which either: (a) supply products, parts of products or services that contribute to the company's products or services, or (b) receive products or services from the company."[859]

That means an American business that supplies paper, software, customer support services, banking services, ink toner, or any number of other business-related products would also be subject to the European Union's ESG system. Noncompliant EU companies would be punished with fines and potentially sanctions, effectively forcing them to ensure that they only do business with those companies willing to bend the knee to the European Union's social-credit-score demands.

In March 2022, Gibson Dunn reported that in February 2022 the European Commission, the executive branch of the European Union, published its own ESG directive, "together with a civil liability regime to enforce compliance with the obligations to prevent, mitigate and bring adverse impacts to an end."[860]

Like the European Parliament draft, the European Commission proposal for an ESG framework would apply to large corporations operating in the EU as well as large non-EU corporations and businesses within a relevant company's value chain, although the European Commission draft is thought to be slightly "narrower" in its scope.[861]

The European Commission's draft would establish "mandatory obligations for relevant companies to conduct human rights and environmental due diligence to identify actual or potential adverse impacts across their own operations, their subsidiaries' operations, and the value chains of their 'established business relationships.' In this context, the Directive expressly envisages the development of preventive action plans and the imposition of contractual terms on business partners, and creates an obligation to bring actual adverse impacts to an end."[862]

In other words, the European Union's proposed ESG system would fundamentally transform Europe and could drag much of the American economy down with it.

Before becoming law, the European Commission's ESG proposal will need to be formally adopted by both the European Parliament and the Council of the European Union. The Council of the European Union approved an ESG proposal in late 2022, but it will need to work with the European Parliament once the Parliament formally passes its own amended version before the plan can be enshrined into law.[863] Legal experts expect that both EU bodies are likely to approve a finalized ESG system at some point in 2023, "with subsequent transposition into national law two to four years thereafter."[864]

If the European Union were to institute a mandatory ESG system, it would undoubtedly have a strong influence on U.S. businesses, especially large multinational corporations, many of which already have ESG and "diversity, equity, and inclusion" programs in place. This, in turn, will impact virtually every part of *your* life. It makes little sense for large corporations to design some of their supply chains so that they are in line with EU mandates, while maintaining a more "free market" version for Americans. It would be much more cost-effective for a corporation to simply alter all or nearly all their business products, services, and practices so that they comply with European standards.

More importantly, some of the mandates that will almost certainly be imposed by the European Union will be impossible to comply with unless a corporation alters its practices and policies across its entire business model. For example, one of the European Union's ESG mandates would be a company's carbon footprint. Such a standard would force businesses to change their policies across the board, because by its very nature, a carbon footprint encompasses all that a business does, not just its practices related to one region that it operates in.

If the European Union's social credit proposal goes into effect, it would effectively mean that whatever the European Union wants, the European Union will get. And Americans will have to deal with the consequences, whether they like them or not, so that corporations can continue to make gobs of cash in Europe.

Of course, it's likely many in the European Union fully expect the United States to adopt an ESG system of its own at some point, especially in light of the recent actions taken by the Biden administration. And if that occurs, the United States and Europe will need to work together to establish a unified, internationally recognized ESG model. Having one ESG system for Europe and another for America and another for Canada would be completely unworkable in our modern globalized economy. Lucky for them, the World Economic Forum and other Great Reset groups have already developed such a system.[865] It's almost as if this has been the plan all along.

One of the primary goals of the ESG model plan published in 2020 by the World Economic Forum and the International Business Council (IBC), which we discussed briefly in chapter 1, was to address concerns over the lack of a common international standard that could apply to all corporations. According to the publication introducing their finalized proposal for a new international ESG model, titled *Measuring Stakeholder Capitalism: Toward Common Metrics and Consistent Reporting of Sustainable Value Creation*, the World Economic Forum and IBC wrote, "In its Summer Meeting 2019, IBC members reaffirmed the significance of environmental, social and governance (ESG) aspects of business performance and risk in creating long-term value. They flagged the existence of multiple ESG reporting frameworks and the lack of consistency and comparability of metrics as pain points preventing companies from credibly demonstrating to all stakeholders their progress on sustainability and their contributions to the SDGs."[866]

SDGs stand for "sustainable development goals." These are the targets for global development set by the United Nations in their Agenda 21 and Agenda 2030 reports. (And yes, in case you were wondering, I am talking about *that* Agenda 21.)

To address this problem, the World Economic Forum and the IBC collaborated "to identify a set of universal, material ESG metrics and recommended disclosures that could be reflected in the mainstream annual reports of companies on a consistent basis across industry sectors and countries."[867]

The International Business Council is one of the most influential associations of CEOs in the world, so its commitment to develop an international ESG system that could be used in both Europe and the United States is telling. We should consider it proof that if the European Union were to impose a mandatory ESG model, there wouldn't be significant pushback from American companies making claims about silly things such as national sovereignty or a need for the United States to lead the way. No, America's largest companies have already signed on to the internationalism of the Great Reset, so whatever ESG system comes out of the European Union will most assuredly serve as the starting point for future negotiations.

JOIN OR DIE

The ESG model can only work effectively if everyone is required to participate. If there are any holdouts, then the entire system could eventually collapse, because the more authoritarian it gets, the more likely it is that businesses will opt out. This is why so many in business and government want to make ESG, or something similar to it, mandatory. But what happens if reasonable Republicans and Democrats in Congress decide they aren't interested in Davos's master plan for transforming society? Would that kill the Great Reset? Oh, if only it were that simple.

To ensure that every business on the planet—and no, I'm not exaggerating—has an ESG social credit score, financial services companies have started to roll out algorithms that "predict" an ESG score based on publicly available information. That means even small and medium-sized companies now have ESG scores, even though many of them do not know it.

I already touched on this topic in chapter 6, but it is crucial that you hear it again and understand the significance of this system.

In July 2021, Moody's Investors Service "launched a first-of-its-kind tool to generate real-time predicted environmental, social, and governance (ESG) scores for millions of public and private small- and medium-sized enterprises (SMEs) worldwide."[868]

According to Moody's press release announcing its new ESG tool, "the ESG Score Predictor provides financial institutions with essential quantitative data for portfolio and risk management, and helps companies monitor ESG risk across their global supply chains."[869]

Moody's further noted, "The ESG Score Predictor leverages state-of-the-art advanced analytics to provide 56 ESG scores and sub-scores for any given company using location, sector, and size."[870]

Moody's claims that its score predictor, coupled with its database of self-reported ESG scores, offers customers "perspectives on more than 140 million public and private companies globally."[871]

Again, *more than 140 million companies globally*. Let that one sink in. Moody's ESG database includes just about every business of any consequence at all, located anywhere on the planet. How is that possible? Is the little dry-cleaning place down the street from your house secretly producing an ESG report for its masters in Davos?

Or even more bizarre, is the mid-sized paper supply company in a bustling urban district in a city you've never heard of in Bangladesh also frantically producing ESG reports for Moody's? Of course not. Moody's ESG predictor tool uses an "innovative machine learning" algorithm relying on basic, easy-to-find information such as a company's size, location, and industry to produce a totally made-up ESG score.[872]

On the surface, this might seem like a strange thing for a company such as Moody's to do. Moody's wants businesses to produce their own ESG reports every year. Moody's uses that data to produce vast ESG databases and reports of its own. Access to these reports and associated data are routinely sold to investors and financial institutions for a big profit. Why, then, would Moody's want to create ESG reports using machine learning? Demand from investors for ESG reports developed using algorithms is almost certainly much lower than the higher-quality reports that are developed using detailed, self-reported data. If you stop and think about it for a minute, though, I think you will see the brilliance of this strategy— and I say "brilliance" in the most supervillain sense of the word.

For most companies, especially those willing to adhere to ESG's various woke causes, the absolute worst way to get an ESG score would be to have it produced by an algorithm like Moody's. Imagine that you're the owner of a donut shop. Let's call it Glenn's Delicious Donuts Emporium. The store would be made in the shape of a donut, and every donut would be made on demand, so when you order a donut, it's always hot and fresh out of the fryer. Oh, and the donut shop would have plush leather couches everywhere, and we'd offer a frosting guarantee that promises Glenn's signature frosted donuts will always have more frosting than all the other donut shops in town—or really anywhere in Texas. No, the world. A worldwide frosted donut guarantee. And any customer who dresses up like

George Washington and enters the store yelling "Huzzah!" gets free donuts for life, but anyone who dresses up like Joe Biden is banned forever. (Wow. This donut shop illustration has really gotten away from me. I think I just found a great plan for retirement, though.)

The point is, you're a donut shop owner, and you decide that Glenn's Delicious Donuts Emporium is going to be the "greenest" donut shop in town. All your donut containers are biodegradable. You only buy dairy products from farms with free-range cows, each of which is assigned its own cow masseuse, to help ensure that milk production is as stress-free as possible. You even sell those terrible paper straws that break apart in your mouth after five seconds but supposedly help to save sea turtles off the coast of Bora Bora.

Under this scenario, if you don't produce an adequate ESG report and distribute it to the proper ratings agencies, you run the very real risk of being assigned an algorithm-based ESG report from an agency like Moody's, which means your green donut shop will be treated as though it were just another Styrofoam-using, planet-hating, deplorable donut emporium, like those losers down the street who own Stu's House of Donuts. As a business owner, if you do anything at all that would normally be favored by ESG analysts, you're incentivized to develop and distribute your own comprehensive ESG report. Otherwise, you're going to end up with whatever ESG score Moody's algorithm gives to you.

For elites who want a new Great Narrative, this is a win-win scenario. Either way, Glenn's Delicious Donut Emporium is going to end up with an ESG social credit score—either by choice or by force. And many of those with assigned scores will likely suffer or even be destroyed as a result. For elites, the ESG movement is "join or die."

You know, now that I think about it, maybe this donut-shop fantasy isn't so great after all.

YOUR VERY OWN ESG SCORE

At this point in the chapter, you're probably feeling a little lonely (and hungry). It isn't fair that big multinational corporations, medium-sized businesses, and small-town donut shops all get to participate in the Great Narrative's ESG system but you, the individual, are left out. I mean, sure, even if you weren't assigned an ESG score, you still get to live under Joe Biden's "new world order." And yes, your life is going to be transformed regardless of whether you have a social credit score tied solely to you. But you're probably still upset that the Great Narrative doesn't seem to include personalized ESG scores. Well, fear not. Your very own ESG social credit score is coming to a community near you, and sooner than you think.

In 2022, the coauthor of this book, Justin Haskins, revealed in a report for The Heartland Institute that expert credit analysts are predicting that ESG scores will soon be used by personal credit scoring companies when determining fitness for mortgage and other credit applications.[873]

According to the supremely handsome Haskins—wait, how did "handsome" make it into the text? Nice try, Justin. Let's try that again. According to Haskins:

> Perhaps the most widely used service to check the creditworthiness of individuals and small business is FICO. When banks and credit unions examine applications for loans, FICO is often the first place they turn. In an article published in December 2021 on FICO's website titled "Lending Predictions 2022: From BNPL to ESG (and More)," a FICO senior principal consultant wrote that he believes in 2022 "The ESG Agenda Will Drive the Search for Cleaner Decisions."[874]
>
> "In financial institutions, much of the ESG agenda is delivered at the corporate level," the analyst wrote, "but in 2022 we

expect to see an increased focus on bringing ESG data into more granular lending and investment decisions. This will require increased innovation in the use of alternative data across all kinds of lending. One example would be the inclusion of property energy ratings data in mortgage valuation and decisioning, and CO_2 emission data for small businesses."[875]

He also noted, "Over the longer term, we expect that ESG and climate risk evaluations will become an integral element of credit risk and affordability assessments."[876]

FICO's prediction about the use of personalized ESG scores begs the question, how can ESG scores be applied to individuals if they don't produce ESG reports like businesses do? To some extent, I am going to speculate here, but I think there are several different ways personalized ESG scores could be applied in the near future.

First, instead of an ESG score being imposed on you directly, it's possible it will simply be applied to the property you own. As the analyst for FICO noted, a potential example of an expansion of ESG to individuals is "the inclusion of property energy ratings data in mortgage valuation and decisioning."[877] So *you* might not technically have an ESG score, but perhaps *your home* and *your car* will, and it could be based mostly on environmental concerns, especially at first.

This isn't likely going to be the only way personalized ESG scores will be utilized, however. As I outlined in previous chapters, the technology already exists to track what anyone says on social media and categorize it as *harmful* or *misinformation*. From there, it isn't a big leap to get to a point where social media companies might team up with credit reporting agencies to help them punish anyone stepping out of line.

Individualized ESG reports could be based on other factors as well. For example, perhaps those who drive gasoline-powered cars—or even those who drive electric cars but do so more often than the average person—could be assigned a lower environmental score in a personalized ESG report created by a non-government credit agency. And since everyone involved is a "private" company, individuals who feel as though they are being targeted wouldn't be able to sue under current law. "It's just the free market," they'll argue.

I know some readers, even after the evidence I have presented thus far, might think all this amounts to little more than fear-mongering. But the truth is, millions of people already have individualized ESG scores and don't even know it. You might even be one of them.

For example, Merrill Lynch, an investment management company owned by Bank of America, automatically generates an ESG score for investors enrolled in its Merrill Edge program, which includes individuals and families with low investment amounts, even less than $1,000. According to Merrill, "Since its creation in 2010, Merrill Edge has grown steadily to $184.5 billion in assets and more than 2.4 million accounts."[878]

There's nothing stopping other investment management firms from employing a similar strategy. Many already seem to be laying the groundwork to dramatically expand their efforts to promote ESG, including to individual investors. JP Morgan Asset Management, for example, noted in a July 2020 report that it has developed a "coordinated strategy" to expand sustainable investing that includes "three pillars."[879]

According to JP Morgan's report:

> The *Sustainable Investing Solutions & Product Innovation* pillar partners with our investment and distribution teams to provide expertise in developing a sustainable investing product framework. Building on ESG integration, the team engages with clients on targeted solutions and builds training and marketing

tools to help further accelerate the development of our firmwide capabilities.

The Sustainable Investing Research & Data pillar is focused on developing dedicated ESG research by partnering with our investors across asset classes and with data scientists. The priority over the next two years is building our proprietary ESG scores, as well as thematic research and analytics, with a key focus on climate change and carbon transition.

The Investment Stewardship pillar is responsible for our investment-led, expert-driven stewardship approach, engaging with companies and voting proxies on behalf of clients. The five main priorities: governance, strategy alignment for the long term, human capital management, stakeholder engagement and climate risk.[880]

It's clear from the report by JP Morgan Asset Management, which had a record $3.11 trillion in assets under management at the end of December 2021, that ESG investing, including for individual portfolios, is only going to become more prominent in years ahead.

In 2022, JP Morgan's Private Bank started to provide its customers with "personalized, automated and relatable ESG 'impact reporting.'"[881] (In case you were wondering how the JP Morgan Private Bank compares to JPMorgan Chase & Co., the Private Bank is a high-priced bank meant for the rich and famous. You didn't think they banked at the same old Chase location by the local mall that you're used to, did you?)

According to an article published on the Private Bank's website, "Rather than one-size-fits-all scores," JP Morgan's Private Bank clients "will be able to see their real-world impact in tangible measurements, such as 'tons of carbon avoided' or 'number of refugees hired' across eligible securities. These concrete figures can empower clients to think of and wield their investments as tools for change going forward."[882]

Boy, I bet you're relieved. Finally, you'll be able to bank with someone who is actively tracking the number of "refugees hired" across all your portfolios—well, only if you're filthy rich, of course. If you're not, don't worry, though. Personalized ESG scores are coming for the middle and working classes soon.

JP Morgan and Merrill Lynch are not the exceptions in the financial services industry.[883] Nearly every single large wealth manager and investment management company I've investigated says they offer ESG investment advice, tools, and/or funds for individual investors. And many already have the ability to determine the ESG score of an individual's personal portfolio at the drop of a hat, although it seems many do not yet run such an analysis without first being asked to do so by an investor, unlike Merrill Lynch.

This is an incredibly troubling development. If ESG scores were used solely for the purpose of offering advice to investors, then I wouldn't care one bit that these massive institutions are spending millions upon millions of dollars to roll out ESG systems directed at individuals. But as I have shown throughout this book, that simply isn't the case. ESG is not merely an option; it's being imposed on businesses and corporations of every size. When business owners refuse to participate voluntarily, the powers that be on Wall Street simply invent an ESG score for them. And now, they are laying the groundwork to do the same thing for individuals and families. Are you getting worried yet?

NET-ZERO "HEROES"

In November 2021, more than one hundred world leaders and forty thousand participants gathered in Glasgow, Scotland, for the UN Climate Change Conference of the Parties (COP26), a meeting that was similar in size and importance to the COP that produced the much-talked-about Paris Climate Agreement in 2015.[884] According to the United Nations, the most important outcome of the Glasgow meetings was the Glasgow Climate Pact, which, among other things, included an agreement among nations that signed the pact to "phase-down" coal-fired power and "phase-out" the use of "inefficient" fossil-fuel subsidies.[885]

Representatives in Glasgow also agreed to "present stronger national action plans" in 2022 and to double the financial support given to developing nations to help them adapt to the "impacts of climate change and building resilience," although the United Nations admits that "this won't provide all the funding that poorer countries need."[886]

Many climate activists and political pundits were quick to call the meeting a disappointment. Given that the standard talking point from scaremongers like Joe Biden is that climate change poses an "existential threat" to human life on earth—meaning all of humanity could end up being wiped out by man-caused climate change—pundits were expecting a sweeping set of radical climate-related reforms. For example, Swedish climate activist and darling of the American media Greta Thunberg held a rally outside of the Glasgow event where she told thousands of young people in attendance that Glasgow was a "failure."[887]

"It is not a secret that COP26 is a failure," Thunberg said. "It should be obvious that we cannot solve a crisis with the same methods that got us into it in the first place."[888]

Thunberg also said Glasgow was a "two-week long celebration of business as usual, and blah, blah, blah," and that "We know that our emperors are naked."[889] The most notable moment from Thunberg's appearance outside of COP26, however, was when she and a band of climate alarmists sang a wonderful new protest anthem—"You can shove your climate crisis up your arse!"—which they set to the tune of the American folk classic, "She'll Be Coming 'Round the Mountain."[890]

As much as I'd like to join Greta in all the singing and criticizing of elites in Glasgow, the truth is, some absolutely remarkable reforms occurred at COP26, many more than what Greta and liberal pundits are willing to acknowledge (and no, that's not a good thing). Their negative reaction was not driven by climate zealots' belief that nothing important happened in Glasgow, but rather because in their minds, the only acceptable "solution" to any problem is to dramatically expand the might of government. In Glasgow, that didn't happen—at least not in the most traditional sense—because the representatives there, including President Biden and his Great-Reset-loving "climate czar" John Kerry, knew full well that they wouldn't be able to deliver on any truly extreme climate policies adopted at Glasgow. Contrary to Thunberg's beliefs, most regular, non-insane people in America, Canada, and Europe aren't willing to put government in charge of virtually every part of the global economy in the hopes of stopping a nearly undetectable amount of global warming a hundred years in the future.[891] In other words, it's a big, fat political loser.

This point was proven in America in 2022, when oil and gas prices soared. Fueled by inflation, Russia's invasion of Ukraine, and Europe and America's reaction to that invasion, the national average for a gallon of gasoline in the United States topped $4 in March 2022, the highest price since 2008.[892] In June, it nearly reached $5 per gallon.[893] In California, the average price surged well above $6.[894]

Rather than celebrate the unaffordability of fossil fuels, Americans were furious and demanded that the Biden administration do more to increase domestic oil and gas production—which, again, is something Biden has said is contributing to the *extinction* of humanity. Rasmussen Reports noted 70 percent of likely voters said they "believe the U.S. government should encourage increased oil and gas production to reduce America's dependence on foreign sources of oil and gas."[895]

The White House reluctantly and ineffectively complied, agreeing to resume selling oil and gas drilling leases on federal lands after more than a year of trying to kill the industry, but not selling anywhere near enough leases.[896] Biden also released one million barrels of oil per day from America's strategic oil reserves, one of the most spectacularly stupid public policy decisions in recent memory (which is really saying something, I know).[897] Not only did releasing the strategic reserves do virtually nothing to lower costs, it depleted America's emergency oil supply at a time when Russia had just invaded Ukraine and was threatening other European nations with a nuclear war, and, as a result, put the United States on the brink of being forced into a major military conflict in Europe. Does that sound to you like a good time to burn through strategic oil reserves?

As terrible as the Biden administration's reaction to rising oil and gas prices was, it sent a clear signal to the White House that their understanding of voters' view on oil and gas was at least partially correct. There was and still is absolutely no interest among voters in seeing the Biden administration shift its resources and energy toward battling climate change. So why do I say that Glasgow was a success, at least from the perspective of power-hungry ruling elites? Because thanks to the Great Reset, government doesn't need to pass laws to reform societies and economies. All they need to do is expand their framework for advancing public-private partnerships, and that's exactly what happened in Glasgow in 2021.

By far, the most important thing to happen at COP26 was an announcement by the Glasgow Financial Alliance for Net-Zero that it had struck an agreement with hundreds of financial institutions around the world to impose a quasi-Green New Deal on the global economy.[898] The development was covered in detail in a report published by the *Irish Times*, which wrote:

During a day of talks dominated by climate finance issues, the most significant announcement was $130 trillion in funding over three decades through the Glasgow Financial Alliance for Net-Zero (GFANZ).

Banks and asset managers representing 40 per cent of the world's financial assets, involving 450 firms across 45 countries, have pledged to meet the goals set out in the Paris climate agreement, said UN special envoy on climate Mark Carney, who is co-chairing the initiative with US businessman Michael Bloomberg.

"Ramping up adoption of clean energy and other sustainable infrastructure fast enough to avoid the worst impacts of climate change will require trillions of dollars in new investment—likely in the ballpark of $100 trillion," the GFANZ co-chairs said.

"Most of that will have to come from the private sector, especially after the enormous toll that the pandemic has taken on governmental budgets."[899]

GFANZ, which was first launched in April 2021, bills itself as "a global coalition of leading financial institutions committed to accelerating the decarbonization of the economy." Although it doesn't get the attention it deserves, GFANZ is one of the most important new forces in the Great Reset movement.[900]

All member institutions in GFANZ (and there are already more than 450) must say they are "committed to the same overarching goal: reducing net-zero emissions across all scopes swiftly and fairly in line with the Paris Agreement, with transparent action plans and robust near-term targets." Further, "All actors must meet stringent criteria," including enacting net-zero carbon-dioxide commitments that "use science-based guidelines to reach net-zero emissions across all emissions scopes by 2050."[901] GFANZ members must also "include 2030 interim target settings and commit to transparent reporting and accounting in line with Race to Zero criteria."[902]

This does *not* mean that GFANZ members have merely agreed to enact net-zero commitments within their own companies. Their pledge to make net-zero commitments "across all emissions scopes" is another way of saying that GFANZ members must agree to use their wealth and power to impose net-zero policies on everyone they do business with. Because GFANZ members include much of the financial system used in the West—$130 trillion worth, according to the *Irish Times* report—the GFANZ model is effectively a plan to force everyone in the United States, Canada, and Europe, as well as companies that do business in these regions, to transform their lives and business practices so that they are in line with "green" causes.

GFANZ members are grouped into several different associations, all of which fall under the GFANZ banner: "the Net-Zero Banking Alliance, the Net Zero Asset Managers initiative, the Net-Zero Asset Owner Alliance, the Paris Aligned Investment Initiative, the Net-Zero Insurance Alliance, the Net Zero Financial Service Providers Alliance, or the Net Zero Investment Consultants Initiative."[903]

Member institutions in each of these groups have a special role to play in the plan to impose an international Green New Deal. For example:

+ The Net-Zero Banking Alliance agrees to use the banking system to deny access to capital to noncompliant businesses and individuals.
+ The Net Zero Asset Managers initiative and Net-Zero Asset Owner Alliance use the financial muscle offered by groups like BlackRock to force businesses on Wall Street to give in to GFANZ's demands.

◆ The members of the Net-Zero Insurance Alliance are "committed to individually transitioning their underwriting portfolios to net-zero greenhouse gas emissions by 2050," meaning that over the next three decades, insurance companies are progressively going to stop offering insurance products that cover businesses, homes, cars, and other properties that are not in line with the net-zero movement.[904]

The establishment of GFANZ is the Great Reset movement's biggest victory yet, and it could single-handedly accomplish much of what the Great Reset and Great Narrative movements have been calling for, especially if GFANZ turns its sights to other issue areas, such as "wealth inequality" and "racial equity."

The connection between the Glasgow Financial Alliance for Net Zero, the Biden administration, and the Great Reset is not merely theoretical. There are deeply rooted, well-documented ties between them that prove the Biden White House is a driving force behind the Great Reset. Biden's climate czar John Kerry worked directly with the leadership of GFANZ to launch and expand the initiative, which was officially announced one day before Joe Biden hosted his "Head of State Climate Summit" in April 2021.[905] Treasury Secretary Janet Yellen also appeared with Kerry and GFANZ leadership when the alliance was introduced to the public.[906]

The GFANZ leadership team is full of people with direct ties to President Biden and/or the Great Reset. For example, Mark Carney, co-chair of GFANZ, has served on the Board of Trustees for Klaus Schwab's World Economic Forum.[907]

Former New York City mayor and billionaire Michael Bloomberg is another GFANZ co-chair. For those of you who don't remember, Bloomberg is one of American history's greatest political losers. He will forever be remembered for spending more than $900 million in the 2020 Democratic presidential primaries

despite having absolutely no chance of winning the party's nomi-
nation.[908] In fact, Bloomberg failed to win a single state. He did,
however, manage to capture 58 of the 1,991 delegates needed to be
the party's presidential nominee, about 3 percent of the total. That's
an average campaign cost of $15.51 million per delegate won.

After Bloomberg's presidential campaign burst into flames,
he turned his attention to assisting his political ally, Joe Biden.
Bloomberg committed a whopping $100 million to help blue-collar,
Scranton Joe win the 2020 general election in Florida.[909] Of course,
Joe lost Florida badly. Donald Trump won the state by more than
371,000 votes, a much bigger margin of victory than Trump enjoyed
in 2016. (Barack Obama won Florida in both 2008 and 2012.)

Now that I think about it, maybe Bloomberg's involvement in
the Great Reset is a good thing, since, you know, everything else he
does in politics ends up being a total dumpster fire.

Another GFANZ-Biden connection is Mary Schapiro. She's
the vice chair of GFANZ.[910] She worked alongside Biden in the
Obama administration, where Schapiro served as the chairperson
of the Securities and Exchange Commission.[911]

Two members of GFANZ's Principals Group are also members
of the World Economic Forum's board: Thomas Buberl, CEO of
French insurance giant AXA; and everyone's favorite Wall Street
tyrant, Larry Fink, the head of BlackRock and another Biden ally.
Fink was even rumored to be in the running to become Biden's
Treasury secretary.[912]

It's also worth noting that Brian Moynihan, whose connection to the Great Reset was discussed in chapter 1, is a part of the
GFANZ Principals Group.[913] In case you've forgotten, Moynihan
is CEO and chairman of the board at Bank of America, and he was
one of the leaders behind the publication of *Measuring Stakeholder
Capitalism: Toward Common Metrics and Consistent Reporting of
Sustainable Value Creation*, the model ESG framework released by

the World Economic Forum and International Business Council in September 2020.[914]

When you couple the power of GFANZ with its numerous connections to the Great Reset and Biden White House, I don't think you will struggle to see why I believe the Glasgow Financial Alliance for Net Zero will be a vital part of the movement to impose the Great Reset over the next decade or more.

DIGITAL DOLLARS

As I explained in chapter 1, the radical economic proposal called modern monetary theory (MMT) is the straw that stirs the Great Reset drink. Not everyone in the Great Reset movement will admit it—probably because of how insane modern monetary theory sounds to regular folks—but elites' actions in recent years have proven that they are devoted to MMT (or something like it) for the long haul.

In short, MMT is the belief that debts and deficits don't matter, or matter very little, and that all central banks and governments should be concerned with is addressing inflation and helping an economy reach full employment. If your goal is to control the economy using the financial system, which is exactly what the Great Reset aims to do, then having the ability to create as much money as you want via an MMT monetary system is an extremely appealing proposition.

The best way to control inflation, according to those who believe in the modern monetary theory model, is for government to manage economic activity more closely.[915] So under MMT, if energy prices were driving inflation, a government could impose price controls, offer subsidies, mandate spending limits, or build an elaborate system of ESG incentives and punishments to help bring the price of energy down, and inflation along with it.

None of this actually works, of course. When central banks and governments spend too much money, you end up with horrifically stunted economic growth or inflation—or, if you're really lucky, you'll get both. But you cannot convince government bureaucrats that they do not, in fact, know best. In the end, central planners are gonna plan.

In chapter 4, we talked about how a central bank digital currency could be used to control and manipulate behavior, but it is also worth mentioning that it would be an incredibly useful tool for central planners seeking to alter economic activity too. If government knows at every moment where each digital penny is being spent, stored, and/or invested, it can create rules that would help rein in inflation. Why enact a price control if you can simply program a digital currency so that there are detailed limits on spending in sectors considered to be problem areas? Similarly, think about how great it would be—at least "great" in the minds of the ruling-class elites in charge of the Federal Reserve—if central banks could control the money supply by knowing exactly how many dollars exist in the world, and then destroying currency when there's too much of it or helicopter-dropping it to spur economic activity. Think about how simple it would be for central banks to adjust interest rates as well, and to ensure there's proper wealth "equity," both within and between nations.

A programmable central bank digital currency would be an especially powerful tool if it were tied to individual and business ESG scores. Americans with higher scores could earn more interest on their dollars, for example. Others with high scores might have automatic discounts applied while shopping. Interest rates for holding digital dollars could be raised or lowered based on ESG metrics, or to advance racial or gender equity. The possibilities are scary and endless.

I already detailed my biggest concerns with digital dollars in chapter 4, so there's no need to go over the issue again at a granular level here, but it is important to remember that the creation of a central bank digital currency is something that the Biden administration set the table for in 2022, and the administration has already released plans to further develop a future CBDC in 2023.[916, 917] Although a U.S. digital dollar has not yet been created, if enough digital-dollar-loving progressive Democrats and Republicans were to gain power in Congress in the future, they would almost certainly finish what Biden started. If they did, then for generations to come, a digital currency would play a core role in elites' expansion of the Great Reset and new Great Narrative.

EXPANDING "BIOTECHNOLOGY"

One of the most disturbing topics we've discussed so far in this book is gene editing and bioengineering. Although some forms of bioengineering can offer significant benefits for the world, such as making crops more drought resistant, others can be used to alter the genetic makeup of animals and even people.[918] In chapter 7, I talked about the advances being made in this area, as well as the potential benefits and risks. However, for most people, the scariest aspects of bioengineering and gene editing seem too theoretical to worry about today. But as nutty as it might sound, these technological innovations are not only developing at a rapid pace; they are being officially promoted by the U.S. government.

In September 2022, President Biden released an "Executive Order on Advancing Biotechnology and Biomanufacturing Innovation for a Sustainable, Safe, and Secure American Bioeconomy."[919] The stated primary purposes of the order were to "Grow Domestic Biomanufacturing Capacity," "Expand Market Opportunities for Bio-based Products," "Improve Access to Quality Federal Data," "Advance Biosafety and Biosecurity to Reduce Risk," and "Streamline Regulations for Products of Biotechnology," among other things.[920]

The executive order is sweeping and includes more important statements than I could possibly fit into this chapter, but the most vital comments are made in the order's very first section. According to the order, "Although the power of these technologies is most vivid at the moment in the context of human health, biotechnology and biomanufacturing can also be used to achieve our climate and energy goals, improve food security and sustainability, secure our supply chains, and grow the economy across all of America."[921]

Note the extent of Biden's executive order. The Biden administration believes biotechnology and biomanufacturing could be expanded across numerous parts of the economy, including "in the context of human health."

The next two sentences in the order provide even greater context for this impressive goal, and they are flat-out terrifying:

> For biotechnology and biomanufacturing to help us achieve our societal goals, the United States needs to invest in foundational scientific capabilities. We need to develop genetic engineering technologies and techniques to be able to write circuitry for cells and predictably program biology in the same way in which we write software and program computers; unlock the power of biological data, including through computing tools and artificial intelligence; and advance the science of scale-up production while reducing the obstacles for commercialization so that innovative technologies and products can reach markets faster.[922]

Wait a minute. The White House is now actively promoting that scientists learn "to develop genetic engineering technologies and techniques to be able to write circuitry for cells and predictably program biology in the same way in which we write software and program computers"? And they want to "unlock the power of biological data" too? Whose "data" are they talking about, exactly? Yours? Mine?

Call me crazy, but I don't think it's a good idea for the same government that can't figure out a way to run Amtrak without losing hundreds of millions of dollars every single year to be in the business of "genetic engineering technologies and techniques to be able to write circuitry for cells and predictably program biology in the same way in which we write software and program computers."

This is far too much power for a government in a free society to have, and if the goal here is only to bioengineer crops to help feed more people, then that should have been explicitly stated in the text of the order. As far as I can tell, there isn't a single provision making that clear.

I can't believe that I need to write this, but we must not let the Biden administration—or any other administration, for that matter—play God by rewriting the basic rules of biology. That is a dangerous game, and the last time a major Western power played it, Europe ended up with the Holocaust.

THE "INFLECTION POINT"

Before I wrap up this chapter, let's briefly recap the progress Joe Biden and the wider Great Reset movement have made in recent years toward their goal of building a framework for a new brand of twenty-first century, international fascism:

1. Influential leaders from government, corporations, financial institutions, central banks, think tanks, and activist groups have been actively calling for a "new world order," a Great Reset of capitalism, and a new Great Narrative for the human race, driven in large part by technological advancements and globalization.[923, 924, 925]

2. The Biden administration has started to lay the foundation for the widespread use of ESG scores in the United States. Among other actions, the Biden administration has established

new SEC rules that require companies to create various ESG reports and climate and energy disclosures.[926] This White House has also killed Trump-era OCC regulations that would have stopped banks from using ESG scores and other subjective metrics when evaluating customers, and it has established an official program (the First Movers Coalition) with the World Economic Forum to further expand the U.S. government's public-private partnerships with large corporate interests.[927, 928]

3. Thousands of companies, located in more than fifty countries, have jumped on the ESG bandwagon. This includes 82 percent of large corporations in the United States.[929] Adoption is even more common among the largest corporations. About 96 percent of the G250—"the 250 largest companies by revenue as defined in the *Fortune* 500 ranking"—produce ESG reports.[930]

4. Led by the Biden administration, the G-7 nations—which includes the heads of state of Canada, France, Germany, Japan, Italy, the United States, and the United Kingdom—launched in June 2021 a global "Build Back Better World" initiative, a Great Reset–themed global infrastructure plan.[931]

5. The European Union is now on the verge of creating a mandatory ESG social credit scoring system, one that would apply to the biggest and most influential companies in Europe, America, and Canada. If this mandatory ESG system is adopted, it would have an immediate impact on corporate behavior in the United States, and as a result, it would dramatically change our own markets and culture.[932]

6. Many of the world's most powerful CEOs have collaborated with the World Economic Forum to develop a new international ESG model that could standardize ESG social credit scores across North America and Europe.[933]

7. Moody's Investors Service has developed an ESG score "predictor" tool that institutions are already using to review

ESG scores for almost every small and medium-sized business on the planet, most of which have never once produced an ESG report of their own.[934]

8. Large financial services companies such as Merrill Lynch and JPMorgan have started to develop personalized ESG scores for millions of individual consumers, many of whom have no idea that this has occurred. Further, FICO, America's leading personal credit score agency, has predicted that ESG scores will soon be applied to individuals.[935]

9. With the help of the Biden administration, Mark Carney, Michael Bloomberg, and a number of other elites connected to the White House and/or the World Economic Forum launched the Glasgow Financial Alliance for Net Zero. GFANZ member institutions control more than $130 trillion in assets and have pledged to use their wealth and influence to push countries around the world toward the climate goals of the Great Reset, as well as to destroy as much of the fossil-fuel industry as possible by 2050.[936]

10. In 2022, the Biden administration and Federal Reserve laid the groundwork for the creation of a new central bank digital currency, one that would almost certainly be programmable, trackable, and easily manipulated to promote the Great Reset and a new Great Narrative.[937]

After looking at all the "progress" that has been made by elites seeking to build a foundation for a new Great Narrative, it's easy to lose hope in the future of the West, including the United States. But while it is true that the challenges we face are immense and that the times in which we live truly do represent an "inflection point" in the course of humanity, there are many reasons to think that those of us who still believe in fundamental human rights and the importance of empowering individuals can stop the Great Reset and Great Narrative from gaining a permanent foothold. We must recognize the reality of the dangers, but we shouldn't despair. As I'll show you in chapter 10, there is much we can do, and I have faith that the American people, as well as the citizens of Canada and Europe who are determined to be free, will rise to the occasion.

However, before we can address the best strategies for fighting back against the new Great Narrative and its Great Reset framework, there's one more significant danger we must discuss and be fully attuned to, because if we're not, it could swallow up the pro-liberty movement and push our societies in the direction of full-blown tyranny even more rapidly than what we're seeing with the Great Reset and Great Narrative.

In the wake of the numerous actions taken by the Biden administration, John Kerry, Klaus Schwab and the World Economic Forum, United Nations, International Monetary Fund, Canadian prime minister Justin Trudeau, and various other Great Reset groups in North America and Europe, various authoritarian government regimes—most notably Russia and China—have created an anti-Great Reset movement of their own. But instead of standing for the cause of liberty and individual rights, these regimes are seeking to protect their tyrannical governments and the societies they lord over from being affected by the internationalism of the Great Reset, as well as its nontraditional values on issues such as sexuality.

The governments of Russia, China, and other nations are now selling themselves as the champions of nationalism and traditionalism and as the defenders of their rich cultural heritages, which they say are in grave danger because of the actions taken by supporters of the Great Reset and Great Narrative in North America and Europe. But the truth is, these governments and many of their leaders are horrific and are certainly not friends of freedom nor traditional Western values. In fact, many of them would love nothing more than to see the West collapse.

Like the devotees of the Great Reset, these regimes are led by fascists too, but they are not international fascists like those who support the Great Narrative. They are national fascists, and they have a deep interest in using advanced technologies to impose their will on their own people. As much as we might want to focus all our attention on the fight against the Great Reset and the elimination of freedom in the United States and other nations in the West, we must not lose sight of the trouble brewing in the East. We must fight this war on two fronts.

So what do the national fascistic regimes of countries like Russia and China look like, and how are they trying to transform the world so that it helps them accomplish their own goals? In the next chapter, I will detail the plan to advance national fascism across the globe, focusing on the emerging leader in this movement, Vladimir Putin and his tyrannical regime in Russia.

9

NATIONAL FASCISM, RUSSIA, AND A NEW WORLD WAR

FTER NEARLY A YEAR OF AMASSING TROOPS ALONG THE
eastern and northern borders of Ukraine, Russian president
Vladimir Putin gave the order to his military forces to launch a full-scale invasion on February 24, 2022—a date that will forever live
in infamy in the minds and hearts of tens of millions of people in
Ukraine and around the world.[938]

Just prior to the invasion, 150,000 to 200,000 Russian soldiers
surrounded Ukraine, along with an estimated 2,840 battle tanks.
In the months thereafter, most of those forces entered Ukrainian
territory.[939] The incredibly fierce battles that followed captured
the attention of the world, as everyday Ukrainians took to arms to
valiantly defend their nation. By mid-March, just twenty days after
the war began, 14,000 to 21,000 Russian soldiers had been injured
in the fighting, and more than 7,000 had been killed.[940] To put that

astounding figure into perspective, more Russian soldiers died in Ukraine in three weeks than the total number of Americans killed over two decades of fighting in Afghanistan and Iraq as part of the United States' Global War on Terror.[941]

For the first time since the end of World War II, a full-scale war had broken out in Europe, and as you will see later in this chapter, the Great Reset was at least partially to blame.

By the end of April 2022, Russian forces had seized control of much of the eastern and southeastern regions of Ukraine, including the valuable warm-water port city of Mariupol, which had offered Ukraine access to the Sea of Azov and, by extension, the Black Sea, Istanbul, the Aegean Sea, and the Mediterranean Sea.[942] But the cost to the Russian military for these gains was great. About 21,000 Russian troops had been killed in the fighting by the end of April, along with several Russian military generals and other high-ranking military officials, according to reports by the Ukrainian military.[943] The toll for the Ukrainians had also increased dramatically.

According to admittedly questionable reports from the Ukrainian government, about 2,500 to 3,000 Ukrainian soldiers had died in the fighting through the middle of April, and about 10,000 others had been injured.[944]

At the time of the publication of this book, the war rages on, with seemingly no end in sight. In February 2023, the United Kingdom's Defense Ministry reported that Russia has lost between 40,000 and 60,000 soldiers in the war, including private contractors.[945] Another 140,000 to 160,000 Russian soldiers have been wounded.[946] Accurate estimates about Ukraine's casualties are harder to come by, but U.S. officials estimated in November 2022 that it was greater than 100,000.[947]

Of course, the military casualties only tell a small part of the story. The suffering endured by the civilian population of Ukraine was both breathtaking and unimaginably tragic. In the initial months of the conflict, numerous stories of human rights violations surfaced.

In Manhush, located twelve miles from Mariupol, Russian forces dug two hundred graves to hide thousands of dead civilian bodies they killed in battles throughout the region.[948] The United Nations noted in a report about the war that Russian forces "indiscriminately shelled and bombed populated areas, killing civilians and wrecking hospitals, schools and other civilian infrastructure—actions that may amount to war crimes."[949]

The United Nations further reported at least seventy-five incidents of sexual assault, as well as more than one hundred attacks by Russian forces on medical facilities and "widespread" detentions, all in just the first couple of months of the war.[950]

Ukrainian forces were also accused of committing human rights violations, although not on the scale of the claims made against Russia's military. One of the most notable examples occurred in April 2022, when video footage was released to the public that appeared to show Ukrainian soldiers executing a captured, injured Russian soldier.[951]

On March 13, 2023, the United Nations' human rights office reported 13,734 Ukrainian civilians had been injured in the conflict and 8,231 others had been killed.[952] Further, in the initial months of the conflict, greater than 11 million Ukrainians had been forced from their homes, with more than 5 million of the displaced leaving the country entirely. About half ended up in Poland, which sits to the west of Ukraine.[953]

A NEW WORLD WAR

Following Putin's unprecedented attack, Great Reset–aligned European and North American leaders, including President Joe Biden, rallied to wage a truly historic economic, financial, and public-relations war of their own against Russia's government, economy, and even some prominent Russian figures.

Within just the first two months of the war, dozens of economic sanctions were imposed on Russian businesses, individuals, and government entities. The United States issued sanctions prohibiting new investment in Russia and limiting access to two important Russian banks, Sberbank and Alfa Bank.[954] Russian flights were prohibited from entering the airspace of Canada, the European Union, United States, and United Kingdom.[955] The United Kingdom and European Union banned the export of luxury goods such as cars and artwork to Russia.[956] High levies, some surpassing 30 percent, were placed on a variety of Russian imports, including vodka.[957]

The European Union, United Kingdom, and United States also imposed sanctions on at least one thousand individual Russian citizens and businesses, including Kremlin-linked Russian oligarchs and Putin's own adult children.[958] In some cases, governments seized the property of Russian citizens located outside of Russia, typically without proving a crime had been committed. A $90 million yacht owned by Viktor Vekselberg was seized in Spain.[959] British authorities captured a $50 million yacht in London in March 2022.[960] The French government seized twelve residences belonging to billionaire Russian oligarch Roman Abramovich, including a $120 million mansion in France's Riviera region.[961]

Additionally, the United States banned the import of Russian oil and natural gas, and the United Kingdom announced that it would totally phase out Russian oil by the end of 2022.[962] EU member states, some of which rely heavily on Russian energy, pledged to end their dependence on Russian energy "well before 2030."[963]

The most important and far-reaching sanctions, however, sought to undermine Russia's financial and monetary systems. In an article published by the BBC outlining the many sanctions taken by Western nations against Russia, the BBC reported, "Western countries have frozen the assets of Russia's central bank, to stop it using its $630bn (£470bn) of foreign currency reserves. This caused the value of the rouble to slump by 22%, which has pushed up the price of imported goods and led to a 14% rise in Russia's rate of inflation."[964]

The BBC further reported, "The United States has barred Russia from making debt payments using the $600m it holds in US banks, making it harder for Russia to repay its international loans."

Without access to its foreign currency reserves, Russia was unable to pay many of its obligations, causing credit ratings agencies to downgrade Russian bonds and other investments.

According to the BBC, "Credit ratings agency S&P … declared Russia to be in 'selective default' (this means a debtor has defaulted on a specific obligation but not its entire debt) after it attempted to make interest payments on roubles for two dollar-denominated bonds. The agency said this was because investors were unlikely to be able to convert the roubles into dollars."[965]

These and dozens of other sanctions resulted in massive energy-price increases across the globe. Gasoline and oil prices were already high before Russia's invasion of Ukraine. This was largely because of the Biden administration's anti-fossil-fuel policies and a global supply chain crisis that was primarily caused by reckless governments choosing to lock down huge swaths of their economies in 2020 and 2021 as part of a futile attempt to stop the COVID-19 pandemic. So when North America and Europe waged war on Russia's energy industry, the result was soaring energy prices.

According to the *Wall Street Journal*, "Events in Ukraine caused oil prices to skyrocket, pouring gasoline on what was already a smoldering fire. Brent crude topped $130 a barrel in early March, and gasoline prices recently hit a record $4.331 a gallon, putting them up more than 15% from where they stood a month earlier, according to AAA."[966]

Of course, in a Great Reset world, government never walks alone. Hundreds of the largest and most powerful corporations in North America and Europe imposed their own "sanctions" on Russian businesses and communities. According to a remarkable report by the Yale School of Management, by March 2023, "Over 1,000 companies have publicly announced they are voluntarily curtailing operations in Russia to some degree beyond the bare minimum legally required by international sanctions."[967]

Among the more than one thousand businesses that are working hand in hand with Western governments to punish Russia are MasterCard, BlackRock, Salesforce, UPS, VISA, Mercedes-Benz, Snapchat, eBay, John Deere, Ford, Amazon, Coca-Cola, Delta, FICO, Hilton, Boeing, Prada, Uber, Reebok, Nike, Adidas, Microsoft, PayPal, Apple, Marriott, and fast-food giant McDonald's, which closed all eight hundred and fifty of its restaurants just two weeks after Russia's invasion started.[968,969]

In an April 7, 2022, article in the *New York Times* celebrating the moves by corporations against Russia, Yale's Jeffrey Sonnenfeld and Steven Tian noted that although it's "still too early to tell whether their moves will help force Russia to end the war," the "sanctions from Ukraine's allies have already shaken Russia's economy. The country's stock market is on an IV drip, and the Kremlin has imposed strict controls to prop up the value of the ruble."[970]

"Our goal is absolute, and some might even say extreme," Sonnenfeld and Tian also wrote. "Every corporation with a presence in Russia must publicly commit to a total cessation of business there. Russians who rely on the food or medicine those companies make or jobs they provide may suffer hardship. But if that's what it takes to stop Mr. Putin from killing innocent Ukrainians, that's what businesses must do."[971]

A THREAT UNLIKE ANY OTHER

The financial and economic assault on Russia that occurred in 2022 and 2023 by Western governments and businesses was stunning and something that hadn't occurred at that scale in modern history.

It was, in effect, a public-private economic blockade, one that put Russia on track for "its deepest recession since the aftermath of the collapse of the Soviet Union."[972]

Now, at this point, you might ask, "What's wrong with that, Glenn? Aren't you glad a unified Western world turned on Putin and pressured him to end the war?"

Before I answer that question, which isn't nearly as simple as you might believe, I want to make it abundantly clear that Vladimir Putin is a monster, and what the Russian military has done in Ukraine is nothing short of evil. Putin should, at the very least, be tried for war crimes, convicted, and locked away in a tiny prison cell for the rest of his life—again, at the very least. And if that whole trial thing doesn't work out, they can just send Mr. Putin to Texas; I assure you, the good people here will know *exactly* what to do with him.

I am not in any way a sympathizer of Vladimir Putin or his tyrannical regime, a fact that will be made even more obvious later in this chapter. I have been warning my audiences about the dangers of Putin and the evil people who surround him for many years, long before anyone in the media bothered to pay significant attention to him. And unlike most in the mainstream press, I warned my audience about *real* issues surrounding Putin, Russia, and Ukraine, not witch hunts about "golden showers" and secret videotapes, fairytales about Facebook ads changing the results of the 2016 election, or Donald Trump being recruited to become a super-secret Russian agent.

But just because I think Putin and his allies are truly horrific people does not mean I am eager to celebrate the news that the Great Reset Death Star has become fully armed and operational, and that's exactly what has happened in the wake of Putin's assault on Ukraine. Never before in history have we seen the kind of close coordination between banks, businesses, and governments as we have since Russia's invasion.

The Russian economy was largely brought to its knees by a public-private partnership. It's exactly the sort of thing people like Klaus Schwab and BlackRock's Larry Fink fantasize about, and that alone is reason enough for us to be very cautious.

Think about it. Russia is the eleventh-largest economy in the world.[973] Russia has more land than any other nation, and it has the sixth-largest supply of proven oil reserves.[974] Russia's population, at 142 million, is the ninth largest, and it has the biggest nuclear arsenal on the planet.[975] (Yes, even larger than the United States'.)

Russia is one of the most powerful countries in existence, and its economy was crushed in mere months by an alliance of businesses, banks, and governments in the West. And Russia probably wouldn't have survived had it not been for the support of China. (More on that later in this chapter.)

The Great Reset machine has become so powerful that it is now capable of taking down *entire countries*. And we're not talking about nations like Moldova and Latvia, either. We're talking about one of the top ten most important countries on earth. We're talking about the people who put the first man in space. We're talking about a country that pours vodka on its cereal for breakfast, and the nation that killed Apollo Creed and *almost* beat Rocky. If the Great Reset movement can nearly destroy a nuclear-armed country such as Russia, what do you think it can do to businesses and individual Americans like *you* who stand in its way?

If you are skeptical that the Great Reset movement had anything to do with the West's reaction to Russia's invasion of Ukraine, know that you don't have to take my word for it. Supporters of the Reset and a new Great Narrative have repeatedly tied the war to the advancement of key parts of the Great Reset. For example, in chapter 8, I showed you how many Reseters have made the connection between the war and the birth of a "new world order," including Joe Biden, Klaus Schwab, and the globalists at the World Government Summit.[976, 977]

But perhaps the most important statement revealing how the Great Reset machine has been utilized to defeat Russia came from BlackRock CEO Larry Fink, who, don't forget, serves as a World Economic Forum board member.[978] (Warning: I'm going to quote from Fink heavily throughout the remainder of the subsection of this chapter. I know reading long quotes by Larry Fink isn't exactly the most exciting thing in the world to do, but please stick with me. This is one of the most revealing and important pieces of evidence about the Great Reset and Great Narrative I have ever found.)

In a jaw-dropping letter to BlackRock investors distributed on March 24, 2022, one month after the Russian invasion commenced, Fink warned shareholders that because of Russia's aggression in Ukraine, "the world is undergoing a transformation."[979]

"In consultation with our stakeholders, BlackRock has also joined the global effort to isolate Russia from financial markets," wrote Fink.[980]

"The ramifications of this war are not limited to Eastern Europe," he added. "They are layered on top of a pandemic that has already had profound effects on political, economic, and social trends. The impact will reverberate for decades to come in ways we can't yet predict."[981] (What Fink is describing here are the conditions for a Great Reset of capitalism—the "golden opportunity" of the COVID-19 pandemic, as I explained in chapter 1 of this book and in much more detail in my 2022 book, *The Great Reset*.[982])

Fink then claimed that although "the Russian invasion of Ukraine has put an end to the globalization we have experienced over the last three decades," it has also "catalyzed nations and governments to come together to sever financial and business ties with Russia."[983]

"United in their steadfast commitment to support the Ukrainian people," Fink wrote, governments and businesses "launched an 'economic war' against Russia. Governments across the world almost unanimously imposed sanctions, including taking the unprecedented step of barring the Russian central bank from deploying its hard currency reserves."[984]

Fink then bragged that although governments worked swiftly to stifle Russia's economy, financial institutions and companies "have gone even further" in this "economic war."

"Capital markets, financial institutions and companies have gone even further beyond government-imposed sanctions," Fink said. "As I wrote in my letter to CEOs earlier this year [in 2022], access to capital markets is a privilege, not a right. And following Russia's invasion, we saw how the private sector quickly terminated long-standing business and investment relationships."[985]

Did you catch it? Fink said "access to capital markets is a privilege, not a right." A privilege? A privilege offered by whom, exactly? Well, Larry Fink and his pals, of course. And if it's a *privilege*, then it can be taken away whenever Fink and his friends want. So as Fink makes very clear, don't you or anyone else stand in their way, or you will also be destroyed.

"BlackRock has been committed to doing our part," Fink continued. "Grounded in our fiduciary duty, we moved quickly to suspend the purchase of any Russian securities in our active or index portfolios. Over the past few weeks, I've spoken to countless stakeholders, including our clients and employees, who are all looking to understand what could be done to prevent capital from being deployed to Russia."[986]

Fink then spiked the football even harder, proudly declaring, "The speed and magnitude of company actions to amplify sanctions has been incredible. Iconic American consumer brands have suspended their operations of non-essential products. And financial services companies have taken similar steps to further isolate the Russian economy from the global financial system."[987]

Before Fink moved on to other topics in his lengthy letter, he made one final, impossible-to-miss statement about the power of "capital markets"—a clear allusion to the forces behind the Great Reset—stating, "These actions taken by the private sector demonstrate the power of the capital markets: how the markets can provide capital to those who constructively work within the system and how quickly they can deny it to those who operate outside of it. Russia has been essentially cut off from global capital markets, demonstrating the commitment of major companies to operate consistent with core values. This 'economic war' shows what we can achieve when companies, supported by their stakeholders, come together in the face of violence and aggression."[988]

If you take anything from this book at all, remember Fink's statement that the Western world's reaction to the Russian invasion of Ukraine shows "how the markets can provide capital to those who constructively work within the system and how quickly they can deny it to those who operate outside of it." This is, in Fink's own words, an "economic war" waged by companies and governments to defend their "core values."[989]

If that doesn't chill you to the bone, then you haven't been paying attention. Fink couldn't possibly have been any clearer: you either play ball with them, or they'll crush you. And if you don't think they are serious, Fink suggests you look carefully at what just happened to Russia.

But as important as it is for us to understand how the Great Reset is connected to the West's response to the Russian invasion of Ukraine, it is not the only link. I believe the best available evidence also shows that the Great Reset movement and its supporters' obsession with imposing internationalism on the rest of the world was one of the primary *causes* of the war as well.

LIGHTING THE FUSE

What sparked Putin's decision to invade? Like many in the media, that question plagued me when Russia first crossed into Ukrainian territory. On the surface, the decision appeared to make little sense. After the invasion, Russia became, almost instantaneously, the enemy of the entire Western world. Putin and his closest allies in Russia were ostracized by much of the global community. Russia's economy was pummeled by an onslaught of North American and European sanctions. Tens of thousands of Russian soldiers, including numerous military generals and other leaders were killed.[990]

Of course, it is true that the war went far worse than planned for Vladimir Putin's regime. The resistance and resiliency of the Ukrainian people, the billions of dollars in weapons and aid provided by the United States, and the unexpected heroic leadership of Volodymyr Zelenskyy—Ukraine's president and, believe it or not, a former sitcom star—took Russia by surprise, embarrassing Putin. If Russian forces had quickly steamrolled Ukraine's resistance, perhaps the decision to invade wouldn't seem quite as foolhardy as it does to so many today.

But even under the best conditions, a war on the scale pursued by Putin has made little sense to most pundits, world leaders, and military analysts. I mean, did Russia really expect that it could seize a large foreign capital city and then occupy a nation of more than 44 million mostly Russian-hating people forever?

Occupying regions with large populations of Russian-speaking people, notably in the Ukrainian territories of Luhansk and Donetsk, is morally horrific, but nothing like the dramatic move Putin ended up making in the initial weeks of Russia's attack.[991] There had been Russian-supporting rebels in Luhansk and Donetsk for many years. And there was little interest in the West for escalating the conflict over areas occupied mostly by ethnic Russians. As America's gaffe-machine president suggested, in what might be one of the most spectacularly stupid foreign policy statements of all time, a "minor incursion" into eastern Ukraine would likely not have triggered an aggressive reaction from America and other European nations.[992] So, then, why did Putin pursue a more dangerous, bloody course?

In the wake of the invasion, virtually every theory imaginable was presented to help explain Russia's actions, but one in particular seemed to gain more popularity than the rest: Vladimir Putin has lost his mind.

In March 2022, the *Washington Post* reported, "Russia's invasion of Ukraine has prompted comments from numerous U.S. observers—from White House press secretary Jen Psaki to Sen. Marco Rubio (R-Fla.), as well as former U.S. officials such as Condoleezza Rice and HR McMaster—and speculation that Russian President Vladimir Putin has become unhinged, perhaps due to pandemic isolation or illness."[993]

Similarly, a writer for the *New York Daily News* wondered, "Is Putin clinically insane?"[994] The *Daily Beast* adamantly declared, "Putin Isn't Just Insane. It's Far Worse Than That."[995] *New York Magazine* argued, "Putin's War Looks Increasingly Insane."[996]

I must admit that at various times during the initial days of the attack, I, too, shared some of these thoughts about Putin's mental state. But the more I looked closely at statements made by Putin himself, as well as by key intellectual and government figures in Russia, the more obvious it became that Putin's decision wasn't driven by insanity—at least, not clinically speaking—but rather by an intense, albeit violent and authoritarian, desire to defeat the Great Reset and its brand of twenty-first-century international fascism.

To understand why I have come to this conclusion, you first need a foundational understanding of the recent history between Russia and Ukraine, as well as a firm grasp on the often-ignored views held by many Russian thought leaders about the role globalists in America and much of Europe have played in creating increasingly more tension in the region.

CHAOS, REVOLUTION, AND REVENGE

As strange as it might sound to many Americans, Putin, along with many other influential figures in Moscow, believes that the long-standing alliance between European and North American states poses a clear and present danger to the sovereignty of Russia. This is why Putin has repeatedly identified the potential expansion of the North Atlantic Treaty Organization (NATO) into Ukraine as one of his primary geopolitical concerns.[997] In Russia, NATO is often spoken of as an extremely dangerous institution. In America, most people don't even know what NATO is.

Beginning with the creation of modern Ukraine, which secured its sovereignty in 1991 following the collapse of the Soviet Union, numerous Ukrainian leaders have increasingly turned to American and European institutions, including NATO, to build stronger economic and military ties with the Western world.[998] As the BBC has rightfully noted, Putin has "sought to reverse that, seeing the fall of the Soviet Union as the 'disintegration of historical Russia.' He has claimed Russians and Ukrainians are one people, denying Ukraine its long history and seeing today's independent state merely as an 'anti-Russia project.'"[999]

According to Putin's worldview, Ukraine is part of Russia, regardless of what your map at home tells you, what European and North American governments claim, or even what Ukrainians themselves say. This position has been clearly and repeatedly expressed in numerous speeches and official communications. For instance, in a speech delivered in February 2022, just days before the invasion started, Putin said, "Ukraine is not just a neighboring country for us. It is an inalienable part of our own history, culture, and spiritual space. Since time immemorial, the people living in the southwest of what has historically been Russian land have called themselves Russians."[1000]

How, then, did Ukraine become its own nation? For Putin, the birth of modern Ukraine arose out of foolish decisions made by the leadership of "Bolshevik Communist Russia," which Putin says was too eager in the twentieth century to appease "zealous nationalists" in Ukraine as part of an attempt to shore up political support for the Soviet Union.[1001] Then, following the collapse of the Soviet Union—something Putin has called "a major geopolitical disaster of the century"[1002]—European and American forces began to exert increasingly more influence in Eastern Europe, especially in Ukraine.

According to statements by Putin and his political allies, the West's involvement in Ukraine reached a tipping point in 2013 and 2014, when widespread protests in the country broke out following a decision by Ukraine's former president, Viktor Yanukovych, to reverse course on an agreement for Ukraine to expand its ties to the European Union. Instead of moving Ukraine further in the direction of Europe, Yanukovych, who was considered by many analysts to be a "man of the oligarchs"[1003] with Russian sympathies, sought to strengthen economic bonds between Ukraine and Putin's government.[1004] Perhaps most importantly, Yanukovych's decision was made despite the fact the democratically elected Ukrainian parliament had already backed the proposal to increase economic relations with the European Union.

Following Yanukovych's policy reversal in November 2013, thousands of pro-European protesters took to the streets in the Ukrainian capital of Kyiv, demanding constitutional reforms and eventually Yanukovych's removal from office. Violence ensued, and the protests turned to riots, which carried over into early 2014.[1005] The Yanukovych regime maintained its commitment to Russia and attempted to crush the increasingly more destructive riots, but the more violent Yanukovych's government became, the more the Ukrainian people protested.

During the bloodiest days of the riots in Kyiv, from February 18–21, 2014, nearly ninety protesters were killed by government forces, sparking international outrage and calls within Ukraine for greater American and European involvement in the conflict.[1006] In late February, Ukraine's parliament deposed Yanukovych with the support of Western governments. A new government was then established and legal reforms were made. Western countries immediately recognized the validity of the new government, but Putin called it an illegal "revolution." Putin also claimed that because of this "revolution," his government "reserves the right to use all available options, including force as a last resort."[1007]

Putin's arguments were accepted by many Russians and large Russian-speaking populations in Ukraine, and they were bolstered in the years that followed by countless reports of widespread corruption within the Ukrainian government, a reality that Joe Biden himself repeatedly acknowledged while serving as vice president. Of course, Biden had the advantage of knowing firsthand about Ukrainian corruption. He and his family profited from corrupt arrangements in the country for years.[1008]

Following the installment of Ukraine's new government, many Russian-speaking communities in eastern Ukraine and Crimea rebelled. Some demanded that their communities become part of Russia. One voter referendum in Crimea backed by Putin, for example, showed substantial support for unifying the breakaway territory with Russia.[1009]

In March 2014, Russia took advantage of the precarious situation, deploying troops to Crimea. Putin then annexed the region, formally bringing the peninsula into the Russian Federation for the first time in decades.[1010]

European and North American countries were outraged by the actions of Putin's government, as were tens of millions of Ukrainians. The West was unified in its position that Putin's annexation of Crimea was illegal, but rather than spark a new war in Europe, the newly elected Ukrainian government settled for an uneasy peace agreement with Putin.

Although most Americans at the time of Russia's annexation and since have viewed the move as a victory for Putin, in many respects, Putin's government and many leaders in Russia believed not nearly enough had been accomplished. Putin saw the new pro-Western government in Ukraine as a dangerous "colony with a puppet regime," as well as a country that had been "placed under [the] external control" of Western forces that had helped rebels impose a "coup d'état."[1011]

In Russia, what had occurred in Ukraine in 2013 and 2014 was uniformly considered to be a threat to Russian interests and an unjust and illegal revolution, an opinion that was further solidified by a number of additional developments and legal reforms that occurred in the years leading up to Russia's invasion in 2022.

In 2019, Ukrainian courts found former Ukrainian president and Putin ally Yanukovych guilty of treason for his treatment of protesters in 2014. According to a report published by *The Guardian*, "Yanukovych was also charged with asking Vladimir Putin to send Russian troops to invade Ukraine after he had fled the country."[1012] Yanukovych was never arrested, however, because he had left Ukraine long ago and was living in exile in—you guessed it, Russia.[1013]

Also in 2019, former Ukrainian president Petro Poroshenko, the man who had been elected to lead Ukraine following the removal of Yanukovych, signed into law a constitutional amendment pledging the country to "submit a request for EU membership and receive a NATO membership action plan no later than 2023."[1014] According to one news report about the reform, "European Council President

Donald Tusk attended the signing of the constitutional amendment in the parliament building. Addressing the lawmakers in Ukrainian, Tusk, who is Polish, said that 'there can be no Europe without Ukraine.'"[1015] Although most Americans largely ignored these developments, Russia viewed the possible inclusion of Ukraine into NATO as a plausible, totally unacceptable, extremely dangerous development.

Further, from 2014 to the 2022 invasion, Russian-aligned separatist groups in eastern Ukraine's Luhansk and Donetsk regions waged war against the Ukrainian government. Millions were forced to relocate from the area, and the local economy collapsed. In many respects, these regions remained in a state of war for years leading up to Putin's 2022 attack. Thousands of explosions rocked Luhansk and Donetsk *every month* from 2014 through the Russian invasion in 2022, and 75,000 soldiers occupied the area.[1016]

Throughout this period, Putin repeatedly asked Western governments, including the United States, to agree to keep Ukraine out of NATO. Failure to do so, Putin warned, could lead to further military conflict. And although NATO never formally accepted Ukraine into its fold prior to Putin's invasion in 2022, many NATO leaders—most notably, Joe Biden—flat-out refused to make a long-term commitment to Putin that Ukraine would forever be kept from joining the alliance.

In early 2021, Putin attempted to prove to the world that he wasn't bluffing about his warnings against Ukraine and NATO. He started to amass troops along Ukraine's border, causing President Zelenskyy—who had defeated Poroshenko in the nation's 2019 election, largely by promising to end corruption—to increase his calls for Ukraine to join NATO.[1017]

This move greatly concerned Putin. If Ukraine were to enter into NATO, not only would it create the possibility that other European nations and perhaps America could soon be drawn into the conflict in Luhansk and Donetsk, but it would also effectively put Western nuclear powers on Russia's doorstep, making future Russian advancements in Ukraine all but impossible.

Many foreign policy experts believe the idea that North American and European powers could soon be advancing farther westward didn't only concern Putin because of the obvious military implications, but also due to fears that Ukraine could become a staging ground for subversive operations meant to undermine Putin's authority at home. As one academic who specializes in Russia at the University of Toronto noted, "I think the bigger threat for him [Putin] is a regime threat, not an actual military invasion. He thinks the West wants to subvert his regime the way they did in Ukraine. That's why NATO is only a part of [the] threat."[1018]

After all the outlandish accusations made by the American media during the Trump era about Putin's role in the 2016 election, how could anyone blame Putin for being paranoid that a Biden-controlled army of CIA, NSA, military, and other national security officers could use Ukraine as a base of operations against Putin?

Putin and other Russian leaders also began to worry about a number of Great Reset–related economic developments that occurred throughout 2021. For example, in the runup to the invasion, Reset-affiliated North American and European world leaders, as well as their allies in business, repeatedly promised that they would soon dismantle the world's fossil-fuel industry, an essential part of the Russian economy.

As I explained in detail in chapter 8, tens of thousands of people and more than one hundred world leaders gathered in November 2021 in Glasgow, Scotland, to discuss, among other far-reaching topics, how to push the reset button on the energy sector. The most important thing to come out of Glasgow was the Glasgow Financial Alliance for Net-Zero (GFANZ), an agreement by hundreds of banks, investors, investment management groups, insurance companies, and other financial institutions to phase out all or nearly all fossil-fuel use over the next few decades, beginning immediately.[1019] Together these institutions control $130 trillion in assets.[1020]

If the members of GFANZ were to follow through on their promise, it would be a huge blow to Putin and the Russian economy. In 2020, Russia was the third-largest oil producer in the world, ranking only behind the United States and Saudi Arabia.[1021] Russia supplies about 10 percent of the global oil supply, and fossil-fuel-related revenues accounted for about 45 percent of Russia's federal budget in 2021.[1022, 1023] For Russia to be successful for the remainder of this century, it needs a large chunk of the world to continue using oil and natural gas, and perhaps coal as well—the very opposite of what the elites at Glasgow promised.

I am not trying to suggest that the decision made by many Western leaders to phase out fossil fuels contributed to Russia invading Ukraine. If America and Germany, for example, were to decide to transition away from oil and natural gas, Russia would find other markets to sell their products in. But the Glasgow alliance is much bigger than that and reaches much further. GFANZ members have pledged to use the financial and corporate might of the West to force *everyone* everywhere to stop using fossil fuels. If you were Vladimir Putin, that would have to, at the very least, affect your thinking and long-term strategic planning for Russia.

And if all that weren't enough, consider that in February 2021, the Ukrainian government targeted a close friend of Putin's, Viktor Medvedchuk. Medvedchuk is a lawyer and Ukrainian politician who had been heavily involved with the country's largest opposition party. According to the *Washington Post*, Medvedchuk was one of Ukraine's "most influential behind-the-scenes political brokers for more than three decades."[1024]

Medvedchuk was not only a politician, but he was also an important figure in Ukraine's television industry. Medvedchuk had a "media empire" that included "a 25 percent stake in Ukraine's most popular TV channel."[1025]

"When the conflict with Moscow-supported separatists ignited in eastern Ukraine in 2014, Ukrainian officials found Medvedchuk to be a useful go-between who could pass messages to Russian officials and help negotiate prisoner exchanges with the militants," the *Washington Post* reported.[1026]

However, his "mediator role came to an abrupt end with Zelensky's victory in Ukraine's presidential election in 2019," the *Post* further reported. "In February 2021, Zelenskyy signed a decree that accused Medvedchuk of financing terrorism, freezing his assets. In May, prosecutors accused Medvedchuk of high treason and placed him under house arrest."[1027] This move reportedly enraged Putin, who had developed such a strong relationship with Medvedchuk over the years that he agreed to be the godfather of his daughter.[1028]

Let's a take a moment to think this through. I'm not asking you to agree with Putin's perspective on foreign policy or history. I don't, that's for sure. But you do not have to share Putin's perspective to understand why he might be seriously concerned about NATO potentially getting involved in a civil war with pro-Russian separatists fighting along Russia's border. You don't have to agree with him about climate change or the importance of fossil fuels to understand why Putin would be angry that Western corporations and financial institutions were (and still are) actively working to eliminate Russia's oil and gas industries. I also don't think you need to be pals with Putin to imagine why he would be angry about Yanukovych's ousting in 2014 or the arrest of his personal friend and pro-Russian opposition leader Viktor Medvedchuk.

Putin is an authoritarian tyrant. He's a thug and a world-class egomaniac. He's a fascist too. You can and should call Vladimir Putin many things, but don't call him insane. He's far too cunning and much too dangerous for a name like that.

PUTIN AND THE WEST

Whenever I have to speculate, as opposed to outline well-documented facts and information, I always try to give you a fair warning, and you deserve one now. I think the motivations behind Putin's decisions I outlined in the previous section of this chapter almost certainly explain much, but likely not all, of why Russia invaded Ukraine in 2022. However, I also believe—and this is where some speculation comes into play—that the Great Reset itself was top of mind for Putin when he finally made the choice to attack.

Based on numerous speeches, articles, and books by leading intellectuals who have had or still have some degree of influence on Putin's thinking, as well as comments from Putin himself, I think the best evidence shows that NATO expansion, the West's involvement in Ukraine, North America and Europe's reaction to the annexation of Crimea in 2014, and the Great Reset/Great Narrative are all linked together in the minds of some of the most powerful figures in Russia, including its president.

For Putin and other Russian intellectual and political leaders, North America and Europe are hell-bent on imposing their political ideas, values, and other cultural and religious (or, in actuality, non-religious) beliefs on most other nations, including Russia. This is especially problematic for Putin, because he believes that Western culture is destroying itself and is in extreme decline. Putin sees himself as a great defender of Russian traditionalism, not merely of Russia's military might or national borders.

The Great Reset and calls for a new Great Narrative pose a grave danger to traditionalist ideas everywhere, as they seek to reimagine and reform society through the vast influence of corporations, financial institutions, governments, universities, and media, all of which are using breakthrough technologies like those I have discussed throughout this book to increase their power and wealth. Putin and many of those advising him know this, and they are deeply troubled by it.

Before I get to the evidence showing why I believe the Great Reset and Great Narrative are linked to many of Russia's recent geopolitical moves, please keep one more important warning in mind: there are some truly incredible statements by Vladimir Putin and others included in the next couple of sections of this chapter that you will actually agree with. (No, I'm not joking. You really will. Just wait.) At times, you might even be tempted to think, *Huh, maybe I've got this Putin character all wrong!* (Again, I'm not joking. You may be tempted to think that.) However, and I cannot stress this point enough, by the time you get through the end of this chapter and have seen *all* the evidence, you're not going to be rooting for Vladimir Putin nor the Russian military. You will see Putin for who he truly is—an evil, highly authoritarian, quasi-dictator. But that doesn't mean he is stupid or crazy, and it doesn't mean he's wrong about literally every view he holds. As you'll soon see, he and others allied with him are very intelligent people who do have *some* legitimate criticisms of the West that help shed light on their true motivations for the war in Ukraine.

One of the best illustrations of Putin's views comes from an October 2021 meeting of the Valdai Discussion Club, a highly influential Russian nonprofit project founded by a partnership of think tanks and educational institutions, many of which have ties to the Russian government.[1029] At the event, Vladimir Putin delivered a long speech about the "global shake-up in the twenty-first century," specifically as it relates to "values," "the state," and "the individual."[1030] Throughout the address, Putin listed many of his concerns about changes occurring in the world, including ongoing cultural changes in the West.

For example, Putin noted that Russians "look in amazement at the processes underway in the countries which have been traditionally looked at as the standard-bearers of progress," specifically "the social and cultural shocks that are taking place in the United States and Western Europe."[1031]

Putin then said, "Some people in the West believe that an aggressive elimination of entire pages from their own history, 'reverse discrimination' against the majority in the interests of a minority, and the demand to give up the traditional notions of mother, father, family and even gender, they believe that all of these are the mileposts on the path towards social renewal."[1032]

Later in the speech, Putin went even further, saying, "In a number of Western countries, the debate over men's and women's rights has turned into a perfect phantasmagoria." (For those of you who aren't elite wordsmiths such as me, a *phantasmagoria* is a series of illusions, like something you might experience in a dream.)

"Zealots of these new approaches even go so far as to want to abolish these concepts altogether," Putin said. "Anyone who dares mention that men and women actually exist, which is a biological fact, risk being ostracized. 'Parent number one' and 'parent number two,' 'birthing parent' instead of 'mother,' and 'human milk' replacing 'breastmilk' because it might upset the people who are unsure about their own gender."[1033]

Putin then decried the "truly monstrous things" that occur "when children are taught from an early age that a boy can easily become a girl and vice versa. That is, the teachers actually impose on them a choice we all supposedly have. They do so while shutting the parents out of the process and forcing the child to make decisions that can upend their entire life." This, Putin argued, "verges on a crime against humanity, and it is being done in the name and under the banner of progress."[1034]

(Are you feeling a bit confused yet? Remember what I said at the outset of this section: avoid making any judgments until you finish the chapter.)

Putin then warned the audience that although a "technological revolution, impressive achievements in artificial intelligence, electronics, communications, genetics, bioengineering, and medicine" are opening up "enormous opportunities," they are also raising "philosophical, moral and spiritual questions that were until recently the exclusive domain of science fiction writers."[1035]

"What will happen if machines surpass humans in the ability to think?" Putin asked. "Where is the limit of interference in the human body beyond which a person ceases being himself and turns into some other entity? What are the general ethical limits in the world where the potential of science and machines are becoming almost boundless? What will this mean for each of us, for our descendants, our nearest descendants—our children and grandchildren?"[1036]

Boy, all of this sounds right up Klaus Schwab's alley, doesn't it? Isn't it incredible how seemingly every global leader on the planet is thinking and talking about these issues, but everyday Americans have been totally left in the dark about these concepts by most of the establishment media? Maybe, and I'm just spitballing here, you should strongly consider running away as fast as you can from the deceivers and ignorant fools at places like the New York Times and CNN and, I don't know, instead subscribe to BlazeTV, where these issues are actually being talked about.

Putin further noted that many new and incredibly complex cultural, technological, and economic issues are presenting every society with serious problems and concerns, but in Putin's opinion, North America and Europe are woefully unprepared to deal with them effectively. This doesn't mean Putin wants to impose his values on the West, though. Quite the contrary. He repeatedly stated "we are keeping out" of the West's cultural war. However, he also said, "we would like to ask them to keep out of our business as well."[1037]

"We have a different viewpoint, at least the overwhelming majority of Russian society—it would be more correct to put it this way—has a different opinion on this matter," Putin said. "We believe that we must rely on our own spiritual values, our historical tradition, and the culture of our multiethnic nation."[1038]

This doesn't mean that Putin believes Russia or any other nation should ignore international problems. However, whatever global challenges might exist must be dealt with through *cooperation* between independent states, not by all-powerful international institutions or a cabal of Great Reset elites seeking to impose their ideas on everyone else.

"We understand all too well that resolving many urgent problems the world has been facing would be impossible without close international cooperation," Putin said. "However, we need to be realistic: most of the pretty slogans about coming up with global solutions to global problems that we have been hearing since the late twentieth century will never become reality. In order to achieve a global solution, states and people have to transfer their sovereign rights to supra-national structures to an extent that few, if any, would accept."[1039]

It is clear throughout the address that Putin believes that international institutions, including the United Nations, can serve a purpose, but only if they recognize the sovereignty and unique perspectives of each nation. In Putin's view, the West hasn't been doing that. Instead, America and Europe have pursued a course of "Western domination," a plan that has "failed." And as a result, a "re-alignment of the balance of power" is about to occur.[1040]

"To put it bluntly," Putin said, "the Western domination of international affairs, which began several centuries ago and, for a short period, was almost absolute in the late 20th century, is giving way to a much more diverse system."[1041]

That "much more diverse system" Putin referenced is cooperation among nationalist states, such as Russia, China, and numerous other countries. I'll explain more about this later in the chapter, but for now, remember that a key theme in Putin's thinking is that much of the West is led by internationalists desiring "Western domination," and that they are opposed by nationalist leaders like him in numerous other countries.

Now, it's true that Putin never used the words "Great Reset" or "Great Narrative" in his presentation before the Valdai Discussion Club, but the concepts presented throughout his presentation, as well as in countless other speeches he has given over the past several years, seem to be directly at odds and a direct reaction to *some* of the views of the supporters of the Great Reset and the World Economic Forum. (By the way, it is well documented that Putin is familiar with the Great Reset and WEF, even if he hasn't mentioned it publicly. For example, Putin has spoken at Davos events before, including one in 2021 that heavily promoted the Great Reset–related "Davos Agenda."[1042])

This doesn't mean Putin opposes government involvement in the economy. In fact, Putin very clearly stated at several points in his Valdai speech that government involvement is great, and that Russia needs more of it. At one point, he even went so far as to say that it is "essential" for Russia to "build a social welfare state."[1043] Again, Putin's primary criticisms of the West are not that North American and European nations have big governments and Russia doesn't, but rather that they are being led by internationalists who are trying to impose their culture, values, and political and social norms on other nations. This, of course, is the primary point of the Great Reset.

With that said, if all the evidence I could find were speeches by Putin like the one I referenced, then I'm not sure I would be totally convinced that Russia's invasion of Ukraine had much, if anything, to do with the Great Reset movement—even though it's undeniable that Putin has thought and spoken at length about issues connected closely with the Reset and a new Great Narrative. However, there is *much* more evidence to consider, evidence that appears to show that we're already in the midst of a new world war between the international twenty-first-century fascists of the Great Reset and the traditionalist, national fascists of Russia and China. I also think the proof I've uncovered reveals that it is very likely Russia's government had this "war" among the fascistic groups of the world in mind when it attacked Ukraine.

THE NEW RASPUTIN

Unless you have been listening to my radio show and watching me on television over the past few years, you probably have never heard of Alexander Dugin. He has been one of Russia's most influential political philosophers since the fall of the Soviet Union.[1044] Dugin is an activist, former advisor to key Russian politicians, and the founder of the Eurasia Party.[1045] He's a prolific writer, the author of more than thirty books, and a popular speaker. Oh, and I almost forgot; he's also *one of the most dangerous men in the world*, one who could very well end up causing a nuclear holocaust—and no, that's not an exaggeration.

We cannot be 100 percent certain that Dugin personally knows Vladimir Putin, even though the two have run in the same circles for decades and some analysts have suggested he's in "Putin's inner circle."[1046, 1047] What we do know beyond any doubt, however, is that

Dugin's ideas have become wildly popular in the highest echelons of Russian government, including at the Kremlin and with Putin. For many years, foreign policy analysts have referred to Dugin as "Putin's brain" and even "Putin's Rasputin."[1048] (Rasputin was a bizarre mystic and political advisor who greatly contributed to the downfall of Russia's last monarch, Czar Nicholas II, head of the Romanov dynasty.[1049])

Writer Cathy Young notes that like Rasputin, Dugin "has had a lifelong obsession with the occult, ranging from the legacy of magician and huckster Aleister Crowley (a 1995 video shows [Dugin] reciting a poem at a ceremony honoring Crowley in Moscow) to much more sinister Nazi occultism."[1050] Although at times Dugin has been described as a "hipster" and a "guitar-playing poet," he often presents himself as an exceptionally serious, religious academic with fascistic traditionalist views.[1051]

In an article published on Stanford University's Europe Center website, John Dunlop, a senior fellow at the Hoover Institution and a well-known expert on Russian politics, outlined the tremendous impact Dugin—especially his most notable book—has had on international affairs in Russia.

"There probably has not been another book published in Russia during the post-communist period that has exerted an influence on Russian military, police, and statist foreign policy elites comparable to that of [Aleksander] Dugin's 1997 neo-fascist treatise, *Foundations of Geopolitics*," Dunlop wrote. "The impact of this intended 'Eurasianist' textbook on key elements among Russian elites testifies to the worrisome rise of fascist ideas and sentiments during the late [Boris] Yeltsin and Putin periods."[1052]

Young notes that in the 1990s and early 2000s, Dugin's *Foundations of Geopolitics* "became part of the curriculum at the General Staff Academy, other military and police academies, and some elite institutions of higher learning."[1053] The success of the book propelled Dugin to increasingly higher levels of influence in Russia's government.

Dunlop recorded that in 1998, "Dugin's career took a key step forward when he was named an adviser on geopolitics to Gennadii Seleznev. Seleznev was chairman (or 'speaker') of the Russian State Duma and a major player in Russian politics."[1054]

Although Dugin's views are complex and cover a wide array of topics, one of the overarching ideas is that the world is on the brink of immense change and a transformation pitting land-based traditionalist societies and empires against more technology-focused, anti-religious, nontraditional sea-based nations, like those in Europe and North America.

In an article for the *Washington Post*, David von Drehle succinctly summarizes Dugin's primary beliefs well. In von Drehle's words, Dugin believes, "Before modernity ruined everything, a spiritually motivated Russian people promised to unite Europe and Asia into one great empire, appropriately ruled by ethnic Russians. Alas, a competing sea-based empire of corrupt, money-grubbing individualists, led by the United States and Britain, thwarted Russia's destiny and brought 'Eurasia'—his term for the future Russian empire—low."[1055]

Von Drehle notes that in *Foundations of Geopolitics*, Dugin "mapped out a game plan" for the development of a new Eurasian, traditionalist empire, one that Putin has "followed ... to the letter."[1056] Under Dugin's plan, "Russian agents should foment racial, religious and sectional divisions within the United States while promoting the United States' isolationist factions. . . . In Great Britain, the psy-ops effort should focus on exacerbating historic rifts with Continental Europe and separatist movements in Scotland, Wales and Ireland. Western Europe, meanwhile, should be drawn in Russia's direction by the lure of natural resources: oil, gas and food. NATO would collapse from within."[1057]

Young rightly notes that in *Foundations of Geopolitics* and his other, later writings, Dugin, who is now in his sixties, has repeatedly emphasized his core themes of "community, faith, service, and the subordination of the individual to the group and to authority," ideas regularly espoused by Putin.[1058] In contradistinction, many in the West are devoted to "mobility, trade, innovation, rationality, political freedom, and individualism," which have, according to Dugin, eroded North American and European societies.[1059]

Dugin has suggested for many years that Ukraine has an important role to play in Russia's future ambitions for building Eurasia. Back in 2014, when Russia annexed Crimea, the BBC conducted an interview with Dugin, who said that a much larger war between Russia and Ukraine "is inevitable" and necessary "to save Russia's moral authority." According to the BBC, Dugin believes "the next step" following the takeover of Crimea "is military intervention in eastern Ukraine, which he [Dugin] regularly calls Novorossiya (New Russia). It is a name that has also been used by President Putin."[1060]

In Dugin's mind, Ukraine is part of historic Russia and must be brought under the rulership of Putin. Sound familiar? As I mentioned earlier in this chapter, that is exactly the same argument Putin has been making all along. Let's revisit what Putin said about Ukraine, which I quoted earlier in this chapter: "Ukraine is not just a neighboring country for us. It is an inalienable part of our own history, culture, and spiritual space. Since time immemorial, the people living in the southwest of what has historically been Russian land have called themselves Russians."[1061]

For Dugin—and I believe for Putin too—all of this is wrapped up in the fight against the Great Reset, which Dugin sees as a battle against internationalism, traditionalism, and even our basic understanding of what it means to be a human being. Dugin made this connection abundantly clear in a book titled

The Great Awakening vs. The Great Reset, which he published in September 2021, just one month before Putin made his address to the Valdai Discussion Club and less than six months before Russia invaded Ukraine.[1062]

In *The Great Awakening vs. The Great Reset*, Dugin claims that the following three phases of historical development in the West have led to the rise of the Great Reset, which now threatens all of humanity. (It is clear from Dugin's writing, as you'll soon see, that he ties the dangers posed by technological development to the Great Reset as well.)

Phase One. According to Dugin, the birth of Protestantism and rejection of Catholicism in the West in the sixteenth century led to a greater emphasis on the individual over the collective. The notion of "collective identity" eroded over time, and the concept of individual rights naturally led to capitalism and a greater importance of property rights.[1063]

Phase Two. Capitalism faced major challenges in the nineteenth and twentieth centuries. Movements to reject individualism developed, leading to the creation of socialism, social democrats, and communists, many of whom were internationalists. Revolutions occurred and communist governments took over various countries. At the same time, national socialists (fascists) emerged as a reaction to extreme collectivism, and the European ideological spectrum shifted to a new conception of left-versus-right. It was no longer limited government versus big government, but rather national fascism versus international collectivism, including socialism, communism, and certain branches of progressivism. Capitalists managed to defeat both fascistic groups, and in the wake of World War II, both socialism and fascism gave rise to a kind of capitalistic globalism, but one that Dugin says was heavily impacted by collectivist thinking.[1064]

Phase Three. "Gender and Posthumanism" is Dugin's third phase. According to Dugin, "After defeating its last ideological foe, the socialist camp, capitalism has come to a crucial point. Individualism, the market, the ideology of human rights, democracy, and Western values had won on a global scale. It would seem that the agenda is fulfilled—no one opposes 'individualism' and nominalism with anything serious or systemic anymore."[1065]

Dugin further writes, "In this period, capitalism enters its third phase. On closer inspection, after defeating the external enemy, liberals have discovered two more forms of collective identity. First of all, gender. After all, gender is also something collective: either masculine or feminine. So, the next step was the destruction of gender as something objective, essential, and irreplaceable."[1066] (Sounds an awful lot like something Putin would say, doesn't it?)

Then Dugin claims that after Western culture wars about sexuality ended with a victory for the left, liberal individualists turned to humanity itself, since the concept of humanity is also a collective thought. The "last step" for the left, which has yet to occur, is "to abolish humans" and "replace humans, albeit partially, by cyborgs, artificial intelligence networks, and products of genetic engineering. The optional human logically follows optional gender."[1067]

Are you picking up on the similarities between Dugin's book and Putin's speech at the Valdai Discussion Club? Nearly every single one of Dugin's concerns was echoed by Putin, who just a few months later, invaded Ukraine.

After laying out the immense stakes of what's ahead, Dugin makes this incredible comment about modern international liberalism:

So, we have determined our place on the scale of history. And in doing so, we got a fuller picture of what the Great

Reset is all about. It is nothing less than the beginning of the "last battle." The globalists, in their struggle for nominalism, liberalism, individual liberation, and civil society, appear to themselves as "warriors of light," bringing progress, liberation from thousands of years of prejudice, new possibilities—and perhaps even physical immortality and the wonders of genetic engineering, to the masses. All who oppose them are, in their eyes, "forces of darkness." And by this logic, the "enemies of open society" must be dealt with in their own severity. "If the enemy does not surrender, he will be destroyed." The enemy is anyone who questions liberalism, globalism, individualism, nominalism in all their manifestations. This is the new ethic of liberalism. It's nothing personal. Everyone has the right to be a liberal, but no one has the right to be anything else.[1068]

Reading Dugin's work is terrifying but incredibly interesting. There are very few, if any, thinkers like him in America, where the ideological divide has always been individual freedom against the power of government and other collectivist forces working with government. Dugin's approach, which I fully believe is shared by Putin, is that individualism is the cause of all the West's problems. In total opposition to everything pro-liberty Americans believe, Dugin argues freedom leads to international tyrannical governments and systems who will stop at nothing to rid the world of all of its "old" ideas. This is an ideological war the likes of which we have never seen before.

According to Dugin, "These are the conditions under which Biden has come to head the United States. American soil itself is burning under the feet of globalists. And this gives the situation of 'the final battle' a special, additional dimension. This is not the West against the East, not the U.S. and NATO against everyone else, but liberals against humanity—including that segment of humanity which finds itself on the territory of the West itself, but which is turning more and more away from its own globalist elites."[1069]

From Dugin's perspective, how can the traditionalist forces win against the might of the Great Reset? Dugin says the "Great Awakening" is the answer. It is a call to nationalism, traditionalism (including religious traditionalism), and a rejection of the emphasis on the individual. This must be a populist movement, and it must occur across the world for it to be effective, but it cannot be a "globalist" movement. In other words, Dugin believes sovereign nations must work toward common goals without giving up their power to a supranational institution. For Dugin, internalization is the enemy.

How does Russia fit into this vision for the future? According to Dugin, the "most important" role "is intended for Russia," because Dugin says Russians have "always prioritized the common" despite being influenced by the West, putting them at an advantage to reject liberalism and its destructive obsession with the individual. And unlike most other nations, Russians have borrowed the best ideas from Western and Eastern nations. Dugin says this allows Russia to play a "special role" in defeating the Great Reset and the rise of globalism, but only if Russia pursues and inspires an "imperial renaissance."[1070]

Dugin writes, "Therefore, the imperial awakening of Russia is called upon to be a signal for a universal uprising of peoples and cultures against the liberal globalist elites. Through rebirth as an empire, as an Orthodox empire, Russia will set an example for other empires—the Chinese, Turkish, Persian, Arab, Indian, as well as the Latin American, African . . . and the European. Instead of the dominance of one single globalist 'empire' of the Great Reset, the Russian awakening should be the beginning of an era of many empires, reflecting and embodying the richness of human cultures, traditions, religions, and value systems."[1071]

RUSSIA'S GREAT AWAKENING

Whether Vladimir Putin had this "Great Awakening" in mind when he invaded Ukraine is something we might never know with absolute certainty. But ask yourself, is there anything that Alexander Dugin has said that doesn't fit with what we've seen from Vladimir Putin? For more than two decades, Putin has been laying the groundwork to build a new Eurasia, gobbling up land and resources and making strategic alliances that could be used to combat what we now think of as the Great Reset and new Great Narrative. Ukraine was the obvious next step in pursuing the goal of building a traditionalist Russian-Eurasian empire, just like the one Dugin has been dreaming of, writing about, and advocating for in the halls of power in Russia for more than twenty years.

I am not the only one to make this connection, either. In von Drehle's *Washington Post* article, after an intense study of Dugin and Putin, he wrote, "With the undermining of the West going so well, Putin has turned to the pages of Dugin's text in which he declared: 'Ukraine as an independent state with certain territorial ambitions represents an enormous danger for all of Eurasia,' and 'without resolving the Ukrainian problem, it is in general senseless to speak about continental politics.'"[1072]

My argument that Russia is attempting to usher in an "imperial renaissance" like the one supported by Dugin is bolstered by what occurred in the months following the invasion. In reaction to the numerous strict and far-reaching sanctions imposed on Russia following its entrance into Ukraine in 2022, Russia didn't back down.[1073] It didn't whimper away with its tail tucked between its legs, even as it struggled economically and militarily. Putin knew what was coming, and he and others affiliated with his administration used the West's all-out economic assault on Russia to build stronger ties with many of the same nations referenced by Dugin in his book about the Great Awakening.

For example, *Foreign Policy* reported in late March 2022 that despite intense pressure from America and European leaders for Saudi Arabia to condemn Russia, as well as "entreaties to raise oil production," the "Saudi Crown Prince Mohammed bin Salman allegedly declined to speak with U.S. President Joe Biden a week after speaking with Russian President Vladimir Putin."[1074]

Foreign Policy further reported, "By refusing to compensate for Russian oil [being pushed off the market in many Western nations], the crown prince is facilitating Putin's aggression by allowing him to weaponize energy in the face of sanctions imposed by the international community and hold energy-dependent European countries hostage to Russian oil and gas."[1075]

On April 29, 2022, *Business Insider* reported "China and Russia are working on homegrown alternatives" to the U.S.-backed SWIFT international payment system, which would allow them to quickly make payments across borders without being under the influence or control of America or Europe. Russia's payment system has largely only been used for domestic transactions, but *Business Insider* noted "Moscow is working with Beijing to connect it" with China's CIPS international payment system, in order to help Russia "work around the SWIFT ban."[1076] Both India and Saudi Arabia have reportedly said they are considering a switch to either the Chinese or Russian model to escape the SWIFT system.[1077]

One of the most important and remarkable developments that occurred following Russia's invasion of Ukraine was the focus of an important April 2022 interview of Sergey Glazyev, the minister responsible for Integration and Macroeconomics at the Eurasian Economic Commission (EEC).[1078] From 2012 to 2019, Glazyev was an adviser to President Putin. It is very likely Glazyev left the Kremlin to take his position at the EEC at the direction of Putin himself. The interview was conducted by Pepe Escobar, "a columnist at *The Cradle*, editor-at-large at *Asia Times* and an independent geopolitical analyst focused on Eurasia."[1079]

According to its website, Glazyev's EEC "is the permanent regulatory body of the Eurasian Economic Union (EAEU). It started work on February 2, 2012. The main purpose of the Eurasian Economic Commission is ensuring the functioning and development of the EAEU, and developing proposals for the further development of integration."[1080] At the time of publication of this book, the EEC has five member countries: Armenia, Belarus, Kazakhstan, the Kyrgyz Republic, and Russia.

During the interview with Glazyev, Escobar noted that the EEC is "at the forefront of a game-changing geo-economic development: the design of a new monetary/financial system via an association between the EAEU and China, bypassing the US dollar, with a draft soon to be concluded."[1081]

Escobar then asked Glazyev to explain "some of the features of this system," to which Glazyev responded, "In a bout of Russophobic hysteria, the ruling elite of the United States played its last 'trump ace' in the hybrid war against Russia. Having 'frozen' Russian foreign exchange reserves in custody accounts of western central banks, financial regulators of the US, EU, and the UK undermined the status of the dollar, euro, and pound as global reserve currencies. This step sharply accelerated the ongoing dismantling of the dollar-based economic world order."[1082]

Glazyev then went on to explain that "the current dollar-centric global financial system will be superseded by a new one, based on a consensus of the countries who join the new world economic order."[1083] (Wait. There's *another* "new world order"? Something tells me this isn't going to end well.)

The transition outlined by Glazyev has three phases. (Why everyone in Russia is obsessed with "three phases," I don't know.) The first phase involves "currency swaps" between like-minded nations, which will, depending on the nation, slowly or quickly shift away from Western currency reserves to Eastern currencies and gold. This phase, according to Glazyev, was nearly over in late April 2022, and it's likely tied to the stories I referenced earlier in this chapter about SWIFT.

"The second stage of the transition will involve new pricing mechanisms that do not reference the dollar," Glazyev said. "Price formation in national currencies involves substantial overheads, however, it will still be more attractive than pricing in 'un-anchored' and treacherous currencies like dollars, pounds, euro, and yen. The only remaining global currency candidate—the yuan—won't be taking their place due to its inconvertibility and the restricted external access to the Chinese capital markets."

Finally, Glazyev said, "The third and the final stage on the new economic order transition will involve a creation of a new digital payment currency founded through an international agreement." It will be backed by a basket of national currencies and perhaps "an index of prices of main exchange-traded commodities: gold and other precious metals, key industrial metals, hydrocarbons, grains, sugar, as well as water and other natural resources."[1084]

Although at the time of publication of this book it remains to be seen whether a new digital world reserve currency led by China, Russia, and other nations will be widely adopted, the transition away from the U.S. dollar as the world reserve currency and SWIFT as the international payment system of choice for many Eastern nations is already underway. As scary as it might seem, this could very well be the foundation of the Great Awakening alliance described and promoted by Alexander Dugin.

There's also good reason to believe that a military alliance between Russia, Iran, and China could be developing. In January 2022, one month *before* Russia's invasion of Ukraine, Radio Free Europe reported:

Iran, Russia, and China are holding their third joint naval drill in the northern Indian Ocean, amid speculation that the three countries are teaming up in the face of growing regional tensions with the United States.

Russian vessels, together with the Chinese and Iranian navies, performed "joint tactical maneuvering and practiced artillery fire at a naval target as well as search-and-rescue missions at sea," the Russian Defense Ministry said on January 21, adding that the sides also "practiced inspection and liberation of a ship that was supposedly captured by pirates."

Eleven Iranian vessels were joined by three Russian ships and two Chinese vessels, Iranian Rear Admiral Mostafa Tajoldini earlier told state TV. Iran's Islamic Revolutionary Guards Corps (IRGC) are also participating in the exercises, with smaller ships and helicopters.

Since coming to office in June 2021, Iran's hard-line President Ebrahim Raisi has pursued a policy to deepen ties with both Moscow and Beijing. Russia, Iran, and China are subject to Western sanctions imposed over various issues, including Russia's threats on Ukraine's territorial integrity, human rights abuses in China, and Iran's nuclear program.[1085]

Further, since the outbreak of the war in Ukraine, Russia has been caught using Iranian military equipment, including unmanned aerial attack drones, and U.S. Secretary of State Antony Blinken has said China is "almost certainly" providing Russia with "non-lethal" support for the war.[1086, 1087]

Perhaps most importantly, during an April 2022 meeting of the Boao Forum (an annual economic meeting of Asian countries promoting regional cooperation and integration), two months into the Russia-Ukraine war, China's national fascistic leader Xi Jinping announced the launch of a China-led Global Security Initiative.[1088]

During the announcement, Xi noted that the Global Security Initiative is needed because the world must reform its "security governance system" in order to shore up "territorial integrity." Xi also called on countries to "reject the Cold War mentality" and "block confrontation," apparent criticisms of the West's financial war on Russia.[1089]

Writing for the *Epoch Times* about the announcement of the Global Security Initiative, China expert Antonio Graceffo noted that although there wasn't "much concrete detail" provided about the Global Security Initiative at the Boao Forum, Xi said the initiative would focus in part on "indivisible security." According to Graceffo, "Russian President Vladimir Putin used the exact words to justify his confrontation with Ukraine in a Feb. 2 phone call with British Prime Minister Boris Johnson."[1090]

Graceffo concluded his analysis of the announcement by stating, "Although it is unclear exactly what form this security initiative will take, it seems clear that it seeks to legitimize the Russian invasion of Ukraine and support the CCP's position to take Taiwan. Geopolitical scholars from Europe, India, Australia, and the United States agree that these are the greatest threats to global security."[1091]

NATIONAL FASCISM

After spending a substantial amount of time and energy researching, thinking, and being scared to death about the Great Narrative and its brand of international fascism, it's easy for those who haven't studied Russia and other nationalistic countries to be drawn to the siren song of Dugin and Putin's Great Awakening. In fact, Dugin's *The Great Awakening vs. The Great Reset* book was written in large part to persuade right-leaning Americans to join his cause, which is why he spends a substantial amount of the book talking about how unfairly Donald Trump was treated throughout his presidency.[1092]

But having any sympathy at all for the Dugin-Putin view would be a massive mistake.

A seemingly endless number of media reports, books, data, and government and nongovernment analyses overwhelmingly show that Vladimir Putin's regime, as well as many of the foreign regimes it has allied itself with, is as anti-freedom as it gets. Putin is a violent, ruthless tyrant, and Russia is a nation where freedom is merely tolerated—and only when it serves the interests of Putin.

Vladimir Putin and the government he has been building for more than two decades is undoubtedly fascistic. Like the governments imagined by the supporters of the Great Reset, Putin believes government should use the might of corporations and big businesses to control and shape society, a hallmark of fascism, and he believes individual liberties should always give way to the best interests of the collective. But rather than define "collective" as the entire world, an essential part of Great Reset and Great Narrative ideology, Putin believes every policy decision should be laser-focused on improving the power, wealth, and prestige of Mother Russia, as well as the Russian peoples living in other countries, including places such as Ukraine.

What is life like in Russia under Putin's vision of national fascism? For starters, most large-scale economic decisions are made by Putin, his administration, or oligarchs who are closely tied to him. Further, the Russian people have become increasingly more dependent on government services and government-run businesses in recent years. Putin has repeatedly said that he believes the welfare state must be *expanded*, not limited, a point I made earlier when citing his October 2021 Valdai Discussion Club speech. Rather than support a free-market capitalist economy, Putin favors a mixed economic system that's comparable to the one utilized by the Communist Party of China.[1093] In fact, Putin and his allies have repeatedly praised China's "mixed" model, even going so far as to suggest that it will be the downfall of the West, unless countries like the United States adopt it too.

For example, during the Valdai speech, Putin praised the use of public-private partnerships in the handling of Russia's 2008–09 financial crisis, as well as the "quite effective" Chinese model. "Other countries also had positive experiences in making the state and the market work in tune with each other," Putin said. "The People's Republic of China is a case in point. While the Communist Party retains its leading role there, the country has a viable market and its institutions are quite effective. This is an obvious fact."[1094]

I don't think I would describe the Communist Party of China's one- and two-child policies, the execution of citizens for basic drug possession, the imprisonment of millions of religious and ethnic minorities, the construction of gigantic "ghost cities" with absolutely no people in them, a mass surveillance state, the repeated theft of private property, the elimination of most forms of political dissent, a state-controlled media, or the mismanagement of the economy to the tune of hundreds of millions of impoverished people as "quite effective." But if I were a bloodthirsty wannabe emperor like Putin, I suppose I would be really impressed with what is going on in China too.

Putin also said during the Valdai address that "wild capitalism does not work" and inevitably leads to significant societal problems, such as wealth inequality. Instead, Putin said he sees managing the economy "like art."[1095] He then immediately added, again referencing how government must manage economic activity, "You need to understand when to place a bigger emphasis on something: when to add more salt, and when to use more sugar."

Yes, I know. The whole "salt" and "sugar" reference has nothing to do with "art," but hey, I don't write the mixed metaphors and similes for the world's dictators, so you'll have to file your complaints with Mr. Putin. (I suggest that you do it really, really nicely.)

As I have already highlighted, some of the most important industries controlled by Putin's government are those tied to natural resources such as oil, coal, and natural gas. The Russian government is heavily reliant on revenues from fossil fuels such as oil and natural gas, as well as its extensive mining operations. According to the Russian Ministry of Natural Resources, about 60 percent of the country's GDP is composed of the value of natural resources such as diamonds, gold, iron, coal, oil, and gas.[1096] All of these industries are tightly controlled or outright owned by Putin's government or by a Russian oligarch tied to Putin—absolutely not what you would see in a country that embraces free-market economics.

Jack McPherrin, a research fellow at The Heartland Institute who has written extensively about Russia, noted in a comprehensive 2023 report about Putin, "establishing control over the oligarchs running the energy companies responsible for extracting those resources is the lynchpin of Putin's entire vertical power structure."[1097]

McPherrin also detailed Putin's artfully authoritarian method of managing a carefully selected group of "oligarchs," who together, along with Putin's government, effectively control most of Russia's economy. According to McPherrin,

> To dominate the energy industries—as well as other sectors of the Russian economy such as the media, transportation, and the banking industries—Putin acquired the loyalty of some oligarchs, and replaced others with close allies. Media titans Vladimir Gusinsky and Boris Berezovsky—at that point, two of the richest men in Russia—were forced to flee into exile within a year of Putin's ascension, with many of their assets subsequently seized by the state and redistributed to Putin loyalists. Gazprom chairman Riem Viakhirev was forced to resign, paving the way for Putin to appoint close childhood friend Dimitri Medvedev in his stead. When Medvedev later resigned to briefly

take over for Putin as president [of Russia], control of Gazprom was handed to Alexey Miller and Viktor Zubkov, close Putin confidantes who still run Gazprom as CEO and Chairman of the Board, respectively. Controlling this company alone gives Putin access to a revenue stream of approximately $90 billion per year. Putin also prioritized control over the transport of his natural resources. He appointed long-time business associate Nikolai Tokarev president of Transneft, Russia's monopolistic state-owned pipeline company. Putin's friend Vladimir Yakunin was appointed president of Russian Railways, another state-run monopoly enterprise. Igor Sechin was handed control over Russia's shipbuilding monopoly. Overseeing each of these companies, and others, allows Putin complete control over all resource extraction, domestic transportation, and exportation.[1098]

Putin's authoritarianism doesn't stop at his management of Russia's economy either. Virtually every part of Russian life is deeply impacted by Putin and his allies. Steven Lee Myers, the former bureau chief at the *New York Times*, says Putin has effectively become Russia's "new Tsar,"[1099] and Human Rights Watch claims that Russia's current government "is more repressive than it has ever been in the post-Soviet era."[1100]

According to Human Rights Watch, under Putin, "The authorities crack down on critical media, harass peaceful protesters, engage in smear campaigns against independent groups, and stifle them with fines. Foreign organizations are increasingly banned as 'undesirable,' and Russian nationals and organizations are penalized for supposed involvement with them. A new law enables Russian authorities to partially or fully block access to the internet in Russia in the event of undefined 'security threats' and gives the government control of the country's internet traffic, enhancing its capacity to conduct fine-grain censorship. Impunity for egregious abuses by security officials in Chechnya remains rampant."[1101]

There is also little privacy or political freedom in Putin's Russia. Four powerful intelligence agencies—the Federal Protection Service (FSO), Main Intelligence Directorate (GRU), the Foreign Intelligence Service (SVR), and the Federal Security Service (FSB)—use breakthrough technology to help Putin's regime keep a tight grip on society.[1102] Putin is especially fond of using the FSB— an agency Putin once led—to squash dissent and instill fear in political opponents.

As McPherrin noted in his detailed report about Putin's authoritarianism, Putin has "used FSB agents to assert control over the Russian media institutions by raiding offices, seizing records, coercing the sale of company shares via threats of imprisonment."[1103] Further, McPherrin wrote, "The FSB is regularly employed to arrest any rival political figures such as regional governors, and to redistribute economic resources from those deemed insufficiently loyal to his more arduous supporters. It is linked to the poisoning of former Ukrainian leader Viktor Yushchenko, among many other foreign political targets."[1104]

Prisoners in Russia, including political prisoners, are routinely abused and violently attacked. In a 2020 report by Human Rights Watch, the organization noted that throughout 2019, "Torture and other ill-treatment remained widespread" in Russia, "especially in pretrial detention and prisons."[1105] In October 2021, the BBC reported that a Belarusian whistleblower who spent time in a Russian prison leaked more than a thousand videos of prisoners being abused or tortured. According to the BBC, "One video appears to show a naked man being abused with a stick at a prison hospital in the city of Saratov," while another "appears to show a man . . . face-down with his hands taped behind him, as a guard presses a boot into his back."[1106]

Putin's government has also cracked down on religious minority groups in recent years, relying on an incredibly broad law against "extremism." Human Rights Watch reported that in February 2019, "a court in Oryol sentenced Dennis Christensen, a Jehovah's Witness and a Danish citizen, to six years' imprisonment on extremism charges. In November, a court in Tomsk handed down the same sentence to another Jehovah's Witness, Sergei Klimov. At least 285 Jehovah's Witnesses have been convicted or were facing trial or under investigation in Russia in 2019" for their "extremist" religious views.[1107]

Limiting free speech on the Internet, throwing political dissenters in prison, torture, assassinations, mass surveillance, arresting religious minorities, expanding the welfare state, owning or controlling entire industries, praising the Chinese Communist Party's model for public-private partnerships and manipulation of Chinese society—does any of this sound like the sort of thing free-market, pro-liberty Americans would support? Of course not. But these terrifying, deeply authoritarian policies are an essential part of Putin's strategy for maintaining and expanding power. As I have said repeatedly throughout this book, Putin might be a traditionalist, at least in some sense, and he might be opposed to the internationalism of the Great Reset and Great Narrative movements, but he is a fascist nonetheless, and one of the world's most dangerous, tyrannical, and ruthless men.

A THIRD WAY

The world is currently at war, both figuratively and, in some regions, literally. On one side of the battle are Great Reset–affiliated international fascists seeking to create a new Great Narrative for humanity. On the other side are the traditionalistic national fascists of countries such as Russia, China, Turkey, and Iran. And caught in the middle are billions of regular people and their families who wake up every morning seeking to build a better life for their children, take care of their elderly parents, earn an honest living, buy a home of their own, worship (or not worship) God in accordance with their conscience, and live in peace. These are the people suffering in decaying towns in the American Rust Belt because of the reckless policies of Washington, the heroes dying by the thousands in the streets of Ukraine to defend their nation, and the parents across the United States who have been labeled domestic terrorists for daring to push back against school boards who are corrupting the educa-tion of their children.[1108]

Making matters worse, the technological developments of the Fourth Industrial Revolution will soon create unprecedented levels of disruption, a problem that is going to become increasingly worse as this decade continues to progress. This era will undeniably be marked by a tremendous growth in opportunities for humankind, but the elites of the Great Reset and tyrants of Dugin's Great Awakening will attempt to use these new technologies to further expand their own power—and to destroy anyone who stands against them.

There is, however, another way. Americans, as well as those from all other parts of the world who still yearn to breathe free, do not need to subject themselves to the shackles of the Great Reset nor the national fascistic movements dominating Russia and China. There is a third path, one that can harness the might of the Fourth Industrial Revolution to cure cancer, travel to distant planets, grow more than enough food to feed the global population, make home-ownership more affordable, improve education, and dramatically increase the quality of life for *all* people. But in order to pursue this course, we must remember and reform our own Great Narrative, a story that has inspired hundreds of millions of people around the world and lifted more people out of poverty and authoritarianism than any other ideology in human history.

It is a narrative that harnesses the advantages of innovation without destroying the dignity of humanity, one that seeks to decentralize power and liberate the common man from the domination of the ruling class. It is a narrative Americans used to teach their children, but one many of us have since forgotten or neglected. It is the story of the American way, and it's the subject of my next and final chapter.

— 10 —

A GREATER NARRATIVE

A T THE 2018 ANNUAL MEETING OF THE WORLD ECONOMIC Forum, noted historian Yuval Harari delivered what could someday be considered one of this century's most forward-thinking speeches.[1109] Standing before an audience of hundreds of the richest, most influential, most powerful people on the planet, with thousands more watching remotely, Harari, a prolific author who has published numerous international bestsellers, outlined his vision of the future in the Fourth Industrial Revolution.

In the span of just seventeen minutes, Harari expertly navigated the potential dangers of the emerging technological revolution and then offered advice to the WEF's guests about the best way for humanity to thrive in the twenty-first century and beyond.

Although Harari is just one of many voices discussing the Fourth Industrial Revolution, his unique ideas have had an astonishing impact on elites in Europe and North America, an assertion captured well by Harari's introduction at Davos in 2018 by Gillian Tett, managing editor at the *Financial Times*'s U.S. division.

Prior to Harari starting his presentation, Tett told the audience, "There are not many historians who would be put on the main stage of the conference center of the World Economic Forum sandwiched between Angela Merkel and [Emmanuel] Macron."[1110] (Merkel and Macron were at the time chancellor of Germany and president of France, respectively.)

"I think there are even fewer who could fill the room almost as much as Angela Merkel," Tett added. "And almost none who would have the experience as we were waiting in the green room, and Angela Merkel came through, Chancellor Merkel came through, she took care to stop, go up to Yuval and say, 'I have read your book.'"[1111]

Tett further noted that Harari's ideas "have really shaped the debate—not just inside governments, but inside many businesses and many nongovernmental organizations too."[1112]

Following Tett's gushing introduction, Harari took the stage and carefully, persuasively, and passionately offered his beliefs about the trajectory of mankind and the radical evolution of society and humanity that has already commenced.

Harari warned that the "future masters of the planet" will be chosen "by the people who own the data."[1113]

"Those who control the data control the future, not just of humanity but the future of life itself," Harari said. "Because today, data is the most important asset in the world."[1114]

Harari went on to explain that once the infotech revolution combines with the growing biotech revolution, algorithms will emerge that will allow computers and those running them to know you better than you know yourself. "If we are not careful, the outcome might be the rise of digital dictatorships," Harari said.[1115]

Harari went on to explain to the audience, "In the twentieth century, democracy generally outperformed dictatorship because democracy was better at processing data and making decisions."[1116] This is why, Harari rightly argued, the relatively free markets of the

United States were able to dramatically outperform the command-and-control societies of the Soviet Union and other populated communist nations.

However, Harari claimed "this is true only under the unique technological conditions of the twentieth century. In the twenty-first century, new technological revolutions, especially AI and machine learning, might swing the pendulum in the opposite direction. They might make centralized data processing far more efficient than distributed data processing. And if democracy cannot adapt to these new conditions, then humans will come to live under the rule of digital dictatorships."[1117]

For Harari, the perils of digital dictatorships are not limited to merely possessing knowledge or the tools to make great sums of money. Harari is concerned that the concentration of data, mixed with the machines of the future, "might enable human elites to do something even more radical than just build digital dictatorships."[1118]

"By hacking organisms, elites may gain the power to re-engineer the future of life itself," Harari said. "Because once you can hack something, you can usually also engineer it. And if indeed we succeed in hacking and engineering life, this will be not just the greatest revolution in the history of humanity, this will be the greatest revolution in biology since the very beginning of life four billion years ago."[1119]

Harari claimed that there are dangers inherent in a system that allows "big corporations" to control most of our data, but "mandating governments to nationalize the data may curb the power of the big corporations only in order to give rise to digital dictatorships."[1120]

"And politicians really (many politicians at least) are like musicians," he added. "And the instrument they play on is the human emotional biochemical system. A politician gives a speech and there is a wave of fear all over the country. A politician Tweets, and there is an explosion of anger and hatred. Now, I don't think we should give these musicians the most sophisticated instruments to play on, and I certainly don't think they are ready to be entrusted with the future of life in the universe. Especially as many politicians and governments seem incapable of producing meaningful visions of the future and instead what they sell the public are nostalgic fantasies about going back to the past."[1121]

In another speech at Davos, this time in 2020, Harari warned, "If you know enough biology and have enough computing power and data, you can hack my body and my brain and my life, and you can understand me better than I understand myself. You can know my personality type, my political views, my sexual preferences, my mental weaknesses, my deepest fears and hopes. You know more about me than I know about myself. And you can do that not just to me, but to everyone. A system that understands us better than we understand ourselves can predict our feelings and decisions, can manipulate our feelings and decisions, and can ultimately make decisions for us."[1122]

So who should own the world's data? And who should have control over the tools necessary to alter and manipulate human civilization?

In 2018, Harari responded to those questions with, "I, frankly, don't know. I think the discussion has just begun."[1123] What Harari said he *does* know with certainty, however, is that "The future, not just of humanity, but the future of life itself, may depend on the answer to this question."[1124]

In the mind of Yuval Harari, humanity cannot even begin to deal with these difficult problems until "the fragile global order" is repaired. We cannot put our own nations first, Harari says, and we especially cannot be like leaders such as President Donald Trump, who sought to "neglect" the global order and "even deliberately undermine it."[1125]

If we return to the "jungle" of competition between nations, "our species will probably annihilate itself" with the "powerful new technologies of the twenty-first century," Harari concluded.[1126]

THE DAVOS WAY

I have read and watched more speeches, books, and articles written by the friends of the World Economic Forum than I care to admit. But of all the speakers and writers in the Davos-sphere, I think Yuval Harari is my favorite. He, like so many others who have become swept up in the Great Narrative movement, is what I like to call "a true believer." Many in the World Economic Forum attend meetings to be part of a spectacle, eat free shrimp cocktails at George Soros soirees, or to plot schemes to attain greater wealth or power for themselves, their business, or government. But not Yuval Harari.

Harari believes the Fourth Industrial Revolution is imminent, as I do. He suspects the world is on the brink of descending into catastrophe. I believe that one as well. He thinks the emerging breakthroughs in technology will lead to the further consolidation of power. I agree. He suggests we could soon descend into a "digital dictatorship." I would argue that this has already started to occur.

Yuval Harari and I agree about a lot. Anyone who takes the time to carefully study the Fourth Industrial Revolution would likely share our views as well. But where we fundamentally and vehemently disagree is what ought to be done about it.

The reason Harari has received numerous invitations to Davos is because, despite his many warnings about "elites," he believes "global cooperation" among elites is the answer to solving the world's biggest problems. And other true believers in Davos—along with the not-so-true believers—share the sentiment. It is really the one unbreakable rule that Davos has: no matter who you are or what you think about all sorts of different issues, you *must* agree that some form of globalism is the answer.

Through global cooperation, Harari hopes rules for society and businesses can be written that will protect human rights and stave off disaster. I wouldn't say that he's optimistic this will occur; at times he seems downright fatalistic. But in the end, he thinks it is the only chance for humanity to survive. For him and many others in Davos, the answer always leads back to "international cooperation," an expanded role for the United Nations, greater coordination between powerful multinational corporations—really anything that rallies the Western world behind one common cause.

The wildly idealistic vision of internationalism presented by the World Economic Forum, Harari, and others sounds nice. It really does. I would love to live in a world where people of every nation, tribe, and tongue work harmoniously together in peace and harmony. But there is absolutely no evidence—none whatsoever—that globalist institutions deliver on these sort of pie-in-the-sky promises they so often make.

The United Nations, WEF, multinational corporations, and big Wall Street firms have shown that they are far more interested in elevating their own statuses and amassing as much power as possible than they are devoted to fighting for the "little guy" and the "stakeholders" they claim to care so much about. As I noted in chapter 1, the most obvious proof of this reality is elites' close relationship with China's Communist Party.

China is one of the biggest human rights violators on the planet, so why are so many compassionate, kind, bleeding-heart institutions so willing to do business with China? If corporations care so much about the marginalized and oppressed, why would they jump into bed with a nation that has locked away more than a million Uyghurs, an ethnic and religious minority in China, in a "sprawling network of camps" designed for "re-education"?[1127]

The Chinese Communist Party and its allies have also worked to limit exposure to material considered to normalize homosexuality. Citizens of China can't even watch certain parts of the television series *Friends* anymore, because of concerns about a plotline involving one of the character's lesbian ex-wives.[1128] Does this sound like a policy Davos would support?

And don't forget about China's addiction to coal-fired energy. A February 2022 Reuters report noted, "China started building 33 gigawatts of new coal-fired power generation capacity last year, the most since 2016, research published on Thursday showed, a sign the country is falling back on fossil fuels as economic worries mount."[1129]

According to Reuters, the Centre for Research on Energy and Clean Air and the Global Energy Monitor say China's "newly added capacity under construction was three times more than the rest of the world combined."[1130]

American, Canadian, and European corporations claim that carbon dioxide emissions are causing a climate crisis that could wipe out all life on earth. That's one of the reasons we need a new Great Narrative in the first place, they say. So why are they supporting, directly and indirectly, a country committed to *increasing* its CO_2 emissions like China? And how can they in good conscience profit from the affordable energy provided by China's coal plants, energy used to produce thousands of different products sold by U.S. companies?

The only reasonable explanation for Great Reset–aligned corporations' decision to look the other way while China oppresses hundreds of millions of people is that they actually *don't* care about the many causes they regularly advocate for. For many elites, building a globalist Great Narrative for the twenty-first century is all about wealth, power, and satisfying their immense savior complexes. That's not true of everyone, of course. I think true believers like Harari really do see the trouble ahead and want to find a way to help humanity survive it. But he's the exception, not the rule.

Even if you could prove, however, that most of those seeking to create a new Great Narrative have the best intentions in mind, there's no reason to believe that they have the ability to deliver on their romantic, dreamy promise that globalist institutions can use the technology of the Fourth Industrial Revolution to alleviate all suffering and despair. Men such as Klaus Schwab and Joe Biden imagine themselves to be a cross between Franklin Delano Roosevelt, Ray Kurzweil, Jay Gatsby, and Jesus Christ. In reality, they have more in common with Jimmy Carter and the guys who ran Enron into the ground—with perhaps a dash of every James Bond villain.

For well over a century, progressives such as Schwab and Biden have insisted that, when armed with the latest and greatest technological tools, an expert class of elites and an army of administrative "experts" could guide society to the promised land. But whenever they have tried, nations have ended up riddled with debt, bogged down by an endless sea of bureaucracy, and stuck with an increasingly larger power-and-wealth gap between the rich and poor. And the more influence globalist institutions have had on the world, the worse these problems have become.

The payoff for allowing greater centralization of power and international coordination among elite institutions is that it will supposedly ensure the security and continuing stability of the new world order. (The Emperor in *Star Wars* made the same promise, by the way. And it didn't turn out too well for regular folks living in that far, far away galaxy either.[1131]) But that's never how the story ends. Instead, individuals end up suffering greatly, because it is a law of human nature that the more authority you vest in the hands of a small class of people, the greater the risk of extreme abuse, bloodshed, and tyranny becomes.

Intellectuals such as Yuval Harari might be correct in saying, "In the twentieth century, democracy generally outperformed dictatorship because democracy was better at processing data and making decisions," while, "In the twenty-first century, new technological revolutions, especially AI and machine learning, might swing the pendulum in the opposite direction."[1132] It's possible that machines could make up for the incredible *economic* deficiencies that normally come with greater centralization. Humans are terrible central planners, but the machines of the future might be pretty good at it.

However, achieving greater productivity and efficiency shouldn't be our highest value. And for most Americans, it isn't. Of course, we all want a better quality of life, more affordable goods and services, and additional time away from work to enjoy our lives. But should the free people of the world trade their liberty and autonomy for those comforts? Powerful machines *might* soon make greater centralization more effective in terms of macro-level economic output, but the history of human civilization has clearly shown that centralization will never result in more liberty. And you will never be able to convince me that cold, metallic, ultra-rationalistic machines will do any better in that regard. If anything, they have the potential to be much, much worse.

There's also the very real possibility that the geniuses over at the World Economic Forum and the White House fail spectacularly in their attempt to design technology intelligent enough to manage the most sophisticated parts of our lives. Instead of building the fascism Ferrari they think they are, perhaps they are constructing the world's biggest Ford Pinto, exploding gas tanks and all.

No one can predict the future, so although many of the best and brightest minds think technology will soon usher in radical disruption and transformation, and that much of that technology will be controlled by a small number of elite corporations and governments, it's entirely possible that the Fourth Industrial Revolution will fail long before Klaus and his friends succeed in building an ESG utopia. That might sound like good news, but history has shown repeatedly that the only thing bloodier than a fascistic plan gone *right* is a fascistic plan gone *wrong*. Take a few minutes to read brief histories of the Soviet Union and Nazi Germany and you will see the truth for yourself.

A BETTER PATH FORWARD

Davos believes through international coordination, more powerful global institutions, and the development of tools such as ESG social credit scores, it can shape the technology of the future so that it is "human-centered," inclusive, and benefits all people.[1133] But the only way to ensure people remain free in the midst of massive economic, societal, and technological disruption is for the exact opposite to occur.

The world desperately needs to be radically decentralized, so that as much decision-making as possible is made by individuals and families, not large institutions. This does not mean we should embrace technophobic policies that aim to destroy or limit most forms of innovation. That would be a catastrophic mistake, because if the only societies in the world willing to make technological improvements are those who have few, if any, real protections for individual rights, then humanity will surely enter its bloodiest, most tyrannical era yet. And free societies will eventually become dependent and perhaps even subservient to those ruthless regimes who seek power at all costs.

Navigating the Fourth Industrial Revolution utilizing the principles of the American way will require embedding new and emerging technologies with values, but not those found in the Davos Manifesto, the Constitution of the People's Republic of China, or the Constitution of the Russian Federation. Instead, the techno-logical innovations of the Fourth Industrial Revolution should be built on a framework that translates the values of the Bill of Rights and Declaration of Independence into guardrails for the next wave of new technology. This will require dramatic shifts in the way most Americans think about existing political and social divides, as well as the dismantling of old ideological ideas that might have made sense two decades ago but have since become significantly harmful.

Perhaps the greatest hurdle for many who read this book will be altering the way we think about political and ideological dividing lines. We are no longer living in the political environment of 1997, 2007, or even 2017. A remarkable ideological shift is occurring that could unite groups that appear on the surface to have completely different attitudes.

For example, countless open-minded liberals and moderates are now starting to realize that many of the people who pretend to be on their side in Davos are actually just *using* leftists to help them further their own goals.

Kim Iversen, a popular liberal political commentator who previously cohosted The Hill's *Rising* video program and still hosts the popular *Kim Iversen Show*,[1134] had a perspective-changing revelation about the Great Reset back in 2022.[1135]

On an episode of *Rising* that aired in January 2022, Iversen said, "Glenn Beck was on Tucker Carlson's show last week touting what has been called a right-wing conspiracy theory and discussing his new book, *The Great Reset: Joe Biden and the Rise of Twenty-First-Century Fascism*."[1136]

"Well, maybe that all sounds a little bit loony—and believe me, I do think Glenn Beck tends to be a loon," she said. "But maybe this isn't such a crazy conspiracy theory after all. And after seeing everything we've seen with the governments enacting all sorts of authoritarian controls and many other conspiracy theories coming true, maybe there's something to be concerned about. So, what is the Great Reset? The name even sounds conspiratorial, but believe it or not, it's a real thing."[1137]

Iversen continued by outlining some of the most troubling things said by Great Reset and Great Narrative elites, using their own words, just as I have been doing from day one, to show her audience why this topic is worth taking seriously.

"You'll own nothing and you will be happy: That's what they're saying," Iversen noted. "And with inflation sky high and no signs of it slowing down, they might be right."[1138]

"We are on our way to becoming a nation of renters. But don't worry, it's nothing to fear ... don't worry, everything is being done under the premise that this is all ... being done for our own good, the benefit of a collective society, and we will be happy," she said sneeringly.[1139]

Iversen concluded her lengthy segment on the Great Reset by hammering the Davos crowd and anyone who would defend them.

"Who thinks it's a good idea that a bunch of corporate millionaire and billionaires and world leaders are getting together and coming up with what's best for we the little people?" she asked. "I mean, who thinks that that's a really good idea? And who thinks that they are going to be doing it for our benefit? But, of course they're going to frame it like 'Oh, this is good for you. You're going to rent. You'll own nothing and you'll be happy. Don't worry about it' ... When you look at the actual list of partners with the World Economic Forum, they control everything. They control media. They control health. They control business. They control everything, and so then it does become, how do we people fight against that?"[1140]

Shortly after the segment aired, I contacted Kim to see if she would be open to speaking with me on my radio show. She not only came on the show to discuss the Great Reset, but she also sat down with me in-studio for a really enlightening conversation about the war in Ukraine, free speech, and a whole bunch of other topics.[1141] We didn't agree on everything, and we still don't. That's OK. We don't have to have the same position on every single topic to both believe that standing up to the ruling class is going to be essential to save our country. And we do not need to share all the same ideas in order for us to hold similar values about basic human rights, such as freedom of speech and religious liberty. On those, and many other essential issues, Kim and I do agree—and there are millions of others, Democrats and Republicans alike, who hold the same values in common. We must work tirelessly to find those who share this devotion to freedom and be willing to work with people and groups who we have in the past thought of as adversaries.

SACRED COWS

Another vital change conservatives and libertarians must make is to kill many of the old sacred cows that still haunt the free-market movement, first among them being unfettered support for large corporate interests. Advocates for freedom have long promoted the idea that limiting regulations, taxes, and controls on large corporations helps to spur economic growth, create jobs, lower costs, and raise the standard of living for families. And I haven't seen a single shred of evidence to suggest that this view is wrong. The freer that markets become, the greater the economic growth.

But the intermingling of large corporations, financial institutions, and Wall Street firms with governments and central banks throughout the Western world has effectively made many of these institutions the henchmen of big government. The close coordination between government and large corporations has become so horrendous in recent years that it is virtually impossible to tell who is really behind decisions being made in both business and government.

I know I already mentioned President Biden's degenerate son Hunter in a previous chapter, but the coordination between government and Big Tech to silence everyday Americans and large media institutions from even talking about Hunter's infamous laptop is a perfect example of how intermingled government and private corporations have become.

When tech companies such as Twitter and Meta banned their users from sharing the *New York Post*'s investigation of Hunter Biden's laptop and its damaging material about Joe Biden just weeks before the 2020 election, most people, including yours truly, thought this was yet another example of large technology companies doing everything they could to help a Democrat win an important election.[1142] It took nearly two full years for the American people to find out that many of the tech companies that stifled free speech about the Hunter Biden laptop story were doing so as a direct reaction to warnings issued by the FBI.[1143]

During a 2022 interview with popular podcaster Joe Rogan, Meta CEO Mark Zuckerberg said, "The background here is that the FBI came to us—some folks on our team—and was like 'hey, just so you know, you should be on high alert. We thought there was a lot of Russian propaganda in the 2016 election, we have it on notice that basically there's about to be some kind of dump that's similar to that.'"[1144]

Because the Hunter Biden laptop story was said to "fit the pattern," Meta labeled the story as "misinformation," then later reversed course after realizing that the story had merit.[1145]

Had the FBI come to Meta, Twitter, and other platforms and said, "The Hunter Biden story is misinformation. Take it down now," that would be a violation of the First Amendment. But that's not what the FBI did. It gave social media companies the ammunition they needed to justify taking the story down on their own. You might call it a public-private partnership.

Many of the advocates for freedom who say they are deeply concerned about the dangers associated with expanding the size and influence of government, who say they are concerned about how big tech companies are using their power to target and silence disfavored groups, and who say they want truly free markets, are the same people passionately arguing in favor of allowing corporations and governments to work hand in hand to undermine your liberties. "It's just the free market," they say. But it isn't the free market. Large corporate interests, as well as the interests of banks, insurance companies, and Wall Street firms, have become so intertwined with government that there is, in effect, little difference between them.

Anyone who argues that large corporations operating in the public marketplace should have the authority to stifle free speech, freedom of association, religious freedom, or any other liberty included in the Bill of Rights is either uninformed, wildly corrupt, unbelievably foolish, or completely ignorant of the Great Reset and Great Narrative movements. Whatever the case may be, such a person or organization has become a useful idiot for Davos and is therefore just as dangerous to free societies as the World Economic Forum and its partners have ever been.

Corporations are no longer truly separated from government. Publicly traded corporations, financial institutions, and many large Wall Street firms benefit immensely from special legal and tax advantages that do not apply to individuals and many small businesses. They regularly receive bailouts and government funding. They often work directly alongside government agencies, and many have obtained lucrative government contracts. And, most importantly, many of the trillions of new dollars created by the Federal Reserve in recent years have poured into corporate coffers, yielding massive profits and record-high stock returns, even when the global economy had largely been shut down as part of an attempt to slow the spread of the coronavirus.[1146] Without the Fed's vast money-printing, corporations would have suffered huge losses during the 2020 and 2021 lockdowns, and ESG systems would likely not exist at the scale they do today, because businesses and investors couldn't afford to use them.

If powerful financial institutions, corporations, and governments are allowed to continue to work together to control society to *their* benefit, then *our* "rights" will become nothing more than meaningless scribbles on old pieces of parchment. This should be an ideal that reasonable liberals, moderates, and conservatives can all agree upon. And it is essential that they do. Without a unified approach to tackling this high level of cronyism, the problem will only get worse.

A BLUEPRINT FOR THE FUTURE

How can we ensure that the relevant liberties enshrined in the Bill of Rights become the foundation of the Fourth Industrial Revolution, instead of the national fascism of Russia and China or the international soft (at least for now) fascism of the Great Narrative?

That is, admittedly, an extremely difficult question to answer. However, the following five principles offer a good road map for starting the conversation. A lot more will need to be done in the years ahead, and it's going to require minds a lot smarter than mine. But if we stick with these five principles, I think it's possible America, Canada, and freedom-focused nations in Europe could not only survive the coming disruption, but they could also thrive in the midst of it and then emerge from the Fourth Industrial Revolution stronger and freer than ever.

PRINCIPLE I: WE MUST DISMANTLE CORPORATE AND GOVERNMENT SOCIAL CREDIT SCORES

Environmental, social, and government metrics, along with all other social credit scores, are some of the most important tools elites are using today to manipulate society, often without any laws needing to be passed. And the worst part is, ESG is still in its infancy. As it continues to grow, it will have increasingly more impact on people's daily lives. If ESG and other social credit scoring systems are torn down, it will be very difficult for elites to reshape society or embed their values in new technologies. You can think of ESG like a gigantic control dial for Davos and its allies. If you rip the sucker out, the machinery it's attached to might still be in place, but it can't be easily moved in one direction or another.

Unfortunately, stopping the use of ESG is much easier said than done. Some estimates show that more than 90 percent of companies in the S&P 500 already have ESG systems in place.[1147] Even worse, the European Union has been laying the groundwork to impose a mandatory ESG system in 2023 or 2024, a move that would eventually force many large U.S. companies to adhere to whatever ESG rules are passed in Europe.[1148]

The only way for Americans to protect themselves from the ESG movement is for state and federal lawmakers to put rules into place that prevent the most disconcerting uses of ESG. This does not mean that investors should be barred from using ESG metrics when deciding where to invest their own hard-earned money. If you want to jump off the ESG cliff, that should be your right. However, ESG should *not* be used by pensions and governments to invest other people's money, a practice that has become common in many states—including states run by Republicans. When public pensions and governments invest in ESG, they are effectively forcing taxpayers to fund causes they don't believe in. This practice must be stopped.

Further, banks and financial institutions regularly use ESG as a way to screen out certain businesses and industries, as well as to reward the "good" companies willing to play ball with Davos and its friends.[1149] This is a particularly dangerous development, because if businesses are required to have a high ESG social credit score to access banking, insurance, and other financial services, they have no choice but to participate in this corrupt system, whether they want to or not. Even more troubling, there is strong evidence to suggest that financial institutions will soon start using ESG as a tool to punish and reward *individuals*, not just businesses, making ESG one of the biggest threats to freedom in America today.[1150]

When I first started talking about the Great Reset and ESG scores back in 2020, almost no one in Washington or state capitol buildings understood what ESG scores were or cared to stop them. So in 2020 and 2021, I dedicated numerous radio and television shows to covering these topics, and then I published *The Great Reset* book in January 2022. Concerns about ESG spread like wildfire, eventually capturing the attention of countless state and federal lawmakers. I wish I could take all the credit for the anti-ESG movement, but the real heroes of this story are the members of my audience and their friends and family members who took the time to teach people about what's really going on.

In 2021 and especially 2022, lawmakers in Congress and in more than twenty states proposed legislation designed to slow or stop the rise of ESG.[1151] In some states—including Kentucky, West Virginia, Tennessee, Utah, and Texas—policymakers sought to enact rules that would stop state pension and other government funds from investing with firms promoting ESG.[1152] In other states—such as New Hampshire, Kansas, Idaho, and Arizona—lawmakers also focused on preventing financial institutions from using their might to impose an ESG agenda.[1153]

In March 2021, U.S. senator Kevin Cramer, a Republican from North Dakota, introduced the Fair Access to Banking Act, which would require large banks to base lending and other business decisions on financial considerations, rather than on subjective ESG metrics like determining whether a business has the "right" ratio of Asian to Hispanic workers.[1154] Sen. Cramer's bill quickly gained support from many Republicans in the Senate, earning a whopping thirty-three cosponsors. Among those senators backing the bill were Marsha Blackburn (R-TN), Rick Scott (R-FL), Mike Braun (R-IN), Tim Scott (R-SC), Mike Crapo (R-ID), Josh Hawley (R-MO), Marco Rubio (R-FL), and Ted Cruz (R-TX).[1155] In the House of Representatives, Representative Andy Barr (R-KY) introduced a companion bill featuring eighty cosponsors.[1156]

The opposition to these bills from some Democrats and many bank lobbyists, both at the federal and state levels, was fierce. In many state legislatures, weak Republicans beholden to corporate interests, not Democrats, were the primary forces responsible for bills failing. In other cases, establishment so-called conservative groups and think tanks helped to kill important bills, often in an effort to get weaker legislation passed. As a result, anti-ESG laws or regulations were only passed in a handful of states, and often due to the work of state treasurers such as Riley Moore in West Virginia and Marlo Oaks in Utah.

At the time this book was sent to the publisher in early 2023, lawmakers in twenty states were considering anti-ESG legislation or had already rejected bills. Five other states were considered likely to adopt anti-ESG policies soon, according to experts I spoke with at The Heartland Institute, a free-market think tank. And lawmakers in another nine states had passed some kind of anti-ESG legislation, regulation, or rule, either through a legislature, regulatory body, governor's office, or state treasurer's office.[1157]

The anti-ESG legislative defeats that have occurred so far might appear disheartening, but in reality, there is a lot to be excited about. It is practically unheard of for a topic to garner so much support from lawmakers in such a short period. And it's not uncommon for legislative campaigns to take multiple attempts over several years before really strong bills are passed. Grassroots activists and experts at think tanks have told me that they expect the remainder of 2023 and 2024 to be huge years for the anti-ESG movement. And I have personally met with many lawmakers, including members of the U.S. Senate, who say that they are committed to passing legislation to stop social credit scores such as ESG.

Perhaps most encouraging of all is that some of the biggest leaders of the conservative movement are now joining the fight. In July and August 2022, Florida governor Ron DeSantis announced a package of legislative and regulatory proposals targeting the use of ESG in his state, including provisions that would "prohibit big banks, credit card companies and money transmitters from discriminating against customers for their religious, political, or social beliefs."[1158] At the time this book was sent to the publisher, Florida lawmakers had formally proposed DeSantis's plan and appeared to be on the verge of passing a tough anti-ESG bill.[1159]

We won't know until after this book has gone to the printer whether all of DeSantis's proposals will be passed in the Florida Legislature, but DeSantis has already used his executive authority to stop state public pensions from being used to support ESG, a significant blow to supporters of ESG.[1160]

A lot more work is needed, but a growing number of lawmakers have shown a big interest in making ESG a focus in upcoming legislative sessions. With additional pressure from voters, it's possible laws could soon be passed that would severely restrict the authority of ESG. That would not solve all the problems outlined in this book, but it would be a gigantic step forward.

PRINCIPLE 2: THINK LOCAL—REALLY, REALLY LOCAL

No one understands better than I do how easy it is to get swept up in national political debates. Who doesn't love bashing Alexandria Ocasio-Cortez when she goes all Fidel Castro on social media? And who can resist the allure of talking about Joe Biden's latest catastrophic policy decision or episode of creepy touching and hair-sniffing? And who has the strength and self-restraint to ignore yet another Kamala Harris cackle-fest?

The issues that occur in Washington and around the world matter. They matter a lot. But the best way to insulate yourself from the disastrous policies being imposed by big corporations, big government, and the United Nations is not to obsess over what's happening in faraway halls of power, but rather to think local. It's really hard to get good bills passed in Washington and nearly as hard in many state capitols. However, local rules and programs are much easier to fix—but only if patriotic Americans are willing to get involved.

Consider running for your local school board. At the very least, consider going to your local school board meetings and seeing what board members are up to. If you have the knowledge, try to join local zoning and planning boards. Find out who your state lawmakers are and what they believe. Contact them and ask them lots of questions about where they stand on ESG and other issues related to the Great Narrative. If you're not happy with their answers and cannot run for office yourself, find reliable people who will. Or support groups you trust who are seeking to identify good candidates for office.

You do not need to get deeply involved in politics to make a difference, either. You can start by simply buying from local vendors instead of large corporations. That includes shopping at a farmer's market if you have one nearby. If you do not, try getting in touch with farmers directly. Many offer "farm shares," which allow you to regularly purchase products directly from them for a set fee.

I know that big-box stores and gigantic multinational retailers often have the best prices, but many of them are using their wealth and power to destroy freedom, or, at the very least, they are partic- ipating in elites' ESG scheme because they are afraid of suffering if they don't. Local businesses are not nearly as affected by ESG at this time, so by supporting them instead, you're taking money out of the ESG system. Small businesses have also had it rougher than just about anyone over the past few years. They need your support more than ever. Help them. Maybe that means buying less or spending more, but it's worth it. Our country is at stake.

In addition to shopping locally, you need to try to find a way to bank locally. That's not always possible, and it's sometimes hard to figure out which local banks are using ESG (or something similar). It's going to take some time and legwork on your part. You need to talk to local bank managers and find out if they are using ESG, and if they are, find out why. Credit unions could be a better option, but it's not a guarantee. What is guaranteed, however, is that if you continue to do all your banking at one of the big guys, such as JPMorgan Chase & Co., Wells Fargo, Citi, or Bank of America, you're helping some of the biggest ESG bullies in the world impose elites' values on the rest of society.

PRINCIPLE 3: LARGE CORPORATIONS SHOULD BE REQUIRED TO ADHERE TO THE BILL OF RIGHTS TOO

As I mentioned earlier, one of the biggest sacred cows in need of being slaughtered is the idea that all regulations imposed on large corporations are bad because the "free market" works best when corporations are allowed to run wild. Now, I agree that *if* we had a truly free marketplace, then most regulations would be completely unnecessary. But thanks to corrupt Democratic *and* Republican politicians working to undermine our interests over the past few decades, America's economy has become a funhouse-mirror distortion of what capitalism should be.

America is not a socialist nation—not yet, anyway—but it doesn't have a truly free market either. Corporations, including social media companies, receive all sorts of special tax breaks, bailouts, subsidies, regulatory benefits, protections for intellectual property, and legal carve-outs that give them advantages over individuals and many small businesses. They get these benefits through taxpayer-funded government institutions and programs. Many of them also coordinate with government officials and lobby to have laws written in a way that favors them.

If large corporations are going to benefit from governments paid for by and accountable to all Americans, then they should have to treat all Americans equally. Imposing most of the Bill of Rights on public for-profit corporations, which have effectively become government partners in recent years, would protect individual rights and prevent many of the worst-case scenarios from developing in the coming Fourth Industrial Revolution.

How would this play out in real life? The Bill of Rights forbids censorship of many forms of free speech, including religious speech. So large corporate social media companies such as Twitter and Meta should not be allowed to censor speech normally protected by the First Amendment. And that should apply not only to the social media platforms themselves but also to any other products and services created in the future, such as the metaverse, future application stores, and virtual reality devices.

Similarly, large corporations that own rental homes shouldn't be allowed to ban activities that are protected by the Bill of Rights either. For example, corporate rental homes shouldn't be allowed to prevent individuals from possessing a legally owned gun, a Second Amendment right, or from hosting political meetings.

This would also mean large banks and other financial institutions wouldn't be allowed to deny services or access to capital on the basis of characteristics that fall under the Bill of Rights, such as political affiliation.

This approach would not require that small businesses or individuals be held to the same standards. They are not working hand in hand with government in the same way most large corporations do, and the rights of individuals must always be protected from government, including the right to discriminate based on ESG considerations. Nonprofit advocacy organizations should also be exempt from these requirements, because they exist to promote ideas, not serve a public market in an effort to earn a profit. They are designed in many cases to effectively act as a voice for many individuals seeking to promote specific religious or political ideas, and they should be allowed to continue doing that work without the restraints of the Bill of Rights.

Some might think that taking this position is dangerous because it could create a slippery slope that leads to left-wing ideas being imposed on corporations too. With all due respect to the freedom-focused readers who still think this way, when it comes to big corporations, the slippery-slope argument is about as dumb as it gets. We've already slipped down the slope. Actually, we've been callously tossed down the side of a mountain. We're currently clinging to the side of a cliff with our trembling hand desperately clutching a shriveled root tenuously growing out of the mountain's rocky ground. And it looks like it could snap at any moment. We are out of options. We either fight this battle now or we're toast.

What's more, it's worth noting that the idea that large corporations should be held to a different standard than small businesses and individuals has existed for many decades, both among liberals and conservatives. My favorite example comes from a Supreme Court decision handed down in 1946 in a case called *Marsh v. Alabama*.

In *Marsh*, the U.S. Supreme Court ruled that a private corporation could not prohibit a member of a Jehovah's Witness church from distributing religious materials in a company-owned town. According to the Supreme Court, the ban was in violation of the First Amendment, even though the land was privately owned.

Writing for the majority, Justice Hugo Black declared, "Ownership does not always mean absolute dominion. The more an owner, for his advantage, opens up his property for use by the public in general, the more do his rights become circumscribed by the statutory and constitutional rights of those who use it. Thus, the owners of privately held bridges, ferries, turnpikes and railroads may not operate them as freely as a farmer does his farm."[1161]

This makes perfect sense, and it's a rule that has already been applied in many respects. For example, businesses are not allowed to deny service to customers on the basis of race, religious membership, skin color, disability, gender, and other characteristics.[1162] Why? Because everyone understands that businesses exist to serve the public—the whole public—and bans on people based on these characteristics effectively shut off whole parts of our society to groups on a purely discriminatory basis. All I'm suggesting is that we expand this concept to include many other liberties included in the Bill of Rights.

PRINCIPLE 4: DATA PROTECTIONS SHOULD BE ENHANCED

In chapter 6 of this book, I explained how important data collection and control will be in the Fourth Industrial Revolution. He who has the gold makes the rules, and data will, in so many ways, be more valuable than gold throughout the remainder of this century. Also, the further collection of data and consolidation of its ownership, mixed with more powerful machines and the development of advanced forms of artificial intelligence, could soon lead to, in the words of WEF intellectual Yuval Harari, "digital dictatorships."[1163]

It is essential that individuals' data are protected from abuse, but what can policymakers do to make sure that this happens? Well, for starters, we absolutely cannot allow the federal government to take over the management of data. If government bureaucrats and career politicians are allowed to get their grubby little hands on the massive amount of data that will be collected in the Fourth Industrial Revolution, then they will almost certainly use it to substantially expand the influence of government in our everyday lives.

Of course, large corporations that control vast amounts of data are already abusing their power, and if America stays on its current trajectory, the problem will get increasingly worse. We will have a digital dictatorship, to be sure, shared by Google, Meta, Apple, and Microsoft, our new benevolent rulers.

In order to stop things from getting out of hand, America desperately needs a comprehensive national privacy law that would allow corporations to collect data—something that essentially has to occur, to some degree, in order for the United States to compete globally—but that would also severely restrict its management and ownership. For example, a comprehensive law could stop corporations from selling or sharing data with third parties. It could also mandate that users provide permission in writing for the continued use of data after a specified period, perhaps a year or two. If express permission to continue using the data is not given in writing, the data would be automatically deleted.

Certain kinds of data collection, such as those related to health care, already have some rules in place, but many more could be added. And laws could be written to ensure that data are only used for a specified, approved purpose, and that agreements to use data are written in plain language and kept very short.

This shouldn't be a controversial proposal. Many people on both the ideological left and right want to limit corporations' control of data, including Alexandria Ocasio-Cortez, a number of Republicans in the House, and writers at the *New York Times*.[1164, 1165, 1166] Most Americans are just as worried. A poll conducted in 2019 by the Pew Research Center found that 81 percent of Americans believe the "potential risks" associated with data collection by companies "outweigh the benefits."[1167] When asked about government data collection, 66 percent said the risks outweigh the benefits.[1168]

PRINCIPLE 5: THE FEDERAL RESERVE NEEDS TO BE DRAMATICALLY REFORMED

In my ideal world, the U.S. Federal Reserve system would be completely destroyed and replaced with a much better, more stable model. That probably isn't going to happen, but hey, a guy can dream, right?

In the spirit of offering more realistic solutions, a good fifth principle for protecting freedom in the Fourth Industrial Revolution era is to reform the Federal Reserve and U.S. monetary policy, so that our central bank cannot be used as a weapon to manipulate society. Much of the Great Narrative's goals for the future depend on access to cheap dollars and continuously low or negative interest rates. The Fed is fueling the current Great Reset, and elites plan on the Fed (or some other, similar institution) fueling the Great Narrative era for decades to come.

There are a number of ways the Federal Reserve should be reformed. Let's start with the easiest one: Americans should know who the Fed banks really are, how they make decisions, and every action that they perform. As crazy as it sounds, Americans don't know much about what goes on at the Federal Reserve. Some of their deliberations are made public, but a lot of their decisions are shrouded in mystery. Americans aren't even allowed to know all the transactions made by the Fed with foreign banks and countries, although we do know the Fed has purchased massive stakes in foreign assets.

U.S. senator Rand Paul, a Republican from Kentucky, has been trying to audit the Fed for years. In 2021, Paul reintroduced the Federal Reserve Transparency Act, which would have required "the nonpartisan, independent Government Accountability Office (GAO) to conduct a thorough audit of the Federal Reserve's Board of Governors and reserve banks within one year of the bill's passage and to report back to Congress within 90 days of completing the audit."[1169] Representative Thomas Massie, also a Republican from Kentucky, sponsored the companion bill in the House.[1170]

Under Paul's bill, the GAO would have been empowered to "fully audit"

> Transactions for or with a foreign central bank, government of a foreign country, or nonprivate international financing organization;
>
> Deliberations, decisions, or actions on monetary policy matters, including discount window operations, reserves of member banks, securities credit, interest on deposits, and open market operations;
>
> Transactions made under the direction of the Federal Open Market Committee; or a part of a discussion or communication among or between members of the Board and officers and employees of the Federal Reserve System related to clauses (1)–(3) of this subsection.[1171]

Democrats killed the Paul-Massie bill in the House and Senate, despite the fact that many House Democrats had expressed support for the measure in previous congressional sessions.[1172] Even Bernie Sanders has voted in favor of the bill in the past.[1173]

Auditing the Fed is just the start, though. Strict rules need to be put in place that would explicitly forbid the Federal Reserve from using its power to advance social justice or environmental goals. The Fed's mission ought to be solely to keep the U.S. currency stable. That's it.

The Federal Reserve should also be forbidden from working directly with private Wall Street firms and others with a clear conflict of interest. For example, the Fed should never again be allowed to hire firms like BlackRock, a notorious champion of the Great Reset, to help the government purchase bonds, as it did in 2020.[1174]

Most important of all, the Federal Reserve should never be allowed to create a programmable digital currency, an effort the Biden administration is working feverishly to accomplish.[1175] As I explained at length in chapter 4, a programmable digital dollar would give the government or Federal Reserve unprecedented amounts of power. A programmable currency could be tracked, manipulated, easily replicated, and it would almost certainly encourage lawmakers to push the United States much deeper into debt.

Rather than give the Fed unprecedented levels of power, policymakers should run screaming in the opposite direction. The Fed should have strict limits on creating new dollars, and it should be required to ask for permission from Congress, the people's representatives, to engage in some of its more radical tactics to boost economic output.

Finally, although cryptocurrencies do not fall under the jurisdiction of the Fed, it's worth mentioning here that everything possible should be done to guard against a government takeover of the cryptocurrency market. In chapter 6, I explained how cryptocurrencies have the potential to dramatically disrupt the financial services industry, and most of those disruptions would be for the better. Cryptocurrencies offer Americans who want to avoid the perils of the "official" monetary system an off-ramp. If cryptocurrencies are allowed to flourish, regular people could effectively become their own banks, peer-to-peer lending and other services could become commonplace, and there would be an option for investors to store their wealth outside the watchful eye of government and its lackies at the Federal Reserve.

Or, I suppose we could just go back to the whole obliterate-the-Fed plan I led this section off with. It's not the most elegant solution, but it sure would get the job done.

A GREATER NARRATIVE

There's one final principle that must guide Americans' journey through the Fourth Industrial Revolution. I know I only numbered five earlier in the chapter, but having a "six-principle plan to save the world" just doesn't flow quite as well. Besides, this one deserves to stand apart from the rest.

There's a reason why Klaus Schwab and his marketing department at the World Economic Forum chose to build a campaign called the Great Narrative. Their vision for the future is going to require humanity to adopt a completely new way of thinking. It's the only way people will ever voluntarily choose to submit themselves to the corporate-techno-globalist-fascistic world imagined by Schwab. With a new Great Narrative in mind, people would be less selfish, less egotistical, and more willing to accept the guidance of the strong hand of their betters in Davos.

But there's a much better narrative, one that rarely comes up at World Economic Forum annual meetings because it's a dangerous idea. So dangerous, in fact, that when it is discussed by elites in places such as Davos, it's often used as an example of greed or recklessness. The truth, however, is that history unequivocally shows that despite opposition from the educated masterminds of Europe, Washington, and New York, this other "Great Narrative" offers more hope for the future than anything dreamed up by Schwab, Biden, or even a panel of "experts" at the latest and greatest World Government Summit. It's the story of America, and imperfect as it might be, it's humanity's best chance to flourish in the decades to come.

When people think of American history, they often conjure up dates, places, and important figures. And there's nothing wrong with that. America is, at least in some ways, a country like every other country, and it certainly has a history worthy of respect and careful study. But the United States is so much more than a place. It's a powerful idea. It's an opportunity. It's a dream.

For the vast majority of the years humans have walked the earth, they have, by their own design, been subjugated to ruling-class elites—to tribal leaders, monarchs, emperors, and warlords. It's only within the past few centuries that anyone ever imagined that a society of ordinary men and women could govern themselves—and even more dangerously, that men and women had the God-given *authority* to govern themselves. From its very first moments, Americans have believed this truth with every fiber of their being. They haven't always applied it equally, justly, or fairly, but the idea has consistently remained with them, serving as a guidepost for navigating the treacherous roads to the future.

Some have suggested that Americans have a long history of seeking to hide away from the rest of the world, only agreeing to come out when duty demanded it or imperial affections encouraged it. But nothing could be further from the truth. The United States has at times wisely avoided many of the conflicts of Europe, Africa, Asia, and South and Central America, but its people have never shied away from wanting the world to watch and learn from their great experiment.

When the Pilgrims arrived in New England in the early seventeenth century, they came as religious refugees. Much of Europe had turned against them, and those with similar views faced intense persecution in England. The Pilgrims hoped that if they were to build a community of people bound together in a common love of God, they would be blessed, and the world would see this blessing and be inspired to live as they were.

In one of the most famous speeches in American history, John Winthrop, governor of the Massachusetts Bay Colony and founder of Boston, said in a 1630 sermon, "For we must consider that we shall be as a city upon a hill. The eyes of all people are upon us. So that if we shall deal falsely with our God in this work we have undertaken, and so cause him to withdraw his present help from us, we shall be made a story and a by-word through the world."[1176]

For Winthrop and many of the other early founders of America, the stakes for their venture couldn't be higher. If they failed, they reasoned that the rest of the world would use their failure as proof that their ideas were false. "We shall open the mouths of enemies to speak evil of the ways of God, and all professors for God's sake," Winthrop said. "We shall shame the faces of many of God's worthy servants, and cause their prayers to be turned into curses upon us till we be consumed out of the good land whither we are going."[1177]

Americans' attitudes and religious beliefs have evolved over time, to be sure, but the idea that we stand as a "city upon a hill" for all continents to see has never dissipated. America has always been the best hope for the world. Why? Because in promising its inhabitants the ability to pursue their own passions and chart their own course, the United States has become a beacon for the most ingenious, artistic, brave, and hardworking people the planet has to offer. They have come by the tens of millions to build a better life for themselves, and in the process, they have contributed their talents to the further expansion of the American dream for all those who were blessed enough to already live here. The American way is the way of freedom, hard work, respect, and love. Who *wouldn't* want to live in a place that offers a vision for life such as that?

As the American colonies grew in size and strength in the eighteenth century, they naturally sought to shake free from the shackles of imperialist England. A nation ruled by inept monarchs half a world away could never truly be a shining city upon a hill. In the process of forming a common identity, Americans developed a shared understanding that their liberties come from a power that's higher, greater, and nobler than any earthly king ever could be. They come from God and from the natural world that God created. Once this idea entered the American bloodstream, revolution wasn't only inevitable, it was *necessary*.

In the Declaration of Independence, Thomas Jefferson wrote, "When in the Course of human events, it becomes necessary for one people to dissolve the political bands which have connected them with another, and to assume among the powers of the earth, the separate and equal station to which the Laws of Nature and of Nature's God entitle them, a decent respect to the opinions of mankind requires that they should declare the causes which impel them to the separation."[1178]

Jefferson added, "We hold these truths to be self-evident, that all men are created equal, that they are endowed by their Creator with certain unalienable Rights, that among these are Life, Liberty and the pursuit of Happiness. That to secure these rights, Governments are instituted among Men, deriving their just powers from the consent of the governed."[1179]

This was truly a history-changing idea, one that would shake the foundations of Europe and consume the minds of hundreds of millions of people located on every continent. Had the earliest Americans lived in perfect harmony with these words, applying them equally to all those people who lived in their midst, the United States would be a far better place than it is today. Just as Winthrop warned in 1630, moral failures have been used by its enemies to injure the beliefs of the American people, including cultural, religious, and political ideas.

But a fair analysis of the history of the United States shows that it has steadily—one might even say *progressively*—increased freedom for all people, to the point where no one is now denied equal treatment under the law, regardless of race, religion, sexual orientation, or anything else. And the freer America has become, the more attractive it has been to those exceptional people the world over who want to live peacefully, with their lives, families, property,

and liberties protected. This, more than anything else, has accelerated the development of the United States.

This, of course, is not the story of America young people hear
in many schools throughout the country. Instead, they are taught
only the most horrifying, darkest moments of our collective past,
as though the American narrative has nothing to offer but shat-
tered dreams and hypocrisy. As a result, millions of people have
forgotten what it means to be from the United States. Their narrative, shaped by decades of public-school propaganda, is ugly and
devoid of historical context, making many of our neighbors susceptible to Davos's sweet-sounding offers of collectivism, management
by educated elites, and globalism. Such a strategy has never yielded
the exceptionalism promised by America, the very same exceptionalism that still lures the best and brightest to come to our shores,
from every corner of the earth.

I am not sure anyone has ever captured the spirit of America better
than Emma Lazarus. Her poem titled "The New Colossus" was written
in November 1883 as part of an effort to pay for the foundation of the
Statue of Liberty in New York.[1180] Lazarus died in 1887, just one year
after the Statue of Liberty had been officially dedicated, and it wasn't
until 1903 that her poem made its way to a plaque that sits at the feet
of the statue. The poem only became well-known after Lazarus's friend,
Georgina Schuyler, led a public campaign to have her work commem-
orated.[1181] Emma Lazarus would be stunned to know that her largely
unknown poem has become one of the most famous ever written—
well, one line of it anyway.

Everyone has heard Lazarus's line, "Give me your tired, your
poor, your huddled masses yearning to breathe free." But most
Americans have never bothered to read the rest of the poem, or to
even try to understand what the poem is about. If you polled one
hundred people walking down the street about the meaning of that
famous line, almost all of them would say it's about immigration.

You might be thinking that very thing now. But "The New Colossus" isn't about immigration at all—not really. It's about who we are as Americans. It's about our story. Our Greater Narrative.

Lazarus's poem begins:

> Not like the brazen giant of Greek fame,
> With conquering limbs astride from land to land;
> Here at our sea-washed, sunset gates shall stand
> A mighty woman with a torch, whose flame
> Is the imprisoned lightning, and her name
> Mother of Exiles.[1182]

The "brazen giant of Greek fame" is an allusion to the Colossus of Rhodes, a wonder of the ancient world. It allegedly stood at the entrance to the harbor for the city of Rhodes, which was located on an island in Greece with the same name.

Lazarus's description of "imprisoned lighting" is not only a reference to the Statue of Liberty's famous torch, but also to Americans' technological achievements. Thomas Edison's light bulb had first been demonstrated to the public in New Jersey on New Year's Eve in 1879, less than four years before Lazarus wrote her poem.[1183]

Lazarus's "New Colossus" continues,

> From her beacon-hand
> Glows world-wide welcome; her mild eyes command
> The air-bridged harbor that twin cities frame.
> "Keep, ancient lands, your storied pomp!" cries she
> With silent lips. "Give me your tired, your poor,
> Your huddled masses yearning to breathe free,
> The wretched refuse of your teeming shore.
> Send these, the homeless, tempest-tost to me,
> I lift my lamp beside the golden door!"

At first glance, it's tempting to think solely of immigration when you read Lazarus's poem, and there's no doubt that this was in the poet's mind when she wrote it. But if you read the text carefully, you'll see that the true meaning is much richer.

Note that Lazarus put, "Keep, ancient lands, your storied pomp!" in quotation marks in her text. That's because it's meant to be read as though the Statue of Liberty were saying it. Her "lips" might be "silent" but the message is clear as the statue looks out across the ocean to Europe and says, Americans don't want your "ancient lands" and "your storied pomp!"

For Lazarus, the Statue of Liberty was crying out to Europe as the "Mother of Exiles," calling immigrants to her shores, yes, but also rejecting the old ways of Europe.

"Give me your tired, your poor, Your huddled masses," the Statue screams across the Atlantic Ocean.

Hammering the point home, Lazarus further described the exiles as "The wretched refuse of your teeming shore," "the homeless," and the "tempest-tost." In other words, the statue, representing all of America, tells Europe that it doesn't care about its wealth and history. It doesn't care about its castles and kingdoms. It doesn't care about its wars or international agreements. What it does care about, however, is its people, no matter how poor or "wretched" or beaten up by the storms of life they might be.

But—and this is a *huge* but—the statue doesn't welcome just anyone to America's shores. It wants those "yearning to breathe free."

"Send these," the statue says. "I lift my lamp beside the golden door!"

What is the "golden door"? It's the entrance, the portal to a free world, made available to all those who want to live the American way. *This* is the true Great Narrative.

The Fourth Industrial Revolution is going to create levels of disruption humanity has never seen before. People will be confused, excited, terrified, and willing to reevaluate many of the ideas that have long been part of their lives and cultures. The World Economic Forum and the Biden administration would have Americans tackle these challenges by handing much of their authority and decision-making abilities over to international institutions, governments, and massive corporations. The era of the selfish individual is over, they say. Global cooperation is the only path that ensures humanity can survive. But I disagree.

Rather than become more like Europe, Americans should strive to build a technologically rich, freedom-focused utopia of our own. We should be proud of our exceptional heritage, however imperfect it might be. We should stand firm against the internationalism of Europe, adamantly declaring that they can keep their "storied pomp," "ancient lands," and prestigious globalist organizations. But we should also avoid at all costs the violent national fascism of nations such as Russia and China. Let Europe celebrate Davos and its allegedly "progressive" vision of the future. They can have it. Let China celebrate Mao, and let Russia glorify Vladimir Putin. We have no use for their wretched ideas here.

We are Americans. We ought to be a shining city on a hill for the rest of the world to see, standing by the golden door of freedom, carrying a torch of imprisoned lighting. We must show the world that humanity can thrive in the Fourth Industrial Revolution while embracing both the benefits of emerging technologies and a passionate commitment to inalienable, unchangeable, eternal human rights. That cannot happen if we submit ourselves to the World Economic Forum's Great Narrative.

The road ahead will be extremely difficult, to be sure, and undoubtedly fraught with ethical, technological, economic, and societal challenges that no one today can foresee. Thriving in the Fourth Industrial Revolution while maintaining a devotion to individual freedom cannot be accomplished without great struggle. But who said saving the world would be easy?

I, alongside the millions of other Americans who truly yearn to breathe free, stand by the golden door, where imprisoned lighting illuminates the future, offering hope and true progress to all those who sincerely desire to become part of our Greater Narrative. And I've written this book to ask you and your family to join me.

Will humanity's future be bright, full of technological achievement *and* liberty, or will we soon descend into fascistic darkness? That's the decision we all must make. Whose side are *you* on?

NOTES

Chapter I: The Great Reset Was Just the Beginning

1   U.S. National Park Service, "Ike, Gettysburg, and the Cold War," NPS.gov, accessed
    April 4, 2022, https://www.nps.gov/eise/index.htm.

2   Dwight D. Eisenhower Presidential Library, Museum, and Boyhood Home,
    "The Eisenhowers," accessed April 4, 2022, https://www.eisenhowerlibrary.
    gov/eisenhowers.

3   See the "Reading Copy" of President Dwight Eisenhower's "Farewell Address,"
    made available by the Dwight D. Eisenhower Presidential Library, Museum, and
    Boyhood Home, accessed April 4, 2022, https://www.eisenhowerlibrary.gov/sites/
    default/files/research/online-documents/farewell-address/reading-copy.pdf.

4   President Eisenhower's full speech has been made available online by the Lillian
    Goldman Law Library at Yale Law School. See Dwight Eisenhower, "Military-
    Industrial Complex Speech," delivered on January 17, 1961, accessed April 4, 2022,
    https://avalon.law.yale.edu/20th_century/eisenhower001.asp.

5   Dwight Eisenhower, "Military-Industrial Complex Speech."

6   Bernie Sanders @Bernie Sanders, "We Must Have the Guts to Take on
    Wall Street," June 27, 2019, https://twitter.com/berniesanders/status/
    1144446944472907776?lang=en.

7   Letter by Dwight Eisenhower to Professor Theodore R. Kennedy, June 21, 1967.
    Made available online by the Dwight D. Eisenhower Presidential Library, Museum,
    and Boyhood Home, accessed April 4, 2022, https://www.eisenhowerlibrary.gov/
    sites/default/files/research/online-documents/farewell-address/1967-06-21-dde-
    to-kennedy.pdf.

8   Dwight Eisenhower, "Military-Industrial Complex Speech."

9   Dwight Eisenhower, "Military-Industrial Complex Speech."

10   Dwight Eisenhower, "Military-Industrial Complex Speech."

11   Dwight Eisenhower, "Military-Industrial Complex Speech."

12   "President Biden's Economic Strategy and Fiscal Responsibility Decreasing Deficit by More Than $1.3 Trillion—Largest One-Year Decline in U.S. History," White House, March 28, 2022, https://www.whitehouse.gov/omb/briefing-room/2022/03/28/president-bidens-economic-strategy-and-fiscal-responsibility-decreasing-deficit-by-more-than-1-3-trillion-largest-one-year-decline-in-u-s-history.

13   Kyle Smith, "How Dem officials, the media and Big Tech worked in concert to bury the Hunter Biden story," New York Post, March 18, 2022, https://nypost.com/2022/03/18/how-big-tech-media-and-dems-killed-the-hunter-biden-story.

14   Mariem Del Rio, "Coca-Cola Asks Its Workers to Be 'Less White' to Fight Racism," Entrepreneur, February 25, 2021, https://www.entrepreneur.com/article/366132.

15   Nicole Goodkind, "Hundreds of CEOs are taking a stand against new Republican voting laws," Fortune, April 14, 2021, https://fortune.com/2021/04/14/ceos-republican-voting-laws-voter-suppression-apple-amazon-blackrock-facebook-warren-buffett.

16   Adam Brewster and Caitlin Huey-Burns, "What Georgia's new voting law really does—9 facts," CBS News, cbsnews.com, April 7, 2021, https://www.cbsnews.com/news/georgia-voting-law-9-facts.

17   Eamon Barrett, "Wells Fargo Is the Last of the Big Six Banks to Issue a Net-Zero Climate Pledge. Now Comes the Hard Part," Fortune, March 9, 2021, https://fortune.com/2021/03/09/wells-fargo-climate-carbon-neutral-net-zero.

18   Lucas Manfredi, "DeSantis says Disney 'crossed the line' for criticizing Parental Rights in Education bill," Fox Business, foxbusiness.com, March 30, 2022, https://www.foxbusiness.com/politics/disney-desantis-parental-rights-education.

19   Jessica Chasmar, "Florida's DeSantis signs Parental Rights in Education bill, hits back at Hollywood critics," Fox News, foxnews.com, March 28, 2022, https://www.foxnews.com/politics/florida-desantis-signs-parental-rights-education-bill.

20   Glenn Beck and Justin Haskins, The Great Reset: Joe Biden and the Rise of Twenty-First Century Fascism (Mercury Ink, 2022).

21   World Economic Forum, "The Great Reset: Hello and Welcome," last updated June 3, 2020, archived version made available by Archive.org, https://web.archive.org/web/20200720025411/https://www.weforum.org/great-reset/live-updates.

22   Justin Haskins, "Al Gore Joins Global Elites Calling for Eco-Socialist 'Great Reset' Proposal," StoppingSocialism.com, June 22, 2020, https://stoppingsocialism.com/

2020/06/al-gore-great-reset, citing "Al Gore Talks Climate Crisis: 'This is the Time for a Great Reset,'" *TODAY*, NBC, June 19, 2020, https://www.today.com/video/al-gore-talks-climate-crisis-this-is-the-time-for-a-great-reset-85439045592.

23   Andrew Ross Sorkin et al., "Larry Fink Defends Stakeholder Capitalism," *New York Times*, January 18, 2022, https://www.nytimes.com/2022/01/18/business/dealbook/fink-blackrock-woke.html.

24   Anna Bruce-Lockhart and Ross Chainey, "'Normal Wasn't Working' – John Kerry, Phillip Atiba Goff and Others on the New Social Contract Post-COVID," World Economic Forum, June 24, 2020, https://www.weforum.org/agenda/2020/06/great-reset-social-contract-john-kerry-phillip-goff.

25   See, for example, David Gelles, "In Its 50th Year, Davos Is Searching for Its Soul," *New York Times*, January 19, 2020, https://www.nytimes.com/2020/01/19/business/davos-50th-year.html.

26   Klaus Schwab, "Now is the Time for a 'Great Reset,'" World Economic Forum, June 3, 2020, https://www.weforum.org/agenda/2020/06/now-is-the-time-for-a-great-reset.

27   Klaus Schwab, "Now is the Time for a 'Great Reset.'"

28   Klaus Schwab, "Now is the Time for a 'Great Reset.'"

29   See World Economic Forum, "About: The Great Reset: A Unique Twin Summit to Begin 2021," weforum.org, accessed July 14, 2020, https://www.weforum.org/great-reset/about.

30   See "Klaus Schwab Releases 'Stakeholder Capitalism'; Making the Case for a Global Economy that Works for Progress, People and Planet," press release, World Economic Forum, January 29, 2021, https://www.weforum.org/press/2021/01/klaus-schwab-releases-stakeholder-capitalism-making-the-case-for-a-global-economy-that-works-for-progress-people-and-planet, citing Klaus Schwab and Peter Vanham, *Stakeholder Capitalism: A Global Economy that Works for Progress, People and Planet* (World Economic Forum, 2021).

31   See "Klaus Schwab Releases 'Stakeholder Capitalism'; Making the Case for a Global Economy that Works for Progress, People and Planet," press release, World Economic Forum.

32   Klaus Schwab, "Now is the Time for a 'Great Reset.'"

33   Klaus Schwab, "Now is the Time for a 'Great Reset.'"

34   Kate Whiting, "How the World Can 'Reset' Itself After COVID-19 – According to These Experts," World Economic Forum, June 3, 2020, https://www.weforum.org/agenda/2020/06/covid19-great-reset-gita-gopinath-jennifer-morgan-sharan-burrow-climate.

35 Anna Bruce-Lockhart and Ross Chainey, "'Normal Wasn't Working' – John Kerry, Phillip Atiba Goff and Others on the New Social Contract Post-COVID."

36 Anna Bruce-Lockhart and Ross Chainey, "'Normal Wasn't Working' – John Kerry, Phillip Atiba Goff and Others on the New Social Contract Post-COVID."

37 See "The Great Reset," *TIME*, October 21, 2020, https://time.com/collection/great-reset.

38 For some examples, see Kate Whiting, "How the World Can 'Reset' Itself After COVID-19–According to These Experts" and Kristalina Georgieva, "Remarks to World Economic Forum," speech given to the World Economic Forum, June 3, 2020, https://www.imf.org/en/News/Articles/2020/06/03/sp060320-remarks-to-world-economic-forum-the-great-reset.

39 Glenn Beck and Justin Haskins, *The Great Reset: Joe Biden and the Rise of Twenty-First Century Fascism*, Chapter 5: "The Great Reset: Building a Twenty-First Century Fascism Machine."

40 Beth Stackpole, "Why sustainable business needs better ESG ratings," Massachusetts Institute of Technology Sloan School of Business, December 6, 2021, https://mitsloan.mit.edu/ideas-made-to-matter/why-sustainable-business-needs-better-esg-ratings#:~:text=There's%20ambiguity%20around%20ESG%20ratings,MSCI)%20was%20on%20average%200.61.

41 Jonathan Walter, lead author, *Measuring Stakeholder Capitalism: Toward Common Metrics and Consistent Reporting of Sustainable Value Creation*, World Economic Forum, September 2020, http://www3.weforum.org/docs/WEF_IBC_Measuring_Stakeholder_Capitalism_Report_2020.pdf.

42 Jonathan Walter, lead author, *Measuring Stakeholder Capitalism: Toward Common Metrics and Consistent Reporting of Sustainable Value Creation*.

43 Jonathan Walter, lead author, *Measuring Stakeholder Capitalism: Toward Common Metrics and Consistent Reporting of Sustainable Value Creation*.

44 Jonathan Walter, lead author, *Measuring Stakeholder Capitalism: Toward Common Metrics and Consistent Reporting of Sustainable Value Creation* and "Valuation Guide: Giving in Numbers Survey," CECP, "VII. The S in ESG: Total Social Investment," pp. 27-34, https://cecp.co/wp-content/uploads/2022/01/CECP-Giving-in-Numbers-General-Valuation-Guide-Final.pdf.

45 Kyle Smith, "How Dem officials, the media and Big Tech worked in concert to bury the Hunter Biden story."

46 Richard Threlfall et al., *The Time Has Come: The KPMG Survey of Sustainability Reporting 2020*, KPMG, December 2020, https://assets.kpmg/content/dam/

kpmg/xx/pdf/2020/11/the-time-has-come.pdf.

47 Mikelle Street, "RuPaul Has a Huge Holiday Campaign with Old Navy," *Out*, October 26, 2020, https://www.out.com/fashion/2020/10/26/rupaul-has-huge-holiday-campaign-old-navy.

48 See, for example, Lee Edwards, "The Legacy of Mao Zedong is Mass Murder," The Heritage Foundation, heritage.org, February 2, 2010, https://www.heritage.org/asia/commentary/the-legacy-mao-zedong-mass-murder.

49 Matthew Hill, David Campanale, and Joel Gunter, "'Their goal is to destroy everyone': Uighur camp detainees allege systematic rape," BBC News, February 2, 2021, https://www.bbc.com/news/world-asia-china-55794071.

50 Colum Murphy, "Being Gay in China Has Gotten Harder Under Xi Jinping," Bloomberg.com, February 17, 2022, https://www.bloomberg.com/news/newsletters/2022-02-17/being-gay-in-china-has-gotten-harder-under-xi-jinping.

51 Stephen McDonell, "China allows three children in major policy shift," BBC News, bbc.com, May 31, 2021, https://www.bbc.com/news/world-asia-china-57303592.

52 David Stanway, "China starts building 33 GW of coal power in 2021, most since 2016 -research," Reuters.com, February 23, 2022, https://www.reuters.com/markets/commodities/china-starts-building-33-gw-coal-power-2021-most-since-2016-research-2022-02-24.

53 Talib Visram, "ESG investing continued to soar in 2021. The government could boost it even more," *Fast Company*, December 28, 2021, https://www.fastcompany.com/90706552/esg-investing-continued-to-soar-in-2021-the-government-could-boost-it-even-more#:~:text=2021%20was%20a%20record%20year,the%20%2451%20billion%20of%202020.

54 Talib Visram, "ESG investing continued to soar in 2021. The government could boost it even more."

55 Principles for Responsible Investment, "About the PRI," unpri.org, accessed Jan. 12, 2021, https://www.unpri.org/pri/about-the-pri.

56 Principles for Responsible Investment, "About the PRI."

57 See Dorothy Neufeld, "Visualizing the $94 Trillion World Economy in One Chart," December 22, 2021, *Visual Capitalist*, https://www.visualcapitalist.com/visualizing-the-94-trillion-world-economy-in-one-chart.

58 Tommy Wilkes and Patturaja Murugaboopathy, "ESG funds set for first annual outflows in a decade after bruising year," Reuters, reuters.com, December 19, 2022, https://www.reuters.com/business/sustainable-business/esg-funds-set-first-annual-outflows-decade-after-bruising-year-2022-12-19.

59 Dan Weil, "BlackRock Hits $10 Trillion Assets Under Management," *The Street*, January 14, 2022, https://www.thestreet.com/investing/blackrock-10-trillion-dollars-assets.

60 "Our Clients," BlackRock, accessed April 8, 2022, https://www.blackrock.com/institutions/en-axj/our-client.

61 Gautam Naik, "How BlackRock CEO's latest letter to execs will shape the ESG conversation," January 20, 2022, S&P Global, https://www.spglobal.com/esg/insights/how-blackrock-ceo-s-latest-letter-to-execs-will-shape-the-esg-conversation.

62 Gautam Naik, "How BlackRock CEO's latest letter to execs will shape the ESG conversation."

63 Matt Phillips, "Exxon's Board Defeat Signals the Rise of Social-Good Activists," *New York Times*, June 9, 2021, https://www.nytimes.com/2021/06/09/business/exxon-mobil-engine-no1-activist.html.

64 Evie Fordham, "Flashback: Kamala Harris said she would support eating less meat if elected president," FoxNews.com, April 27, 2021, https://www.foxnews.com/politics/kamala-harris-red-meat-climate-change-beef.

65 Matt Phillips, "Exxon's Board Defeat Signals the Rise of Social-Good Activists."

66 Matt Phillips, "Exxon's Board Defeat Signals the Rise of Social-Good Activists."

67 Matt Phillips, "Exxon's Board Defeat Signals the Rise of Social-Good Activists."

68 "Leadership and Governance," World Economic Forum, weforum.org, accessed September 26, 2021, https://www.weforum.org/about/leadership-and-governance.

69 Larry Fink, "The Power of Capitalism," BlackRock, January 17, 2022, https://www.blackrock.com/corporate/investor-relations/larry-fink-ceo-letter.

70 Jonathan Walter, lead author, *Measuring Stakeholder Capitalism: Toward Common Metrics and Consistent Reporting of Sustainable Value Creation*.

71 Emphasis in quote added by the author.

72 Emphasis in quote added by the author.

73 Jonathan Walter, lead author, *Measuring Stakeholder Capitalism: Toward Common Metrics and Consistent Reporting of Sustainable Value Creation*.

74 Larry Fink, "The Power of Capitalism."

75 Emphasis in quote added by the author. Larry Fink, "The Power of Capitalism."

76 Ross Kerber, "Fund leader Vanguard pushes for diverse boards, but avoids targets," Reuters, December 15, 2020, https://www.reuters.com/article/global-race-vanguard/fund-leader-vanguard-pushes-for-diverse-boards-but-avoids-targets-idUSKBN28P1FJ.

77 Ross Kerber, "Fund leader Vanguard pushes for diverse boards, but avoids targets."

78 Ross Kerber, "Fund leader Vanguard pushes for diverse boards, but avoids targets."

79 Ross Kerber, "Fund leader Vanguard pushes for diverse boards, but avoids targets."

80 Amy Whyte, "State Street to Turn Up the Head on All-Male Boards," *Institutional Investor*, September 27, 2018, https://www.institutionalinvestor.com/article/b1b4fh28ys3mr9/State-Street-to-Turn-Up-the-Heat-on-All-Male-Boards.

81 Amy Whyte, "State Street to Turn Up the Head on All-Male Boards."

82 Dan Weil, "BlackRock Hits $10 Trillion Assets Under Management."

83 This list changes slightly from year to year, but there is generally very little movement among the top 20 firms. See Tim Lemke, "The 10 Largest Investment Management Companies Worldwide," *The Balance*, last updated August 6, 2021, https://www.thebalance.com/which-firms-have-the-most-assets-under-management-4173923.

84 Glenn Beck and Justin Haskins, *The Great Reset: Joe Biden and the Rise of Twenty-First Century Fascism*, Chapter 5: "The Great Reset: Building a Twenty-First Century Fascism Machine," p. 191, citing Lucian Bebchuk and Scott Hirst, "The Specter of the Giant Three," *Boston University Law Review* 99, no. 721 (2019), https://scholarship.law.bu.edu/cgi/viewcontent.cgi?article=1601&context=faculty_scholarship.

85 "Corporate Bonds," U.S. Securities and Exchange Commission, last accessed April 8, 2022, https://www.investor.gov/introduction-investing/investing-basics/investment-products/bonds-or-fixed-income-products.

86 "Corporate Bonds," U.S. Securities and Exchange Commission.

87 "ESG in Credit," FitchRatings, July 2021, https://www.fitchratings.com/whitepapers/esg-in-credit.

88 "ESG in Credit," FitchRatings.

89 "ESG in Credit," FitchRatings.

90 "ESG in Credit," FitchRatings.

91 See Stephanie Kelton, *The Deficit Myth: Modern Monetary Theory and the Birth of the People's Economy* (New York: PublicAffairs, 2019).

92 Board of Governors of the Federal Reserve System, "M1 (M1SL)," retrieved from FRED, Federal Reserve Bank of St. Louis, last accessed February 27, 2023, https://fred.stlouisfed.org/series/M1SL.

93 "2022 has been a year of brutal inflation," *The Economist*, economist.com, December 21, 2022, https://www.economist.com/finance-and-economics/2022/12/21/2022-has-been-a-year-of-brutal-inflation.

94 Walter J. Williams, "Alternate Inflation Charts," ShadowStats.com, last updated

March 10, 2022, http://www.shadowstats.com/alternate_data/inflation-charts.

95 U.S. Census Bureau and U.S. Department of Housing and Urban Development, "Average Sales Price of Houses Sold for the United States," retrieved from FRED, Federal Reserve Bank of St. Louis, https://fred.stlouisfed.org/series/ASPUS.

96 Dan Weil, "BlackRock Hits $10 Trillion Assets Under Management."

97 Dan Weil, "BlackRock Hits $10 Trillion Assets Under Management."

98 Isabel Vincent, "Inside BLM cofounder Patrisse Khan-Cullors' million-dollar real estate buying binge," *New York Post*, April 10, 2021, https://nypost.com/2021/04/10/inside-blm-co-founder-patrisse-khan-cullors-real-estate-buying-binge.

99 "The Great Narrative," World Economic Forum, accessed April 11, 2022, https://www.weforum.org/events/the-great-narrative-2021/about.

Chapter 2: The "Great Narrative" in the Fourth Industrial Revolution

100 Klaus Schwab and Thierry Malleret, *The Great Narrative* (Forum Publishing, 2021), World Economic Forum.

101 Klaus Schwab and Thierry Malleret, *The Great Narrative*.

102 For example, see Klaus Schwab, *The Fourth Industrial Revolution* (Currency, 2017).

103 Klaus Schwab and Thierry Malleret, *The Great Narrative*.

104 Elizabeth Schulze, "Everything you need to know about the Fourth Industrial Revolution," CNBC.com, last updated January 22, 2019, https://www.cnbc.com/2019/01/16/fourth-industrial-revolution-explained-davos-2019.html.

105 Klaus Schwab, "We must move on from neoliberalism in the post-COVID era," and Klaus Schwab and Thierry Malleret, *The Great Narrative*.

106 Elizabeth Schulze, "Everything you need to know about the Fourth Industrial Revolution."

107 Elizabeth Schulze, "Everything you need to know about the Fourth Industrial Revolution."

108 Elizabeth Schulze, "Everything you need to know about the Fourth Industrial Revolution."

109 "Fourth Industrial Revolution," World Economic Forum, accessed April 12, 2022, https://www.weforum.org/focus/fourth-industrial-revolution?msclkid=e-2587530ba4d11ecb35673e7ce0296ca.

110 Elizabeth Schulze, "Everything you need to know about the Fourth Industrial Revolution."

111 "Fourth Industrial Revolution," World Economic Forum.

112 Klaus Schwab, "We must move on from neoliberalism in the post-COVID era,"

World Economic Forum, October 12, 2020, https://www.weforum.org/agenda/
2020/10/coronavirus-covid19-recovery-capitalism-environment-economics-
equality.

113 Klaus Schwab, "We must move on from neoliberalism in the post-COVID era."

114 Klaus Schwab, "We must move on from neoliberalism in the post-COVID era."

115 Klaus Schwab and Thierry Malleret, *The Great Narrative*.

116 "The Great Narrative," World Economic Forum, weforum.org, accessed April 12,
2022, https://www.weforum.org/events/the-great-narrative-2021.

117 "The Great Narrative," World Economic Forum.

118 Klaus Schwab and Mohammad Abdullah Al Gergawi, "Narrating the Future,"
discussion at The Great Narrative conference, hosted by the World Economic
Forum and Government of the United Arab Emirates, November 10, 2021,
https://www.weforum.org/events/the-great-narrative-2021/sessions/a-call-for-
the-great-narrative.

119 Klaus Schwab and Mohammad Abdullah Al Gergawi, "Narrating the Future."

120 Klaus Schwab and Mohammad Abdullah Al Gergawi, "Narrating the Future."

121 Klaus Schwab and Mohammad Abdullah Al Gergawi, "Narrating the Future."

122 Klaus Schwab and Mohammad Abdullah Al Gergawi, "Narrating the Future."
Emphasis in quote added by the authors.

123 Klaus Schwab and Mohammad Abdullah Al Gergawi, "Narrating the Future."

124 Klaus Schwab and Mohammad Abdullah Al Gergawi, "Narrating the Future."

125 Klaus Schwab and Mohammad Abdullah Al Gergawi, "Narrating the Future."

126 Klaus Schwab, "Now is the Time for a 'Great Reset,'" World Economic Forum,
June 3, 2020, https://www.weforum.org/agenda/2020/06/now-is-the-time-for-a-
great-reset.

127 Klaus Schwab and Mohammad Abdullah Al Gergawi, "Narrating the Future."

128 Klaus Schwab, "Now is the Time for a 'Great Reset.'"

129 Susie Mesure, "Klaus Schwab: The secret of Schwab's success," *Independent* (U.K.),
accessed April 13, 2022, https://www.independent.co.uk/news/business/analysis-
and-features/klaus-schwab-the-secret-of-schwab-s-success-433891.html.

130 Peter Goodman, "'He has an Incredible Knack to Smell the Next Fad': How
Klaus Schwab Built a Billionaire Circus at Davos," *Vanity Fair*, January 18, 2022,
https://www.vanityfair.com/news/2022/01/how-klaus-schwab-built-a-billion-
aire-circus-at-davos.

131 Klaus Schwab and Mohammad Abdullah Al Gergawi, "Narrating the Future."

132 Klaus Schwab and Mohammad Abdullah Al Gergawi, "Narrating the Future."

133 Klaus Schwab and Mohammad Abdullah Al Gergawi, "Narrating the Future."

134 Klaus Schwab and Thierry Malleret, *The Great Narrative*.

135 Klaus Schwab and Thierry Malleret, *The Great Narrative*.

136 Klaus Schwab and Mohammad Abdullah Al Gergawi, "Narrating the Future."

137 Klaus Schwab and Thierry Malleret, *The Great Narrative*.

138 Klaus Schwab and Thierry Malleret, *The Great Narrative*.

139 Klaus Schwab and Thierry Malleret, *The Great Narrative*.

140 See Glenn Beck and Justin Haskins, *The Great Reset: Joe Biden and the Rise of Twenty-First Century Fascism*, Chapter 5: "The Great Reset: Building a Twenty-First Century Fascism Machine."

141 Ollie Williams, "118 Private Jets Take Leaders To COP26 Climate Summit Burning Over 1,000 Tons Of CO_2," *Forbes*, November 5, 2021, https://www.forbes.com/sites/oliverwilliams1/2021/11/05/118-private-jets-take-leaders-to-cop26-climate-summit-burning-over-1000-tons-of-co2/?sh=1f61fa9453d9.

142 Joe Bastardi, "If Obama's worried about warming, why buy a house headed under water?" CFACT, cfact.org, December 14, 2019, https://www.cfact.org/2019/12/14/if-obamas-worried-about-warming-why-buy-a-house-headed-under-water.

143 U.S. Energy Information Administration, "What countries are the top producers and consumers of oil?" eia.gov, last updated December 8, 2021, https://www.eia.gov/tools/faqs/faq.php?id=709&t=6.

144 Klaus Schwab and Thierry Malleret, *The Great Narrative*, citing Steve Morgan, "Cybercrime To Cost The World $10.5 Trillion Annually By 2025," *Cybercrime Magazine*, November 13, 2020, https://cybersecurityventures.com/cybercrime-damages-6-trillion-by-2021.

145 Ben Russell, "Cybercrime to Top $6 Trillion in 2021, According to Cybersecurity Ventures," NBC DFW, nbcdfw.com, May 19, 2021, https://www.nbcdfw.com/news/tech/cybercrime-to-top-6-trillion-in-2021-north-texas-security-firm-says/2636083.

146 Klaus Schwab and Thierry Malleret, *The Great Narrative*.

147 Klaus Schwab and Thierry Malleret, *The Great Narrative*.

148 Klaus Schwab and Thierry Malleret, *The Great Narrative*.

149 Klaus Schwab and Thierry Malleret, *The Great Narrative*.

150 Klaus Schwab and Thierry Malleret, *The Great Narrative*.

151 Klaus Schwab and Thierry Malleret, *The Great Narrative*.

152 Klaus Schwab, "Now is the Time for a 'Great Reset.'"

153 "Artificial Intelligence for Children," World Economic Forum, weforum.org,

March 29, 2022, https://www.weforum.org/reports/artificial-intelligence-for-children.

154 "Artificial Intelligence for Children," World Economic Forum.

155 "Artificial Intelligence for Children," World Economic Forum.

156 Doug Irving, "How AI could increase the risk of nuclear war," RAND Corporation, in collaboration with the World Economic Forum, weforum.org, April 25, 2018, https://www.weforum.org/agenda/2018/04/how-ai-could-increase-the-risk-of-nuclear-war.

157 Doug Irving, "How AI could increase the risk of nuclear war."

158 Doug Irving, "How AI could increase the risk of nuclear war."

159 Doug Irving, "How AI could increase the risk of nuclear war."

160 "When did the United Kingdom leave the European Union?" Government of the Netherlands, government.nl, accessed April 14, 2022, https://www.government.nl/topics/brexit/question-and-answer/when-will-the-united-kingdom-leave-the-european-union.

161 Klaus Schwab, "Now is the Time for a 'Great Reset.'" Emphasis in quote added by the authors.

162 *The Matrix*, directed by Lana Wachowski and Lilly Wachowski (Warner Bros., 1999).

Chapter 3: The Age of Disruption, Part I: The Automation Bomb

163 Richard Conniff, "What the Luddites Really Fought Against," *Smithsonian Magazine*, March 2011, https://www.smithsonianmag.com/history/what-the-luddites-really-fought-against-264412/#:~:text=Then%2C%20on%20March%2011%2C%201811,machinery%20in%20a%20nearby%20village.

164 Richard Conniff, "What the Luddites Really Fought Against."

165 Kevin Binfield, *Writings of the Luddites* (Johns Hopkins University Press, 2004).

166 Richard Conniff, "What the Luddites Really Fought Against."

167 Kevin Binfield, *Writings of the Luddites*.

168 Richard Conniff, "What the Luddites Really Fought Against."

169 Kevin Binfield, *Writings of the Luddites*.

170 "The Struggle for Democracy: Getting the Vote," National Archives of the United Kingdom, last accessed July 27, 2022, https://www.nationalarchives.gov.uk/pathways/citizenship/struggle_democracy/getting_vote.htm.

171 "1832 Reform Act," British Library, bl.uk, accessed online September 12, 2022, https://www.bl.uk/learning/timeline/item107685.html.

172 "The Struggle for Democracy: Getting the Vote," National Archives of the United Kingdom.

173 Kevin Binfield, *Writings of the Luddites*.

174 *Passengers*, directed by Morten Tyldum (Columbia Pictures et al., 2016).

175 Joe Guszkowski, "AI's latest job? Making sure the coffee's fresh," *FSD*, April 13, 2022, https://www.foodservicedirector.com/technology-equipment/ais-latest-job-making-sure-coffees-fresh.

176 Amanda Kavanagh, "Restaurant kiosks: everything you need to know," Flipdish, February 10, 2022, https://www.flipdish.com/us/resources/blog/restaurant-kiosks.

177 Amanda Kavanagh, "Restaurant kiosks: everything you need to know."

178 Amanda Kooser, "Flippy, the fast-food robot who makes fries at White Castle, gets an upgrade," CNET, November 7, 2021, https://www.cnet.com/culture/internet/flippy-the-fast-food-robot-makes-fries-at-white-castle-gets-an-upgrade.

179 See Amanda Kooser, "Flippy, the fast-food robot who makes fries at White Castle, gets an upgrade."

180 Amanda Kooser, "Flippy, the fast-food robot who makes fries at White Castle, gets an upgrade."

181 Sean Salai, "Fast-food chains outsource work to robots," *Washington Times*, February 2, 2023, https://www.washingtontimes.com/news/2023/feb/2/fast-food-chains-outsource-work-robots.

182 Miso Robotics, "White Castle Expands Partnership with Miso Robotics to Install Flippy 2 in 100 New Locations," PRNewswire, February 15, 2022, https://www.prnewswire.com/news-releases/white-castle-expands-partnership-with-miso-robotics-to-install-flippy-2-in-100-new-locations-301482275.html.

183 Thai Phi Le, "The new faces of labor? Meet the robots of the National Restaurant Association Show," *Restaurant Dive*, May 23, 2022, https://www.restaurantdive.com/news/labor-saving-robots-at-national-restaurant-association-show/624167.

184 Thai Phi Le, "The new faces of labor? Meet the robots of the National Restaurant Association Show."

185 Thai Phi Le, "The new faces of labor? Meet the robots of the National Restaurant Association Show."

186 Thai Phi Le, "The new faces of labor? Meet the robots of the National Restaurant Association Show."

187 Thai Phi Le, "The new faces of labor? Meet the robots of the National Restaurant Association Show."

188   Khristopher Brooks, "Banks could soon suffer massive wave of job losses, analysts say," CBSNews.com, October 1, 2021, https://www.cbsnews.com/news/banking-100000-jobs-wells-fargo-analysts-automation.

189   Khristopher Brooks, "Banks could soon suffer massive wave of job losses, analysts say."

190   Khristopher Brooks, "Banks could soon suffer massive wave of job losses, analysts say."

191   Kevin Dwyer, "Will Cryptocurrencies and Blockchain Replace Banking and Finance?" coinmarketcap.com, 2021, https://coinmarketcap.com/alexandria/article/will-cryptocurrencies-and-blockchain-replace-banking-and-finance.

192   "Census Bureau Estimates Show Average One-Way Travel Time to Work Rises to All-Time High," census.gov, U.S. Census Bureau, March 18, 2021, https://www.census.gov/newsroom/press-releases/2021/one-way-travel-time-to-work-rises.html.

193   This estimate assumes a person works about 48 weeks per year, commutes an average of four hours per week, and works from the ages of 21 to 65.

194   Prasenjit Mitra, "What is 5G? An electrical engineer explains," The Conversation, January 10, 2022, https://theconversation.com/what-is-5g-an-electrical-engineer-explains-173196.

195   Prasenjit Mitra, "What is 5G? An electrical engineer explains."

196   "Bandwidth," Verizon.com, accessed August 23, 2022, https://www.verizon.com/info/definitions/bandwidth.

197   Prasenjit Mitra, "What is 5G? An electrical engineer explains."

198   Prasenjit Mitra, "What is 5G? An electrical engineer explains."

199   "Building A CASE For Connected And Autonomous Vehicles With 5G Connectivity," T-Mobile for Business, Forbes, August 27, 2021, https://www.forbes.com/sites/tmobile/2021/08/27/building-a-case-for-connected-and-autonomous-vehicles-with-5g-connectivity/?sh=5322de527c31.

200   Kersten Heineke et al., "Development in the mobility technology ecosystem—how can 5G help?" McKinsey & Co., June 27, 2019, https://www.mckinsey.com/industries/automotive-and-assembly/our-insights/development-in-the-mobility-technology-ecosystem-how-can-5g-help.

201   Daniel Ren, "Self-driving cars will eventually be safer than those driven by people, says Chinese search engine giant Baidu," South China Morning Post, November 7, 2021, https://www.scmp.com/business/companies/article/3155196/self-driving-cars-will-eventually-be-safer-those-driven-people.

202 Chris Isidore, "Self-driving cars are already really safe," CNN Business, March 21, 2018, https://money.cnn.com/2018/03/21/technology/self-driving-car-safety/index.html.

203 Alex Davies, "Heat-Seeking Cameras Could Help Keep Self-Driving Cars Safe," WIRED, April 21, 2018, https://www.wired.com/story/self-driving-cars-thermal-image-cameras.

204 R. Spencer Hallyburton et al., "Security Analysis of Camera-LiDAR Fusion Against Black-Box Attacks on Autonomous Vehicles," 31st USENIX Security Symposium, August 10-12, 2022, made available by sciencedaily.com, https://www.sciencedaily.com/releases/2022/03/220314142029.htm.

205 For example, see K. Holt, "Waymo's autonomous vehicles have clocked 20 million miles on public roads," Engadget, August 19, 2021, https://www.engadget.com/waymo-autonomous-vehicles-update-san-francisco-193934150.html#:~:text=The%20company's%20vehicles%20have%20autonomously,20%20billion%20miles%20in%20simulations.

206 Chris Isidore, "Self-driving cars are already really safe."

207 U.S. National Highway Traffic Safety Administration, "Automated Vehicles for Safety," nhtsa.gov, accessed August 26, 2022, https://www.nhtsa.gov/technology-innovation/automated-vehicles-safety.

208 U.S. National Highway Traffic Safety Administration, "Automated Vehicles for Safety."

209 U.S. National Highway Traffic Safety Administration, "Automated Vehicles for Safety."

210 Richard Mudge et al., "America's Workforce and the Self-Driving Future," Securing America's Future Energy, June 2018, https://avworkforce.secureenergy.org/wp-content/uploads/2018/06/Americas-Workforce-and-the-Self-Driving-Future_Realizing-Productivity-Gains-and-Spurring-Economic-Growth.pdf.

211 Richard Mudge et al., "America's Workforce and the Self-Driving Future."

212 Greg Rosalsky, "Is There Really A Truck Driver Shortage?" National Public Radio, npr.org, May 25, 2021, https://www.npr.org/sections/money/2021/05/25/999784202/is-there-really-a-truck-driver-shortage.

213 "Driving the Rural Delivery Route," uspsoig.gov, Office of the Inspector General of the U.S. Postal Service, February 7, 2022, https://www.uspsoig.gov/blog/driving-rural-delivery-route.

214 Matt McFarland, "Amazon generally delivers later than competitors. That can be terrifying for some of its drivers," CNN, cnn.com, updated December 21,

2021, https://www.cnn.com/2021/12/21/tech/amazon-delivery-night/index.
html#:~:text=Amazon%20(AMZN)%20relies%20on%203%2C000,deliver%20
packages%2C%20according%20to%20Amazon.

215 Jennifer Cheeseman Day and Andrew Hait, "Number of Truckers at All-Time
High," census.gov, U.S. Census Bureau, June 6, 2019, https://www.census.gov/
library/stories/2019/06/america-keeps-on-trucking.html.

216 "Nearly 400 car crashes in 11 months involved automated tech, companies tell
regulators," Associated Press, article appearing on npr.org, June 15, 2022, https://
www.npr.org/2022/06/15/1105252793/nearly-400-car-crashes-in-11-months-
involved-automated-tech-companies-tell-regul.

217 Neil Winton, "Computer Driven Autos Still Years Away Despite Massive
Investment," *Forbes*, February 27, 2022, https://www.forbes.com/sites/
neilwinton/2022/02/27/computer-driven-autos-still-years-away-despite-massive-
investment/?sh=5c57a2b518cc.

218 Luc Olinga, "Elon Musk Promises Full Self-Driving Teslas in 2022," *TheStreet*,
January 27, 2022, https://www.thestreet.com/lifestyle/cars/elon-musk-promises-
full-self-driving-teslas-in-2022.

219 Luc Olinga, "Elon Musk Promises Full Self-Driving Teslas in 2022."

220 Andrei Nedelea, "Musk Says Teslas Will Be Fully-Autonomous, Not Require
Driver Next Year," *Inside EVs*, May 23, 2022, https://insideevs.com/news/
587531/elon-musk-tesla-autonomous-no-driver-2023.

221 Steve Dent, "Tesla's *FSD* driver assist beta is now available to anyone who wants to
pay," *Engadget*, November 24, 2022, https://www.engadget.com/tesla-fsd-driver-
assist-available-to-all-drivers-114916660.html.

222 Cameron Schoppa, "Top Autonomous Vehicles Companies to Watch in 2023," *AI
Time Journal*, updated February 2, 2023, https://www.aitimejournal.com/autono-
mous-vehicles-companies-to-watch.

223 Luc Olinga, "Tesla's New Car Is a Fantasy for Sci-Fi Fans," *TheStreet*, April 21,
2022, https://www.thestreet.com/technology/tesla-has-a-new-car-without-a-
steering-wheel-or-pedals-for-2024.

224 Sean Fleming, "A short history of jobs and automation," World Economic Forum,
weforum.org, September 3, 2020, https://www.weforum.org/agenda/2020/09/
short-history-jobs-automation.

225 Sara Brown, "A new study measures the actual impact of robots on jobs. It's
significant," MIT Sloan School of Management, mitsloan.mit.edu, July 29, 2020,
https://mitsloan.mit.edu/ideas-made-to-matter/a-new-study-measures-actual-

impact-robots-jobs-its-significant.

226 Sara Brown, "A new study measures the actual impact of robots on jobs. It's significant."

227 Sara Brown, "A new study measures the actual impact of robots on jobs. It's significant."

228 Sara Brown, "A new study measures the actual impact of robots on jobs. It's significant."

229 Sara Brown, "A new study measures the actual impact of robots on jobs. It's significant."

230 Timothy Aeppel, "Robots marched on in 2021, with record orders by North American firms," Reuters, February 2, 2022, https://www.reuters.com/technology/robots-marched-2021-with-record-orders-by-north-american-firms-2022-02-02.

231 Timothy Aeppel, "Robots marched on in 2021, with record orders by North American firms."

232 Timothy Aeppel, "Robots marched on in 2021, with record orders by North American firms."

233 Timothy Aeppel, "Robots marched on in 2021, with record orders by North American firms."

234 Yuri Kageyama, "Smart robots do all the work at Nissan's 'intelligent' plant," Associated Press, posted by ABC News, abcnews.go.com, October 8, 2021, https://abcnews.go.com/Technology/wireStory/smart-robots-work-nissans-intelligent-plant-80473171.

235 Yuri Kageyama, "Smart robots do all the work at Nissan's 'intelligent' plant."

236 Yuri Kageyama, "Smart robots do all the work at Nissan's 'intelligent' plant."

237 There are numerous connections between PwC and the World Economic Forum, including that they have co-published reports and studies together. See, for example, "Upskilling for Shared Prosperity," *Insight Report*, World Economic Forum, in collaboration with PwC, January 2021, https://www.pwc.com/gx/en/issues/upskilling/shared-prosperity/upskilling_for_shared_prosperity_final.pdf.

238 "How will automation impact jobs?" PwC, pwc.co.uk, last accessed August 27, 2022, https://www.pwc.co.uk/automation.

239 "How will automation impact jobs?" PwC.

240 "How will automation impact jobs?" PwC.

241 "How will automation impact jobs?" PwC.

242 "How will automation impact jobs?" PwC.

243 IBM Cloud Education, "Artificial Intelligence (AI): What is Artificial Intelligence?" IBM, ibm.com, June 3, 2020, https://www.ibm.com/cloud/learn/what-is-artificial-intelligence.

244 Archil Cheishvili, "The Future Of Artificial General Intelligence," *Forbes*, July 16, 2021, https://www.forbes.com/sites/forbestechcouncil/2021/07/16/the-future-of-artificial-general-intelligence/?sh=1c8dfa6a3ba9.

245 Naveen Joshi, "7 Types Of Artificial Intelligence," June 19, 2019, *Forbes*, https://www.forbes.com/sites/cognitiveworld/2019/06/19/7-types-of-artificial-intelligence/?sh=795bef33233e.

246 Naveen Joshi, "7 Types Of Artificial Intelligence."

247 Bernard Marr, "The 10 Best Examples Of How AI Is Already Used In Our Everyday Life," *Forbes*, December 16, 2019, https://www.forbes.com/sites/bernardmarr/2019/12/16/the-10-best-examples-of-how-ai-is-already-used-in-our-everyday-life/?sh=5e2a9061171f.

248 Bernard Marr, "The 10 Best Examples Of How AI Is Already Used In Our Everyday Life."

249 Bernard Marr, "The 10 Best Examples Of How AI Is Already Used In Our Everyday Life."

250 Bernard Marr, "The 10 Best Examples Of How AI Is Already Used In Our Everyday Life."

251 Bernard Marr, "The 10 Best Examples Of How AI Is Already Used In Our Everyday Life."

252 "Succeeding in the AI supply-chain revolution," McKinsey & Company, mckinsey.com, April 30, 2021, https://www.mckinsey.com/industries/metals-and-mining/our-insights/succeeding-in-the-ai-supply-chain-revolution.

253 "Succeeding in the AI supply-chain revolution," McKinsey & Company.

254 Kevin Roose, *Futureproof: 9 Rules for Humans in the Age of Automation* (Random House Publishing, 2021).

255 Kevin Roose, *Futureproof: 9 Rules for Humans in the Age of Automation.*

256 Kevin Roose, *Futureproof: 9 Rules for Humans in the Age of Automation.*

257 Kevin Roose, *Futureproof: 9 Rules for Humans in the Age of Automation.*

258 "ChatGPT: Optimizing Language Models for Dialogue," OpenAI, chat.openai.com, November 30, 2022, https://openai.com/blog/chatgpt.

259 The exact prompt given to ChatGPT was: "Describe what ChatGPT is and how it could possibly impact jobs across numerous industries, in the style of Glenn Beck," OpenAI, chat.openai.com, https://chat.openai.com/chat.

260 James Manyika et al., "Jobs lost, jobs gained: What the future of work will mean for jobs, skills, and wages," McKinsey Global Institute, mckinsey.com, November 28, 2017, https://www.mckinsey.com/featured-insights/future-of-work/jobs-lost-jobs-gained-what-the-future-of-work-will-mean-for-jobs-skills-and-wages.

261 James Manyika et al., "Jobs lost, jobs gained: What the future of work will mean for jobs, skills, and wages."

262 "The future of work after COVID-19," McKinsey Global Institute, mckinsey.com, February 18, 2021, https://www.mckinsey.com/featured-insights/future-of-work/the-future-of-work-after-covid-19.

263 "How will automation impact jobs?" PwC.

264 "Forrester's Future-Of-Jobs Forecast: 12 Million Jobs Will Be Lost To Automation Across Europe By 2040," Forrester Research, forrester.com, January 20, 2022, https://www.forrester.com/press-newsroom/forresters-future-of-jobs-forecast-12-million-jobs-will-be-lost-to-automation-across-europe-by-2040.

265 Saadia Zahidi et al., "The Future of Jobs Report 2020," World Economic Forum, weforum.org, October 2020, https://www3.weforum.org/docs/WEF_Future_of_Jobs_2020.pdf.

266 Klaus Schwab and Mohammad Abdullah Al Gergawi, "Narrating the Future," discussion at The Great Narrative conference, hosted by the World Economic Forum and Government of the United Arab Emirates, November 10, 2021, https://www.weforum.org/events/the-great-narrative-2021/sessions/a-call-for-the-great-narrative; also see Chapter 2 of this book for more quotes.

267 See preface to Saadia Zahidi et al., "The Future of Jobs Report 2020."

268 See preface to Saadia Zahidi et al., "The Future of Jobs Report 2020."

269 See preface to Saadia Zahidi et al., "The Future of Jobs Report 2020."

270 See preface to Saadia Zahidi et al., "The Future of Jobs Report 2020."

271 See preface to Saadia Zahidi et al., "The Future of Jobs Report 2020."

272 Saadia Zahidi et al., "The Future of Jobs Report 2020."

273 Note that in the WEF report, the Open Society Institute is listed, not Open Society Foundations. That's because the name of the organization has changed from Open Society Institute to Open Society Foundations. To avoid confusion, we used the current name in the text of this book.

274 Christopher Alessi, "'A golden opportunity' - HRH the Prince of Wales and other leaders on the Forum's Great Reset," World Economic Forum, weforum.org, June 3, 2020, https://www.weforum.org/agenda/2020/06/great-reset-launch-prince-charles-guterres-georgieva-burrow.

275 Wilson Pang, "Human-centric tech will make AI faster and fairer. Here's how," World Economic Forum, weforum.org, June 7, 2021, https://www.weforum.org/agenda/2021/06/human-centric-tech-will-make-ai-faster-and-fairer-here-s-how.

276 Kevin Roose, *Futureproof: 9 Rules for Humans in the Age of Automation*.

277 Kevin Roose, *Futureproof: 9 Rules for Humans in the Age of Automation*.

278 Kevin Roose, *Futureproof: 9 Rules for Humans in the Age of Automation*.

279 Author's note: The best fake blood is not made with water. That's for amateurs. If you really want to freak out your friends with an old-fashioned fake blood gag, you'll need corn syrup. That will give your substance the classic bloody look you've been looking for.

Chapter 4: The Age of Disruption, Part 2: Virtual Reality, Digital Money, Quantum Computers, and the Metaverse

280 "What is Virtual Reality?" The Virtual Reality Society, vrs.org.uk, accessed September 1, 2022, https://www.vrs.org.uk/virtual-reality/what-is-virtual-reality.html.

281 "What is Virtual Reality?" The Virtual Reality Society.

282 "What is Virtual Reality All About?" Meta Quest, oculus.com, September 10, 2021, https://www.oculus.com/blog/what-is-virtual-reality-all-about.

283 "What is Virtual Reality All About?" Meta Quest.

284 "AR/VR," 3M, futures.3m.com, accessed September 1, 2022, https://futures.3m.com/AR-VR?utm_term=corp-cces-sci-en_us-ba-futures-cpc-google-na-learn-na-feb22-na.

285 Bernard Marr, "10 Best Examples Of Augmented And Virtual Reality In Retail," *Forbes*, September 13, 2021, https://www.forbes.com/sites/bernardmarr/2021/09/13/10-best-examples-of-augmented-and-virtual-reality-in-retail/?sh=6bc3da1b6626.

286 Bernard Marr, "10 Best Examples Of Augmented And Virtual Reality In Retail."

287 Bernard Marr, "10 Best Examples Of Augmented And Virtual Reality In Retail."

288 "Implementing VR & AR in Medicine and Medical Training," Onix Systems, onix-systems.com, August 15, 2022, https://onix-systems.com/blog/implementing-virtual-reality-in-medicine-and-medical-training.

289 "Implementing VR & AR in Medicine and Medical Training," Onix Systems.

290 "Implementing VR & AR in Medicine and Medical Training," Onix Systems.

291 "Implementing VR & AR in Medicine and Medical Training," Onix Systems.

292 "Robotic Surgery," Mayo Clinic, mayoclinic.org, accessed September 2, 2022,

https://www.mayoclinic.org/tests-procedures/robotic-surgery/about/pac-20394974.

293 Bernard Marr, "A Short History Of The Metaverse," *Forbes*, March 21, 2022, https://www.forbes.com/sites/bernardmarr/2022/03/21/a-short-history-of-the-metaverse/?sh=44e99bb35968.

294 Salvador Rodriguez, "Facebook changes company name to Meta," CNBC, cnbc. com, October 28, 2021, https://www.cnbc.com/2021/10/28/facebook-changes-company-name-to-meta.html.

295 Mike Isaac, "Meta spent $10 billion on the metaverse in 2021, dragging down profit," *New York Times*, February 2, 2022, https://www.nytimes.com/2022/02/02/technology/meta-facebook-earnings-metaverse.html.

296 "What is the metaverse?" Meta, about.facebook.com, accessed September 2, 2022, https://about.facebook.com/what-is-the-metaverse.

297 See "Our Partners," World Economic Forum, weforum.org, accessed September 2, 2022, https://www.weforum.org/partners.

298 "Environment, Social, Governance Resources," Meta Investor Relations, Meta, accessed September 2, 2022, https://investor.fb.com/esg-resources/default.aspx.

299 See Jonathan Walter, lead author, *Measuring Stakeholder Capitalism: Toward Common Metrics and Consistent Reporting of Sustainable Value Creation*, World Economic Forum, September 2020, http://www3.weforum.org/docs/WEF_IBC_Measuring_Stakeholder_Capitalism_Report_2020.pdf.

300 See Chapter 6, "The Great Reset: Building a 21st Century Fascism Machine" in Glenn Beck and Justin Haskins, *The Great Reset: Joe Biden and the Rise of Twenty-First Century Fascism* (Mercury Ink, 2022).

301 "We're empowering people and organizations to advance the United Nations Sustainable Development Goals by 2030," Meta Investor Relations, Meta, accessed September 2, 2022, https://about.fb.com/sdg.

302 "Environment, Social, Governance Resources," Meta Investor Relations, Meta, accessed September 2, 2022, https://investor.fb.com/esg-resources/default.aspx.

303 Maxine Williams, "How We're Helping Build the Metaverse with Diversity, Equity and Inclusion in Mind," Meta, about.fb.com, June 16, 2022, https://about.fb.com/news/2022/06/how-were-helping-build-the-metaverse-with-diversity-equity-and-inclusion-in-mind.

304 Emphasis in quote appears in the original. Maxine Williams, "How We're Helping Build the Metaverse with Diversity, Equity and Inclusion in Mind."

305 Maxine Williams, "How We're Helping Build the Metaverse with Diversity,

Equity and Inclusion in Mind."

306 Andrew Chow, "An Industry-Backed Group Thinks the Metaverse Can Avoid
     the Ills of Social Media. Here's How," *Time*, January 6, 2022, https://time.com/
     6133271/oasis-safety-metaverse.

307 Andrew Chow, "An Industry-Backed Group Thinks the Metaverse Can Avoid the
     Ills of Social Media. Here's How."

308 Tanya Basu, "This group of tech firms just signed up to a safer metaverse," *MIT
     Technology Review*, January 20, 2022, https://www.technologyreview.com/2022/
     01/20/1043843/safe-metaverse-oasis-consortium-roblox-meta.

309 Tanya Basu, "This group of tech firms just signed up to a safer metaverse."

310 Andrew Bosworth and Nick Clegg, "Building the Metaverse Responsibly," Meta,
     about.fb.com, updated May 25, 2022, https://about.fb.com/news/2021/09/
     building-the-metaverse-responsibly.

311 Andrew Bosworth and Nick Clegg, "Building the Metaverse Responsibly."

312 Andrew Bosworth and Nick Clegg, "Building the Metaverse Responsibly."

313 "Partners," World Economic Forum, weforum.org, accessed September 5, 2022,
     https://initiatives.weforum.org/defining-and-building-the-metaverse/partners.

314 "Partners," World Economic Forum.

315 "Partners," World Economic Forum.

316 Cathy Li, "How to build an economically viable, inclusive and safe metaverse,"
     World Economic Forum, weforum.org, May 25, 2022, https://www.weforum.
     org/agenda/2022/05/how-to-build-an-economically-viable-inclusive-and-safe-
     metaverse.

317 Cathy Li, "How to build an economically viable, inclusive and safe metaverse."

318 "What is a blockchain?" Coinbase, Coinbase.com, accessed September 5, 2022,
     https://www.coinbase.com/learn/crypto-basics/what-is-a-blockchain.

319 Luke Conway, "What Is a Blockchain? The Simple Explanation," *TheStreet*,
     updated September 21, 2021, https://www.thestreet.com/crypto/bitcoin/what-is-
     a-blockchain-the-simple-explanation.

320 Luke Conway, "What Is a Blockchain? The Simple Explanation," *TheStreet*.

321 Luke Conway, "What Is a Blockchain? The Simple Explanation," *TheStreet*.

322 Luke Conway, "What Is a Blockchain? The Simple Explanation," *TheStreet*.

323 Adam Hayes, "Blockchain Facts: What Is It, How It Works, and How It Can
     Be Used," *Investopedia*, updated June 24, 2022, https://www.investopedia.com/
     terms/b/blockchain.asp.

324 Michell Clark, "Blockchain, Explained," *The Verge*, September 9, 2021, https://

www.theverge.com/22654785/blockchain-explained-cryptocurrency-what-is-stake-nft.

325 Michell Clark, "Blockchain, Explained."

326 Kate Ashford, "What Is Cryptocurrency?" *Forbes*, June 6, 2022, https://www.forbes.com/advisor/investing/cryptocurrency/what-is-cryptocurrency.

327 Kate Ashford, "What Is Cryptocurrency?"

328 Kate Ashford, "What Is Cryptocurrency?"

329 Kate Ashford, "What Is Cryptocurrency?"

330 Adam Hayes, "What Happens to Bitcoin After All 21 Million Are Mined?" *Investopedia*, updated March 5, 2022, https://www.investopedia.com/tech/what-happens-bitcoin-after-21-million-mined.

331 See "Bitcoin," CoinDesk, coindesk.com, last accessed September 5, 2022, https://www.coindesk.com/price/bitcoin.

332 See "Litecoin," CoinDesk, coindesk.com, last accessed September 5, 2022, https://www.coindesk.com/price/litecoin/#:~:text=In%20May%202021%2C%20LTC%20price,in%20the%20following%20six%20months.

333 Nicholas Rossolillo, "Types of Cryptocurrency," *The Motley Fool*, updated June 28, 2022, https://www.fool.com/investing/stock-market/market-sectors/financials/cryptocurrency-stocks/types-of-cryptocurrencies.

334 Nicholas Rossolillo, "Types of Cryptocurrency."

335 Nicholas Rossolillo, "Types of Cryptocurrency."

336 "What is Ada?" Cardano Foundation, cardano.org, accessed September 5, 2022, https://cardano.org/what-is-ada.

337 "What is Ada?" Cardano Foundation.

338 "What is Cardano?" Coinbase, coinbase.com, accessed September 5, 2022, https://www.coinbase.com/learn/crypto-basics/what-is-cardano.

339 "What are smart contracts on blockchain?" IBM, ibm.com, accessed September 5, 2022, https://www.ibm.com/topics/smart-contracts.

340 Benedikt Eikmanns, Isabell Welpe, and Philipp Sandner, "Decentralized Finance Will Change Your Understanding Of Financial Systems," *Forbes*, https://www.forbes.com/sites/philippsandner/2021/02/22/decentralized-finance-will-change-your-understanding-of-financial-systems/?sh=24b92d6b5b52.

341 Benedikt Eikmanns, Isabell Welpe, and Philipp Sandner, "Decentralized Finance Will Change Your Understanding Of Financial Systems."

342 Nathan Reiff, "Algorand (ALGO)," *Investopedia*, updated September 1, 2022, https://www.investopedia.com/algorand-algo-definition-5217725#:~:text=Al-

gorand%20(ALGO)%20is%20a%20blockchain,like%20a%20major%20
payments%20processor.&text=ALGO%2C%20the%20native%20coin%20
of,and%20reward%20the%20platform's%20operators.

343 "What is LBRY exactly? Is it a protocol, an app, a website, or a company?" LBRY,
accessed September 6, 2022, https://lbry.com/faq/what-is-lbry.

344 "Use Filecoin to store and retrieve data," Filecoin, accessed September 6, 2022,
https://filecoin.io/store.

345 "Rally (RLY)," Coinbase: Getting Started, accessed September 6, 2022, https://
help.coinbase.com/en/coinbase/getting-started/crypto-education/rly.

346 Robyn Conti, "What Is An NFT? Non-Fungible Tokens Explained," *Forbes
Advisor*, April 8, 2022, https://www.forbes.com/advisor/investing/cryptocur-
rency/nft-non-fungible-token.

347 "The 10 Most Expensive NFTs Ever Sold," Binance Academy, academy.binance.
com, updated June 2, 2022, https://academy.binance.com/en/articles/the-most-
expensive-nfts-ever-sold.

348 "The 10 Most Expensive NFTs Ever Sold," Binance Academy.

349 "The 10 Most Expensive NFTs Ever Sold," Binance Academy.

350 "The 10 Most Expensive NFTs Ever Sold," Binance Academy.

351 James Bowden and Edward Thomas Jones, "NFTs are much bigger than an art
fad – here's how they could change the world," *The Conversation*, April 26, 2021,
https://theconversation.com/nfts-are-much-bigger-than-an-art-fad-heres-how-
they-could-change-the-world-159563.

352 Shine Li, "Blockchain-Based Driving Licenses in South Korea Hit One Million
Drivers," *Blockchain.News*, August 13, 2020, https://blockchain.news/news/
blockchain-based-driving-licenses-south-korea-hit-one-million-drivers.

353 Werner Vermaak, "What Is Web 3.0?" Coinmarketcap.com, updated February
2022, https://coinmarketcap.com/alexandria/article/what-is-web-3-0.

354 See Ian DeMartino, "Glenn Beck Says Blockchain Technologies Can Help Fight
Fascism," *CoinTelegraph*, February 10, 2015, https://cointelegraph.com/news/
glenn-beck-says-blockchain-technologies-can-help-fight-fascism.

355 See "Executive Order on Ensuring Responsible Development of Digital Assets,"
whitehouse.gov, March 9, 2022, https://www.whitehouse.gov/briefing-room/
presidential-actions/2022/03/09/executive-order-on-ensuring-responsible-devel-
opment-of-digital-assets.

356 "FACT SHEET: President Biden to Sign Executive Order on Ensuring Responsible Development of Digital Assets," whitehouse.gov, March 9, 2022, https://

www.whitehouse.gov/briefing-room/statements-releases/2022/03/09/fact-sheet-president-biden-to-sign-executive-order-on-ensuring-responsible-innovation-in-digital-assets.

357   "FACT SHEET: President Biden to Sign Executive Order on Ensuring Responsible Development of Digital Assets," whitehouse.gov.

358   Thomas Wade, "Tracker: Crypto and Fintech Developments in the Biden Administration," American Action Forum, americanactionforum.org, last updated August 24, 2022, https://www.americanactionforum.org/insight/tracker-crypto-and-fintech-developments-in-the-biden-administration.

359   Thomas Wade, "Tracker: Crypto and Fintech Developments in the Biden Administration."

360   Thomas Wade, "Tracker: Crypto and Fintech Developments in the Biden Administration."

361   Sergey Nazarov, "The missing link between blockchains and enterprises," World Economic Forum, weforum.org, December 15, 2020, https://www.weforum.org/agenda/2020/12/the-missing-link-between-blockchain-and-existing-systems.

362   Sergey Nazarov, "The missing link between blockchains and enterprises."

363   Sergey Nazarov and Punit Shukla, lead authors, "Bridging the Governance Gap: Interoperability for blockchain and legacy systems," World Economic Forum, weforum.org, December 2020, https://www.weforum.org/whitepapers/bridging-the-governance-gap-interoperability-for-blockchain-and-legacy-systems.

364   Brandon Rearick, "ISO 20022 Cryptos: 5 Compliant Cryptos to Keep an Eye on in 2022," *Investor Place*, December 22, 2021, https://www.yahoo.com/video/iso-20022-cryptos-5-compliant-194204661.html.

365   Brandon Rearick, "ISO 20022 Cryptos: 5 Compliant Cryptos to Keep an Eye on in 2022."

366   Brandy Betz, "BlackRock to Offer Crypto for Institutional Investors Through Coinbase Prime," CoinDesk, August 4, 2022, https://www.coindesk.com/business/2022/08/04/blackrock-to-offer-crypto-for-institutional-investors-through-coinbase-prime.

367   Brandy Betz, "BlackRock to Offer Crypto for Institutional Investors Through Coinbase Prime."

368   "What is a Central Bank Digital Currency?" U.S. Federal Reserve Banks, federalreserve.gov, last accessed September 7, 2022, https://www.federalreserve.gov/faqs/what-is-a-central-bank-digital-currency.htm.

369   "What is a Central Bank Digital Currency?" U.S. Federal Reserve Banks.

370 See "Today's Central Bank Digital Currencies Status," CBDC Tracker, cbdctracker. com, updated September 6, 2022, https://cbdctracker.org.

371 See "Today's Central Bank Digital Currencies Status," CBDC Tracker.

372 "Central Bank Digital Currency (CBDC): Frequently Asked Questions," Board of Governors of the Federal Reserve System, accessed September 7, 2022, https:// www.federalreserve.gov/cbdc-faqs.htm.

373 "Programmable Money: How Smart Contracts Make Money Better," Algorand, algorand.com, August 26, 2021, https://www.algorand.com/resources/blog/ programmable-money-smart-contracts-make-money-better.

374 See "Executive Order on Ensuring Responsible Development of Digital Assets," whitehouse.gov.

375 Also see "FACT SHEET: President Biden to Sign Executive Order on Ensuring Responsible Development of Digital Assets," whitehouse.gov.

376 "FACT SHEET: President Biden to Sign Executive Order on Ensuring Responsible Development of Digital Assets," whitehouse.gov.

377 "FACT SHEET: President Biden to Sign Executive Order on Ensuring Responsible Development of Digital Assets," whitehouse.gov.

378 "FACT SHEET: President Biden to Sign Executive Order on Ensuring Responsible Development of Digital Assets," whitehouse.gov.

379 See "Executive Order on Ensuring Responsible Development of Digital Assets," whitehouse.gov.

380 See "Executive Order on Ensuring Responsible Development of Digital Assets," whitehouse.gov.

381 "FACT SHEET: White House Releases First-Ever Comprehensive Framework for Responsible Development of Digital Assets," Office of President Joe Biden, whitehouse.gov, September 16, 2022, https://www.whitehouse.gov/briefing- room/statements-releases/2022/09/16/fact-sheet-white-house-releases-first- ever-comprehensive-framework-for-responsible-development-of-digital-assets.

382 See "Executive Order on Ensuring Responsible Development of Digital Assets," whitehouse.gov.

383 See "Executive Order on Ensuring Responsible Development of Digital Assets," whitehouse.gov.

384 "Background Press Call by Senior Administration Officials on the President's New Digital Assets Executive Order," whitehouse.gov, March 9, 2022, https:// www.whitehouse.gov/briefing-room/press-briefings/2022/03/09/background- press-call-by-senior-administration-officials-on-the-presidents-new-digital-assets-

executive-order.

385 "Background Press Call by Senior Administration Officials on the President's New Digital Assets Executive Order," whitehouse.gov.

386 "Background Press Call by Senior Administration Officials on the President's New Digital Assets Executive Order," whitehouse.gov.

387 "Background Press Call by Senior Administration Officials on the President's New Digital Assets Executive Order," whitehouse.gov.

388 "Background Press Call by Senior Administration Officials on the President's New Digital Assets Executive Order," whitehouse.gov.

389 See Laura Taylor, "Navigating the ABCs of CBDCs—Central Bank Digital Currencies," The Federal Reserve Bank of St. Louis, June 30, 2021, https://www.stlouisfed.org/open-vault/2021/june/navigating-the-abcs-of-central-bank-digital-currencies.

390 See video in Laura Taylor, "Navigating the ABCs of CBDCs—Central Bank Digital Currencies."

391 See video in Laura Taylor, "Navigating the ABCs of CBDCs—Central Bank Digital Currencies."

392 See video in Laura Taylor, "Navigating the ABCs of CBDCs—Central Bank Digital Currencies."

393 Jeff Desjardins, "The Rising Speed of Technological Adoption," Visual Capitalist, February 14, 2018, https://www.visualcapitalist.com/rising-speed-technological-adoption.

394 April Montgomery and Ken Mingis, "The evolution of Apple's iPhone," Computer World, September 14, 2022, https://www.computerworld.com/article/2604020/the-evolution-of-apples-iphone.html#slide2.

395 Jeff Desjardins, "The Rising Speed of Technological Adoption."

396 Tibi Puiu, "Your smartphone is millions of times more powerful than the Apollo 11 guidance computers," ZME Science, May 13, 2021, https://www.zmescience.com/science/news-science/smartphone-power-compared-to-apollo-432.

397 "Moore's Law," Encyclopedia Britannica, last updated September 2, 2022, https://www.britannica.com/technology/Moores-law.

398 "Meet two of the most powerful supercomputers on the planet," IBM, ibm.com, https://www.ibm.com/thought-leadership/summit-supercomputer.

399 "Moore's Law," Encyclopedia Britannica.

400 Ann Kelleher, "Moore's Law – Now and in the Future," Intel Newsroom, February 16, 2022, https://www.intel.com/content/www/us/en/newsroom/opinion/

moore-law-now-and-in-the-future.html#gs.cdq1tv.

401 Allison Linn, "With new Microsoft breakthroughs, general purpose quantum
computing moves closer to reality," Microsoft, microsoft.com, September 25, 2017,
https://news.microsoft.com/features/new-microsoft-breakthroughs-general-
purpose-quantum-computing-moves-closer-reality.

402 Van Bryan, "Jeff Brown and Glenn Beck Discuss Quantum Computing," Brown-
stone Research, brownstoneresearch.com, November 28, 2019, https://www.
brownstoneresearch.com/bleeding-edge/jeff-brown-and-glenn-beck-discuss-
quantum-computing.

403 Michael Tabb, Andrea Gawrylewski, and Jeffery DelViscio, "How Does a
Quantum Computer Work?" *Scientific American*, July 7, 2021, https://www.scien-
tificamerican.com/video/how-does-a-quantum-computer-work.

404 Van Bryan, "Jeff Brown and Glenn Beck Discuss Quantum Computing."

405 Daphne Leprince-Ringuet, "Quantum computing: This new 100-qubit processor
is built with atoms cooled down near to absolute zero," *ZDNet*, July 9, 2021,
https://www.zdnet.com/article/quantum-computing-this-new-100-qubit-
processor-is-built-with-atoms-cooled-down-near-to-absolute-zero.

406 Elizabeth Gibney, "Quantum gold rush: the private funding pouring into quantum
start-ups," *Nature*, October 2, 2019, https://www.nature.com/articles/d41586-
019-02935-4.

407 "Traveling salesman problem (TSP)," *Tech Target*, last updated June 2020, https://
www.techtarget.com/whatis/definition/traveling-salesman-problem.

408 Michal Stechly, "Solving the Traveling Salesman Problem Using Quantum
Computer," *Medium*, March 15, 2019, https://medium.com/@michal.
stechly/solving-the-traveling-salesman-problem-using-quantum-computer-
bb00438de223.

409 Allison Linn, "With new Microsoft breakthroughs, general purpose quantum
computing moves closer to reality," Microsoft, September 25, 2017, https://news.
microsoft.com/features/new-microsoft-breakthroughs-general-purpose-quantum-
computing-moves-closer-reality/.

410 Frank Arute, et al., "Quantum supremacy using a programmable uperconducting
processor," *Nature*, October 23, 2019, https://www.nature.com/articles/s41586-
019-1666-5.

411 Adrian Cho, "IBM casts doubt on Google's claims of quantum supremacy," *Science*,
October 23, 2019, https://www.science.org/content/article/ibm-casts-doubt-
googles-claims-quantum-supremacy.

412 Devin Coldewey, "Google's 'quantum supremacy' usurped by researchers using ordinary supercomputer," *Tech Crunch*, August 5, 2022, https://techcrunch.com/2022/08/05/googles-quantum-supremacy-usurped-by-researchers-using-ordinary-supercomputer/.

413 Matthew Sparkes, "IBM creates largest ever superconducting quantum computer," *New Scientist*, November 15, 2021, https://www.newscientist.com/article/2297583-ibm-creates-largest-ever-superconducting-quantum-computer/.

414 "IBM Unveils 400 Qubit-Plus Quantum Processor and Next-Generation IBM Quantum System Two," IBM Newsroom, press release, newsroom.ibm.com, November 9, 2022, https://newsroom.ibm.com/2022-11-09-IBM-Unveils-400-Qubit-Plus-Quantum-Processor-and-Next-Generation-IBM-Quantum-System-Two.

415 "IBM Unveils 400 Qubit-Plus Quantum Processor and Next-Generation IBM Quantum System Two," IBM Newsroom.

416 "Research project successful: Volkswagen IT experts use quantum computing for traffic flow optimization," Volkswagen Newsroom, March 20, 2017, https://www.volkswagen-newsroom.com/en/press-releases/research-project-successful-volkswagen-it-experts-use-quantum-computing-for-traffic-flow-optimization-1303.

417 Dr. Elena Yndurain, et al., "Exploring quantum computing use cases for financial services," IBM Institute for Business Value, September 2019, https://www.ibm.com/thought-leadership/institute-business-value/report/exploring-quantum-financial.

418 Matthias Evers, Anna Heid, and Ivan Ostojic, "Pharma's digital Rx: Quantum computing in drug research and development," McKinsey & Company, June 18, 2021, https://www.mckinsey.com/industries/life-sciences/our-insights/pharmas-digital-rx-quantum-computing-in-drug-research-and-development.

419 Maya Posch, "Quantum Computing and the End of Encryption," Hackaday, June 11, 2020, https://hackaday.com/2020/06/11/quantum-computing-and-the-end-of-encryption/.

420 Michael Bahar, Chris Bloomfield, and Mary Jane Wilson-Bilik, "Getting ready for quantum computing: Managing the quantum threat," JSUPRA, August 5, 2022, https://www.jdsupra.com/legalnews/getting-ready-for-quantum-computing-6995870.

421 "H.R.6227 – National Quantum Initiative Act," Congress.gov, https://www.congress.gov/bill/115th-congress/house-bill/6227/text.

422 "National Quantum Initiative," Quantum.gov, https://www.quantum.gov.

423 Brian Wang, "China will open a $10 billion quantum computer center and others also investing in quantum computing," Next Big Future, October 10, 2017, https://www.nextbigfuture.com/2017/10/china-will-open-a-10-billion-quantum-computer-center-and-others-also-investing-in-quantum-computing.html.

424 Although the principle "A man's home is his castle" has been an important part of American jurisprudence and culture for centuries, its origins are found in the writings of Sir Edward Coke, an English jurist who lived in the sixteenth and seventeenth centuries. See "Sir Edward Coke declares that your house is your 'Castle and Fortress' (1604)," Online Library of Liberty, the Liberty Fund, accessed September 13, 2022, https://oll.libertyfund.org/quote/sir-edward-coke-declares-that-your-house-is-your-castle-and-fortress-1604.

Chapter 5: In the Future, You Will Own Nothing

425 Ida Auken, "Welcome to 2030. I own nothing, have no privacy, and life has never been better," World Economic Forum, weforum.org, Nov 11, 2016, made available by archive.org, accessed August 10, 2022, https://web.archive.org/web/20200919081413/https://www.weforum.org/agenda/2016/11/shopping-i-can-t-really-remember-what-that-is?utm_content=buffer60978&utm_medium=social&utm_source=twitter.com&utm_campaign=buffer.

426 Ida Auken, "Welcome to 2030. I own nothing, have no privacy, and life has never been better."

427 Ida Auken, "Welcome to 2030. I own nothing, have no privacy, and life has never been better."

428 Reuters Staff, "Fact check: The World Economic Forum does not have a stated goal to have people own nothing by 2030," Reuters, reuters.com, February 25, 2021, https://www.reuters.com/article/uk-factcheck-wef/fact-check-the-world-economic-forum-does-not-have-a-stated-goal-to-have-people-own-nothing-by-2030-idUSKBN2AP2T0.

429 Ida Auken, "Welcome to 2030. I own nothing, have no privacy, and life has never been better."

430 "The History of Home Movie Entertainment," Reel Rundown, reelrundown.com, March 30, 2022, https://reelrundown.com/film-industry/The-History-Of-Home-Movie-Entertainment.

431 Ian Bogost, "Rest in Peace, VCR," The Atlantic, July 26, 2016, https://www.theatlantic.com/technology/archive/2016/07/vrc-is-dead/492992.

432 Sarah Whitten, "The death of the DVD: Why sales dropped more than 86% in 13 years," CNBC, November 8, 2019, https://www.cnbc.com/2019/11/08/the-death-of-the-dvd-why-sales-dropped-more-than-86percent-in-13-years.html.

433 Sarah Whitten, "The death of the DVD: Why sales dropped more than 86% in 13 years.

434 "What's the future of DVDs and Blu-rays?" Diverse Tech Geek, diversetechgeek.com, Oct 12, 2021, https://www.diversetechgeek.com/whats-future-dvds-blu-rays.

435 Jason Bailey, "'Gone With the Wind' and Controversy: What You Need to Know," New York Times, last updated May 25, 2021, https://www.nytimes.com/2020/06/10/movies/gone-with-the-wind-controversy.html.

436 Jason Bailey, "'Gone With the Wind' and Controversy: What You Need to Know."

437 Rebecca Alter, "Every Blackface Episode and Scene That's Been Pulled From Streaming So Far," Vulture, vulture.com, June 29, 2020, https://www.vulture.com/2020/06/blackface-tv-episodes-scenes-removed-streaming.html.

438 Rebecca Alter, "Every Blackface Episode and Scene That's Been Pulled From Streaming So Far."

439 Bryan Pietsch, "Disney Adds Warnings for Racist Stereotypes to Some Older Films," New York Times, October 18, 2020, https://www.nytimes.com/2020/10/18/business/media/disney-plus-disclaimers.html.

440 Jacob Stolworthy, "Spotify quietly removes 113 episodes of Joe Rogan's podcast amid 'misinformation' and 'horrible' N-word clips," Independent, February 7, 2022, https://www.independent.co.uk/arts-entertainment/music/news/joe-rogan-podcast-episodes-removed-b2009035.html.

441 Ryan Parker, "Macaulay Culkin Among Those Who Want Donald Trump Removed from 'Home Alone 2,'" The Hollywood Reporter, January 14, 2021, https://www.hollywoodreporter.com/movies/movie-news/macaulay-culkin-among-those-who-want-donald-trump-removed-from-home-alone-2-4116354.

442 Angela Brown, "Homeowner advantages: 5 benefits of owning a home," Fox Business, foxbusiness.com, February 23, 2021, https://www.foxbusiness.com/money/homeowner-benefits-of-owning-a-home.

443 Michelle Fox, "With rising inflation and a hot housing market, here's what you need to know about buying a home right now," CNBC, cnbc.com, November 23, 2021, https://www.cnbc.com/2021/11/23/rising-inflation-hot-housing-market-what-you-need-to-know-about-buying-a-home.html.

444 Odeta Kushi, "Homeownership Remains Strongly Linked to Wealth-Building,"

First American, blog.firstam.com, November 5, 2020, https://blog.firstam.com/economics/homeownership-remains-strongly-linked-to-wealth-building.

445 Kevin Leacock, "A Brief History of Housing Policy in the U.S.," National Nurse-Led Care Consortium, nurseledcare.phmc.org, October 29, 2019, https://nurseledcare.phmc.org/advocacy/policy-blog/item/641-a-brief-history-of-housing-policy-in-the-u-s.html.

446 "The Clinton-Gore Administration: A Record of Progress," Clinton White House Archives, accessed August 10, 2022, https://clintonwhitehouse5.archives.gov/WH/Accomplishments/housing_accomps.html.

447 "Homeownership Policy Book," George W. Bush White House Archives, accessed August 10, 2022, https://georgewbush-whitehouse.archives.gov/infocus/homeownership/homeownership-policy-book-background.html.

448 "Homeownership Rate in the United States," Federal Reserve Bank of St. Louis, accessed August 10, 2022, https://fred.stlouisfed.org/series/RHORUSQ156N.

449 "Average Sales Price of Houses Sold for the United States," Federal Reserve Bank of St. Louis, accessed August 10, 2022, https://fred.stlouisfed.org/series/ASPUS.

450 "Average Sales Price of Houses Sold for the United States," Federal Reserve Bank of St. Louis.

451 "Average Sales Price of Houses Sold for the United States," Federal Reserve Bank of St. Louis.

452 Kim Parker, Juliana Menasce Horowitz, and Rachel Minkin, "Americans Are Less Likely Than Before COVID-19 To Want To Live in Cities, More Likely To Prefer Suburbs," Pew Research Center, December 16, 2021, https://www.pewresearch.org/social-trends/2021/12/16/americans-are-less-likely-than-before-covid-19-to-want-to-live-in-cities-more-likely-to-prefer-suburbs.

453 Alexandra Ciuntu, "Would-Be Millennial Homebuyers Fuel the Rise of Lifestyle Renting in 2021," *RentCafe*, December 3, 2021, https://www.rentcafe.com/blog/rental-market/market-snapshots/millennial-lifestyle-renting.

454 See "California housing crisis: Lawmakers reach deal on bills to boost homebuilding," Associated Press, republished by CBS News Bay Area, cbsnews.com, August 25, 2022, https://www.cbsnews.com/sanfrancisco/news/california-housing-crisis-lawmakers-deal-ab2011-sb6.

455 "Blackstone Reports Fourth Quarter and Full Year 2021 Results," Blackstone, January 27, 2022, https://s23.q4cdn.com/714267708/files/doc_financials/2021/q4/Blackstone4Q21EarningsPressRelease.pdf.

456 Kerry Curry, "Invitation to a Housing Revolution," *D*, April 8, 2018, https://www.

dmagazine.com/publications/d-ceo/2018/april/invitation-homes-rental-dallas.

457   "Blackstone to buy $1 billion worth of Tampa Bay homes for rentals," *Tampa Bay Times*, September 24, 2012, https://www.tampabay.com/news/business/realestate/blackstone-to-buy-1-billion-worth-of-tampa-bay-homes-for-rentals/1252624.

458   "Blackstone to buy $1 billion worth of Tampa Bay homes for rentals," *Tampa Bay Times*.

459   Larry Getlen, "How corporations are buying up houses – robbing families of the American Dream," *New York Post*, July 18, 2020, https://nypost.com/2020/07/18/corporations-are-buying-houses-robbing-families-of-american-dream.

460   Angela Gonzales, "Phoenix again tops nation in single-family home rent growth, despite Covid-19 effects," *Phoenix Business Journal*, bizjournals.com, September 15, 2020, https://www.bizjournals.com/phoenix/news/2020/09/15/phoenix-tops-nation-single-family-rent-growth.html.

461   "Blackstone's Invitation Homes raises $1.54 billion in IPO: Source," CNBC, cnbc.com, January 31, 2017, https://www.cnbc.com/2017/01/31/invitation-homes-raises-154-billion-in-ipo-source.html.

462   James Kleimann, "Blackstone gets back into the single-family rental game," *Housing Wire*, September 1, 2020, https://www.housingwire.com/articles/blackstone-gets-back-into-the-single-family-rental-game.

463   "Blackstone to buy Home Partners of America in $6 bln deal," Reuters, reuters.com, June 22, 2021, https://www.reuters.com/business/blackstone-buy-home-partners-america-6-billion-deal-wsj-2021-06-22.

464   Maureen Farrell, "Blackstone expands further into rental housing in the United States," *New York Times*, February 16, 2022, https://www.nytimes.com/2022/02/16/business/blackstone-real-estate-acquisition.html.

465   Vishesh Raisinghani, "Blackstone is preparing a record $50 billion vehicle to scoop up real estate bargains during the downturn – here's how to lock in higher yields than the big money," *MoneyWise*, reposted to Yahoo.com, August 5, 2022, https://www.yahoo.com/now/blackstone-preparing-record-50-billion-120000092.html.

466   Kevin Schaul and Jonathan O'Connell, "Investors bought a record share of homes in 2021. See where," *Washington Post*, February 16, 2022, https://www.washingtonpost.com/business/interactive/2022/housing-market-investors.

467   Francesca Mari, "A $60 Billion Housing Grab by Wall Street," *New York Times Magazine*, last updated October 22, 2021, https://www.nytimes.com/2020/03/04/magazine/wall-street-landlords.html.

468 Dan Budzyn, "Institutions Set To Own 40% Of Single-Family Rental Homes
     – How Can You Get Your Share?" *Benzinga*, August 22, 2022, https://www.
     benzinga.com/real-estate/22/08/28584067/institutions-set-to-own-40-of-single-
     family-rental-homes-how-can-you-get-your-share.

469 Ryan Dezember, "How I Bought a House and Joined the Foreclosure Generation,"
     The Daily Beast, August 2, 2020, https://www.thedailybeast.com/how-i-bought-a-
     house-and-joined-the-foreclosure-generation.

470 Ryan Dezember, "How I Bought a House and Joined the Foreclosure Generation."

471 Ryan Dezember, "How I Bought a House and Joined the Foreclosure Generation."

472 Matthew Ponsford, "House-flipping algorithms are coming to your neighborhood,"
     MIT Technology Review, April 13, 2022, https://www.technologyreview.com/
     2022/04/13/1049227/house-flipping-algorithms-are-coming-to-your-neighbor-
     hood.

473 Matthew Ponsford, "House-flipping algorithms are coming to your neighborhood."

474 Matthew Ponsford, "House-flipping algorithms are coming to your neighborhood."

475 John Gittelsohn, "U.S. Moves Toward Home 'Rentership Society,' Morgan Stanley
     Says," Bloomberg, July 20, 2011, https://www.bloomberg.com/news/articles/
     2011-07-20/u-s-moves-to-rentership-society-as-owning-tumbles-morgan-stanley-
     says.

476 Larry Getlen, "How corporations are buying up houses – robbing families of the
     American Dream."

477 "Our Partners," World Economic Forum, weforum.org, accessed September 28,
     2022, https://www.weforum.org/partners/#m.

478 Ida Auken, "Welcome to 2030. I own nothing, have no privacy, and life has never
     been better."

479 "Blackstone to buy $1 billion worth of Tampa Bay homes for rentals," *Tampa Bay
     Times*.

480 Karl Smith, "America Should Become a Nation of Renters," Bloomberg, June
     17, 2021, https://www.bloomberg.com/opinion/articles/2021-06-17/america-
     should-become-a-nation-of-renters#xj4y7vzkg.

481 Shane Phillips, "Renting Is Terrible. Owning Is Worse," *The Atlantic*, March 11,
     2021, https://www.theatlantic.com/ideas/archive/2021/03/why-its-better-to-
     rent-than-to-own/618254.

482 Sarah Paynter, "US will 'become a renter nation,' says real estate investor," *Yahoo!
     Finance*, October 8, 2020, https://www.yahoo.com/now/us-will-become-a-renter-
     nation-says-investor-183327180.html.

483 Steven Richmond, "4 Things Landlords Are Not Allowed to Do," *Investopedia*, last
     updated July 31, 2022, https://www.investopedia.com/articles/personal-finance/
     061515/4-things-landlords-are-not-allowed-do.asp.

484 Stephen Michael White, "Why You Need A No-Party Clause In Your Rental
     Agreement," rentprep.com, April 6, 2021, https://rentprep.com/landlord-tips/
     stop-your-rental-property-from-becoming-party-central.

485 "Just found a 'no alcohol' clause in our rental agreement. Is this legal?" Reddit,
     reddit.com, https://www.reddit.com/r/exmormon/comments/ylgs6/just_
     found_a_no_alcohol_clause_in_our_rental.

486 George Khoury, "Can My Landlord Ban Gun Ownership," Find Law, August 18,
     2017, https://www.findlaw.com/legalblogs/law-and-life/can-my-landlord-ban-
     gun-ownership.

487 Francisco Da Cunha and Filipa Belchior Coimbra, "The Impact of Social Good on
     Real Estate," Deloitte, deloitte.com, https://www2.deloitte.com/ce/en/pages/real-
     estate/articles/the-impact-of-social-good-on-real-estate.html.

488 Ida Auken, "Welcome to 2030. I own nothing, have no privacy, and life has never
     been better."

489 Kalin Bracken et al., "A Framework for the Future of Real Estate," World
     Economic Forum, weforum.org, April 2021, https://www3.weforum.org/docs/
     WEF_A_Framework_for_the_Future_of_Real_Estate_2021.pdf.

490 Kalin Bracken et al., "A Framework for the Future of Real Estate."

491 Kalin Bracken et al., "A Framework for the Future of Real Estate."

492 "LA County Coordinated Entry System," Los Angeles Homeless Services
     Authority, accessed August 10, 2022, https://www.lahsa.org/ces.

493 Virginia Eubanks, *Automating Inequality: How High-Tech Tools Profile, Police, and
     Punish the Poor* (St. Martin's Press, January 2018).

494 Nuala Bishari, "San Francisco Rations Housing by Scoring Homeless People's
     Trauma. By Design, Most Fail to Qualify," San Francisco Public Press, April 14,
     2022, https://www.sfpublicpress.org/san-francisco-rations-housing-by-scoring-
     homeless-peoples-trauma-by-design-most-fail-to-qualify.

495 Virginia Eubanks, *Automating Inequality: How High-Tech Tools Profile, Police, and
     Punish the Poor.*

496 This is an allusion to Karl Marx's famous quote, "From each according to his
     ability, to each according to his needs," which was published in Marx's *Critique of
     the Gotha Programme* in 1875.

497 Virginia Eubanks, *Automating Inequality: How High-Tech Tools Profile, Police, and*

Punish the Poor.

498 Darrell Etherington, "Lyft says nearly 250k of its passengers ditched a personal car in 2017," *Tech Crunch,* January 16, 2018, https://techcrunch.com/2018/01/16/lyft-says-nearly-250k-of-its-passengers-ditched-a-personal-car-in-2017.

499 "Transit Horizons: Toward a New Model of Public Transportation," Uber, uber.com, https://www.uber.com/us/en/transit/horizons-paper.

500 David Zipper, "Can Uber Help Save Public Transit?" Bloomberg, January 26, 2021, https://www.bloomberg.com/news/articles/2021-01-26/what-to-make-of-uber-s-bid-to-help-public-transit.

501 Winnie Yeh, "3 circular economy approaches to reduce demand for critical metals," World Economic Forum, weforum.org, July 18, 2022, https://www.weforum.org/agenda/2022/07/3-circular-approaches-to-reduce-demand-for-critical-mineral.

502 Jason Silverstein, "Airbnb, Lyft, Uber allowing service to be denied to Unite the Right marchers," CBS News, August 10, 2018, https://www.cbsnews.com/news/unite-the-right-dc-uber-airbnb-lyft-allowing-service-to-be-denied-to-marchers.

503 Sharon Bernstein, "Uber, Lyft ban conservative activist after anti-Muslim tweets," Reuters, November 1, 2017, https://www.reuters.com/article/new-york-attack-uber-loomer-idCNL2N1N801Z.

504 Alex Pappas, "GOP interns: Uber driver refused us service because of MAGA hats," Fox News, foxnews.com, July 13, 2018, https://www.foxnews.com/politics/gop-interns-uber-driver-refused-us-service-because-of-maga-hats.

505 "Together on the road to zero emissions," Uber, uber.com, https://www.uber.com/us/en/drive/services/electric.

506 Ida Auken, "Welcome to 2030. I own nothing, have no privacy, and life has never been better."

507 Kevin Stone, "California Bans the Sale of All Small Off-Road Internal Combustion Engines," *Heartland Daily News,* November 1, 2021, https://heartlanddailynews.com/2021/11/california-bans-the-sale-of-all-small-off-road-internal-combustion-engines.

508 "Ag and Food Sectors and the Economy," Economic Research Service, U.S. Department of Agriculture, ers.usda.gov, accessed March 8, 2023, https://www.ers.usda.gov/data-products/ag-and-food-statistics-charting-the-essentials/ag-and-food-sectors-and-the-economy.

509 "Ag and Food Sectors and the Economy," Economic Research Service.

510 "Agriculture," Digital History, digitalhistory.uh.edu, https://www.digitalhistory.uh.edu/disp_textbook.cfm?smtID=11&psid=3837.

511 Jayson Lusk, "The Evolution of American Agriculture," *Jayson Lusk Blog*, June 27, 2016, http://jaysonlusk.com/blog/2016/6/26/the-evolution-of-american-agriculture.

512 Jayson Lusk, "The Evolution of American Agriculture."

513 "Farmland Value," Economic Research Service, U.S. Department of Agriculture, https://www.ers.usda.gov/topics/farm-economy/land-use-land-value-tenure/farmland-value.

514 Ariel Shapiro, "America's Biggest Owner Of Farmland Is Now Bill Gates," *Forbes*, January 14, 2021, https://www.forbes.com/sites/arielshapiro/2021/01/14/americas-biggest-owner-of-farmland-is-now-bill-gates-bezos-turner/?sh=69691c986096.

515 "Why Bill Gates Is Buying Up U.S. Farmland," CNBC, made available on youtube.com, August 21, 2021, https://www.youtube.com/watch?v=MJVL9HegCr4.

516 "Farmland Ownership and Tenure," Economic Research Service, U.S. Department of Agriculture, https://www.ers.usda.gov/topics/farm-economy/land-use-land-value-tenure/farmland-ownership-and-tenure.

517 Chris McGreal, "How America's food giants swallowed the family farms," *The Guardian*, theguardian.com, March 9, 2019, https://www.theguardian.com/environment/2019/mar/09/american-food-giants-swallow-the-family-farms-iowa.

518 Rahul Kanwal et al., "Redefining Food Systems with Emerging Technologies," World Economic Forum, weforum.org, May 26, 2022, https://www.weforum.org/event_player/a0P68000001Kd0vEAC/sessions/redefining-food-systems-with-emerging-technologies.

519 John Blasberg et al., "How companies can accelerate and galvanize food system transformation," World Economic Forum, weforum.org, May 25, 2022, https://www.weforum.org/agenda/2022/05/companies-can-accelerate-and-galvanize-food-system-transformation.

520 Kate Whiting, "Food systems can lead the way to net zero, if we act now," World Economic Forum, weforum.org, March 16, 2022, https://www.weforum.org/agenda/2022/03/food-systems-net-zero.

521 "Dutch gov't sets targets to cut nitrogen pollution, farmers to protest," Reuters, reuters.com, June 10, 2022, https://www.reuters.com/world/europe/dutch-govt-sets-targets-cut-nitrogen-pollution-farmers-protest-2022-06-10.

522 "Dutch gov't sets targets to cut nitrogen pollution, farmers to protest," Reuters.

523 Mike Corder, "EXPLAINER: Why are Dutch farmers protesting over emissions?" ABC News, abcnews.go.com, June 28, 2022, https://abcnews.go.com/Business/

wireStory/explainer-dutch-farmers-protesting-emissions-85848026.

524 Aanya Wipulasena and Mujib Mashal, "Sri Lanka's Plunge Into Organic Farming Brings Disaster," *New York Times*, December 7, 2021, https://www.nytimes.com/2021/12/07/world/asia/sri-lanka-organic-farming-fertilizer.html.

525 Aanya Wipulasena and Mujib Mashal, "Sri Lanka's Plunge Into Organic Farming Brings Disaster."

526 Uditha Jayasinghe and Devjyot Ghoshal, "Fertiliser ban decimates Sri Lankan crops as government popularity ebbs," Reuters, reuters.com, March 3, 2022, https://www.reuters.com/markets/commodities/fertiliser-ban-decimates-sri-lankan-crops-government-popularity-ebbs-2022-03-03.

527 Chris Kenning and Christina Fernando, "Protests, a president's exit and a crackdown: What's next in Sri Lanka's economic crisis?" *USA Today*, usatoday.com, July 31, 2022, https://www.usatoday.com/story/news/world/2022/07/31/sri-lanka-debt-crisis-economic-collapse/10147198002/?gnt-cfr=1.

528 Rhea Mogul and Iqbal Athas, "Sri Lanka's economy has 'completely collapsed,' Prime Minister says," CNN, cnn.com, last updated June 23, 2022, https://www.cnn.com/2022/06/23/asia/sri-lanka-economy-collapse-prime-minister-intl-hnk/index.html.

529 Ranil Wickremesinghe, "Sir Lanka PM: This is how I will make my country rich by 2025," World Economic Forum, weforum.org, August 29, 2018, https://www.weforum.org/agenda/2018/08/this-is-how-we-will-make-sri-lanka-rich-by-2025.

530 "Japan-World Bank Program for Mainstreaming Disaster Risk Management in Developing Countries – List of Projects (South Asia)," World Bank, worldbank.org, June 1, 2022, https://www.worldbank.org/en/data/interactive/2020/03/01/tokyo-drm-hub-south-asia.

531 "New Vision for Agriculture," World Economic Forum, weforum.org, https://www3.weforum.org/docs/WEF_CO_NVA_Overview.pdf.

532 "New Vision for Agriculture," World Economic Forum.

533 Jen Skerritt, "Trudeau Spars With Farmers on Climate Plan Risking Grain Output," Bloomberg, bloomberg.com, July 27, 2022, https://www.bloomberg.com/news/articles/2022-07-27/trudeau-spars-with-farmers-on-climate-plan-cutting-fertilizer-grain-output.

534 Jen Skerritt, "Trudeau Spars With Farmers on Climate Plan Risking Grain Output."

535 Jen Skerritt, "Trudeau Spars With Farmers on Climate Plan Risking Grain Output."

536 H. Claire Brown, "The Biden Administration Will Pay Farmers More Money Not to Farm," Governing, governing.com, May 2, 2021, https://www.governing.com/now/the-biden-administration-will-pay-farmers-more-money-not-to-farm.

537 "How to apply for a lump sum payment to leave or retire from farming," uk.gov, last updated April 12, 2022, https://www.gov.uk/government/publications/apply-for-a-lump-sum-payment-to-leave-or-retire-from-farming/how-to-apply-for-a-lump-sum-payment-to-leave-or-retire-from-farming.

538 Sean Fleming, "Good grub: why we might be eating insects soon," World Economic Forum, weforum.org, July 16, 2018, https://www.weforum.org/agenda/2018/07/good-grub-why-we-might-be-eating-insects-soon.

539 Antoine Hubert, "Why we need to give insects the role they deserve in our food systems," World Economic Forum, weforum.org, July 12, 2021, https://www.weforum.org/agenda/2021/07/why-we-need-to-give-insects-the-role-they-deserve-in-our-food-systems.

540 Amrou Awaysheh and Christine J. Picard, Ph.D., "5 reasons why eating insects could reduce climate change," World Economic Forum, weforum.org, February 9, 2022, https://www.weforum.org/agenda/2022/02/how-insects-positively-impact-climate-change.

541 Aly Lancione, "World's largest cricket processing plant coming to London, Ont.," CBC, last updated July 20, 2020, https://www.cbc.ca/news/canada/london/worlds-largest-cricket-processing-plant-coming-to-london-1.5655813.

542 Rebecca Zandbergen, "Massive cricket-processing facility comes online in London, Ont.," CBC, last updated July 1, 2022, https://www.cbc.ca/news/canada/london/cricket-farm-london-ontario-1.6506606.

543 Kate Whiting, "How soon will we be eating lab-grown meat?" World Economic Forum, weforum.org, October 16, 2020, https://www.weforum.org/agenda/2020/10/will-we-eat-lab-grown-meat-world-food-day.

544 Ida Auken, "Welcome to 2030. I own nothing, have no privacy, and life has never been better."

545 Ida Auken, "Welcome to 2030. I own nothing, have no privacy, and life has never been better."

Chapter 6: A "New Blueprint" for Society

546 For specific figures and citations, see Chapter 4: "Socialist Utopias and Their Bloody History of Failure," in Glenn Beck, *Arguing with Socialists* (Threshold Editions, 2020).

547 "Khmer Rouge: Cambodia's years of brutality," BBC News, bbc.com, November 16, 2018, https://www.bbc.com/news/world-asia-pacific-10684399.

548 "Khmer Rouge," History Channel, history.com, updated August 21, 2018, https://www.history.com/topics/cold-war/the-khmer-rouge.

549 "Documenting Numbers of Victims of the Holocaust and Nazi Persecution," *Holocaust Encyclopedia*, U.S. Holocaust Memorial Museum, accessed September 14, 2022, https://encyclopedia.ushmm.org/content/en/article/documenting-numbers-of-victims-of-the-holocaust-and-nazi-persecution.

550 Kathrin Hille, "China's 'sent-down' youth," *Financial Times*, ft.com, September 20, 2013, https://www.ft.com/content/3d2ba75c-1fdf-11e3-8861-00144feab7de.

551 Kathrin Hille, "China's 'sent-down' youth."

552 Ann Schecter, "New details of torture, cover-ups in China's internment camps revealed in Amnesty International report," NBC News, nbcnews.com, June 10, 2021, https://www.nbcnews.com/news/world/new-details-torture-cover-ups-china-s-internment-camps-revealed-n1270014.

553 See, for example, Anna Fifield, "New images show North Korea's extensive network of 'reeducation' camps," *Washington Post*, October 26, 2017, https://www.washingtonpost.com/world/asia_pacific/new-images-show-north-koreas-extensive-network-of-re-education-camps/2017/10/25/894afc1c-b9a7-11e7-9b93-b97043e57a22_story.html.

554 Charles Darwin, *The Descent of Man*, revised edition (Prometheus Publishing, 1997).

555 Karen Matthews, "Sanger's name to be dropped from NYC clinic over eugenics," Associated Press, apnews.com, July 21, 2020, https://apnews.com/article/birth-control-health-us-news-manhattan-new-york-ddef4d3812cfe106b-7c0844536ac37ec.

556 Nikita Stewart, "Planned Parenthood in N.Y. Disavows Margaret Sanger Over Eugenics," *New York Times*, July 21, 2020, https://www.nytimes.com/2020/07/21/nyregion/planned-parenthood-margaret-sanger-eugenics.html.

557 Andrea DenHoed, "The Forgotten Lessons of the American Eugenics Movement," *The New Yorker*, April 27, 2016, https://www.newyorker.com/books/page-turner/the-forgotten-lessons-of-the-american-eugenics-movement.

558 Edwin Black, "Hitler's debt to America," *The Guardian*, theguardian.com, February 4, 2004, https://www.theguardian.com/uk/2004/feb/06/race.usa.

559 See Chapter 7: "Saints, Sinners, and Socialists," in Glenn Beck, *Arguing with Socialists* (Threshold Editions, 2020).

560 Leon Trotsky, *Literature and Revolution*, originally published by Leon Trotsky, April 11, 1924, made available online by Marxist.com, https://www.marxist.com/literature-and-revolution.htm.

561 Leon Trotsky, *Literature and Revolution*.

562 Leon Trotsky, *Literature and Revolution*.

563 Leon Trotsky, *Literature and Revolution*.

564 Joy Pullmann, *The Education Invasion: How Common Core Fights Parents for Control of America's Kids* (Encounter Books, 2017).

565 Joy Pullmann, *The Education Invasion: How Common Core Fights Parents for Control of America's Kids*.

566 Joy Pullmann, *The Education Invasion: How Common Core Fights Parents for Control of America's Kids*.

567 Joy Pullmann, *The Education Invasion: How Common Core Fights Parents for Control of America's Kids*.

568 Joy Pullmann, *The Education Invasion: How Common Core Fights Parents for Control of America's Kids*.

569 Joy Pullmann, *The Education Invasion: How Common Core Fights Parents for Control of America's Kids*.

570 Naomi Schaefer Riley, "'The 1619 Project' Enters American Classrooms," *Education Next*, educationnext.org, accessed September 15, 2022, https://www.educationnext.org/1619-project-enters-american-classrooms-adding-new-sizzle-slavery-significant-cost.

571 Naomi Schaefer Riley, "'The 1619 Project' Enters American Classrooms."

572 Mary Grabar, *Debunking the 1619 Project: Exposing the Plan to Divide America* (Regnery History, 2022).

573 Mary Grabar, *Debunking the 1619 Project: Exposing the Plan to Divide America*.

574 See, for example, Lyndsey Layton, "How Bill Gates pulled off the swift Common Core revolution," *Washington Post*, June 7, 2014, https://www.washingtonpost.com/politics/how-bill-gates-pulled-off-the-swift-common-core-revolution/2014/06/07/a830e32e-ec34-11e3-9f5c-9075d5508f0a_story.html.

575 "Partners," World Economic Forum, weforum.org, accessed September 15, 2022, https://www.weforum.org/partners/#B.

576 "Open Society Foundations Announce $220 Million for Building Power in Black Communities," press release, Open Society Foundations, opensocietyfoundations.org, July 13, 2020, https://www.opensocietyfoundations.org/newsroom/open-society-foundations-announce-220-million-for-building-power-in-black-communities.

577 Cheryl Chumley, "George Soros meddles in America again," *Washington Times*, September 9, 2021, https://www.washingtontimes.com/news/2021/sep/9/george-soros-meddles-america-again.

578 "Our Mission," 1619 Freedom School, 1619freedomschool.org, last accessed March 27, 2023, https://www.1619freedomschool.org/leadership.

579 "Leadership Team," 1619 Freedom School, 1619freedomschool.org, last accessed September 15, 2022, https://www.1619freedomschool.org/leadership.

580 Joseph Losavio, "George Floyd: these are the injustices that led to the protests in the United States," World Economic Forum, weforum.org, June 5, 2020, https://www.weforum.org/agenda/2020/06/this-is-what-has-led-to-george-floyd-protests-in-the-united-states.

581 Mike Gonzalez, "Marxism Underpins Black Lives Matter Agenda," Heritage Foundation, heritage.org, September 8, 2021, https://www.heritage.org/progressivism/commentary/marxism-underpins-black-lives-matter-agenda.

582 Joseph Losavio, "George Floyd: these are the injustices that led to the protests in the United States."

583 See "Klaus Schwab Releases 'Stakeholder Capitalism'; Making the Case for a Global Economy that Works for Progress, People and Planet," press release, World Economic Forum, January 29, 2021, https://www.weforum.org/press/2021/01/klaus-schwab-releases-stakeholder-capitalism-making-the-case-for-a-global-economy-that-works-for-progress-people-and-planet, citing Klaus Schwab and Peter Vanham, Stakeholder Capitalism: A Global Economy that Works for Progress, People and Planet (World Economic Forum, 2021).

584 See chapters 1 and 2 for more information.

585 Klaus Schwab and Mohammad Abdullah Al Gergawi, "Narrating the Future," discussion at The Great Narrative conference, hosted by the World Economic Forum and Government of the United Arab Emirates, November 10, 2021, https://www.weforum.org/events/the-great-narrative-2021/sessions/a-call-for-the-great-narrative.

586 Klaus Schwab and Mohammad Abdullah Al Gergawi, "Narrating the Future."

587 Klaus Schwab and Mohammad Abdullah Al Gergawi, "Narrating the Future."

588 See Bernard Marr, "How Much Data Do We Create Every Day? The Mind-Blowing Stats Everyone Should Read," *Forbes*, May 21, 2018, https://www.forbes.com/sites/bernardmarr/2018/05/21/how-much-data-do-we-create-every-day-the-mind-blowing-stats-everyone-should-read/?sh=4ec0b51d60ba.

589 See Bernard Marr, "How Much Data Do We Create Every Day? The Mind-

Blowing Stats Everyone Should Read."

590 See data in Felix Richter, "Smartphones Cause Photography Boom," Statista, statista.com, August 31, 2017, https://www.statista.com/chart/10913/number-of-photos-taken-worldwide.

591 See Jeff Desjardins, "How much data is generated each day?" World Economic Forum, weforum.org, April 17, 2019, https://www.weforum.org/agenda/2019/04/how-much-data-is-generated-each-day-cf4bddf29f, citing content from Raconteur.

592 Daisy Quaker, "Amazon Stats: Growth, sales, and more," Amazon, sell.amazon.com, March 31, 2022, https://sell.amazon.com/blog/grow-your-business/amazon-stats-growth-and-sales.

593 Maryam Mohsin, "10 Amazon Statistics You Need to Know in 2022," Oberlo, oberlo.com, July 10, 2022, https://www.oberlo.com/blog/amazon-statistics.

594 Nicole Martin, "How Much Does Google Really Know About You? A lot," Forbes, forbes.com, March 11, 2019, https://www.forbes.com/sites/nicolemartin1/2019/03/11/how-much-does-google-really-know-about-you-a-lot/?sh=28ce5ccc7f5d.

595 Nicole Martin, "How Much Does Google Really Know About You? A lot."

596 Nicole Martin, "How Much Does Google Really Know About You? A lot."

597 Chris Albrecht, "LG and Samsung to Show Off New Food Identifying Smart Fridges at CES Next Week," The Spoon, January 2, 2020, https://thespoon.tech/lg-and-samsung-to-show-off-new-food-identifying-smart-fridges-at-ces-next-week.

598 Medea Giordano, "The Best Smart Bulbs to Light Up Your Room," WIRED, wired.com, February 3, 2022, https://www.wired.com/gallery/best-smart-bulbs.

599 Mohammad Hasan, "State of IoT 2022: Number of connected IoT devices growing 18% to 14.4 billion globally," IOT Analytics, May 18, 2022, https://iot-analytics.com/number-connected-iot-devices.

600 Mohammad Hasan, "State of IoT 2022: Number of connected IoT devices growing 18% to 14.4 billion globally."

601 "Fitbit Inspire 3," Fitbit.com, https://www.fitbit.com/global/us/products/trackers/inspire3.

602 Mallory Hackett, "Fitbit begins smart blood pressure tracking study," Mobi Health News, April 08, 2021, https://www.mobihealthnews.com/news/fitbit-begins-smartwatch-blood-pressure-tracking-study.

603 "Fitbits of the future: What's next for biometric data in health?" Aetna, https://www.aetnainternational.com/en/about-us/explore/future-health/fitbit-biometric-

tech-health-care.html.

604   Dan Robitzski, "Brutal Startup Is Using Eye Tracking to Force You to Watch Ads,"
       Futurism, March 22, 2019, https://futurism.com/moviepass-eye-tracking-ads.

605   Jeff Desjardins, "How much data is generated each day?"

606   "eDiscovery Best Practices: The Number of Pages in Each Gigabyte Can Vary
       Widely," CloudNine, accessed September 22, 2022, https://cloudnine.com/
       ediscoverydaily/electronic-discovery/ediscovery-best-practices-the-number-of-
       pages-in-each-gigabyte-can-vary-widely.

607   Verlyn Klinkenborg, "Trying to Measure the Amount of Information That
       Humans Create," *New York Times*, November 12, 2003, https://www.nytimes.
       com/2003/11/12/opinion/editorial-observer-trying-measure-amount-informa-
       tion-that-humans-create.html.

608   "Our Alliance is creating smart city governance," World Economic Forum,
       weforum.org, accessed last on September 22, 2022, https://www.weforum.org/
       impact/smart-cities-governance-alliance.

609   "Our Alliance is creating smart city governance," World Economic Forum.

610   "Our Alliance is creating smart city governance," World Economic Forum.

611   "Our Alliance is creating smart city governance," World Economic Forum.

612   "Our Alliance is creating smart city governance," World Economic Forum.

613   "Our Alliance is creating smart city governance," World Economic Forum.

614   See Jeff Desjardins, "This is what the cities of the future could look like," World
       Economic Forum, weforum.org, January 9, 2019, https://www.weforum.org/
       agenda/2019/01/the-anatomy-of-a-smart-city.

615   See Jeff Desjardins, "This is what the cities of the future could look like."

616   See Jeff Desjardins, "This is what the cities of the future could look like."

617   See Jeff Desjardins, "This is what the cities of the future could look like."

618   See Jeff Desjardins, "This is what the cities of the future could look like."

619   See Jeff Desjardins, "This is what the cities of the future could look like."

620   See Jeff Desjardins, "This is what the cities of the future could look like."

621   Robert Adams, "Turning urban sprawl into a net-zero city. Lessons from
       Melbourne," World Economic Forum, weforum.org, November 16, 2021, https://
       www.weforum.org/global_future_councils/gfc-on-cities-of-tomorrow/articles/
       urban-sprawl-to-net-zero-melbourne.

622   Robert Adams, "Turning urban sprawl into a net-zero city. Lessons from
       Melbourne."

623   Kunal Kumar and Mridul Kaushik, "'My Carbon': An approach for inclusive and

sustainable cities," World Economic Forum, weforum.org, September 14, 2022, https://www.weforum.org/agenda/2022/09/my-carbon-an-approach-for-inclusive-and-sustainable-cities.

624 Kunal Kumar and Mridul Kaushik, "'My Carbon': An approach for inclusive and sustainable cities."

625 Kunal Kumar and Mridul Kaushik, "'My Carbon': An approach for inclusive and sustainable cities."

626 Kunal Kumar and Mridul Kaushik, "'My Carbon': An approach for inclusive and sustainable cities."

627 Kunal Kumar and Mridul Kaushik, "'My Carbon': An approach for inclusive and sustainable cities."

628 Kunal Kumar and Mridul Kaushik, "'My Carbon': An approach for inclusive and sustainable cities."

629 Kunal Kumar and Mridul Kaushik, "'My Carbon': An approach for inclusive and sustainable cities."

630 Kunal Kumar and Mridul Kaushik, "'My Carbon': An approach for inclusive and sustainable cities."

631 Kunal Kumar and Mridul Kaushik, "'My Carbon': An approach for inclusive and sustainable cities."

632 Kunal Kumar and Mridul Kaushik, "'My Carbon': An approach for inclusive and sustainable cities."

633 Justine Calma, "A utility company locked thousands of customers out of their smart thermostats in Colorado," *The Verge*, theverge.com, September 5, 2022, https://www.theverge.com/2022/9/5/23337864/xcel-locked-out-customers-smart-thermostats-colorado-heatwave.

634 Jaclyn Allen, "Thousands of Xcel customers locked out of thermostats during 'energy emergency,'" Denver 7 News, denver7.com, August 31, 2022, https://www.denver7.com/news/contact-denver7/thousands-of-xcel-customers-locked-out-of-thermostats-during-energy-emergency.

635 Justine Calma, "A utility company locked thousands of customers out of their smart thermostats in Colorado."

636 Justine Calma, "A utility company locked thousands of customers out of their smart thermostats in Colorado."

637 See, for example, Klaus Schwab, "Globalization 4.0 will help us tackle climate change. Here's how," World Economic Forum, weforum.org, January 14, 2019, https://www.weforum.org/agenda/2019/01/globalization-4-0-will-help-us-

tackle-climate-change-here-s-how.

638 Mark Smith, "Quantum computing: Definition, facts & uses," Live Science, livescience.com, March 18, 2022, https://www.livescience.com/quantum-computing.

639 Scott Aaronson, "What Makes Quantum Computing So Hard to Explain?" *WIRED*, wired.com, June 13, 2021, https://www.wired.com/story/what-makes-quantum-computing-so-hard-to-explain.

640 Jory Denny, "What is an algorithm? How computers know what to do with data," *The Conversation*, theconversation.com, October 16, 2020, https://theconversation.com/what-is-an-algorithm-how-computers-know-what-to-do-with-data-146665.

641 Lucas Downey, "What an Algorithm Is and Implications for Trading," *Investopedia*, May 27, 2022, https://www.investopedia.com/terms/a/algorithm.asp.

642 Jory Denny, "What is an algorithm? How computers know what to do with data."

643 Jory Denny, "What is an algorithm? How computers know what to do with data."

644 Sara Brown, "Machine Learning, Explained," MIT Sloan School of Management, mitsloan.mit.edu, April 21, 2021, https://mitsloan.mit.edu/ideas-made-to-matter/machine-learning-explained.

645 Sara Brown, "Machine Learning, Explained."

646 Sara Brown, "Machine Learning, Explained."

647 Archil Cheishvili, "The Future Of Artificial General Intelligence," *Forbes*, July 16, 2021, https://www.forbes.com/sites/forbestechcouncil/2021/07/16/the-future-of-artificial-general-intelligence/?sh=1c8dfa6a3ba9.

648 Archil Cheishvili, "The Future Of Artificial General Intelligence."

649 Gary Marcus, "Artificial General Intelligence Is Not as Imminent as You Might Think," *Scientific American*, July 1, 2022, https://www.scientificamerican.com/article/artificial-general-intelligence-is-not-as-imminent-as-you-might-think1.

650 See "Artificial Intelligence Aids Consumer Lending, but With Risks," Fitch Ratings, fitchratings.com, February 7, 2022, https://www.fitchratings.com/research/structured-finance/artificial-intelligence-aids-consumer-lending-with-risks-07-02-2022.

651 Lael Brainard, "Supporting Responsible Use of AI and Equitable Outcomes in Financial Services," speech before the AI Academic Symposium, January 12, 2021, https://www.federalreserve.gov/newsevents/speech/brainard20210112a.htm.

652 Lael Brainard, "Supporting Responsible Use of AI and Equitable Outcomes in Financial Services."

653 Lael Brainard, "Supporting Responsible Use of AI and Equitable Outcomes in Financial Services."

654 Stephanie Hughes, "Bank of Canada taps quantum computing startup to tackle complex financial problems," *Financial Post*, April 18, 2022, https://financialpost.com/fp-finance/cryptocurrency/bank-of-canada-taps-quantum-computing-startup-to-tackle-complex-financial-problems.

655 Stephanie Hughes, "Bank of Canada taps quantum computing startup to tackle complex financial problems."

656 Stephanie Hughes, "Bank of Canada taps quantum computing startup to tackle complex financial problems."

657 Andrea Lorenzoni, "Transforming claims and underwriting with AI," Accenture, accenture.com, August 3, 2022, https://www.accenture.com/us-en/insightsnew/insurance/ai-transforming-claims-underwriting.

658 "How can AI help ESG investing?" S&P Global, spglobal.com, February 25, 2020, https://www.spglobal.com/en/research-insights/articles/how-can-ai-help-esg-investing.

659 "How can AI help ESG investing?" S&P Global.

660 Moody's ESG Solutions, "Moody's Launches First-of-Its-Kind ESG Score Predictor to Provide Transparency on ESG Risk for Millions of SMEs Worldwide," BusinessWire, press release, July 13, 2021, https://www.businesswire.com/news/home/20210713005792/en/Moodys-Launches-First-of-Its-Kind-ESG-Score-Predictor-to-Provide-Transparency-on-ESG-Risk-for-Millions-of-SMEs-Worldwide.

661 Robert Muggah, "How smart tech helps cities fight terrorism and crime," World Economic Forum, weforum.org, June 15, 2018, https://www.weforum.org/agenda/2018/06/cities-crime-data-agile-security-robert-muggah.

662 Robert Muggah, "How smart tech helps cities fight terrorism and crime."

663 "Deep Learning," IBM Cloud Education, IBM, ibm.com, May 1, 2020, https://www.ibm.com/cloud/learn/deep-learning.

664 "Deep Learning," IBM Cloud Education.

665 "Neural Networks," IBM Cloud Education, IBM, ibm.com, August 17, 2020, https://www.ibm.com/cloud/learn/neural-networks.

666 "Deep Learning," IBM Cloud Education.

667 Robert Muggah, "How smart tech helps cities fight terrorism and crime."

668 Isabelle Qian et al., "Four Takeaways From a Times Investigation Into China's Expanding Surveillance State," *New York Times*, updated July 26, 2022, https://

www.nytimes.com/2022/06/21/world/asia/china-surveillance-investigation.
html.

669 Isabelle Qian et al., "Four Takeaways From a Times Investigation Into China's
Expanding Surveillance State."

670 Isabelle Qian et al., "Four Takeaways From a Times Investigation Into China's
Expanding Surveillance State."

671 Isabelle Qian et al., "Four Takeaways From a Times Investigation Into China's
Expanding Surveillance State."

672 Isabelle Qian et al., "Four Takeaways From a Times Investigation Into China's
Expanding Surveillance State."

673 Isabelle Qian et al., "Four Takeaways From a Times Investigation Into China's
Expanding Surveillance State."

674 See, for example, Lofred Madzou et al., "This is best practice for using facial recognition in law enforcement," World Economic Forum, weforum.org, October 5,
2021, https://www.weforum.org/agenda/2021/10/facial-recognition-technology-
law-enforcement-human-rights.

675 Lofred Madzou et al., "This is best practice for using facial recognition in law
enforcement."

676 Lofred Madzou et al., "This is best practice for using facial recognition in law
enforcement."

677 Klaus Schwab, "Now is the time for a 'great reset,'" World Economic Forum,
weforum.org, June 3, 2020, https://www.weforum.org/agenda/2020/06/now-is-
the-time-for-a-great-reset.

678 Anthony Leonardi, "New York Post stuck in 'Twitter jail' one week after publishing
Hunter Biden laptop stories," Washington Examiner, October 21, 2020, https://
www.washingtonexaminer.com/news/new-york-post-stuck-in-twitter-jail-one-
week-after-publishing-hunter-biden-laptop-stories.

679 Nandita Bose, "Exclusive: White House working with Facebook and Twitter to
tackle anti-vaxxers," Reuters, reuters.com, February 19, 2021, https://www.reuters.
com/article/us-health-coronavirus-white-house-exclus/exclusive-white-house-
working-with-facebook-and-twitter-to-tackle-anti-vaxxers-idUSKBN2AJ1SW.

680 Vivek Ramaswamy and Jed Rubenfeld, "Twitter Becomes a Tool of Government
Censorship," Wall Street Journal, August 17, 2022, https://www.wsj.com/articles/
twitter-becomes-a-tool-of-government-censors-alex-berenson-twitter-facebook-
ban-covid-misinformation-first-amendment-psaki-murthy-section-230-antitrust-
11660732095.

681 "Censorship Coordination Deepens," Editorial Board, *Wall Street Journal*, July 16, 2021, https://www.wsj.com/articles/censorship-coordination-deepens-11626474643.

682 See David B. McGarry, "The federal government has been caught spying on American citizens (again)," The Center Square, March 29, 2022, https://www.thecentersquare.com/opinion/op-ed-the-federal-government-has-been-caught-spying-on-american-citizens-again/article_e9e8bb50-af7e-11ec-8301-ef4de84ef8e4.html.

683 "Dr. Rand Paul Sends Letter to the NSA Demanding an Investigation on the Spying and Unmasking of Tucker Carlson," Office of Senator Rand Paul, press release, July 12, 2021, https://www.paul.senate.gov/news/dr-rand-paul-sends-letter-nsa-demanding-investigation-spying-and-unmasking-tucker-carlson.

684 For example, see "NSA Spying Complaint," ACLU, aclu.org, last accessed September 23, 2022, https://www.aclu.org/legal-document/nsa-spying-complaint.

685 See "Trump Really Was Spied on," *Wall Street Journal*, wsj.com, February 14, 2022, https://www.wsj.com/articles/donald-trump-really-was-spied-on-2016-clinton-campaign-john-durham-court-filing-11644878973.

686 See Kaylee McGhee, "Yes, Hillary Clinton spied on Donald Trump—while he was president," *Washington Examiner*, washingtonexaminer.com, February 13, 2022, https://www.washingtonexaminer.com/opinion/yes-hillary-clinton-spied-on-donald-trump-while-he-was-president.

687 See Margot Cleveland, "IG Report Proves Obama Administration Spied On Trump Campaign Big Time," *The Federalist*, January 28, 2020, https://thefederalist.com/2020/01/28/ig-report-proves-obama-administration-spied-on-trump-campaign-big-time.

688 Marisa Iati, "Ocasio-Cortez wants to ax Homeland Security. Some conservatives didn't want it to begin with," *Washington Post*, July 11, 2019, https://www.washingtonpost.com/history/2019/07/11/ocasio-cortez-wants-axe-homeland-security-some-conservatives-didnt-want-it-begin-with.

689 "Artificial Intelligence: On a mission to Make Clinical Drug Development Faster and Smarter," Pfizer, phizer.com, accessed last on September 19, 2022, https://www.pfizer.com/news/articles/artificial_intelligence_on_a_mission_to_make_clinical_drug_development_faster_and_smarter#:~:text=AI%20could%20assist%20pharma%20companies,that%20support%20any%20pharmaceutical%20product.

690 See Luis Voloch, "How Machine Learning Can Unlock Cures For Tomorrow's

Diseases," *Forbes*, May 5, 2021, https://www.forbes.com/sites/forbestechcouncil/2021/05/05/how-machine-learning-can-unlock-cures-for-tomorrows-diseases/?sh=11bfca926a25.

691 Karthik Krishnan, "5 technologies that will transform our lives," World Economic Forum, weforum.org, August 15, 2022, https://www.weforum.org/agenda/2022/08/these-five-key-technologies-will-transform-our-lives.

692 Max Tegmark, *Life 3.0: Being Human in the Age of Artificial Intelligence* (Knopf Doubleday, 2017, p. 100).

693 Oluwakemi Adesina et al., "Embracing Biological Solutions to the Sustainable Energy Challenge," Chem, Cell Press, cell.com, https://www.cell.com/chem/pdf/S2451-9294(16)30274-1.pdf.

694 I highly recommend you read the work of Alex Epstein if you're interested in learning more about affordable energy. See, for example, Alex Epstein, *The Moral Case for Fossil Fuels* (Portfolio, 2014).

695 Kai-Fu Lee, "The Third Revolution in Warfare," *The Atlantic*, September 11, 2021, https://www.theatlantic.com/technology/archive/2021/09/i-weapons-are-third-revolution-warfare/620013.

696 Kai-Fu Lee, "The Third Revolution in Warfare."

697 Kai-Fu Lee, "The Third Revolution in Warfare."

698 Max Tegmark, *Life 3.0: Being Human in the Age of Artificial Intelligence*.

699 Federico Berruti, Pieter Nel, and Rob Whiteman, "An executive primer on artificial general intelligence," McKinsey and Company, mckinsey.com, April 29, 2020, https://www.mckinsey.com/capabilities/operations/our-insights/an-executive-primer-on-artificial-general-intelligence.

700 Stephen Johnson, "The Turing test: AI still hasn't passed the 'imitation game,'" Big Think, bigthink.com, March 7, 2022, https://bigthink.com/the-future/turing-test-imitation-game.

701 Alan Turing, "Computing Machinery and Intelligence," *MIND* (Volume 59, No. 246, October 1950), https://tinyurl.com/3kpnxk9y.

702 Will Oremus, "Google's AI passed a famous test—and showed how the test is broken," *Washington Post*, June 17, 2022, https://www.washingtonpost.com/technology/2022/06/17/google-ai-lamda-turing-test.

703 Nitasha Tiku, "The Google engineer who thinks the company's AI has come to life," *Washington Post*, June 11, 2022, https://www.washingtonpost.com/technology/2022/06/11/google-ai-lamda-blake-lemoine.

704 Nitasha Tiku, "The Google engineer who thinks the company's AI has come to life."

705 Nitasha Tiku, "The Google engineer who thinks the company's AI has come to life."

706 Nitasha Tiku, "The Google engineer who thinks the company's AI has come to life."

707 Nitasha Tiku, "The Google engineer who thinks the company's AI has come to life."

708 Will Oremus, "Google's AI passed a famous test—and showed how the test is broken."

709 Will Oremus, "Google's AI passed a famous test—and showed how the test is broken."

710 Will Oremus, "Google's AI passed a famous test—and showed how the test is broken."

711 Will Oremus, "Google's AI passed a famous test—and showed how the test is broken."

712 Louis Rosenberg, "Mind of its own: Will 'general AI' be like an alien invasion?" Big Think, bigthink.com, February 23, 2022, https://bigthink.com/the-future/general-ai-artificial-intelligence.

713 Matt McFarland, "Elon Musk: 'With artificial intelligence we are summoning the demon,'" *Washington Post*, washingtonpost.com, October 24, 2014, https://www.washingtonpost.com/news/innovations/wp/2014/10/24/elon-musk-with-artificial-intelligence-we-are-summoning-the-demon.

714 Rory Cellan-Jones, "Stephen Hawking warns artificial intelligence could end mankind," BBC, bbc.com, December 2, 2014, https://www.bbc.com/news/technology-30290540.

715 Rory Cellan-Jones, "Stephen Hawking warns artificial intelligence could end mankind."

716 Sam Harris, "Can We Build AI Without Losing Control Over It?" TED Talks, posted to YouTube on October 19, 2016, https://youtu.be/8nt3edWLgIg.

717 Sam Harris, "Can We Build AI Without Losing Control Over It?"

718 Sam Harris, "Can We Build AI Without Losing Control Over It?"

719 Sam Harris, "Can We Build AI Without Losing Control Over It?"

720 Sam Harris, "Can We Build AI Without Losing Control Over It?"

721 Hein de Haan, "The AI Box Experiment," Medium, medium.com, October 1, 2020, https://medium.com/the-singularity/the-ai-box-experiment-c92a0a389eb7.

722 Sidney Gray, "How a Superintelligent AI Could Convince You That You're a

Simulation," *VICE*, vice.com, May 6, 2015, https://www.vice.com/en/article/539ajz/the-superintelligent-ai-says-youre-just-a-daydream.

723 Sidney Gray, "How a Superintelligent AI Could Convince You That You're a Simulation."

724 "Our Team," Machine Intelligence Research Institute, intelligence.org, accessed September 24, 2022, https://intelligence.org/team.

725 Hein de Haan, "The AI Box Experiment."

Chapter 7: A "Second Wave of Human Evolution"

726 Klaus Schwab and Mohammad Abdullah Al Gergawi, "Narrating the Future," discussion at The Great Narrative conference, hosted by the World Economic Forum and Government of the United Arab Emirates, November 10, 2021, https://www.weforum.org/events/the-great-narrative-2021/sessions/a-call-for-the-great-narrative.

727 Klaus Schwab and Mohammad Abdullah Al Gergawi, "Narrating the Future."

728 Klaus Schwab and Mohammad Abdullah Al Gergawi, "Narrating the Future."

729 Pranshu Verma, "Your next sexual harassment training could be in virtual reality," *Washington Post*, April 19 2022, https://www.washingtonpost.com/technology/2022/04/19/virtual-reality-sexual-harassment-training.

730 Pranshu Verma, "Your next sexual harassment training could be in virtual reality."

731 Pranshu Verma, "Your next sexual harassment training could be in virtual reality."

732 Pranshu Verma, "Your next sexual harassment training could be in virtual reality."

733 Pranshu Verma, "Your next sexual harassment training could be in virtual reality."

734 Pranshu Verma, "Your next sexual harassment training could be in virtual reality."

735 Liam Farrell, "UMD, Google Unit Partner on Developing VR Training Platform for Police," *Maryland Today*, University of Maryland, October 27, 2021, https://today.umd.edu/umd-google-unit-partner-on-developing-vr-training-platform-for-police.

736 Liam Farrell, "UMD, Google Unit Partner on Developing VR Training Platform for Police."

737 Liam Farrell, "UMD, Google Unit Partner on Developing VR Training Platform for Police."

738 Eric Swedlund, "Anti-Racism Project Uses Virtual Reality to Let People 'Walk in Someone Else's Shoes,'" news.arizona.edu, University of Arizona, https://news.arizona.edu/story/anti-racism-project-uses-virtual-reality-let-people-walk-someone-elses-shoes.

739 Pranshu Verma, "Your next sexual harassment training could be in virtual reality."

740 Brad Polumbo, "George Floyd Riots Caused Record-Setting $2 Billion in Damage, New Report Says. Here's Why the True Cost Is Even Higher," FEE, fee.org, September 16, 2020, https://bit.ly/3xxs0l5.

741 See "Fatal Force" database, *Washington Post*, washingtonpost.com, last accessed September 17, 2022, https://www.washingtonpost.com/graphics/investigations/police-shootings-database.

742 Justyn Melrose, "Suspect killed in officer-involved shooting outside of Greensboro police headquarters identified; officer in hospital," WGHP-TV, myfox8.com, articled updated August 29, 2021, https://myfox8.com/news/north-carolina/piedmont-triad/suspect-killed-in-officer-involved-shooting-outside-of-greens-boro-police-headquarters-identified.

743 Ali Saeed Bin Harmal Al Dhaheri and Mohamad Ali Hamade, "Experiential learning and VR will reshape the future of education," World Economic Forum, weforum.org, May 23, 2022, https://www.weforum.org/agenda/2022/05/the-future-of-education-is-in-experiential-learning-and-vr.

744 Ali Saeed Bin Harmal Al Dhaheri and Mohamad Ali Hamade, "Experiential learning and VR will reshape the future of education."

745 Ali Saeed Bin Harmal Al Dhaheri and Mohamad Ali Hamade, "Experiential learning and VR will reshape the future of education."

746 Ali Saeed Bin Harmal Al Dhaheri and Mohamad Ali Hamade, "Experiential learning and VR will reshape the future of education."

747 Ali Saeed Bin Harmal Al Dhaheri and Mohamad Ali Hamade, "Experiential learning and VR will reshape the future of education."

748 "Celebrate Black History Month in VR," Meta Quest, occulus.com, accessed February 28, 2022, https://www.oculus.com/blog/black-history-month-2022.

749 "Celebrate Black History Month in VR," Meta Quest.

750 "Celebrate Black History Month in VR," Meta Quest.

751 "Celebrate Black History Month in VR," Meta Quest.

752 "Expanding Our World," Neuralink, neuralink.com, accessed September 19, 2022, https://neuralink.com/about.

753 "Engineering with the Brain," Neuralink, neuralink.com, accessed September 19, 2022, https://neuralink.com/applications.

754 "Interfacing with the Brain," Neuralink, neuralink.com, accessed September 19, 2022, https://neuralink.com/approach.

755 "Interfacing with the Brain," Neuralink.

756 "Interfacing with the Brain," Neuralink.

757 "Engineering with the Brain," Neuralink.

758 "Engineering with the Brain," Neuralink.

759 Albert Murdry, MD, PhD; Mara Mills, PhD, "The Early History of the Cochlear Implant," *JAMA Network*, May 2013, https://jamanetwork.com/journals/jamao-tolaryngology/fullarticle/1688121.

760 Daniel Engber, "The Neurologist Who Hacked His Brain – And Almost Lost His Mind," *WIRED*, January 26, 2016, https://www.wired.com/2016/01/phil-kennedy-mind-control-computer.

761 "Deep brain stimulation," Mayo Clinic, September 03, 2021, https://www.mayoc-linic.org/tests-procedures/deep-brain-stimulation/about/pac-20384562.

762 "Engineering with the Brain," Neuralink.

763 "Engineering with the Brain," Neuralink.

764 See Natasha Bertrand and Eric Wolff, "Nuclear weapons agency breached amid massive cyber onslaught," *Politico*, December 17, 2020, https://www.politico.com/news/2020/12/17/nuclear-agency-hacked-officials-inform-congress-447855.

765 Klaus Schwab and Thierry Malleret, *The Great Narrative* (Forum Publishing, 2021).

766 Klaus Schwab, *The Fourth Industrial Revolution* (Currency, 2017).

767 See interview between Klaus Schwab and Sergey Brin, "Davos 2017 - An Insight, An Idea with Sergey Brin," January 19, 2017, World Economic Forum's 2017 Annual Meeting, video available on youtube.com, https://youtu.be/ffvu6Mr1SVc.

768 Moises Velasquez-Manoff, "The Brain Implants that Could Change Humanity," *New York Times*, August 28, 2020, https://www.nytimes.com/2020/08/28/opinion/sunday/brain-machine-artificial-intelligence.html.

769 Moises Velasquez-Manoff, "The Brain Implants that Could Change Humanity."

770 Moises Velasquez-Manoff, "The Brain Implants that Could Change Humanity."

771 Moises Velasquez-Manoff, "The Brain Implants that Could Change Humanity."

772 Moises Velasquez-Manoff, "The Brain Implants that Could Change Humanity."

773 Moises Velasquez-Manoff, "The Brain Implants that Could Change Humanity."

774 Moises Velasquez-Manoff, "The Brain Implants that Could Change Humanity."

775 Moises Velasquez-Manoff, "The Brain Implants that Could Change Humanity."

776 Sean Fleming, "Could this 'pacemaker for the brain' be the solution to severe depression?" World Economic Forum, weforum.org, October 8, 2021, https://www.weforum.org/agenda/2021/10/brain-implant-could-cure-depression.

777   Lindsey Dodgson, "Scientists have created brain implants that could boost our memory by up to 30%," World Economic Forum, weforum.org, November 16, 2017, https://www.weforum.org/agenda/2017/11/scientists-have-created-brain-implants-that-could-boost-our-memory-by-up-to-30.

778   June Javelosa, "Your smartphone could soon translate your thoughts into text," World Economic Forum, weforum.org, May 4, 2017, https://www.weforum.org/agenda/2017/05/in-5-years-your-smartphone-might-be-able-to-read-your-mind.

779   Dimitra Blana and Andrew Jackson, "Brain implants can let paralysed people move again," World Economic Forum, weforum.org, July 4, 2016, https://www.weforum.org/agenda/2016/07/brain-implants-can-let-paralysed-people-move-again.

780   Judith L. Fridovich-Keil, "Gene Editing," *Encyclopedia Britannica*, last accessed September 19, 2022, https://www.britannica.com/science/gene-editing.

781   Judith L. Fridovich-Keil, "Gene Editing."

782   Aparna Vidyasagar and Nicoletta Lanese, "What is CRISPR?" Live Science, livescience.com, October 20, 2021, https://www.livescience.com/58790-crispr-explained.html.

783   Arlene Weintraub, "Stanford team deploys CRISPR gene editing to fight COVID-19," Fierce Biotech, fiercebiotech.com, June 5, 2020, https://www.fiercebiotech.com/research/stanford-team-deploys-crispr-gene-editing-to-fight-covid-19.

784   Klaus Schwab, *The Fourth Industrial Revolution*.

785   Klaus Schwab, *The Fourth Industrial Revolution*.

786   Klaus Schwab, *The Fourth Industrial Revolution*.

787   Hermione Dace, "Gene Editing in Food Production: Charting a Way Forward," Tony Blair Institute for Global Change, March 17, 2021, https://institute.global/policy/gene-editing-food-production-charting-way-forward.

788   Hermione Dace, "Gene Editing in Food Production: Charting a Way Forward."

789   Hermione Dace, "Gene Editing in Food Production: Charting a Way Forward."

790   Klaus Schwab, *The Fourth Industrial Revolution*.

791   Klaus Schwab, *The Fourth Industrial Revolution*.

792   Klaus Schwab, *The Fourth Industrial Revolution*.

793   Khristopher Brooks, "Bank of America offers zero-down mortgage in minority communities," CBS News, cbsnews.com, September 3, 2022, https://www.cbsnews.com/news/bank-of-america-black-hispanic-mortgage.

794   Khristopher Brooks, "Bank of America offers zero-down mortgage in minority communities."

795 Khristopher Brooks, "Bank of America offers zero-down mortgage in minority communities."

796 For example, see Jonathan Walter, lead author, *Measuring Stakeholder Capitalism: Toward Common Metrics and Consistent Reporting of Sustainable Value Creation*, World Economic Forum, September 2020, http://www3.weforum.org/docs/WEF_IBC_Measuring_Stakeholder_Capitalism_Report_2020.pdf.

797 Klaus Schwab and Mohammad Abdullah Al Gergawi, "Narrating the Future."

798 See "*The Fourth Industrial Revolution*, by Klaus Schwab," World Economic Forum, weforum.org, accessed September 20, 2022, https://www.weforum.org/about/the-fourth-industrial-revolution-by-klaus-schwab.

799 Klaus Schwab, *The Fourth Industrial Revolution*.

800 Klaus Schwab, *The Fourth Industrial Revolution*.

801 Nayef Al-Rodhan, "Will biology change what it means to be human?" World Economic Forum, weforum.org, November 10, 2014, https://www.weforum.org/agenda/2014/11/synthetic-biology-designing-our-existence.

802 Nicholas Davis, "What is the Fourth Industrial Revolution?" World Economic Forum, weforum.org, January 19, 2016, https://www.weforum.org/agenda/2016/01/what-is-the-fourth-industrial-revolution.

803 Simone Schurle, "Here are five things to know about the future of being human," World Economic Forum, weforum.org, May 24, 2018, https://www.weforum.org/agenda/2018/05/5-things-know-future-being-human-enhanced.

804 See comments by Abdullah Al Gergawi in Klaus Schwab and Mohammad Abdullah Al Gergawi, "Narrating the Future."

805 Klaus Schwab, *The Fourth Industrial Revolution*.

806 Klaus Schwab, *The Fourth Industrial Revolution*.

807 Klaus Schwab, *The Fourth Industrial Revolution*.

808 Klaus Schwab, *The Fourth Industrial Revolution*.

809 "Ray Kurzweil," *Encyclopedia Britannica*, britannica.com, accessed September 20, 2022, https://www.britannica.com/biography/Raymond-Kurzweil.

810 Ray Kurzweil, *The Age of Spiritual Machines* (Penguin Publishing, 1999).

811 Ray Kurzweil, *The Age of Spiritual Machines*.

812 See, for example, "FACT SHEET: President Biden to Launch a National Biotechnology and Biomanufacturing Initiative," Office of the White House, whitehouse.gov, September 12, 2022, https://www.whitehouse.gov/briefing-room/statements-releases/2022/09/12/fact-sheet-president-biden-to-launch-a-national-biotechnology-and-biomanufacturing-initiative.

Chapter 8: Joe Biden and the Fundamental Transformation of the West

813   "About Us," Business Roundtable, accessed April 15, 2022, https://www.business-roundtable.org/about-us.

814   "About Us," Business Roundtable.

815   "Business Roundtable Redefines the Purpose of a Corporation to Promote 'An Economy That Serves All Americans,'" Business Roundtable, August 19, 2019, https://www.businessroundtable.org/business-roundtable-redefines-the-purpose-of-a-corporation-to-promote-an-economy-that-serves-all-americans.

816   "Statement on the Purpose of a Corporation," Business Roundtable, August 19, 2019, https://s3.amazonaws.com/brt.org/BRT-StatementonthePurposeofaCorporationJuly2021.pdf, emphasis added.

817   "Statement on the Purpose of a Corporation," Business Roundtable. Emphasis in quote appears in the original manuscript.

818   "Statement on the Purpose of a Corporation," Business Roundtable.

819   See the full quote in Noah Kim, "No, Biden doesn't want to dissolve the stock market," PolitiFact, September 23, 2020, https://www.politifact.com/factchecks/2020/sep/23/facebook-posts/no-biden-doesnt-want-to-dissolve-stock-market.

820   Rebecca Ungarino, "Here are 9 fascinating facts to know about BlackRock, the world's largest asset manager," Business Insider, March 10, 2022, https://www.businessinsider.com/what-to-know-about-blackrock-larry-fink-biden-cabinet-facts-2020-12.

821   Joe Biden, "Remarks by President Biden Before Business Roundtable's CEO Quarterly Meeting," March 21, 2022, posted to WhiteHouse.gov, accessed April 15, 2022, https://www.whitehouse.gov/briefing-room/speeches-remarks/2022/03/21/remarks-by-president-biden-before-business-roundtables-ceo-quarterly-meeting.

822   Tim Smart, "Inflation Soared to 40-Year High of 8.5% in March," U.S. News & World Report, April 12, 2022, https://www.usnews.com/news/national-news/articles/2022-04-12/inflation-soared-to-40-year-high-of-8-5-in-march#:~:text=Inflation%20Soared%20to%2040-Year%20High%20of%208.5%25%20in,that%20are%20at%20their%20highest%20in%2040%20years.?msclkid=289f0e42bccc11ec95159aa831e6336e.

823   Joe Biden, "Remarks by President Biden Before Business Roundtable's CEO Quarterly Meeting."

824   Joe Biden, "Remarks by President Biden Before Business Roundtable's CEO Quarterly Meeting."

825   "Organization," World Government Summit, worldgovernmentsummit.org, last accessed April 15, 2022, https://www.worldgovernmentsummit.org/about.

826   "Organization," World Government Summit.

827   "Leadership," World Government Summit, worldgovernmentsummit.org, last accessed April 15, 2022, https://www.worldgovernmentsummit.org/about/leadership.

828   Klaus Schwab and Mohammad Abdullah Al Gergawi, "Narrating the Future," discussion at The Great Narrative conference, hosted by the World Economic Forum and Government of the United Arab Emirates, November 10, 2021, https://www.weforum.org/events/the-great-narrative-2021/sessions/a-call-for-the-great-narrative.

829   "Are We Ready for a New World Order?" World Government Summit, worldgovernmentsummit.org, last accessed April 15, 2022, https://www.worldgovernmentsummit.org/events/2022/session-detail/a0f3z0are-we-ready-for-a-new-world-order-.

830   Becky Anderson et al., "Are We Ready for a New World Order?" panel discussion, World Government Summit, March 29, 2022. See video of the panel at "World Government Summit 2022 Livestream: Day 1," World Government Summit, YouTube.com, posted March 29, 2022, https://youtu.be/JTTDzH2A1tM.

831   Becky Anderson et al., "Are We Ready for a New World Order?"

832   Becky Anderson et al., "Are We Ready for a New World Order?"

833   Becky Anderson et al., "Are We Ready for a New World Order?"

834   Joe Biden, "Remarks by President Biden Before Business Roundtable's CEO Quarterly Meeting."

835   Becky Anderson et al., "Are We Ready for a New World Order?"

836   Becky Anderson et al., "Are We Ready for a New World Order?"

837   Klaus Schwab, "Our World Today … Why Government Must Act Now?" speech before the World Government Summit, March 29, 2022, https://www.worldgovernmentsummit.org/events/2022/session-detail/a0f3z0our-world-today-why-government-must-act-now-.

838   Klaus Schwab, "Our World Today … Why Government Must Act Now?"

839   Richard Threlfall et al., *The Time Has Come: The KPMG Survey of Sustainability Reporting 2020*, KPMG, December 2020, https://assets.kpmg/content/dam/kpmg/xx/pdf/2020/11/the-time-has-come.pdf.

840   Richard Threlfall et al., *The Time Has Come: The KPMG Survey of Sustainability Reporting 2020*.

841 Richard Threlfall et al., *The Time Has Come: The KPMG Survey of Sustainability Reporting 2020*.

842 Kyle Danish, Michael Platner, and Arthur Singletary, "SEC Unveils Landmark Climate Disclosures Proposal," *National Law Review* (online), March 22, 2022, https://www.natlawreview.com/article/sec-unveils-landmark-climate-disclosures-proposal.

843 Michael Cohn, "Companies prepare for SEC climate-related disclosures," *Accounting Today*, March 7, 2023, https://www.accountingtoday.com/news/companies-prepare-for-sec-climate-related-disclosures.

844 Kyle Danish, Michael Platner, and Arthur Singletary, "SEC Unveils Landmark Climate Disclosures Proposal."

845 Office of the Spokesperson, "Launching the First Movers Coalition at the 2021 UN Climate Change Conference," U.S. Department of State, November 4, 2021, https://www.state.gov/launching-the-first-movers-coalition-at-the-2021-un-climate-change-conference.

846 Office of the Spokesperson, "Launching the First Movers Coalition at the 2021 UN Climate Change Conference."

847 Office of the Spokesperson, "First Movers Coalition Announces Expansion," U.S. Department of State, November 9, 2022, https://www.state.gov/first-movers-coalition-announces-expansion.

848 Davey Alba, "The baseless 'Great Reset' conspiracy theory rises again," *New York Times*, November 17, 2021, https://www.nytimes.com/live/2020/11/17/world/covid-19-coronavirus#the-baseless-great-reset-conspiracy-theory-rises-again.

849 Sonny Mazzone, "Biden Administration Suspends Rule Protecting Businesses from Banking Discrimination," *Reason*, Feb. 2, 2021, https://reason.com/2021/02/11/biden-administration-suspends-rule-protecting-businesses-from-banking-discrimination..

850 See Chapter 1 for a detailed analysis of this problem.

851 Sonny Mazzone, "Biden Administration Suspends Rule Protecting Businesses from Banking Discrimination."

852 See Justin Haskins, "John Kerry reveals Biden's devotion to radical 'Great Reset' movement," *The Hill*, December 3, 2020, https://thehill.com/opinion/energy-environment/528482-john-kerry-reveals-bidens-devotion-to-radical-great-reset-movement.

853 "FACT SHEET: President Biden and G7 Leaders Launch Build Back Better World (B3W) Partnership," WhiteHouse.gov, June 12, 2021, https://www.white-

house.gov/briefing-room/statements-releases/2021/06/12/fact-sheet-president-biden-and-g7-leaders-launch-build-back-better-world-b3w-partnership.

854 "FACT SHEET: President Biden and G7 Leaders Launch Build Back Better World (B3W) Partnership," WhiteHouse.gov.

855 "FACT SHEET: President Biden and G7 Leaders Launch Build Back Better World (B3W) Partnership," WhiteHouse.gov.

856 See Chapter 1.

857 Alex Bevan et al., "EU Signals New Mandatory ESG Due Diligence for Companies Operating in EU," Shearman & Sterling, shearman.com, April 2021, https://www.shearman.com/Perspectives/2021/04/New-Mandatory-Human-Rights-Environmental-and-Governance-Due-Diligence-for-Companies-in-EU-Market.

858 Alex Bevan et al., "EU Signals New Mandatory ESG Due Diligence for Companies Operating in EU."

859 Alex Bevan et al., "EU Signals New Mandatory ESG Due Diligence for Companies Operating in EU."

860 "European Commission Proposes Far-Reaching Human Rights and Environmental Due Diligence Obligations," Gibson Dunn, gibsondunn.com, March 11, 2022, https://www.gibsondunn.com/european-commission-proposes-far-reaching-human-rights-and-environmental-due-diligence-obligations.

861 "European Commission Proposes Far-Reaching Human Rights and Environmental Due Diligence Obligations," Gibson Dunn.

862 "European Commission Proposes Far-Reaching Human Rights and Environmental Due Diligence Obligations," Gibson Dunn.

863 "Council adopts position on due diligence rules for large companies," Council of the European Union, consilium.europa.eu, December 1, 2022, https://www.consilium.europa.eu/en/press/press-releases/2022/12/01/council-adopts-position-on-due-diligence-rules-for-large-companies.

864 "European Commission Proposes Far-Reaching Human Rights and Environmental Due Diligence Obligations," Gibson Dunn.

865 Jonathan Walter, lead author, *Measuring Stakeholder Capitalism: Toward Common Metrics and Consistent Reporting of Sustainable Value Creation*, World Economic Forum, September 2020, http://www3.weforum.org/docs/WEF_IBC_Measuring_Stakeholder_Capitalism_Report_2020.pdf.

866 Jonathan Walter, lead author, *Measuring Stakeholder Capitalism: Toward Common Metrics and Consistent Reporting of Sustainable Value Creation*.

867 Jonathan Walter, lead author, *Measuring Stakeholder Capitalism: Toward Common*

Metrics and Consistent Reporting of Sustainable Value Creation.

868 "Moody's Launches First-of-Its-Kind ESG Score Predictor to Provide Transparency on ESG Risk for Millions of SMEs Worldwide," Moody's Investors Service, press release published by BusinessWire, July 13, 2021, https://www.businesswire.com/news/home/20210713005792/en/Moodys-Launches-First-of-Its-Kind-ESG-Score-Predictor-to-Provide-Transparency-on-ESG-Risk-for-Millions-of-SMEs-Worldwide.

869 "Moody's Launches First-of-Its-Kind ESG Score Predictor to Provide Transparency on ESG Risk for Millions of SMEs Worldwide," Moody's Investors Service.

870 "Moody's Launches First-of-Its-Kind ESG Score Predictor to Provide Transparency on ESG Risk for Millions of SMEs Worldwide," Moody's Investors Service.

871 "Comprehensive ESG Coverage," Moody's Investors Service, moodys.com, accessed April 19, 2022, https://ma.moodys.com/MESG-Comprehensive-Coverage-Pd-Eng.html?gclid=CjwKCAjwu_mSBhAYEiwA5BBmf4CIpiB-VafLbIJAWiIV39ALesfof-lp8o76D4cwff3VwJcfkTU5cxoCV4sQAvD_BwE&gclsrc=aw.ds.

872 "Trusted ESG and Climate Risk Scoring," Moody's Investors Service, published 2020, accessed April 19, 2022, https://www.moodysanalytics.com/-/media/solutions/ESG-Score-Predictor.pdf.

873 Justin Haskins, "Are Financial Institutions Using ESG Social Credit Scores to Coerce Individuals, Small Businesses?" The Heartland Institute, Heartland.org, February 27, 2022, https://www.heartland.org/publications-resources/publications/financial-institutions-are-expanding-esg-social-credit-scores-to-target-individuals-small-businesses.

874 Justin Haskins, "Are Financial Institutions Using ESG Social Credit Scores to Coerce Individuals, Small Businesses?" citing Doug Craddock, "Lending Predictions 2022: From BNPL to ESG (and More)," FICO, fico.com, December 15, 2021, https://www.fico.com/blogs/lending-predictions-2022-bnpl-esg-and-more.

875 Justin Haskins, "Are Financial Institutions Using ESG Social Credit Scores to Coerce Individuals, Small Businesses?" citing Doug Craddock, "Lending Predictions 2022: From BNPL to ESG (and More)."

876 Justin Haskins, "Are Financial Institutions Using ESG Social Credit Scores to Coerce Individuals, Small Businesses?" citing Doug Craddock, "Lending Predictions 2022: From BNPL to ESG (and More)."

877 Justin Haskins, "Are Financial Institutions Using ESG Social Credit Scores to Coerce Individuals, Small Businesses?" citing Doug Craddock, "Lending Predic-

tions 2022: From BNPL to ESG (and More)."

878 "Bank of America to Open 600 More Merrill Edge Investment Centers," Bank of America, press release, bankofamerica.com, March 29, 2018, https://newsroom. bankofamerica.com/press-releases/consumer-banking/bank-america-open-600-more-merrill-edge-investment-centers#:~:text=Since%20its%20creation%20 in%202010,our%20full%20wealth%20management%20offering.

879 "ESG Integration: Investment-Led, Expert Driven," Building Stronger Portfolios series, JP Morgan Asset Management, July 2020, https://am.jpmorgan.com/ content/dam/jpm-am-aem/global/en/institutional/communications/lux-communication/JPMAM_ESG_Integration_Brochure.pdf.

880 "ESG Integration: Investment-Led, Expert Driven," Building Stronger Portfolios series, JP Morgan Asset Management.

881 Josh Levin, "Impact reporting for humans: A paradigm shift in ESG data can unlock individual investors," JP Morgan Private Bank, October 12, 2021, https:// privatebank.jpmorgan.com/gl/en/insights/investing/impact-reporting-for-humans-a-paradigm-shift-in-esg-data-can-unlock-individual-investors.

882 Josh Levin, "Impact reporting for humans: A paradigm shift in ESG data can unlock individual investors."

883 Palash Ghosh, "J.P. Morgan assets under management soar to record in 2021," *Pensions & Investments*, pionline.com, January 14, 2022, https://www.pionline. com/money-management/jp-morgan-assets-under-management-soar-record-2021.

884 "COP26: Together for Our Planet," United Nations, un.org, last accessed April 20, 2022, https://www.un.org/en/climatechange/cop26.

885 "COP26: Together for Our Planet," United Nations.

886 "COP26: Together for Our Planet," United Nations.

887 "COP26: Greta Thunberg tells protest that COP26 has been a 'failure,'" BBC News, November 5, 2021, https://www.bbc.com/news/uk-scotland-glasgow-west-59165781.

888 "COP26: Greta Thunberg tells protest that COP26 has been a 'failure,'" BBC News.

889 "COP26: Greta Thunberg tells protest that COP26 has been a 'failure,'" BBC News.

890 Christopher Hutton, "Greta Thunberg to world leaders: 'Shove your climate crisis up your arse,'" *Washington Examiner*, November 2, 2022, https://www.washingtonexaminer.com/news/greta-thunberg-shove-climate-crisis-up-arse.

891 Michael Bastasch, "Ocasio-Cortez's 'Green New Deal' Would Avert A 'Barely Detectable' Amount Of Global Warming. That's According To EPA's Climate Model," Daily Caller, January 7, 2019, https://dailycaller.com/2019/01/07/ocasio-cortez-green-new-deal-warming.

892 Pippa Stevens, "National average for a gallon of gas tops $4, the highest price at the pump since 2008," CNBC.com, March 6, 2022, https://www.cnbc.com/2022/03/06/national-average-for-a-gallon-of-gas-tops-4-the-highest-price-at-the-pump-since-2008.html.

893 "U.S. Regular All Formulations Retail Gasoline Prices," U.S. Energy Information Administration, accessed March 9, 2023, https://www.eia.gov/dnav/pet/hist/LeafHandler.ashx?n=pet&s=emm_epmr_pte_nus_dpg&f=m.

894 "Weekly California Regular All Formulations Retail Gasoline Prices," U.S. Energy Information Administration, accessed March 9, 2023, https://www.eia.gov/dnav/pet/hist/LeafHandler.ashx?n=PET&s=EMM_EPMR_PTE_SCA_DPG&f=W.

895 Rasmussen Reports, "70% Favor Increased U.S. Oil and Gas Production," rasmussenreports.com, March 7, 2022, https://www.rasmussenreports.com/public_content/politics/current_events/environment_energy/70_favor_increased_u_s_oil_and_gas_production.

896 Josh Lederman and Zoe Richards, "Biden administration to resume leasing for oil and gas drilling on federal lands," CNBC.com, April 15, 2022, https://www.cnbc.com/2022/04/15/biden-administration-to-resume-leasing-for-oil-and-gas-drilling-on-federal-lands.html.

897 "Biden plans a major withdrawal from the country's oil reserves to control gas prices," NPR.org, last updated March 31, 2022, https://www.npr.org/2022/03/31/1089887254/biden-considering-to-tap-oil-reserves-to-control-gas-prices.

898 Kevin O'Sullivan, "Cop26: Unprecedented sums pledged to global transition to net zero emissions," Irish Times, November 3, 2021, https://www.irishtimes.com/news/environment/cop26-unprecedented-sums-pledged-to-global-transition-to-net-zero-emissions-1.4718092.

899 Kevin O'Sullivan, "Cop26: Unprecedented sums pledged to global transition to net zero emissions," Irish Times.

900 "About Us," Glasgow Financial Alliance for Net Zero, gfanzero.org, accessed April 20, 2022, https://www.gfanzero.com/about.

901 "About Us," Glasgow Financial Alliance for Net Zero.

902 "About Us," Glasgow Financial Alliance for Net Zero.

903 "Membership," Glasgow Financial Alliance for Net Zero, accessed April 20, 2022, https://www.gfanzero.com/membership.

904 "Membership," Glasgow Financial Alliance for Net Zero.

905 Simon Jessop, "Carney, Kerry launch global finance plan to boost climate action," Reuters, April 21, 2021, https://www.reuters.com/business/sustainable-business/carney-kerry-launch-global-finance-plan-boost-climate-action-2021-04-21.

906 Simon Jessop, "Carney, Kerry launch global finance plan to boost climate action."

907 Adrian Monck, "World Economic Forum Appoints New Members to Board of Trustees," World Economic Forum, weforum.org, August 22, 2019, https://www.weforum.org/press/2019/08/world-economic-forum-appoints-new-members-to-board-of-trustees.

908 Shane Goldmacher, "Michael Bloomberg Spent More Than $900 Million on His Failed Presidential Run," *New York Times*, March 20, 2020, https://www.nytimes.com/2020/03/20/us/politics/bloomberg-campaign-900-million.html.

909 Mara Liasson, "Mike Bloomberg Commits $100 Million To Help Joe Biden Win Florida," NPR, September 13, 2020, https://www.npr.org/2020/09/13/912454183/mike-bloomberg-commits-100-million-to-help-joe-biden-win-florida.

910 "Mary L. Schapiro," Glasgow Financial Alliance for Net Zero, accessed April 20, 2022, https://www.gfanzero.com/about/mary-schapiro.

911 "Mary L. Schapiro," Glasgow Financial Alliance for Net Zero.

912 Brian Schwartz, "Biden donors privately float big names, including Elizabeth Warren and Larry Fink, for key roles," CNBC.com, April 6, 2020, https://www.cnbc.com/2020/04/06/biden-donors-float-elizabeth-warren-larry-fink-others-for-key-roles.html.

913 "Membership," Glasgow Financial Alliance for Net Zero.

914 Jonathan Walter, lead author, *Measuring Stakeholder Capitalism: Toward Common Metrics and Consistent Reporting of Sustainable Value Creation*, World Economic Forum, September 2020, http://www3.weforum.org/docs/WEF_IBC_Measuring_Stakeholder_Capitalism_Report_2020.pdf.

915 For example, see Stephanie Kelton, *The Deficit Myth: Modern Monetary Theory and the Birth of the People's Economy* (New York: PublicAffairs, 2019).

916 "FACT SHEET: President Biden to Sign Executive Order on Ensuring Responsible Development of Digital Assets," Office of President Joe Biden, whitehouse.gov, March 9, 2022, https://www.whitehouse.gov/briefing-room/statements-releases/2022/03/09/fact-sheet-president-biden-to-sign-executive-order-on-

ensuring-responsible-innovation-in-digital-assets.

917 "FACT SHEET: White House Releases First-Ever Comprehensive Framework for Responsible Development of Digital Assets," Office of President Joe Biden, whitehouse.gov, September 16, 2022, https://www.whitehouse.gov/briefing-room/statements-releases/2022/09/16/fact-sheet-white-house-releases-first-ever-comprehensive-framework-for-responsible-development-of-digital-assets.

918 See Chapter 7 for more.

919 "Executive Order on Advancing Biotechnology and Biomanufacturing Innovation for a Sustainable, Safe, and Secure American Bioeconomy," Office of President Joe Biden, whitehouse.gov, September 12, 2022, https://www.whitehouse.gov/briefing-room/presidential-actions/2022/09/12/executive-order-on-advancing-biotechnology-and-biomanufacturing-innovation-for-a-sustainable-safe-and-secure-american-bioeconomy.

920 "FACT SHEET: President Biden to Launch a National Biotechnology and Biomanufacturing Initiative," Office of President Joe Biden, whitehouse.gov, September 12, 2022, https://www.whitehouse.gov/briefing-room/statements-releases/2022/09/12/fact-sheet-president-biden-to-launch-a-national-biotech-nology-and-biomanufacturing-initiative.

921 "Executive Order on Advancing Biotechnology and Biomanufacturing Innovation for a Sustainable, Safe, and Secure American Bioeconomy," Office of President Joe Biden.

922 "Executive Order on Advancing Biotechnology and Biomanufacturing Innovation for a Sustainable, Safe, and Secure American Bioeconomy," Office of President Joe Biden.

923 Joe Biden, "Remarks by President Biden Before Business Roundtable's CEO Quarterly Meeting."

924 Becky Anderson et al., "Are We Ready for a New World Order?"

925 Klaus Schwab and Mohammad Abdullah Al Gergawi, "Narrating the Future."

926 Kyle Danish, Michael Platner, and Arthur Singletary, "SEC Unveils Landmark Climate Disclosures Proposal."

927 Sonny Mazzone, "Biden Administration Suspends Rule Protecting Businesses from Banking Discrimination."

928 Office of the Spokesperson, "Launching the First Movers Coalition at the 2021 UN Climate Change Conference."

929 Richard Threlfall et al., *The Time Has Come: The KPMG Survey of Sustainability Reporting 2020.*

930 Richard Threlfall et al., *The Time Has Come: The KPMG Survey of Sustainability Reporting 2020.*

931 "FACT SHEET: President Biden and G7 Leaders Launch Build Back Better World (B3W) Partnership," WhiteHouse.gov.

932 Alex Bevan et al., "EU Signals New Mandatory ESG Due Diligence for Companies Operating in EU."

933 Jonathan Walter, lead author, *Measuring Stakeholder Capitalism: Toward Common Metrics and Consistent Reporting of Sustainable Value Creation.*

934 "Trusted ESG and Climate Risk Scoring," Moody's Investors Service.

935 Justin Haskins, "Are Financial Institutions Using ESG Social Credit Scores to Coerce Individuals, Small Businesses?" citing Doug Craddock, "Lending Predictions 2022: From BNPL to ESG (and More)."

936 Kevin O'Sullivan, "Cop26: Unprecedented sums pledged to global transition to net zero emissions," *Irish Times.*

937 "FACT SHEET: President Biden to Sign Executive Order on Ensuring Responsible Development of Digital Assets," WhiteHouse.gov.

Chapter 9: National Fascism, Russia, and a New World War

938 Paul Kirby, "Why has Russia invaded Ukraine and what does Putin want?" BBC, April 17, 2022, https://www.bbc.com/news/world-europe-56720589.

939 Helene Cooper, Julian E. Barnes, and Eric Schmitt, "As Russian Troop Deaths Climb, Morale Becomes an Issue, Officials Say," *New York Times*, March 16, 2022, https://www.nytimes.com/2022/03/16/us/politics/russia-troop-deaths.html.

940 Helene Cooper, Julian E. Barnes, and Eric Schmitt, "As Russian Troop Deaths Climb, Morale Becomes an Issue, Officials Say."

941 Helene Cooper, Julian E. Barnes, and Eric Schmitt, "As Russian Troop Deaths Climb, Morale Becomes an Issue, Officials Say."

942 Paul Kirby, "Why has Russia invaded Ukraine and what does Putin want?"

943 Will Stewart and Chris Pleasance, "ANOTHER Russian colonel is killed in Ukraine as Putin's forces continue to lose battlefield top brass," *Daily Mail* (online), April 20, 2022, https://www.dailymail.co.uk/news/article-10735477/Ukraine-war-Russian-colonel-killed.html.

944 Jeremy Herb, "Exclusive: Zelensky says world should be prepared for possibility Putin could use nuclear weapons," CNN.com, April 16, 2022, https://edition.cnn.com/2022/04/15/politics/tapper-zelensky-interview-cnntv/index.html.

945 Matthew Luxmoore, "Russia's Death Toll From Ukraine War Is as High as 60,000,

U.K. Says," *Wall Street Journal*, updated February 17, 2023, https://www.wsj. com/articles/russias-death-toll-from-ukraine-war-is-as-high-as-60-000-u-k-says-14305ba5.

946 Matthew Luxmoore, "Russia's Death Toll From Ukraine War Is as High as 60,000, U.K. Says."

947 "Ukraine war: US estimates 200,000 military casualties on all sides," BBC News, bbc.com, November 10, 2022, https://www.bbc.com/news/world-europe-63580372.

948 "U.N. rights agency details 'horror story' of violations against civilians in Ukraine," CBS News and Associated Press, updated April 22, 2022, https://www.cbsnews. com/news/un-horror-story-human-rights-violations-ukraine-civilians.

949 "U.N. rights agency details 'horror story' of violations against civilians in Ukraine," CBS News and Associated Press.

950 "U.N. rights agency details 'horror story' of violations against civilians in Ukraine," CBS News and Associated Press.

951 Nathan Hodge, Eoin McSweeney, and Niamh Kennedy, "Video appears to show execution of Russian prisoner by Ukrainian forces," CNN.com, April 8, 2022, https://www.cnn.com/2022/04/07/europe/ukraine-execution-russian-prisoner-intl/index.html.

952 Office of the UN High Commissioner for Human Rights, "Ukraine: civilian casualty update 13 March 2023," United Nations, ohchr.org, March 13, 2023, https://www.ohchr.org/en/news/2023/03/ukraine-civilian-casualty-update-13-march-2023#:~:text=From%201%20to%2012%20March%202023%2C%20the%20Office%20of%20the,not%20yet%20known)%3B%20and.

953 "How many Ukrainians have fled their homes and where have they gone?" BBC, April 22, 2022, https://www.bbc.com/news/world-60555472.

954 "What sanctions are being imposed on Russia over Ukraine invasion?" BBC, April 11, 2022, https://www.bbc.com/news/world-europe-60125659.

955 "What sanctions are being imposed on Russia over Ukraine invasion?" BBC.

956 "What sanctions are being imposed on Russia over Ukraine invasion?" BBC.

957 "What sanctions are being imposed on Russia over Ukraine invasion?" BBC.

958 "What sanctions are being imposed on Russia over Ukraine invasion?" BBC.

959 Tal Yellin, "From yachts to lavish estates, tracking Russian assets seized so far," CNN Business, April 13, 2022, https://www.cnn.com/interactive/business/russian-oligarchs-yachts-real-estate-seizures/index.html.

960 Tal Yellin, "From yachts to lavish estates, tracking Russian assets seized so far."

961 Andrew Court, "Roman Abramovich's $120M Riviera mansion seized by French authorities," *New York Post*, April 13, 2022, https://nypost.com/2022/04/13/roman-abramovichs-120m-riviera-mansion-seized-by-french-authorities.

962 "What sanctions are being imposed on Russia over Ukraine invasion?" BBC.

963 Kate Abnett, "EU rolls out plan to cut Russia gas dependency this year," Reuters, March 8, 2022, https://www.reuters.com/business/energy/eu-rolls-out-plan-cut-russia-gas-dependency-this-year-end-it-within-decade-2022-03-08.

964 "What sanctions are being imposed on Russia over Ukraine invasion?" BBC.

965 "What sanctions are being imposed on Russia over Ukraine invasion?" BBC.

966 Scott Patterson and Sam Goldfarb, "Why Are Gasoline Prices So High? Ukraine-Russia War Sparks Increases Across U.S.," *Wall Street Journal*, April 1, 2022, https://www.wsj.com/articles/why-gas-prices-expensive-11646767172.

967 Jeffrey Sonnenfeld et al., "Over 1,000 Companies Have Curtailed Operations in Russia—But Some Remain," Yale School of Management, last updated March 11, 2023, https://som.yale.edu/story/2022/over-1000-companies-have-curtailed-operations-russia-some-remain.

968 Jeffrey Sonnenfeld et al., "Over 750 Companies Have Curtailed Operations in Russia—But Some Remain."

969 Erin Brady, "McDonald's Closing Restaurants in Russia, Will Keep Paying 62K Workers," *Newsweek*, March 8, 2022, https://www.newsweek.com/mcdonalds-closing-restaurants-russia-will-keep-paying-62k-workers-1686052.

970 Jeffrey Sonnenfeld and Steven Tian, "Some of the Biggest Brands Are Leaving Russia. Others Just Can't Quit Putin. Here's a List," *New York Times*, April 7, 2022, https://www.nytimes.com/interactive/2022/04/07/opinion/companies-ukraine-boycott.html.

971 Jeffrey Sonnenfeld and Steven Tian, "Some of the Biggest Brands Are Leaving Russia. Others Just Can't Quit Putin. Here's a List."

972 Graeme Wearden, "Russia heading for worst recession since end of cold war, says UK," *The Guardian*, April 8, 2022, https://www.theguardian.com/world/2022/apr/08/russia-heading-for-worst-recession-since-end-of-cold-war-says-uk.

973 Caleb Silver, "The Top 25 Economies in the World," *Investopedia*, updated February 3, 2022, https://www.investopedia.com/insights/worlds-top-economies.

974 Samuel Stebbins, "These 15 countries, as home to largest reserves, control the world's oil," *USA Today* (online), May 22, 2019, https://www.usatoday.com/story/money/2019/05/22/largest-oil-reserves-in-world-15-countries-that-control-the-worlds-oil/39497945.

975 James Eagle, "Animated Chart: Nuclear Warheads by Country (1945-2022)," *The Visual Capitalist*, March 21, 2022, https://www.visualcapitalist.com/cp/nuclear-warheads-by-country-1945-2022/#:~:text=The%20U.S.%20and%20Russia%20are,close%20to%204%2C000%20in%20possession, citing data from the Federation of American Scientists, February 2022.

976 Joe Biden, "Remarks by President Biden Before Business Roundtable's CEO Quarterly Meeting," March 21, 2022, posted to WhiteHouse.gov, accessed April 15, 2022, https://www.whitehouse.gov/briefing-room/speeches-remarks/2022/03/21/remarks-by-president-biden-before-business-roundtables-ceo-quarterly-meeting.

977 "Are We Ready for a New World Order?" World Government Summit, worldgovernmentsummit.org, last accessed April 15, 2022, https://www.worldgovernmentsummit.org/events/2022/session-detail/a0f3z0are-we-ready-for-a-new-world-order-.

978 "Leadership and Governance," World Economic Forum, weforum.org, accessed September 26, 2021, https://www.weforum.org/about/leadership-and-governance.

979 Larry Fink, "To Our Shareholders," BlackRock, blackrock.com, March 24, 2022, https://www.blackrock.com/corporate/investor-relations/larry-fink-chairmans-letter.

980 Larry Fink, "To Our Shareholders."

981 Larry Fink, "To Our Shareholders."

982 See Chapters 1, 2, and 5 in Glenn Beck and Justin Haskins, *The Great Reset: Joe Biden and the Rise of Twenty-First Century Fascism* (Mercury Ink, 2022).

983 Larry Fink, "To Our Shareholders."

984 Larry Fink, "To Our Shareholders."

985 Larry Fink, "To Our Shareholders."

986 Larry Fink, "To Our Shareholders."

987 Larry Fink, "To Our Shareholders."

988 Larry Fink, "To Our Shareholders."

989 Larry Fink, "To Our Shareholders."

990 Helene Cooper, Julian E. Barnes, and Eric Schmitt, "As Russian Troop Deaths Climb, Morale Becomes an Issue, Officials Say."

991 Paul Kirby, "Donbas: Why Russia is trying to encircle Ukraine's east," BBC News, April 19, 2022, https://www.bbc.com/news/world-europe-60938544.

992 Stavros Atlamazoglou, "Minor Incursion Or Not: America Wants Russia To

Know It Is Ready For A Ukraine Crisis," 19FortyFive, January 20, 2022, https://www.19fortyfive.com/2022/01/minor-incursion-or-not-america-wants-russia-to-know-it-is-ready-for-a-ukraine-crisis.

993   Roseanne McManus, "Perhaps Putin thinks acting crazy is a good strategy. My research says otherwise," Washington Post, March 6, 2022, https://www.washingtonpost.com/politics/2022/03/06/putin-unstable.

994   Barbara Held, "Is Putin clinically insane?" New York Daily News, March 16, 2022, https://www.nydailynews.com/opinion/ny-oped-is-putin-clinically-insane-20220316-lqlzfqtc7ze3bgnqodwmmniakm-story.html.

995   A. Craig Copetas, "Putin Isn't Just Insane. It's Far Worse Than That," The Daily Beast, March 4, 2022, https://www.thedailybeast.com/putin-isnt-just-insane-he-thinks-hes-gods-man-on-earth.

996   Eric Levitz, "Putin's War Looks Increasingly Insane," New York Magazine, March 4, 2022, https://nymag.com/intelligencer/2022/03/putins-war-looks-increasingly-insane.html.

997   Paul Kirby, "Why has Russia invaded Ukraine and what does Putin want?"

998   Paul Kirby, "Why has Russia invaded Ukraine and what does Putin want?"

999   Paul Kirby, "Why has Russia invaded Ukraine and what does Putin want?"

1000   Zack Beauchamp, "Why is Putin attacking Ukraine? He told us," Vox, February 23, 2022, https://www.vox.com/policy-and-politics/2022/2/23/22945781/russia-ukraine-putin-speech-transcript-february-22.

1001   Zack Beauchamp, "Why is Putin attacking Ukraine? He told us."

1002   "John Bolton Says Vladimir Putin once said, 'The breakup of the Soviet Union was the greatest geopolitical tragedy of the 20th century,'" PolitiFact, March 6, 2014, https://www.politifact.com/factchecks/2014/mar/06/john-bolton/did-vladimir-putin-call-breakup-ussr-greatest-geop.

1003   Olga Shumylo-Tapiola, "Viktor Yanukovych: A Man of the Oligarchs," Carnegie Europe, March 10, 2011, https://carnegieeurope.eu/2011/03/10/viktor-yanukovych-man-of-oligarchs-pub-42942.

1004   Romain Houeix, "From the Maidan protests to Russia's invasion: Eight years of conflict in Ukraine," France 24, February 28, 2022, https://www.france24.com/en/europe/20220228-from-the-maidan-protests-to-russia-s-invasion-eight-years-of-conflict-in-ukraine.

1005   Romain Houeix, "From the Maidan protests to Russia's invasion: Eight years of conflict in Ukraine."

1006   Romain Houeix, "From the Maidan protests to Russia's invasion: Eight years of conflict in Ukraine."

1007 Romain Houeix, "From the Maidan protests to Russia's invasion: Eight years of conflict in Ukraine."

1008 U.S. House Committee on Oversight and Reform, "A President Compromised: The Biden Family Investigations," Interim Staff Report, November 17, 2022, https://oversight.house.gov/wp-content/uploads/2022/11/Interim-Staff-Report-A-President-Compromised-The-Biden-Family-Investigation-1.pdf.

1009 Romain Houeix, "From the Maidan protests to Russia's invasion: Eight years of conflict in Ukraine."

1010 Romain Houeix, "From the Maidan protests to Russia's invasion: Eight years of conflict in Ukraine."

1011 Zack Beauchamp, "Why is Putin attacking Ukraine? He told us."

1012 Andrew Roth, "Ukraine's ex-president Viktor Yanukovych found guilty of treason," January 25, 2019, *The Guardian*, https://www.theguardian.com/world/2019/jan/25/ukraine-ex-president-viktor-yanukovych-found-guilty-of-treason.

1013 Andrew Roth, "Ukraine's ex-president Viktor Yanukovych found guilty of treason."

1014 "Ukraine President Signs Constitutional Amendment On NATO, EU Membership," Radio Free Europe and Radio Liberty, February 19, 2019, https://www.rferl.org/a/ukraine-president-signs-constitutional-amendment-on-nato-eu-membership/29779430.html.

1015 "Ukraine President Signs Constitutional Amendment On NATO, EU Membership," Radio Free Europe and Radio Liberty.

1016 "Conflict in Ukraine's Donbas: A Visual Explainer," last accessed April 27, 2022, International Crisis Group, https://www.crisisgroup.org/content/conflict-ukraines-donbas-visual-explainer.

1017 Romain Houeix, "From the Maidan protests to Russia's invasion: Eight years of conflict in Ukraine."

1018 Zack Beauchamp, "Why is Putin attacking Ukraine? He told us."

1019 Kevin O'Sullivan, "Cop26: Unprecedented sums pledged to global transition to net zero emissions," *Irish Times*, November 3, 2021, https://www.irishtimes.com/news/environment/cop26-unprecedented-sums-pledged-to-global-transition-to-net-zero-emissions-1.4718092.

1020 Kevin O'Sullivan, "Cop26: Unprecedented sums pledged to global transition to net zero emissions."

1021 Angelina Davydova, "Will Russia ever leave fossil fuels behind?" BBC News,

November 23, 2021, https://www.bbc.com/future/article/20211115-climate-change-can-russia-leave-fossil-fuels-behind.

1022 "Why Russian Oil and Gas Matter to the Global Economy," *New York Times*, last updated March 10, 2022, https://www.nytimes.com/explain/2022/03/09/business/gas-oil-russia-ukraine.

1023 Joe Wallace and Anna Hirtenstein, "Russia's Oil Industry, Linchpin of Economy, Feels Sting of Ukraine War Disruptions," *Wall Street Journal*, April 13, 2022, https://www.wsj.com/articles/russias-oil-industry-linchpin-of-economy-feels-sting-of-ukraine-war-disruptions-11649843249.

1024 Maite Fernández Simon and David L. Stern, "Who is Viktor Medvedchuk, the pro-Russia mogul arrested in Ukraine?" *Washington Post*, April 13, 2022, https://www.washingtonpost.com/world/2022/02/28/ukraine-russia-medved-chuck.

1025 Maite Fernández Simon and David L. Stern, "Who is Viktor Medvedchuk, the pro-Russia mogul arrested in Ukraine?"

1026 Maite Fernández Simon and David L. Stern, "Who is Viktor Medvedchuk, the pro-Russia mogul arrested in Ukraine?"

1027 Maite Fernández Simon and David L. Stern, "Who is Viktor Medvedchuk, the pro-Russia mogul arrested in Ukraine?"

1028 Maite Fernández Simon and David L. Stern, "Who is Viktor Medvedchuk, the pro-Russia mogul arrested in Ukraine?"

1029 "About: Valdai Club Foundation," Valdai Discussion Club, accessed April 28, 2022, https://valdaiclub.com/about/valdai.

1030 Vladimir Putin, speech before the Valdai Discussion Club, October 21, 2021, made available by the Kremlin, http://en.kremlin.ru/events/president/news/66975.

1031 Vladimir Putin, speech before the Valdai Discussion Club, October 21, 2021.

1032 Vladimir Putin, speech before the Valdai Discussion Club, October 21, 2021.

1033 Vladimir Putin, speech before the Valdai Discussion Club, October 21, 2021.

1034 Vladimir Putin, speech before the Valdai Discussion Club, October 21, 2021.

1035 Vladimir Putin, speech before the Valdai Discussion Club, October 21, 2021.

1036 Vladimir Putin, speech before the Valdai Discussion Club, October 21, 2021.

1037 Vladimir Putin, speech before the Valdai Discussion Club, October 21, 2021.

1038 Vladimir Putin, speech before the Valdai Discussion Club, October 21, 2021.

1039 Vladimir Putin, speech before the Valdai Discussion Club, October 21, 2021.

1040 Vladimir Putin, speech before the Valdai Discussion Club, October 21, 2021.

1041   Vladimir Putin, speech before the Valdai Discussion Club, October 21, 2021.

1042   Holly Ellyatt, "Putin warns of 'all against all' fight if global tensions are not resolved," CNBC, January 27, 2021, https://www.cnbc.com/2021/01/27/russias-putin-warns-of-a-fight-of-all-against-all-at-wef.html.

1043   Vladimir Putin, speech before the Valdai Discussion Club, October 21, 2021.

1044   See Cathy Young, "The Bizarre Russian Prophet Rumored to Have Putin's Ear," *The Bulwark*, April 27, 2022, https://www.thebulwark.com/aleksandr-dugin-putin-brain-russian-prophet-bizarre.

1045   Steven Pittz, "A Civilizational War?" *City Journal*, March 27, 2022, https://www.city-journal.org/does-putin-take-his-cue-from-alexander-dugin.

1046   Cathy Young, "The Bizarre Russian Prophet Rumored to Have Putin's Ear."

1047   See Ayesha Rascoe's interview with David von Drehle, "Russian intellectual Aleksandr Dugin is also commonly known as 'Putin's brain,'" National Public Radio, npr.com, March 27, 2022, https://www.npr.org/2022/03/27/1089047787/russian-intellectual-aleksandr-dugin-is-also-commonly-known-as-putins-brain.

1048   Anton Barbashin and Hannah Thoburn, "Putin's Brain," *Foreign Affairs*, March 31, 2014, https://www.foreignaffairs.com/articles/russia-fsu/2014-03-31/putins-brain.

1049   Carolyn Harris, "The Murder of Rasputin, 100 Years Later," *Smithsonian Magazine*, December 27, 2016, https://www.smithsonianmag.com/history/murder-rasputin-100-years-later-180961572.

1050   Cathy Young, "The Bizarre Russian Prophet Rumored to Have Putin's Ear."

1051   Cathy Young, "The Bizarre Russian Prophet Rumored to Have Putin's Ear."

1052   John Dunlop, "Aleksandr Dugin's Foundations of Geopolitics," the Europe Center at Stanford University, last accessed April 29, 2022, https://tec.fsi.stanford.edu/docs/aleksandr-dugins-foundations-geopolitics. Originally published in Demokratizatsiya 12.1 (Jan 31, 2004): 41.

1053   Cathy Young, "The Bizarre Russian Prophet Rumored to Have Putin's Ear."

1054   John Dunlop, "Aleksandr Dugin's Foundations of Geopolitics."

1055   David von Drehle, "The man known as 'Putin's brain' envisions the splitting of Europe—and the fall of China," *Washington Post*, March 22, 2022, https://www.washingtonpost.com/opinions/2022/03/22/alexander-dugin-author-putin-deady-playbook.

1056   David von Drehle, "The man known as 'Putin's brain' envisions the splitting of Europe—and the fall of China."

1057 David von Drehle, "The man known as 'Putin's brain' envisions the splitting of Europe—and the fall of China."

1058 Cathy Young, "The Bizarre Russian Prophet Rumored to Have Putin's Ear."

1059 Cathy Young, "The Bizarre Russian Prophet Rumored to Have Putin's Ear."

1060 Dina Newman, "Russian nationalist thinker Dugin sees war with Ukraine," BBC News, July 10, 2014, https://www.bbc.com/news/world-europe-28229785.

1061 Zack Beauchamp, "Why is Putin attacking Ukraine? He told us."

1062 Alexander Dugin, *The Great Awakening vs. The Great Reset* (Arktos Media, 2021).

1063 Alexander Dugin, *The Great Awakening vs. The Great Reset.*

1064 Alexander Dugin, *The Great Awakening vs. The Great Reset.*

1065 Alexander Dugin, *The Great Awakening vs. The Great Reset.*

1066 Alexander Dugin, *The Great Awakening vs. The Great Reset.*

1067 Alexander Dugin, *The Great Awakening vs. The Great Reset.*

1068 Alexander Dugin, *The Great Awakening vs. The Great Reset.*

1069 Alexander Dugin, *The Great Awakening vs. The Great Reset.*

1070 Alexander Dugin, *The Great Awakening vs. The Great Reset.*

1071 Alexander Dugin, *The Great Awakening vs. The Great Reset.*

1072 David von Drehle, "The man known as 'Putin's brain' envisions the splitting of Europe—and the fall of China."

1073 "What sanctions are being imposed on Russia over Ukraine invasion?" BBC.

1074 Khalid Al-Jabri, "Biden Should Punish Saudi Arabia for Backing Russia," *Foreign Policy*, March 22, 2022, https://foreignpolicy.com/2022/03/22/biden-mbs-oil-saudi-arabia-russia-ukraine.

1075 Khalid Al-Jabri, "Biden Should Punish Saudi Arabia for Backing Russia."

1076 Huileng Tan, "China and Russia are working on homegrown alternatives to the SWIFT payment system. Here's what they would mean for the US dollar," *Business Insider*, April 29, 2022, https://www.businessinsider.com/china-russia-alternative-swift-payment-cips-spfs-yuan-ruble-dollar-2022-4.

1077 Huileng Tan, "China and Russia are working on homegrown alternatives to the SWIFT payment system. Here's what they would mean for the US dollar."

1078 "Sergei Glazyev," Eurasian Economic Commission, last accessed April 29, 2022, http://www.eurasiancommission.org/en/act/integr_i_makroec/Pages/director.aspx.

1079 Pepe Escobar, "Exclusive: Russia's Sergey Glazyev introduces the new global financial system," The Cradle, April 14, 2022, https://thecradle.co/Article/interviews/9135.

1080 "About the Eurasian Economic Commission," Eurasian Economic Commission, last accessed April 29, 2022, http://www.eurasiancommission.org/en/Pages/about.aspx.

1081 Pepe Escobar, "Exclusive: Russia's Sergey Glazyev introduces the new global financial system."

1082 Pepe Escobar, "Exclusive: Russia's Sergey Glazyev introduces the new global financial system."

1083 Pepe Escobar, "Exclusive: Russia's Sergey Glazyev introduces the new global financial system."

1084 Pepe Escobar, "Exclusive: Russia's Sergey Glazyev introduces the new global financial system."

1085 "Iran, Russia, China Hold Joint Naval Drill Amid Growing Ties," Radio Free Europe/RadioLiberty, with reporting by Reuters, AP, and TASS, January 21, 2022, https://www.rferl.org/a/iran-russia-china-exercises/31663080.html.

1086 Danica Kirka, "US officials point to Russia using Iranian drones in Ukraine," Associated Press, apnews.com, February 14, 2023, https://apnews.com/article/russia-ukraine-iran-politics-defense-intelligence-agency-drones-fecf53c964f09e24bd9a187715ac8598.

1087 Charlie Campbell, "Is China Providing Russia With Military Support? It's Hard to Tell, and That's the Point," *TIME*, time.com, March 2, 2023, https://time.com/6259688/china-russia-dual-use-military-civil-fusion-strategy.

1088 Antonio Graceffo, "China Unveils Global Security Initiative: A Move Toward CCP-Led Globalism," *Epoch Times*, May 5, 2022, https://www.theepoch-times.com/china-unveils-global-security-initiative-a-move-toward-ccp-led-globalism_4441863.html.

1089 Antonio Graceffo, "China Unveils Global Security Initiative: A Move Toward CCP-Led Globalism."

1090 Antonio Graceffo, "China Unveils Global Security Initiative: A Move Toward CCP-Led Globalism."

1091 Antonio Graceffo, "China Unveils Global Security Initiative: A Move Toward CCP-Led Globalism."

1092 Alexander Dugin, *The Great Awakening vs. The Great Reset*.

1093 Vladimir Putin, speech before the Valdai Discussion Club, October 21, 2021.

1094 Vladimir Putin, speech before the Valdai Discussion Club, October 21, 2021.

1095 Vladimir Putin, speech before the Valdai Discussion Club, October 21, 2021.

1096   Ivan Tkachev and Alina Fadeeva, "55 trillion in reserve: how the authorities assessed all the natural resources of Russia," RBC, March 14, 2019, https://www.rbc.ru/economics/14/03/2019/5c8931029a7947b028b8886c?from=-from_main.

1097   Jack McPherrin, "The Road to Totalitarianism: Lessons from Russia," Policy Brief, The Heartland Institute, heartland.org, February 24, 2023, https://heartland.org/publications/the-road-to-totalitarianism-lessons-from-russia.

1098   Jack McPherrin, "The Road to Totalitarianism: Lessons from Russia."

1099   Steven Lee Myers, *The New Tsar: The Rise and Reign of Vladimir Putin* (Vintage, 2016).

1100   "Russia," Human Rights Watch, hrw.org, accessed May 9, 2022, https://www.hrw.org/europe/central-asia/russia#.

1101   "Russia," Human Rights Watch.

1102   Jack McPherrin, "The Road to Totalitarianism: Lessons from Russia."

1103   Jack McPherrin, "The Road to Totalitarianism: Lessons from Russia."

1104   Jack McPherrin, "The Road to Totalitarianism: Lessons from Russia."

1105   "World Report 2020: Russia," Human Rights Watch, hrw.org, published in 2020, last accessed May 20, 2022, https://www.hrw.org/world-report/2020/country-chapters/russia.

1106   "Russia investigates prison torture allegations after videos leaked," BBC News, bbc.com, October 6, 2021, https://www.bbc.com/news/world-europe-58780360.

1107   "World Report 2020: Russia," Human Rights Watch.

1108   Bradford Betz, "Whistleblowers: FBI targeted parents via terrorism tools despite Garland's testimony that it didn't happen," Fox News, foxnews.com, May 11, 2022, https://www.foxnews.com/politics/fbi-targeted-parents-via-terrorism-tools-despite-garland-testimony.

Chapter 10: A Greater Narrative

1109   Yuval Harari, "Will the Future Be Human?" speech before the 2018 Annual Meeting of the World Economic Forum, January 25, 2018, made available by the World Economic Forum on YouTube.com, https://youtu.be/hL9uk4hKyg4.

1110   Yuval Harari, "Will the Future Be Human?"

1111   Yuval Harari, "Will the Future Be Human?"

1112   Yuval Harari, "Will the Future Be Human?"

1113   Yuval Harari, "Will the Future Be Human?"

1114 Yuval Harari, "Will the Future Be Human?"

1115 Yuval Harari, "Will the Future Be Human?"

1116 Yuval Harari, "Will the Future Be Human?"

1117 Yuval Harari, "Will the Future Be Human?"

1118 Yuval Harari, "Will the Future Be Human?"

1119 Yuval Harari, "Will the Future Be Human?"

1120 Yuval Harari, "Will the Future Be Human?"

1121 Yuval Harari, "Will the Future Be Human?"

1122 Yuval Harari, "Read Yuval Harari's blistering warning to Davos in full," World Economic Forum, weforum.org, January 24, 2020, https://www.weforum.org/agenda/2020/01/yuval-hararis-warning-davos-speech-future-predications.

1123 Yuval Harari, "Will the Future Be Human?"

1124 Yuval Harari, "Will the Future Be Human?"

1125 Yuval Harari, "Read Yuval Harari's blistering warning to Davos in full."

1126 Yuval Harari, "Read Yuval Harari's blistering warning to Davos in full."

1127 Matthew Hill, David Campanale, and Joel Gunter, "'Their goal is to destroy everyone': Uighur camp detainees allege systematic rape," BBC News, February 2, 2021, https://www.bbc.com/news/world-asia-china-55794071.

1128 Colum Murphy, "Being Gay in China Has Gotten Harder Under Xi Jinping," Bloomberg.com, February 17, 2022, https://www.bloomberg.com/news/newsletters/2022-02-17/being-gay-in-china-has-gotten-harder-under-xi-jinping.

1129 David Stanway, "China starts building 33 GW of coal power in 2021, most since 2016 -research," Reuters.com, February 23, 2022, https://www.reuters.com/markets/commodities/china-starts-building-33-gw-coal-power-2021-most-since-2016-research-2022-02-24.

1130 David Stanway, "China starts building 33 GW of coal power in 2021, most since 2016 -research."

1131 See "Declaration of a New Order," *Wookieepedia*, starwars.fandom.com, accessed September 27, 2022, https://starwars.fandom.com/wiki/Declaration_of_a_New_Order.

1132 Yuval Harari, "Will the Future Be Human?"

1133 "Advancing Human-Centered Economic Progress in the Fourth Industrial Revolution," G20/T20 Policy Brief, World Economic Forum, weforum.org, May 2017, https://www3.weforum.org/docs/WEF_Advancing_Human_Centred_Economic_Progress_WP_2017.pdf.

1134 Kim Iversen, "Bio," kimiversen.com, accessed April 14, 2022, https://www.
      kimiversen.com.

1135 "'This isn't such a crazy conspiracy theory after all': Journalist concedes 'loony'
      Glenn Beck is RIGHT about the Great Reset," TheBlaze.com, January 19, 2022,
      https://www.theblaze.com/shows/glenn-tv/kim-iversen-the-great-reset?rebell-
      titem=2#rebelltitem2.

1136 "'This isn't such a crazy conspiracy theory after all': Journalist concedes 'loony'
      Glenn Beck is RIGHT about the Great Reset," TheBlaze.com.

1137 "'This isn't such a crazy conspiracy theory after all': Journalist concedes 'loony'
      Glenn Beck is RIGHT about the Great Reset," TheBlaze.com.

1138 "'This isn't such a crazy conspiracy theory after all': Journalist concedes 'loony'
      Glenn Beck is RIGHT about the Great Reset," TheBlaze.com.

1139 "'This isn't such a crazy conspiracy theory after all': Journalist concedes 'loony'
      Glenn Beck is RIGHT about the Great Reset," TheBlaze.com.

1140 "'This isn't such a crazy conspiracy theory after all': Journalist concedes 'loony'
      Glenn Beck is RIGHT about the Great Reset," TheBlaze.com.

1141 Glenn Beck and Kim Iversen, "Is Ukraine a Convenient War for Democrats?"
      The Glenn Beck Podcast, Episode 139, March 26, 2022, https://youtu.be/
      sunZhR1-feo.

1142 David Molloy, "Zuckerberg tells Rogan FBI warning prompted Biden laptop
      story censorship," BBC News, bbc.com, August 26, 2022, https://www.bbc.
      com/news/world-us-canada-62688532.

1143 David Molloy, "Zuckerberg tells Rogan FBI warning prompted Biden laptop
      story censorship."

1144 David Molloy, "Zuckerberg tells Rogan FBI warning prompted Biden laptop
      story censorship."

1145 David Molloy, "Zuckerberg tells Rogan FBI warning prompted Biden laptop
      story censorship."

1146 Hamza Shaban and Heather Long, "The stock market is ending 2020 at
      record highs, even as the virus surges and millions go hungry," *Washington Post*,
      December 31, 2020, https://www.washingtonpost.com/business/2020/12/31/
      stock-market-record-2020.

1147 Lucy Perez et al., "Does ESG really matter—and why?" *McKinsey Quarterly*,
      August 10, 2022, https://www.mckinsey.com/capabilities/sustainability/our-
      insights/does-esg-really-matter-and-why.

1148 "Just and sustainable economy: Commission lays down rules for companies to respect human rights and environment in global value chains," press release, European Commission, ec.europa.eu, February 23, 2022, https://ec.europa.eu/commission/presscorner/detail/en/ip_22_1145.

1149   See the numerous evidences in Justin Haskins, "Are Financial Institutions Using ESG Social Credit Scores to Coerce Individuals, Small Businesses?" , The Heartland Institute, heartland.org, February 27, 2022, https://www.heartland.org/publications-resources/publications/financial-institutions-are-expanding-esg-social-credit-scores-to-target-individuals-small-businesses.

1150   Justin Haskins, "Are Financial Institutions Using ESG Social Credit Scores to Coerce Individuals, Small Businesses?"

1151   See "Environmental, Social, and Governance (ESG) Scores," The Heartland Institute, heartland.org, accessed last on September 29, 2022, https://www.heartland.org/ESG/esg.

1152   See "Environmental, Social, and Governance (ESG) Scores," The Heartland Institute.

1153   See "Environmental, Social, and Governance (ESG) Scores," The Heartland Institute.

1154   "Sen. Cramer: 27 Senators are Cosponsoring the Fair Access to Banking Act," press release, Office of U.S. Senator Kevin Cramer, March 5, 2021, https://www.cramer.senate.gov/news/press-releases/sen-cramer-27-senators-are-cosponsoring-the-fair-access-to-banking-act.

1155   "Sen. Cramer: 27 Senators are Cosponsoring the Fair Access to Banking Act," Office of U.S. Senator Kevin Cramer.

1156   See "H.R.1729 - Fair Access to Banking Act," congress.gov, last accessed September 29, 2022, https://www.congress.gov/bill/117th-congress/house-bill/1729/cosponsors?r=47&s=1.

1157   For updated ESG legislation tracking, see "Environmental, Social, and Governance (ESG) Scores," The Heartland Institute, heartland.org, last visited March 14, 2023, https://heartland.org/esg.

1158   "Governor Ron DeSantis Announces Initiatives to Protect Floridians from ESG Financial Fraud," press release, Office of Governor Ron DeSantis, July 27, 2022, https://flgov.com/2022/07/27/governor-ron-desantis-announces-initiatives-to-protect-floridians-from-esg-financial-fraud.

1159   "Governor Ron DeSantis Announces Legislation to Protect Floridians from the Woke ESG Financial Scam," press release.

1160   "Governor Ron DeSantis Eliminates ESG Considerations from State Pension

Investments," Office of Governor Ron DeSantis, August 23, 2022, https://www.flgov.com/2022/08/23/governor-ron-desantis-eliminates-esg-considerations-from-state-pension-investments.

1161 See *Marsh v. Alabama*, 326 U.S. 501 (1946), https://supreme.justia.com/cases/federal/us/326/501.

1162 "Federal Protections Against National Origin Discrimination," U.S. Department of Justice, justice.gov, accessed September 29, 2022, https://www.justice.gov/crt/federal-protections-against-national-origin-discrimination-1#:~:text=Federal%20laws%20prohibit%20discrimination%20based,%2C%20ances-try%2C%20culture%20or%20language.

1163 Yuval Harari, "Will the Future Be Human?"

1164 Natasha Singer, "The Government Protects Our Food and Cars. Why Not Our Data?" *New York Times*, November 2, 2019, https://www.nytimes.com/2019/11/02/sunday-review/data-protection-privacy.html.

1165 Lauren Feiner, "Republican draft bill would tighten rules for finance firms using customer information," CNBC, cnbc.com, June 23, 2022, https://www.cnbc.com/2022/06/23/gop-draft-bill-would-tighten-rules-for-finance-firms-using-customer-information.html.

1166 See Alexandria Ocasio-Cortez on Twitter.com, @AOC, April 10, 2018, https://twitter.com/aoc/status/983779608607813632.

1167 Brooke Auxier et al., "Americans and Privacy: Concerned, Confused and Feeling Lack of Control Over Their Personal Information," Pew Research Center, pewresearch.org, November 15, 2019, https://www.pewresearch.org/internet/2019/11/15/americans-and-privacy-concerned-confused-and-feeling-lack-of-control-over-their-personal-information.

1168 Brooke Auxier et al., "Americans and Privacy: Concerned, Confused and Feeling Lack of Control Over Their Personal Information."

1169 "Dr. Rand Paul Reintroduces 'Audit the Fed' 2021," Office of U.S. Senator Rand Paul, press release, March 3, 2021, https://www.paul.senate.gov/news/dr-rand-paul-reintroduces-%E2%80%9Caudit-fed%E2%80%9D-2021.

1170 "Dr. Rand Paul Reintroduces 'Audit the Fed' 2021," Office of U.S. Senator Rand Paul.

1171 "Dr. Rand Paul Reintroduces 'Audit the Fed' 2021," Office of U.S. Senator Rand Paul.

1172 Steven Nelson, "Democrats Kill Rand Paul's Audit the Fed Bill, Though Sanders Votes Yes," *U.S. News & World Report*, usnews.com, January 12, 2016, https://

www.usnews.com/news/articles/2016-01-12/democrats-kill-rand-pauls-audit-the-fed-bill-though-sanders-votes-yes.

1173 Steven Nelson, "Democrats Kill Rand Paul's Audit the Fed Bill, Though Sanders Votes Yes."

1174 Dawn Lin, "Federal Reserve Taps BlackRock to Purchase Bonds for the Government," *Wall Street Journal*, March 24, 2020, https://www.wsj.com/articles/federal-reserve-taps-blackrock-to-purchase-bonds-for-the-government-11585085843.

1175 "FACT SHEET: White House Releases First-Ever Comprehensive Framework for Responsible Development of Digital Assets," Office of President Joe Biden, whitehouse.gov, September 16, 2022, https://www.whitehouse.gov/briefing-room/statements-releases/2022/09/16/fact-sheet-white-house-releases-first-ever-comprehensive-framework-for-responsible-development-of-digital-assets.

1176 See John Winthrop's sermon titled "A Model of Christian Charity," with an introduction by Stephen Knott, at "A City upon a Hill," Teaching American History, teachingamericanhistory.com, accessed September 29, 2020, https://teachingamericanhistory.org/document/a-city-upon-a-hill-afp.

1177 See John Winthrop's sermon titled "A Model of Christian Charity," with an introduction by Stephen Knott, at "A City upon a Hill."

1178 Thomas Jefferson, "Declaration of Independence: A Transcription," U.S. National Archives, archives.gov, accessed September 29, 2022, https://www.archives.gov/founding-docs/declaration-transcript.

1179 Thomas Jefferson, "Declaration of Independence: A Transcription."

1180 Deena Zaru, "The story behind 'The New Colossus' poem on the Statue of Liberty and how it became a symbol of immigration," ABC News, abcnews.go.com, August 14, 2019, https://abcnews.go.com/Politics/story-colossus-poem-statue-liberty-symbol-immigration/story?id=64931545#:~:text=The%20poem's%20title%2C%20%22The%20New,escape%20to%20the%20United%20States.

1181 Deena Zaru, "The story behind 'The New Colossus' poem on the Statue of Liberty and how it became a symbol of immigration."

1182 Emma Lazarus, "The New Colossus," made available by the U.S. National Parks Service, accessed September 29, 2022, https://www.nps.gov/stli/learn/history-culture/colossus.htm.

1183 "Edison Light Bulb," Smithsonian Institute, si.edu, November 3, 2011, https://www.si.edu/newsdesk/snapshot/edison-light-bulb.

1184   Thomas Jefferson to Peter Carr, August 10, 1787, quoted in "Jefferson Quotes & Family Letters," Thomas Jefferson Foundation, US Library of Congress, accessed September 26, 2021, https://tjrs.monticello.org/letter/1297.